FODOR'S
NEW YORK STATE

1988

Editor: Andrew E. Beresky
Assistant Editor: Staci Capobianco
Editorial Contributors: Diane Gallo, JoAnn Greco, Brigitte Johnson, Philip C. Johnson, Ira Mayer, Deborah Williams
Drawings: Ted Burwell
Maps: Pictograph

FODOR'S TRAVEL PUBLICATIONS, INC.
New York & London

MANUFACTURED IN THE UNITED STATES OF AMERICA
10 9 8 7 6 5 4 3 2 1

CONTENTS

CONTENTS

FOREWORD

Welcome to New York.

On behalf of all New Yorkers, I cordially invite you to experience the variety of enticing places and pursuits the Empire State offers vacationers from January through December.

The millions of visitors to New York every year enjoy everthing from cosmopolitan crowds in the most civilized settings, to splendid isolation amid unspoiled open space.

Every leisure urge of the four seasons can be satisfied superbly in New York. Our historic sites, museums, parks and beaches, restaurants, performing arts, scenic beauty, recreational opportunities, theaters, entertainment and major league sports are unrivaled for their diversity and allure.

Each region of our State has its own irresistible attraction. The ocean beaches of Long Island, the energy and cultural offerings of New York City, the timeless beauty of the Catskill and Adirondack Mountains, the country charm of the Finger Lakes and Southern Tier, the grandeur of the Great Lakes and Niagara Falls, and the tranquility of the Thousand Islands present you with a multitude of pleasing vacation choices.

Wherever you go and whatever you do, you'll encounter friendly people attuned to the traveler's needs to provide you with lodging, meals, information and assistance.

No wonder I LOVE NEW YORK has become a phrase heard around the world. Why not, when with every visit, the tourist finds more to love?

Come and see.

Governor Mario Cuomo

PREFACE

New York! The mere mention of its name connotes towering skyscrapers, bustling crowds, bright lights, and living in the fast lane in the world's most exciting city. Yes, it is that. But New York State is a lot more, too. The Empire State offers a variety of scenes, adventures, and activities to suit any vacationer's or business tripper's pleasure. There are the comfort and charm of century-old inns along the Hudson River, the informal fun and dining at a Catskill resort, the adventure of hiking or skiing in the rugged Adirondack Mountains; the awe-inspiring sight of mighty Niagara Falls, the headiness of trampling through vineyards and touring a winery; the reliving of history at hallowed Revolutionary War sites.

While every care has been taken to ensure the accuracy of the information contained in this guide, the publishers cannot accept responsibility for any errors which may appear.

All prices quoted in this guide are based on those available to us at the time of writing. In a world of rapid change, however, the possibility of inaccurate or out-of-date information can never be totally eliminated. We trust, therefore, that you will take prices quoted as indicators only, and will double-check to be sure of the latest figures.

Similarly, be sure to check all opening times of museums and galleries. We have found that such times are liable to change without notice, and you could easily make a trip only to find a locked door.

When a hotel closes or a restaurant produces a disappointing meal, let us know, and we will investigate the establishment and the complaint. We are always ready to revise our entries for the following year's edition should the facts warrant it.

Send your letters to the editors of Fodor's Travel Publications, 201 E 50th Street, New York, NY 10022. Continental or British Commonwealth readers may prefer to write to Fodor's Travel Guides, 9-10 Market Place, London W1N 7AG, England.

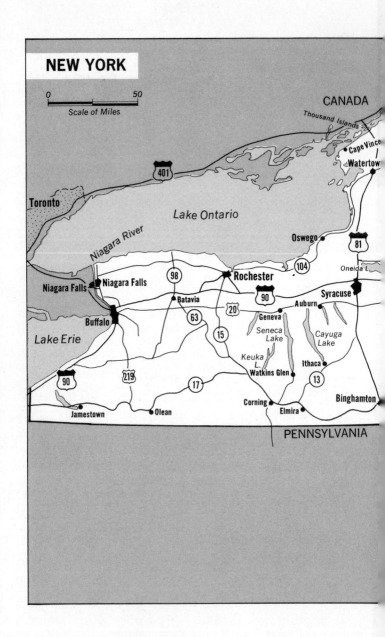

NEW YORK

0 50
Scale of Miles

CANADA

Thousand Islands

Cape Vince

Watertow

Lake Ontario

Toronto

Niagara River

Oswego

81

Oneida L.

98

Rochester

104

Niagara Falls

Niagara Falls

90

Syracuse

Batavia

20

Auburn

Buffalo

63

Geneva

15

Seneca Lake

Cayuga Lake

Lake Erie

Keuka L.

Watkins Glen

Ithaca

13

219

90

17

Corning

Elmira

Binghamton

Jamestown

Olean

PENNSYLVANIA

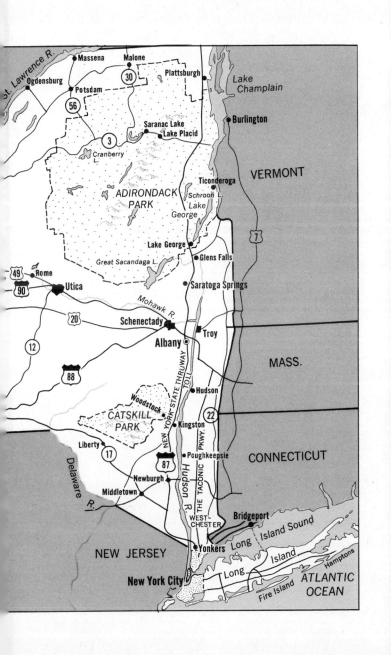

FACTS AT YOUR FINGERTIPS

 FACTS & FIGURES. New York State consists of some 47,000 square miles and a population of more than 17 million people. New York City, whose five boroughs cover a mere 303 square miles, is home to 7 million of those people. The lay of the land takes in vast mountain ranges, forests, and 150 state parks, including Catskill Park and the vast Adirondack Park. There, too, are the wonder of Niagara Falls; the Hudson River and surrounding valley; and scores of national historic sites, including the homes and/or birthplaces of half a dozen United States presidents. Its State Barge Canal System, running from New York City north to the Canadian border and northwest to Buffalo encompasses 800 miles of navigable waterway.

 PLANNING YOUR TRIP. If you don't want to bother with reservations on your own, a travel agent won't cost you a cent, except for specific charges like telegrams. He gets his fee from the hotel or carrier he books for you. A travel agent can also be of help if you prefer to take your vacation on a "package tour"—thus keeping your own planning to a minimum. If you prefer the convenience of standardized accommodations, remember that the various hotel and motel chains publish free directories of their members that enable you to plan and reserve everything ahead of time.

In driving to New York, if you don't belong to an auto club, now is the time to join one. They can be very helpful with routings and providing emergency service on the road. If you plan to route yourself, make certain the map you get is dated for the current year (highways and interstates are being built and extended at an astonishing rate). The American Automobile Association (AAA), which has individual organizations in most states (including New York), does an excellent job in mapping out trips. The national headquarters is at 8111 Gatehouse Rd., Falls Church, VA 22047. The New York office is at 28 East 78th St., New York, NY 10021. However, you must be a member to request materials.

Some of the major oil companies will send maps and mark preferred routes on them if you tell them what you have in mind. Try Exxon Touring Service, Exxon Corp., 1251 Avenue of the Americas, New York, NY 10020; Texaco Travel Service, Box 1459, Houston, TX 77401; or Mobil Oil Corp. Touring Service, Box 25, Versailles, KY 40383. In addition, most states have their own maps, which pinpoint attractions and list historical sites, parks, etc. Chambers of commerce are also good sources of information. Specific addresses are given under *Tourist Information* in this section, and in the *Practical Information* sections of the individual chapters of this book.

 VISITORS INFORMATION. Without question, any visitor to New York State should obtain the most current brochures from the New York State Tourism Division, One Commerce Plaza, Albany, NY 12245; 518–474–4116. The bureau's *I Love NY* series is an excellent collection of guides to state parks and outdoor activities, and to individual areas within the state (including New York City).

TIPS FOR BRITISH VISITORS. Passports. You will need a valid passport and a U.S. visa (which can only be put in a 10-year passport). You can obtain the visa either through your travel agent or from the United States Embassy, Visa and Immigration Department, 24 Grosvenor Square, London, W1. No vaccinations are required to enter the U.S.

Customs. If you are 21 or over, you can take into the U.S. 200 cigarettes, 50 cigars, or 3 lbs of tobacco (not Cuban), 1 liter of alcohol, and duty-free gifts to a value of $100. Do not try to take in meat or meat products, seeds, plants, fruits, etc. And, of course, do not bring in illicit narcotics.

Insurance. We heartily recommend that you insure yourself to cover health and motoring mishaps with Europ Assistance, 252 High St., Croydon CRO INF. Their excellent service is all the more valuable when you consider the high cost of health care in the U.S.

Tour Operators. The price battle that has raged over trans-Atlantic fares has meant that most tour operators now offer excellent budget packages to the U.S. Among those you might consider are: *American Express,* 6 Haymarket, London, SW1; *Thomas Cook Ltd.,* Thorpe Wood, Peterborough, PE3 6SB; *Cosmos,* Cosmos House, 1 Bromley Common, Bromley, Kent BR2 9LX; *Cunard,* 8 Berkeley St., London, W1; *Speedbird,* 200 Buckingham Palace Rd., London SW1

Air Fares. We suggest that you explore the current scene for budget flight possibilities. All the main trans-Atlantic carriers have various discounted fares. Some offer standby tickets as well. If a budget fare can be had going into Newark Airport (as on *Virgin Atlantic*), take it. Newark is readily accessible to Manhattan—in fact, perhaps more easily so than Kennedy or LaGuardia.

Hotels. You may have need of a fast booking service to find a hotel room. One of the very best ways to do this is to contact HBI-HOTAC, Globegate House, Pound Lane, London NW10. They book rooms for most of the large chains, so you can have a choice with only one contact. The company specializes in corporate accounts, but will handle individual requests as well.

Information. One excellent source of information is the *State of New York Division of Tourism,* 25 Bedford Square, London WC1B 3HG (tel. 01-323-0648). They will furnish you with brochures and other information to help you plan your trip.

WHEN TO GO. There are suggestions as to which seasons are best for what activities in the *Practical Information* sections of every chapter in this book. It will be warm to hot everywhere in New York State in the summer months, though New York City is probably the least comfortable in July and August—which is why the Hudson Valley and Catskills are so popular at that time of year. But while some museums and historic sites are closed during the winter, usually because of a combination of fewer tourists and more snow, there are places to visit, activities to be enjoyed, and food and lodging to be had virtually all over the state at any time of the year. For those who can manage it, though, fall is a very special time as the leaves change. Just be sure to make reservations anywhere you want to go at that time of year.

PACKING. What you take will depend largely on where in the state you are headed and what your primary activities are likely to be. If you are going to New York City, for example, and plan to attend the better restaurants, you will need more formal attire; if you are planning to stay at country inns in the Hudson Valley and tour the mansions of the area by day, comfortable weekend clothes will do just fine, though some of the inns may require men to wear jackets in the evenings and prefer women not to wear jeans. Bed-and-breakfast establishments are totally informal.

In terms of weather, be prepared for extremes at any time of year. Layers of clothing are probably easiest to travel with, since you can add or subtract depending on what you need. Temperatures can climb to the 70s in Manhattan in March, and to the 90s in August. Similarly, the mountainous regions will be very warm during summer days, but quite cool in the evenings, when a sweater or jacket will be appropriate. In New York City, most public places are air conditioned to the point of being frigid in the summer, and are overheated in the winter; this is less of a problem elsewhere in the state. Again, depending on your destination, bathing attire may be worth having at any time of year.

CLIMATE. There are substantial variations around the state, though these are a matter of degree (pun intended) rather than vast differences at any given time of year. Shore areas are cooler in the summer than their inland counterparts; there can be a 10–15 degree difference between Manhattan and the New York City beaches of Coney Island or Riis Park, for instance. The Catskills and Adirondacks are also cooler in the summer, and start to feel the bite of fall in late August, while New York City often stays warm through October. Generally, you can figure on the days being in the 80s or higher in midsummer, 60s–70s in fall, 20s–30s in winter (though it does go into the teens at least a few days every year), and 40s–50s in spring.

WHAT IT WILL COST. Your expenses too will vary dramatically depending on the nature of your trip. In New York City, two people treating themselves well but not extravagantly can easily expect to spend $200 a day. But rates outside NYC run the gamut from a pleasant $20 a night bed-and-breakfasts (for two) in the Leatherstocking District to $125 per person, including all meals and facilities, during high season in the Catskills. With the exception of the Hudson Valley, which has quite a few first class restaurants, dining will be cheaper outside New York City than in the Big Apple itself. The same will be true for accommodations. Specific costs are estimated in the *Practical Information* sections of each chapter in this book.

HINTS TO THE MOTORIST. Buckle up! It is against the law to drive anywhere in the state without the driver's and all passengers' seat belts securely fastened. Noncompliance could result in a $50 fine. The maximum speed limit throughout the state is 55 miles per hour, except where posted. Right turn on red is permitted almost everywhere (unless otherwise stated) except New York City proper. Parking is an expensive proposition in New York City—and there is very little street parking available. Also, those signs that say "Tow-Away Zone" mean it, and it will cost $100 in cash—in addition to the parking fine and a great deal of aggravation to get your car back if it is towed. In upstate regions, snow tires and/or chains may be required during the winter. You may wish to join the American Automobile Association, which has individual organizations in most states (including New York), and which provides emergency road service. The national headquarters is at 8111 Gatehouse Rd., Falls Church, VA 22047. The New York office is at 28 East 78th St., New York, NY 10021.

ACCOMMODATIONS. This will be a running theme throughout this book, but it's always best to reserve ahead. Booking a room at the last minute in some parts of the state may not be a problem, but you don't want to be caught at dusk searching for a place to stay in the Hudson Valley, the Catskills, or New York City. This book features an exceptional range of accommodations, including bed-and-breakfasts, inns, lodges, motels, and hotels. Obviously the prices are going to vary widely, as are the services available—and they will vary from one region of the state to the next. A bed-and-breakfast in Manhattan (yes, they do exist) will run $50–$80 a night for two—which is more than the hotel rate in some of the state's smaller cities but substantially less than the rate at many hotels in Manhattan.

Generally, bed-and-breakfasts will offer rooms in the owner's home. There may or may not be a private bath, and there probably won't be a phone or television in the room. Breakfast is usually included, though you likely will have to look elsewhere for other meals. Each area of the state has its own bread-and-breakfast association, which can be contacted through the local chamber of commerce or the area telephone book.

Inns are popping up rapidly all over the state, and they are enormously popular as weekend getaways. Again, rooms may or may not have private bath, and won't have phone or TV. The rooms, however, will often be very individualized—antique is a favored decor—and there will be common sitting areas where guests can mingle. Many inns in New York State have fine dining rooms as well, and are open to the public for dinner.

Lodges, which are popular around ski areas, offer a dormitory-like atmosphere, common meals (often buffet style), and relatively inexpensive accommodations.

Motels and hotels are what you would expect, with all the standard amenities. Among the chains well represented throughout the state are Howard Johnson's, Ramada Inn, and Holiday Inn. Rates will differ markedly from one city to another even within these chains; see the *Practical Information* section for the area you will be visiting.

One type of accommodation truly unique to New York State is the Catskill resort. *Grossinger's,* the *Concord,* and the *Nevele,* to name a few, are miniature cities unto themselves. When you go to one of these resorts you probably won't need to leave the grounds—not for meals (which are all-you-can-eat extravaganzas), not for sports (from golf to tobogganing), not for meeting people (singles weekends are regular attractions, and some resorts have resident matchmakers), not even for a baby sitter (some resorts have a nurse for the newborns!).

The prices at the resorts reflect this all-inclusive nature, but for those who take advantage of the activities and entertainment available, they are actually a bargain at $100–$150 a day. The rooms themselves vary greatly, even within a given hotel/resort, since renovation is an ongoing process when you have, say, 600–1200 rooms.

Because of the wide variety of accommodations and the nature of the different enterprises, it is impossible to generalize according to categories such as *super deluxe, deluxe,* etc. for the entire state. Thus we have included categories where applicable, and brief descriptions with approximate prices for all listings. One area of uniformity: *American Plan* refers to room plus three meals a day (sometimes including a box lunch); *MAP* or *Modified American Plan* means room plus breakfast and dinner; and *European Plan* refers to room alone.

Finally, those seeking to stay at hostels will find quite a few options throughout the state. Contact the national American Youth Hostel Association, 1332

I St., NW, Washington, DC 20005 for membership information and a complete directory.

DINING OUT. As with accommodations, it is always best to have reservations. In New York City this is almost a necessity at the most popular restaurants, and absolutely necessary at the most expensive ones. But even outside the Big Apple, the areas convenient to major cities—especially New York City—fill up rapidly, particularly on weekends, with those fleeing the cities for some serious rest, relaxation, and fine food. Indeed, the best dining in the state is to be found in New York City and the Hudson Valley, and prices will be about the same for comparable food and surroundings—$40 and up for first class nouvelle American or French food.

Of course there are many less expensive options, but here too reservations are well advised. And, once again, when the nature of the restaurants, inns, and resorts varies so drastically, categorizing is not relevant on a statewide basis. Suffice it to say that we've singled out establishments worth a special effort to visit, and have tried to provide guidelines for costs and what you might expect in the way of atmosphere as well as food. Inns and resorts offering accommodations as well as meals often represent excellent values.

TIPPING. Tipping is a personal expression of your appreciation of someone who has taken pleasure and pride in giving you attentive, efficient, and personal service. Because standards of personal service are highly uneven, you should, when you get genuinely good service, feel secure in rewarding it. When you feel that the service you got was slovenly, indifferent, or surly, don't hesitate to show this by withholding or giving a small tip. Remember, in many places the help are paid very little and depend on tips for the better part of their income, which is supposed to give them incentive to serve you well. These days, the going rate on restaurant service is 15 percent on the amount before taxes. This is especially easy to compute in New York City, where the tax on meals is 8¼ percent—doubling that tax amount is common practice for arriving at a tip. Tipping at counters is 10–15 percent of the check.

For bellhops, 50 cents per bag is usual. However, if you load him down with all manner of bag, hatboxes, cameras, etc., you might consider something extra. For one-night stays in most hotels and motels, you leave nothing. If you stay longer, at the end of your stay leave the maid $1–$1.25 per day, or $5 per person per week for multiple occupancy. If you are staying at an American Plan hostelry, $1.50 per day per person for the waiter or waitress is considered sufficient, and is left at the end of your stay. However, if you have been surrounded by an army of servants, add a few extra dollars and give the lump sum to the captain or maitre d'hotel when leaving and ask him to allocate it.

For many other services you may encounter in a big hotel or resort, figure roughly as follows: doorman, 25¢ for taxi handling, 50¢ for helping with baggage; parking attendant, 50¢; bartender, 15 percent; room service, 10–15 percent; laundry or valet service, 15 percent; pool attendant, 50¢ per day; locker attendant, 50¢ per person per day, or $2.50 per week; golf caddies, $1–$2 per bag, or 15 percent of the greens fee for an 18-hole course or $3 on a free course; barbers, 15 percent; shoeshine attendants, 50–75¢; hairdressers, 15 percent, manicurists, $1.

Give 25¢ for any taxi fare under $1, and 15 percent for any above. However, drivers in New York City seem to expect more, though it is hardly mandatory to offer it unless they've been unusually helpful. Limousine drivers—20 percent. Tipping at curbside check-in at airports is about as it is for baggage handling.

SENIOR-CITIZEN AND STUDENT DISCOUNTS. Seniors and students should always carry identification verifying their status. Senior citizen cards or school identification cards are most common. Discount policies vary widely throughout the state; see *Practical Information.*

DRINKING LAWS. The drinking age in New York State is 21; alcohol may be purchased at licensed liquor stores, beer and wine-coolers at supermarkets. If you are caught driving under the influence of alcohol you will rightfully lose your license and possibly face a jail sentence and fine.

BUSINESS HOURS, HOLIDAYS, AND LOCAL TIME. New York State, like the rest of the United States, is on Standard Time from the last Sunday in October until the first Sunday in April. In April, the clock is advanced one hour for Daylight Savings Time, and in October it is turned back an hour. The entire state lies within the Eastern Time Zone, which is five hours earlier than Greenwich Mean Time on local standard (winter) time.

Most businesses, banks, and some restaurants will be closed on New Year's Day (January 1), Washington's Birthday (third Monday in February), Easter Sunday, Memorial Day (last weekend in May), Independence Day (July 4), Labor Day (end of August/beginning of September), Thanksgiving Day (third Thursday in November), and Christmas Day (December 25). In addition, banks and businesses may be closed on Martin Luther King Jr. Day (January 18), Lincoln's Birthday (February 12), Good Friday, Columbus Day (second Monday in October), Election Day (first Tuesday in November), and Veterans' Day (second Monday in November). Of particular importance in New York City, with its large Jewish population, are the Jewish New Year (Rosh Hashana), and the Day of Atonement (Yom Kippur). These fall in mid-September or early October.

SUMMER SPORTS. The New York State Tourism Division's *I Love NY Outdoors* brochure has extensive information on bicycling, boating, fishing, golf, tennis, and horseback riding. In addition, there are good rafting waters; grass skiing at Catamount Mountain in Hillsdale; and lake, oceanfront, and pool swimming. The Atlantic shore in the Rockaways and on parts of Long Island is also excellent for surfing, though, for the safety of bathers, the sport is usually limited to designated beaches. Baseball fans can watch the Yankees and Mets in action.

WINTER SPORTS. New York is a favorite for skiers— the Catskills and the Adirondacks for downhill, and elsewhere for cross-country. The Catskill resorts also offer snowshoeing and tobogganing, while ice skating is available at rinks throughout the state (some in parks, some privately owned). For the spectator, there's professional hockey in New York City and Buffalo as well as basketball in the Big Apple. Colleges throughout the state also field basketball and football teams.

ROUGHING IT. Part of the 2000-mile Appalachian Trail winds through New York State; for hiking details, consult Volume 4 of the *Appalachian Trail Guide Series* (Appalachian Trail Conference, Box 807, Harpers Ferry, WV 25425). Also useful is *Hiking Trails In the Northeast* by Thomas A. Henley and Neesa Sweet (Greatlakes Living Press). Campsites are available in many state parks, as reflected in the *I Love NY Outdoors* brochure, which also includes some hiking information. Sites at state parks can be reserved ahead through Ticketron outlets, by phone with a major credit card or by mail, by writing to State Parks, Albany, NY 12238. Information on cabins that can be rented in state parks is available from the same address. Only a small portion of campsites, though, is available for reservation; most are first-come, first-served.

There are also numerous private campgrounds throughout the state, including some belonging to the Kampgrounds of America chain. Write for their directory at Box 30558, Billings, MT 59114. The AAA also publishes annual camping directories for the state which are free to members. Be forewarned, however: there are neither campgrounds nor trailer parks near New York City. Bringing a drive-it-yourself camper to Manhattan is a mistake; few garages will accept them and street parking is not a good idea—for safety as well as because street parking is so very limited.

 FISHING. Everyone over age 16 needs a license to fish in New York State at anything other than privately stocked ponds. The state's 70,000 miles of rivers and streams offer a wide range of fishing opportunities, with maps to each area available from Outdoor Publications, Box 355, Ithaca, NY 14850. The *I Love NY Outdoors* brochure also lists all the regional fishing offices and fishing hotlines throughout the state.

 STATE PARKS. An extensive state park system exists in New York, with many locations offering outstanding recreational features. An Empire State Pass, available at individual parks or by writing to State Parks, Albany, NY 12238, will take care of all day-use fees for the year in which it is purchased; the pass has in the past cost $25, with day-use fees at various parks typically running about $3.50 per automobile. Camping, boating, and other fees are, of course, extra.

 NATIONAL PARKS. Gateway National Recreation Area extends through Brooklyn, Queens, Staten Island, and New Jersey. The area includes the Jamaica Bay Wildlife Sanctuary and various facilities for outdoor and indoor festivals as well as more "traditional" beachfront and parkland.

 HINTS TO THE DISABLED. Important sources of information in this field are: *Travel Information Center,* Moss Rehabilitation Hospital, 12th St. and Tabor Rd., Philadelphia, PA 19141; *Easter Seal Society for Crippled Children and Adults,* Director of Education and Information Service, 2023 W. Ogden Ave., Chicago, IL 60612. One publication giving valuable information about facilities for the handicapped is *Access to the World,* by Louise Weiss, published by Henry Holt & Co. (212–599–7600). It can be ordered through your local bookstore. (Holt will not accept orders from individuals.)

POSTAGE. At press time, rates for international mail from the United States are as follows: Surface letters to Canada and Mexico are at the U.S. domestic rate of 22¢ for 1 ounce or less, 39¢ for up to 2 ounces. These rates actually get airmail carriage to those countries (and within the U.S.). Airmail letters to countries other than Canada, Mexico, and some Caribbean and South American countries are 44¢ for ½ an ounce, 88¢ for 1 ounce. Postcards are 14¢ domestically and for Canada and Mexico, 25¢ for surface mail elsewhere, and 33¢ for airmail outside the U.S.

SECURITY. Common sense should always be your guideline, especially in cities. Avoid unlit, unpeopled streets. Leave car doors locked at all times. Carry purses securely—which is to say so that they can't be easily grabbed out of your hand, and certainly so that a pickpocket can't easily dig inside. Never carry a wallet in a back pants pocket. Don't leave baggage unattended, or exposed inside a locked car.

CONVERTING METRIC TO U.S. MEASUREMENTS

Multiply:	by:	to find:
Length		
millimeters (mm)	.039	inches (in)
meters (m)	3.28	feet (ft)
meters	1.09	yards (yd)
kilometers (km)	.62	miles (mi)
Area		
hectare (ha)	2.47	acres
Capacity		
liters (L)	1.06	quarts (qt)
liters	.26	gallons (gal)
liters	2.11	pints (pt)
Weight		
gram (g)	.04	ounce (oz)
kilogram (kg)	2.20	pounds (lb)
metric ton (MT)	.98	tons (t)
Power		
kilowatt (kw)	1.34	horsepower (hp)
Temperature		
degrees Celsius	9/5 (then add 32)	degrees Fahrenheit

CONVERTING U.S. TO METRIC MEASUREMENTS

Multiply:	by:	to find:
Length		
inches (in)	25.40	millimeters (mm)
feet (ft)	.30	meters (m)
yards (yd)	.91	meters
miles (mi)	1.61	kilometers (km)
Area		
acres	.40	hectares (ha)
Capacity		
pints (pt)	.47	liters (L)
quarts (qt)	.95	liters
gallons (gal)	3.79	liters
Weight		
ounces (oz)	28.35	grams (g)
pounds (lb)	.45	kilograms (kg)
tons (t)	1.11	metric tons (MT)
Power		
horsepower (hp)	.75	kilowatts
Temperature		
degrees Fahrenheit	5/9 (after subtracting 32)	degrees Celsius

NOTHING BUT THE BEST

An Introduction to New York State

by
DIANE GALLO

Diane Gallo is an award-winning writer specializing in New York State history, tourism, and travel. An authority on New York's Central Leatherstocking Region, she has had articles published in national and regional newspapers, magazines, books, and travel productions.

New York. The Dutch claimed it, the English ruled it, colonials fought for it, and Frank Sinatra loves it.

New York bills itself as having more to see and do than most countries, which is no exaggeration. Besides boasting one of the most diverse and exciting cities in the world, New York has Oceanfront with a capital "O" and fresh water aplenty (more than 4,000 lakes and ponds and 70,000 miles of rivers and streams with some of the finest fishing in the nation). New York also has rolling forests, mountain ranges, high peaks, and plunging cataracts. Natural wonders aside, New York has country fairs and castles, elegant hotels, posh resorts, and dude ranches. From the living history of the American Revolution to the melodic revolutions of modern music, New York has it all.

The state's almost 50,000 square miles are divided into ten geographical regions, each with its own definite flavor. The taste ranges from Broadway and 42nd Street to smalltown Main Street. (This regionalization makes for hot political battles which New Yorkers love to fight.) The regions include New York City and Long Island, the Hudson Valley, the Catskills, Capital–Saratoga, the Adirondacks, Thousand Islands–Seaway, Central Leatherstocking, Finger Lakes, Niagara Frontier, and Chautauqua-Allegheny.

Upstate vs. Downstate

Despite these distinct regions, New York's 18 million people are rather cavalier about their geography. To the brash and brassy city dwellers, anywhere that's not New York City is upstate. For upstaters, anywhere that's not New York City is downstate. Except of course, for those in the Adirondacks who think of themselves as living in the North Country and those who . . . well, you get the idea.

The essence of New York is variety, and that includes the seasons. New York has four distinct seasons of unsurpassed beauty. Winter snows range from Buffalo's infamous whiteouts to the storybook flakes that fall like blessings upon the Hudson Valley Region. All that snow makes for great downhill and cross-country skiing in the Catskills, Adirondacks, and other regions.

From early May through mid-June, flower festivals herald the spring season. There are azaleas on Long Island estates, tulips in Albany, lilacs in Rochester, and roses and apple blossoms from Niagara to Montauk.

In the summer, playing fields and parks come alive. Among the many local and municipal parks and recreational attractions, the New York State park system offers visitors nearly 150 state parks, 35 state historic sites, and a variety of recreational, educational, and cultural facilities—all at a nominal fee. Nearly 50 million people a year run, hike, bike, swim, boat, and play at parks like Niagara Falls State Park and Allegany State Park. As summer turns to autumn, add leaf watching to this list of recreational activities.

Autumn in New York

Autumn is New York's finest season. With its hillsides glowing with scarlet, gold, and orange, New York matches any display the New England countryside can offer. Weekly "leaf reports" alert travelers to the color changes. As the season intensifies, autumn fire burns from Adirondack peaks down through the Hudson Valley and into the Catskills. Pumpkins and cider appear at roadside stands, signaling the harvest.

Despite its reputation as an urban state, New York has farmlands and countryside you rarely hear about except in *I Love New York* commercials. Long Island potatoes are famous, as are Leatherstocking corn and Finger Lakes wheat. Throughout the upstate region, orchards groan with the fruit of apple, pear, and plum trees.

Taste of the Big Apple

With all this bounty, the only way to taste New York is one piece at a time. Start by taking a bite out of the razzle-dazzle Big Apple. New York City is the world headquarters for the arts and entertainment. Artists, actors, musicians, writers, and entertainers; the famous, the infamous, and just plain nice people live and work here. The city is also a center for printing and publishing, shipping and shopping (if shopping could sparkle, New York would blind you), communications and advertising, fashion and sports, and banking and finance (25 percent of the nation's financial transactions occur here).

Viewed at night from the Empire State Building, the city's canyons shimmer with lights and movement. But no matter how you look at it, New York City is the tops. (Except in danger: Despite a switchblade reputation, New York did not even make the list of America's ten most dangerous cities. Still, be careful.)

The city is home to the most diverse ethnic population in the world. In addition to the well-established enclaves of Chinatown and Little Italy, there's a large Indian and Latin American population as well as a growing Russian community. The city's ethnic composition changes so rapidly, it's tough to nail down exactly who is coming from where and when. (In how many places in the world can you find a Peruvian–Chinese bodega?) All over town, strange languages rumble from throats like subways from tunnels.

But whatever language is spoken, the language of the city is always exciting. Greenwich Village. SoHo. Lincoln Center. The New York Aquarium. Radio City Music Hall and the Rockettes (go ahead, kick up those heels!). Skyscrapers. The Statue of Liberty. Central Park. South Street Seaport. Historic art. Modern art. Museums of life, science, nature, and ethnic and creative arts. The performing arts. Broadway theaters. The best restaurants (watch the waistline, please). Discos. Intimate clubs, cafes, and bistros. Explore New York on foot, by subway, taxi, boat, horseback, hansom carriage, and even helicopter. And to cap off a night of revelry, the Staten Island Ferry.

The City's Playground

Although millions come to sample the Big Apple, there's much more to New York than the city—and all of it's within easy reach. New York's superior highway system will quickly get you anywhere you wish. For example, just 45 minutes on the Long Island Expressway will take you from Manhattan's madness to one of the world's premier summer playgrounds—Long Island. A narrow slice of land (23 miles at its widest) with 250 miles of accessible coastline, the island is the place to escape during the long, hot summer. Long Island offers visitors a superb public parks system including Jones Beach, the largest swimming facility in the world. On the Island's smooth beaches, one may ignore the world and swim, jog, sun, clam, surfcast, windsurf, and just plain relax.

On the island's South Shore, the Hamptons offer summer ambience accentuated by fashionable shopping streets, art galleries, theaters, and restaurants. At Montauk Point on the island's eastern tip, the lighthouse built during colonial times still flashes its warning beacon to signal home port to the Northeast's largest fleet of charter and party boats. On the North Shore are the beaches and harbors of Long Island Sound where *Great Gatsby* chateaus politely elbow for room on the Gold Coast.

The Mighty Hudson

If water is a region's lifeblood, then New York is blessed with a great circulatory system. In addition to the Atlantic surf, the state has two Great Lakes, mountain streams, and mighty rivers. Of New York's major waterways, the Hudson River is perhaps the most famous. As you travel north from New York toward Albany, on the west side of the Hudson are the Catskills, and on the east side are the Taconic Mountains, with splendid views from the heights of each. Seven bridges cross the scenic river, allowing travelers to sample the best of both shores.

River towns cluster on the Hudson's banks offering quaint restaurants, museums, art galleries, antique shops, marinas, amusement parks, country fairs, 19th-century mansions, and 17th-century manor houses. The landscape chronicles the names of those who contributed to a young nation's rise—Van Cortlandt, Livingston, Paine, Washington, Fulton, Carnegie, Vanderbilt, Harriman, Rockefeller.

At each turn of the road, you'll follow George Washington's trail as he battled, dined, and snored his way through historic moments of the Revolution. When exploring the Revolutionary War sites, don't miss West Point, the U.S. Military Academy and America's strategic Revolutionary War stronghold.

The Catskills

Northwest from the Hudson Valley is Rip Van Winkle country—the Catskills. Deeply forested, and beautiful as any you could wish for, this is one of many places you'll want to take your foot off the gas pedal and enjoy the scenery.

Pick any hill, climb it, and savor the view, for the Catskills were made for outdoor enjoyment. Skiing, camping, hiking, rock-climbing, and biking in this hilly country are challenges to the aerobically adventurous. But even with all that exercise, your waistline is still in danger. "Eat, eat!" is the rallying cry at the region's resorts and hotels.

The Catskills' famous tradition of hospitality started during the 19th-century resort boom. Thousands of holiday travelers came to escape the city's swelter, to renew health and vigor, and to reclaim contact with nature. Those old-fashioned traditions of hospitality continue at posh resort hotels and at more modest inns and guest farms. After dinner, you can enjoy the show, because the region is the summer home of many big-name performers who provide guests with a wonderfully entertaining nightlife.

Ingratiating Capital

Moving north, the Catskills turn into the gentler terrain of the Capital-Saratoga district. Here, at the juncture of the Mohawk and Hudson rivers, lies Albany. As New York's capital city and regional commercial center, Albany captures and distills the essence of the state.

Albany is immediately ingratiating. The city's rich historic legacy is set within a bustling commercial framework. Despite differences in architectural eras, Albany's stylistic juxtaposition achieves a curious harmony. The modern Empire State Plaza complex provides a spectacular introduction to the city's center. Against the backdrop of the futuristic government plaza stands the state capitol, Albany's star attraction. It is an impressive example of Chateau architecture and boasts the "million-dollar staircase," a Romanesque version of the Paris Opera's elaborately carved baroque stairhall.

Just about 45 minutes' drive north is the smaller but no less sophisticated Saratoga Springs. At the turn of the century, Saratoga was THE place to be for the summer season. Saratoga casinos equaled the opulence of any in the world. It was the fashionable place to indulge oneself. Whether visitors came to take the mineral waters or wager on their favorite racehorse, Saratoga offered a seductive ambience.

Today, Saratoga's summer season still has ambience. It still offers mineral springs, "the sport of kings" at the racetrack, and cultural programs at the Saratoga Performing Arts Center.

"Little Switzerland"

To the north of the Saratoga district begins the slow rise of the Adirondack Mountains. When Robert Louis Stevenson came to cure his tuberculosis, he dubbed the Adirondacks "Little Switzerland."

The key words here are rugged, timeless, remote. There are 42 peaks over 4,000 feet high. Among them are the mile-high Mount Marcy and the east's highest skiing peak, Whiteface Mountain. (For those who do not climb mountains, Whiteface Mountain Memorial Highway leads visitors to one of the Adirondacks' most spectacular views.)

The Adirondacks was the last region of New York to be explored and surveyed. Of the area's almost 11,000 square miles, nearly a third is held by the state to be "forever wild." With 2½ million acres, the vast Adirondack Forest Preserve is America's largest state park. The region's magnificent upland lake district includes Lake Placid, Saranac Lake, Tupper Lake, and Lake George—Queen of the Lakes. Lake George has a "million-dollar beach" and Lake Placid's chair lifts and elevators provide heart-stopping excursions during winter and summer.

Les Milles Isles

Curving northwest around the Adirondacks like a mother's protective arm is the Thousand Islands region. Although the French estimate of Les Milles Isles was poetic, it doesn't do justice to the region. There are actually 1,834 islands clustered in the 50-mile stretch of the St. Lawrence River.

The islands of the St. Lawrence Seaway preserve the romance of 19th-century grand hotels and mansions. Clayton and Alexandria Bay are headquarters for Thousand Island cruises. One popular jaunt is a three-hour trip that includes Boldt Castle, a 300-room replica of a Rhine castle.

The area boasts some of the best fishing on the North American continent. By local custom, a "shore dinner" is fresh-fried by the guide on the nearest island. Every year, fishermen flock to annual trout and salmon derbies at Pulaski and Oswego.

The St. Lawrence Seaway is part of the world's longest unfortified international border. The Thousand Islands International Bridge at Alexandria Bay, a seven-mile, five-span bridge, is a tribute to the neighborly relations between the United States and Canada.

Leatherstocking

Nestled in New York's heartland is the Central Leatherstocking region (so called because of the leather stockings worn by early settlers). Settled by New England pioneers, Leatherstocking's neat farms and white-spired country churches reflect that Yankee heritage. This is dairy country, with hillsides and meadows ripe with corn and alfalfa.

Leatherstocking Country's crown jewel is Cooperstown. Set at the foot of Lake Otsego, Cooperstown bills itself (with good cause) as the village of great museums. The National Baseball Hall of Fame and Museum is here, keeping the memory of Babe Ruth and Hank Aaron alive for today's fans. Cooperstown is also home to the New York State Historic Association, which operates the Fenimore House with its major collection of Americana, and the Farmers' Museum and Village Crossroads, a re-creation of an early frontier village complete with staff in period costume.

The historic theme continues in the Mohawk Valley with its many Revolutionary War sites. Near Utica, the Herkimer "diamond" mines prove that all that glitters is not real. (The "diamonds" are actually quartz crystals.) If it's gems you're after, then mine Leatherstocking's mother lode of bargains at factory outlets that offer everything from fashions to housewares.

Finger Lakes—Water Everywhere

The hills and dairy country of Leatherstocking give way to the Finger Lakes region, which is—if you'll excuse a pun—awash with water. Brooks. Ponds. Streams. Rapids. Rivers. Falls. Little lakes. Fair to middlin' lakes. Mighty lakes. Chains of lakes.

Indian legend says that the Great Spirit put down his hand and water sprang from where his fingers pressed the earth. Certainly it's no hardship to imagine a master's hand at work here. The Finger Lakes district has 11 beautiful lakes, including the five major eastern lakes of Cayuga, Owasco, Skaneateles, Otisco, and Seneca. Unimpeachable sources say that the trout in Seneca Lake weigh in at as much as 32 pounds (the season starts in April). And when you reel in that big one, make sure you've got a bottle of fine Finger Lakes wine on hand, for the Finger Lakes region is justly famous for its vineyards and wineries. When you take your wine tour, make sure it ends with a tasting.

Niagara and Its Mighty Thunder

If Long Island is water on the wave, and the Hudson is water on the move, then Niagara Falls, at the opposite end of the state, is water on the rampage. "Spectacular" is not too strong an adjective to describe Niagara Falls, one of the seven natural wonders of the world. Native Indians who witnessed the dramatic splitting of the short but powerful Niagara River called it "thunder of the waters." At any second, 200,-000 cubic feet of water (weighing more than 62 pounds per foot) rushes over the lip of the falls after having provided upstream the single greatest source of hydroelectric power in North America.

For a heart-stopping journey, do what celebrities like King Edward VII, Prime Minister Nehru, and Marilyn Monroe have done—don a slicker and take a *Maid of the Mist* boat to the very foot of the cataracts. Nearly 10 million people visit this riveting scenic attraction each year. The Niagara Frontier is also home to New York's second city, Buffalo; Lewiston's 200-acre Artpark, a major cultural center; and Darien Lake Theme Park in Darien Center.

Culture in the Wilderness

In New York, fantastic scenery is almost routine. Tucked away in New York's southwest corner, the Chautauqua-Allegheny region is no exception. When pioneers and settlers flowed west from the terminus of the Erie Canal, they largely ignored the southern region and left it relatively undeveloped and sparsely populated.

However, those who did travel south seemed to run out of names. Allegheny, Cattaraugus, and Chautauqua are the region's county names. But they're also lake names, river names, town names, even institute names. Chautauqua is a county, a town, a lake, and an institute. Allegheny is a river and a mountain range. Allegany (note the difference in spelling) is a county park and a state park. Cattaraugus is a county, a town, and a creek.

If you had to briefly characterize Chautauqua-Allegheny, "culture in the wilderness" would do it. No other region offers the curious (but pleasing) contrast of rugged countryside and a nationally known center for the arts, education, religion, and recreation—The Chautauqua Institution.

This westernmost region of New York is a land of small towns, small lakes, a Great Lake, and vast forests. Allegheny County alone has 23 almost untouched state forests and 50,000 acres of publicly owned wild woods. Farther west in Chautauqua County is Allegany State Park. With 94.5 square miles (65,000 acres), Allegany is New York's largest state park as well as one of the most primitive and popular. Wildlife (beavers, raccoons, deer, black bear, game birds) is abundant and birdwatching (over 200 species sighted) is superb. The park also boasts great fishing, hiking, and camping. Here life is stripped down to its most simple components—a sleeping bag and a starry night.

From a still Chautauqua woodland to a windswept Long Island beach to the rush of Broadway and 42nd Street, traveling in New York is like browsing a fabulous gourmet menu. Artful appetizers. Main dishes rich in regional textures and subtly seasoned with history. Side dishes spicy with personality. Sweet desserts.

New York is too much for one meal. You need to come back again and again to savor it fully. Bon appetit!

NEW YORK'S HISTORY

by
DIANE GALLO

New York's first tourists—Henry Hudson and the 18 crewmen of the *Half Moon*—sailed into New York harbor in 1609. Algonquin Indians, no doubt curious about the strange canoe in the river, came to offer greetings. Dressed in deerskins and ceremonial headfeathers, the Algonquins carried gifts of tobacco, sweet berries, corn bread, and furs.

Although the reception was apparently friendly, the crew's chief mate wrote in the log, "We durst not trust them," thus setting the tone for later generations of New York City tourists. (Despite New York City's dangerous reputation and its claim to be tops in everything, it doesn't even make the list of the ten most dangerous American cities.)

At the time Hudson arrived, the region had around 30,000 Indians about evenly divided between Iroquois and Algonquins. The Algonquins were concentrated on Manhattan Island, Long Island, and the lower Hudson Valley and lived in New York thousands of years before Europeans came. Around 1300, small bands of warlike Iroquois began filtering into the hills and valleys of central New York. Gradually the Iroquois conquered their Algonquin neighbors and dominated the region.

Indian Tribes Unite

The Iroquois became a major force in 1570 when the Onondaga chief, Hiawatha, persuaded the Senecas, Cayugas, Onondagas, Oneidas, and Mohawks to unite in the League of Five Nations. For over a century, the confederacy's 2,000 warriors held the fragile balance of power between Britain and France in their hands.

The Iroquois Confederacy ruled the land much as a militant chamber of commerce might—with a policy that nowhere was the grass greener or the water sweeter. The area was rich in wildlife, fertile lands, and the natural waterways which functioned as early superhighways.

Indians taught the settlers how to survive in the wilderness and gave them skills which provided for their future economic well-being. Among other things, the settlers learned how to grow corn—probably the most valuable New York crop since 1650—and how to make maple syrup (New York outproduces Vermont).

Woman's Role Respected

In Iroquois society, women were highly respected. Large family groups deferred to the oldest woman. All real property belonged to women and compensation for a woman's life required twice the amount of wampum as for a man's.

New York's Indian influence is preserved today in museums throughout the state. Native Americana can be seen in Salamanca, the only city in the country located on an Indian reservation and the site of the Seneca-Iroquois National Museum. For a taste of early Indian life, the Owasco Stockaded Indian Village in Auburn is a detailed reconstruction built upon the excavations of an actual Indian village. Other Indian museums include the Indian Heritage Museum in Painted Post (which houses a 20,000-year-old mastodon bone) and the Museum of the Iroquois Indian in Schoharie.

Place names like Saratoga, Manhattan, Poughkeepsie, Niagara Falls, Montauk, and Ticonderoga remind us of the Indian heritage. In towns and hamlets throughout the state, the Indian seasonal festivals like spring maple festivals and autumn harvest festivals are still celebrated.

Going Dutch

When Hudson sailed into the mouth of the "mighty deep-throated river" that would later bear his name, he was convinced he had found the Northwest Passage that would lead across America (17th-century maps showed America as a narrow strip of land) and to the Pacific. Because of Hudson's discoveries, the Dutch claimed the land and named it New Netherland.

Peter Minuit, the first governor, arrived in 1626 with orders from the Dutch West Indian Company to buy Manhattan Island from the Algonquins (more accurately, the Algonkians). With his famous purchase, Minuit struck New York's first marketing coup and became one of the few settlers who ever paid the Indians for anything. The first

Dutch settlements were established at Fort Orange (Albany) and at New Amsterdam on Manhattan Island. New Amsterdam attracted traders from all over the world, and by 1644, eighteen languages were spoken there, causing one cynical observer to note Manhattan had already acquired the "arrogance of Babel."

Although New Netherland lasted only 55 years, the Dutch left a permanent mark with place names like Brooklyn (Breuckelen), Flushing, Yonkers, Rensselaer, Tappan Zee, Kill Van Kull, Peekskill, and folk stories like Rip Van Winkle and *The Legend of Sleepy Hollow.* Today, the Dutch legacy can be traced along the Hudson River in such restorations as the 18th-century Van Cortlandt Manor at Croton-on-Hudson, and in the 17th-century Old Dutch Church at Tarrytown.

The English—Jeweled Hands

In 1664, Peter Stuyvesant, the peg-legged Dutch governor, reluctantly surrendered the beleaguered New Amsterdam to the British. The colony was renamed New York in honor of the Duke of York, who later became King James II. The Duke's interest in New York was purely financial, but the colony proved a disappointing exercise in diminishing returns. Maintaining defenses and enforcing trade regulations in the face of colonial resistance cost more than it brought in.

Despite the costs, New York was Britain's most important outpost. Its geographical position made it a key point in the 100–year struggle between France and Britain for control of North America. Between 1690 and 1760, a series of wars—in America called the French and Indian Wars—were fought by the two powers. During these wars both sides tried to make allies of the powerful Iroquois Confederacy. No master's chess game could have been more tense and convoluted, for with each move, the balance was threatened. Finally, the Iroquois aided the English in driving out the French.

Jeweled hands gripped the uneasy reins of power. English governors gave away valuable tracts of New York land to their friends. Some of these estates, or manors, covered hundreds of square miles. Although many settlers owned their farms, many more were tenants on the manors, which caused much bad feeling.

The British colonial system exhibited a genius for "muddling through." Expansion was difficult because frontier settlements were raided constantly by the French and Indians. Boundary disputes and escalating demands for home rule and the deregulation of economic activities plagued New York. The corrupt land and tenancy system was riddled with speculation and monopoly. By 1691 the treasury was empty and the young colony was in confusion. Mismanagement and sheer incompetence of the colonial rulers had taken its toll.

Self-Rule Evolves

During the time between Dutch rule and the Revolutionary War, New York evolved self-government. By 1710 the Assembly had established a power base which worked through parties with a disciplined membership. The rich merchants of Albany and New York City assembled up on one side. The small farmers in the Hudson Valley and the "Yankee" towns on Long Island lined up on the opposing side. Complicating factors included jealousy between the Dutch and English, factional feuds, and religious splinters.

Colonial New Yorkers were by turn hard drinking, religious, and touchy about their rights. (The same could be said even today.) When Parliament passed the Stamp Act to help pay England's debts from its wars with France, societies of protest, called the Sons of Liberty, retaliated with a boycott. Huge liberty poles were erected and provided the exclamation point for fiery speeches against the English. One of these poles was cut down by English soldiers in 1770 and the ensuing fistfight on Manhattan's lower East Side came to be known as the Battle of Golden Hill—sometimes called the first battle of the Revolution.

Tea Party Encore

In the face of trade losses, Parliament repealed the Stamp Act. However, a few years later it imposed a new set of taxes, including one on tea. When Paul Revere galloped into New York with news of the Boston Tea Party, New Yorkers brewed a pot of their own tea by staging an encore performance in New York harbor.

Day by day, amidst growing religious, political, and economic tensions and fears, a dissatisfied populace eroded the king's Law until there was very little left of "His Majesty's just and undoubted authority, Order and good Government."

New Yorkers realized their dependence on the redcoats for the defense of the frontier. But the French and Indian wars had brought the colonists together and had given them a common cause. Together in hardship, they began to think of themselves as Americans rather than as New Yorkers or Virginians. They had gained the self-reliance and independence which would later flower into . . .

Revolution!

At the outbreak of the Revolutionary War in 1775, New York was still mostly wilderness. Only a fringe of land along the Hudson and the coast of Long Island were settled. Despite its undeveloped state, New York saw a major part of the war. Nearly one-third of all Revolutionary War battles were fought in New York. About 45,000 New Yorkers, or one-quarter of the colony's population, took up arms. Battles were fought at Brooklyn Heights and Harlem Heights. Fully one-fourth of the dwellings on Manhattan Island—a prime objective of the English forces—went up in flames in the great fires of 1776 and 1778.

In the Adirondacks of upstate New York, Ethan Allen and Benedict Arnold, along with a small group of patriots, drove the English garrison from Fort Ticonderoga on May 10, 1775. Known as the "Key to a Continent," Fort Ticonderoga is today a major attraction which has been fully restored and colorfully recalls those turbulent times.

Amidst the gunfire, political life continued. Shortly before the British fleet arrived at New York, the Convention of Representatives of the State of New York met in White Plains and approved the Declaration of Independence on July 9, 1776. When the British advanced on White Plains, the convention moved to what is now the Senate House Museum in Kingston and completed the first state constitution.

French assistance gave the Americans some much needed breathing room. Until 1778 the Iroquois—still allied with the English—were raiding unprotected settlements. In 1779 Washington sent Generals John Sullivan and James Clinton with an army to repel the Iroquois. The annual General Clinton Canoe Regatta—a whitewater canoe race from Lake Otsego in Cooperstown down the Susquehanna River to Bainbridge—retraces the trail Clinton's force took in the campaign that destroyed the power of the Indians in New York forever.

Peace Restored

The final battle of the war was fought in Johnstown in 1781. Two years later, the English signed a peace treaty recognizing American independence. While waiting for the treaty to be signed, George Washington lived for 18 months at Knox Headquarters which is now a state historic Site and regional museum in Newburgh. From there he refused "with surprise and astonishment . . . and abhorrence" the idea that he become the new country's king.

At the end of the hostilities, Washington bade an emotional farewell to his soldiers at Fraunces Tavern on Pearl Street in New York City. Five years later, on April 30, 1789, he stood on the open balcony of the old City Hall—now the Federal Hall Memorial—on Wall Street and took the oath of office.

Throughout New York are state historic sites which recall the drama and courage of the fledgling colonial army. At the Oriskany Battlefield, General Herkimer fought Chief Joseph Brant in "the bloodiest battle of the revolution." At the Saratoga Battle Monument at Schuylerville, British Commander General Burgoyne surrendered. Fort Stanwix in Rome—a reconstructed Revolutionary War outpost and living history program—takes visitors back to 1778. On the Niagara Frontier, the roar you hear may not always be the falls. Roaring cannons, fife and drums, and redcoats armed with muskets are part of the unabashed pageantry at Old Fort Niagara on Lake Ontario.

Explosive Growth

If New York bore the brunt of the Revolutionary War, it also benefited most handsomely. When the war ended, New York's population was about 200,000, ranking it fifth among the 13 states. By 1825 New York held first place in population, commerce, transportation, and agriculture.

No sooner did the sound of gunfire fade from the hills than long lines of Conestoga wagons began to form at Albany. Lumbering westward, the wagons hauled a human river of settlers into the new "western frontier" of New York. Later, New York was the funnel through which hundreds of thousands of settlers flowed farther west.

Travel in the young state was a hardship. The Hudson and Mohawk rivers were the only main thoroughfares. Indian trails usually followed ridges above the valleys and traders and hunters, as well as turnpike, canal, and railroad builders discovered that Indian paths were usually the shortest routes.

As settlement grew, transportation became a priority. Under the leadership of De Witt Clinton, the Erie Canal—"Clinton's Ditch" to its detractors—was built between 1817 and 1825. Via canal, goods from Buffalo and the country's interior could be shipped easily and cheaply to New York City. The 363-mile artery delivered a massive economic jolt to the cities of Albany, Amsterdam, Utica, Syracuse, Rochester, and Buffalo.

Hardly had the canals made New York a driving force than the railroads began to boost the economy and Buffalo (New York's "second city") became one of the world's largest railroad centers. The increased activity encouraged foreign and domestic trade and stimulated manufacturing and commercial agriculture, making New York a leading dairy state.

The period from 1825 to 1865 was the heyday of Manhattan's "merchant princes." These merchants garnered control of well over half the nation's imports and over one-third of its exports, developed new trade, and helped promote pioneer industrialization. In the process they amassed great fortunes. As the 19th century progressed, businessmen like John D. Rockefeller, J. P. Morgan, and Edward H. Harriman made millions in industrial development. These men and others like them made New York the unrivaled financial center of the United States.

New Americans Arrive

New York celebrates its ethnic diversity with hundreds of annual folk festivals, such as the International Celtic Festival, the German Alps Festival, and the Italian Festival held at Hunter and in other towns throughout the state. These festivals recall the vast immigrations of the late 19th and early 20th centuries. Between 1840 and 1860, Irish and German immigrants poured into America. After 1880, waves of immigrants came from southern and eastern Europe—Italians, Poles, Russians, Romanians, and East European Jews. Between 1892 and 1954, 20 million immigrants passed through Ellis Island in New York City—or 90 percent of all immigrants to the United States.

These hopeful new Americans with their varied customs invented a brand-new life style with new cultural and religious patterns. Religious tolerance, which had begun with the Dutch, expanded. Religious revivals blossomed. Central New York earned the term "burned over" because of the successive waves of intense religious fervor that scorched the region. Today, there's a denomination to suit every inclination and New York's houses of worship range from magnificent cathedrals to simple country churches.

Growing out of the religious ardor of the 19th century were the humanitarian movements of social reform—the temperance movement, the worker safety and child labor law crusade, the establishment of the free school system, the abolition of slavery, and the women's rights movement. Perhaps something of the independent Iroquois women's spirit clung to the earth of Seneca Falls. Here in the Iroquois heartland is the Women's Rights National Historical Park where Elizabeth Cady Stanton and Lucretia Mott held the first women's rights convention.

As America marched into the 20th century, New York led the way. The state had one of the finest transportation systems in the country. New York was America's radio broadcast and printing and publishing center. The state was also a major manufacturer of clothing, cameras, typewriters, sewing machines, and electrical equipment.

When World War I exploded, New York's development accelerated. War and prosperity followed in rapid succession. The 1920s was a decade of change in New York. This was due in no small part to the efforts of Governor Alfred E. Smith, who established social reforms that improved working conditions and promoted the public welfare.

Charles A. Lindbergh's famous flight from New York to Paris in 1927 catapulted America into a new age, providing a golden glow that carried all the way into the Great Depression of the 1930s. Native New Yorker Franklin D. Roosevelt served as President of the United States for an unprecedented four terms, guiding the nation through the depression and World War II. His home in Hyde Park is a Historic Site and remains as it was at his death in 1945. (See *Hudson Valley* chapter below.)

Historic Sites Preserved

In the years since Hudson first entered New York harbor, a new world has grown and flourished, but the old world has not been forgotten. New York offers choice slices of history from every era. Fine museums, preservations, and historic sites are dedicated to every aspect of the state's evolution. Led by guides in period dress, you can sample 19th-century country life at Genesee Country Village near Mumford, the Farmers Museum in Cooperstown, or the Old Bethpage Village Restoration on Long Island. Or step into a Gay Nineties castle in Cortland and take a steam train excursion in Arcade on the antique Arcade & Attica Railroad. From the Dutch manors of the Hudson Valley to the whaling museums of Long Island to the Racing Museum at Saratoga, whatever your period of interest, New York's got a museum for you.

Today New York sets the pace for the nation in business, cultural activities, and urban life. From its brash and brassy urban centers to its rolling emerald hillsides, New York truly is "The Empire State"— the microcosm from which America has taken shape and form.

NEW YORK CITY

by
IRA MAYER AND JOANN GRECO

Ira Mayer is president of Presentation Consultants, Inc., New York City, and a travel writer for the New York Post. *JoAnn Greco is a New York City-based free-lance writer specializing in travel subjects.*

New York City has more of everything you could want in the way of culture, entertainment, food, and activities than any other place in the United States. Alas, it also has more of many things you could easily do without, such as crowds, dirt, subway breakdowns, and a pace that can be staggering.

That's the paradox of the Big Apple, and the trade-off between the two is what every New Yorker grapples with daily. There is the excitement of having access to Broadway, major museums, and music of every variety. And there is the sometimes overpowering feeling of helplessness and impersonality as simple chores such as commuting to work or shopping for groceries sap energy to a degree that non-New Yorkers can never fully understand.

To appreciate New York City it is necessary to accept these contradictions, at least for the duration of the visit. New York is a wonderland, and New Yorkers often have to remind themselves of that fact. They don't often look at others on the subway or in elevators, but they do have the chance to hear more jazz and opera than any other city in the country, and they will offer impassioned responses about the best route, the biggest discounts, the most off-the-beaten-track theaters, restaurants, or galleries.

Expect Extremes

Just as the character of New York can be to extreme, so too are the expenses of visiting there. Although we will recommend the most consistently reasonable (by New York standards) establishments there are, no such thing as inexpensive lodging exists in New York—not when compared to other areas of the country. But you can eat cheaply and well, use relatively inexpensive public transportation, and see the sights most reasonably—or you can pay a king's ransom for the best service in the world, including chauffeur-driven limousines and nouvelle American cuisine at $75 (and more) a person.

The key to New York for those on a budget, though, is flexibility:

• You can see a show on or off Broadway, or an opera, ballet, or concert at half-price—if you are willing to wait until the day of the performance and select from what is available at specially designated TKTS booths in the Times Square area or at the World Trade Center.

• By choosing carefully among the city's nightclubs, your minimums can be applied to meals or drinks that are reasonably priced, as at Michael's Pub.

• To dine in opulence, select a pretheater fixed-price dinner at such luxurious restaurants as Central Park's Tavern on the Green—for less than a third what you would pay ordering à la carte. Alternately, New York offers an enormous selection of ethnic eateries where atmosphere is strong, food freshly prepared, and prices low.

No one can see all of New York, not in a single visit, and probably not in a single lifetime. It isn't that the city is particularly large, especially given that most tourists concentrate on Manhattan Island between Wall Street at the south and Lincoln Center at the north. It's the density of the city that makes New York such a challenge for the visitor and native alike. The city towers into the sky and spreads its tentacles below ground, yet there are buildings so narrow that their addresses rise by halves.

Select Your Pleasures

The trick is to be selective—and then narrow your choices. Say your interest is art. You couldn't absorb the entire Metropolitan Museum of Art in one day, let alone such other outstanding museums as the Museum of Modern Art (MOMA), Whitney, and Guggenheim. And this ignores the galleries of 57th Street, upper Madison Avenue, and Soho, the medium-size collections in smaller museums, and the special exhibitions that are invariably placed around town.

Most visitors want to divide their time among the major sites and attractions—a museum or two, the Statue of Liberty, Wall Street, a Broadway or off-Broadway show, the World Trade Center, Chinatown, nightclubs, Greenwich Village, the South Street Seaport, restaurants,

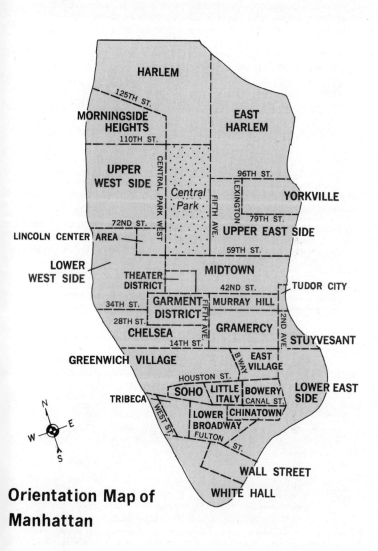

Orientation Map of Manhattan

Rockefeller Center, and so on. A little planning can make the going easier, so that you aren't spending the bulk of your time criss-crossing the city on buses and subways. Grouping the attractions that satisfy your interests saves considerable time as well as transportation costs. It also leaves you feeling less hurried.

You may wish to build your trips around dining. If that is the case, and there are specific restaurants you want to try, make reservations as early as possible, remembering that in order to take advantage of pretheater specials you will probably have to be seated between, say, 5:30 and 7 P.M. (The rules vary from restaurant to restaurant.) Reservations are also recommended for lunch on weekdays at those establishments catering to business executives, and for brunch on weekends.

Shopper's Paradise

You may also want to spend a great deal of time shopping. Macy's and Bloomingdale's are special favorites both for the array of merchandise and the panache with which it is presented. The designer boutiques are on Madison Avenue in the 60s and 70s; the near-wholesale outlets are on the lower East Side along Orchard Street. Second-hand clothes —some eccentric, some outrageous—are to be found on Second Avenue around 10th Street.

However you organize your sightseeing, remember to keep your eyes wide open. There are skyscrapers to be appreciated, windows to be gazed at (especially department stores such as Altman's and Lord & Taylor at Christmas), traffic to watch for (speeding bicycle messengers as well as automobiles, buses, and trucks). Best of all, there are the myriad different people to watch.

New York is a city of constant change, be it the skyline, the streets (forever being ripped open), or the people. The character will be different every time you visit, partly as a function of the different sites you choose to see, partly as a reflection of the city's own mood swings.

EXPLORING NEW YORK CITY

Lower Manhattan encompasses the earliest settlements of the city and includes roughly everything south of Canal Street—an area that is larger today than ever. The reason? Many of the newer skyscrapers and apartment buildings crowding the harbor sit on landfill, accounting for the current position of Water Street, which is quite far inland. Across the East River lies the borough of Brooklyn, connected to Manhattan by (starting farthest downriver and heading north) the Brooklyn, Manhattan, and Williamsburg Bridges. West of the Hudson is New Jersey, and to the south (with the Verrazano-Narrows Bridge in sight) is Staten Island.

The southern tip of Manhattan is known as the financial district because it houses the American and New York Stock exchanges, as well as numerous trading, insurance, and banking firms, though relatively few such companies are actually located on Wall Street itself.

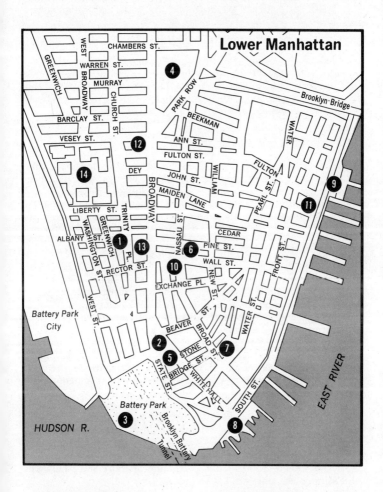

Lower Manhattan

Points of Interest

1) American Stock Exchange
2) Bowling Green
3) Castle Clinton Nat. Monument
4) City Hall
5) Customs House
6) Federal Hall Memorial
7) Fraunces Tavern
8) Ferry to Staten Island
9) Fulton Fish Market
10) N.Y. Stock Exchange
11) South Street Seaport
12) St. Paul's Chapel
13) Trinity Church
14) World Trade Center

This is also the center of much of the city's official business, including City Hall, the Municipal Building, and city, state, and federal courts, and offices.

There are remnants throughout the Wall Street-Battery Park area of the city's actual beginnings. Many of the twisting side streets are filled with historical buildings and references, some of the more important of which are highlighted below. But, the downtown is growing up as well as out: the building of the World Trade Center in the late 1960s sparked a revitalization of the neighborhood and it is now possible to see 70-story buildings jutting over tiny brownstones.

Battery Park and Environs

This area is much improved, thanks to the new Battery Park City, a Cesar Pelli-designed complex of office buildings and apartment houses right on the Hudson. Among the points of interest are:

• World Trade Center. Cortlandt and Church sts. Best known for its gigantic twin towers, the complex consists of seven buildings, all connected by a vast underground network of shops. The 107th floor of Tower No. 2 is an enclosed observation deck (466–7397) that is the highest in the world, although the building is second in height to Chicago's Sears Tower. Admission: $2.95, adults; $1.50, children. Perched way above the city in Tower No. 1 is the famed Windows On The World restaurant. It's very expensive, and a drink at the neighboring Hors d'Oeuvrerie or City Lights bar affords similar views. Business clothing is required at the very least—no leisure suits.

• Battery Park. This park, providing striking waterside views, is home to the Castle Clinton National Monument, a fort built in 1811 to defend New York against British attack. Through the years, the building has also served as a theater and aquarium. Inside, the landmark has been transformed into a free museum, documenting the history of the fort.

• Statue of Liberty. A gift from the French, the statue marked its 100th anniversary in New York Harbor in 1986, at which time Liberty Island was reopened following completion of renovations made for the celebration. On Liberty Island, a visit to the American Museum of Immigration (732–1286) is in order. A ferry ride from Battery Park to the island costs $3.25 for adults ($1.50 for children), and admissions to the statue and museum are included.

Wall Street: Financial Center of the World

Literally speaking, Wall Street is only a few narrow blocks along which once ran the northernmost wall of the city, but the street name has become synonymous for the area. Worth seeing are:

• The Stock Exchanges. The New York Stock Exchange, 20 Broad St. (656–5167) and the American Stock Exchange, 86 Trinity Pl. (306–1000) offer free tours and/or exhibits during trading hours. You can look down from a balcony as hundreds of brokers shout and wave papers, all the while running at incredible speeds. It's a grade-school civics textbook come to life.

- Trinity Church. Broadway and Wall Street (602–0700). The Gothic Revival structure (designed by Richard Upjohn) that currently occupies the site is the third Trinity Church. The graveyard dates from before 1697; much history is written on its headstones. If the gate is open you can wander along its tree-lined paths to seek out the final resting places of Robert Fulton and Alexander Hamilton.
- Federal Hall. 15 Pine St. (264–8711). This national memorial is administered by the National Park Service. The site of George Washington's inauguration in 1789, the building now houses permanent exhibits of early historical documents (reproductions of which are on sale), including the Bill of Rights. You can even listen to a tape recounting the proceedings of the John Peter Zenger trial, the famous 1765 "freedom of the press" case.
- U.S. Customs House. At the intersection of State, Whitehall, and Bridge sts. This ornate granite building is on the site where Peter Minuit allegedly purchased Manhattan from the Indians. The current building, built in 1907, features the famous rotunda filled with artworks from the Works Progress Administration.
- Fraunces Tavern. 54 Pine St. (269–0144). This legendary restaurant is where George Washington bade farewell to his troops before retiring as commander-in-chief. It was here that the original Chamber of Commerce of the State of New York was founded in 1768 to help fight against the Stamp Act and the tea tax. The current building (erected in 1907) is a faithful duplication of the original. Downstairs is a restaurant and bar, upstairs is a small museum, centering around Washington. Both the restaurant and museum are closed on weekends.

South Street Seaport

The newly renovated seaport, at Fulton St., might justifiably be called the new center of downtown. The complex revolves around the three-story Fulton Market Building which is replete with restaurants (traditional and fastfood), take-out markets, and boutiques. A good introduction to the area is "South Street Venture," a multimedia presentation shown hourly every day ($4.25 adults, $2.75 children).

Last year saw the opening of another mall, Pier 17. From the outside, especially at night, it is like a giant, illuminated gingerbread house jutting into the East River. It features more exclusive food and shopping establishments—and a walkway right on the edge of the water.

The side streets of the Seaport are filled with more shops, some of them unusual and interesting, most familiar outlets of large chains. Among the more notable: Caswell Massey at 21 Fulton St. is a wonderful outlet brimming with lovely scents and sensibilities. Down the block at 18 Fulton St., Brookstone is filled with hardware extraordinaire. Booklovers will also want to check out the new downtown branch of the Strand bookstore, at 159 John St. Although much smaller than the celebrated store in Greenwich Village, this one is slicker, more modern, and easier to get around.

The Seaport Museum, Visitor's Center, and the museum's shops are on Museum Block, and certainly worth a visit. Not to be missed are the five late-19th-century and early-20th-century square-rigged sailing ships on view: the four-masted bark *Peking,* the *Ambrose Lightship,* the three-masted *Wavertree,* and the schooners *Lattie G. Howard* and *Pioneer.* The latter can be chartered for up to 40 people for about $800. Generally, the Seaport is great for people-watching, especially on week-day evenings and weekends, when the throngs who work on Wall Street take to the air (and local bars), causing incredible congestion and merrymaking.

As for dining, a few suggestions: Sweets, 2 Fulton St., and Sloppy Louie's right around the corner on South St., are still the area's best, and certainly most consistent. They've spruced up a bit with the com-ing of the Seaport, but they maintain long traditions of serving fresh seafood in unique surroundings. Sweets is the more formal, and not inexpensive. Sloppy Louie's has tile floors, leatherette banquettes, and waiters who know your business better than you. The other best bet is to snack from the wide array of international fast-food eateries; the food won't be great, but it will be fun.

In the summer, there is the added attraction of numerous street entertainers and professional musicians playing and passing the hat. You're sure to stumble upon something interesting no matter where you look. There are also several series of summer weekend concerts on one of the piers.

City Hall

Most of the municipal government buildings are near City Hall Park, a favorite of the downtown lunchtime crowds. The beautiful Brooklyn Bridge, now over 100 years old, extends almost into City Hall Park. When touring, be sure to stop at:

• City Hall. The seat of the city's government has been located in City Hall Park at Broadway and Murray sts. since 1811. This beautiful Federal style building is considered to be one of the finest public buildings in America. The Governor's Room contains a notable collec-tion of historic portraits and antique furniture.

• St. Paul's. This chapel at Broadway and Fulton sts. has been standing since 1766, when George Washington first worshiped there. You'll see his boxed pew on the left side of the outer aisle; it's marked with the Great Seal of the United States. The tiny church cemetery remains something of an anachronism, situated as it is in the shadow of the World Trade Center looming overhead.

• Woolworth Building. Once the tallest building in New York, this 1913 Cass Gilbert structure stands 60 stories high. Its towering Gothic Revival spirals are still beautiful, especially in relation to the newer glass towers so prevalent downtown. The building features an observa-tion deck—it's free—and carolers can be heard in December singing (but hidden from view) from the ornate mosaic gallery that surrounds the lobby.

• Brooklyn Bridge. The 6,775-foot suspension bridge is a testament to the immigrant workers who labored for so many years to build it. Underneath the vaulting is a newly instituted museum detailing the long years of toil dedicated to realizing the dream of father-and-son engineers John and Washington Roebling. It is one of the three bridges connecting Manhattan and Brooklyn.

Chinatown

The traditional image of Chinatown is one of mystery and shrouded glances, but the reality is quite different. New York's Chinatown is a cheerful, bustling place brimming with Chinese restaurants, shops, and other ethnic touches (such as the pagoda-style telephone booths). Many shopkeepers still prefer to do their bookkeeping with the ancient abacus; apothecary and herb shops where family medicinal formulas are compounded are also widespread. Visitors shouldn't leave the area without purchasing something particularly characteristic of China, such as the brocaded gowns or tea sets found in almost every store. Chinatown has for the most part escaped becoming overly conscious of its touristy status, so you can find prices quite to your liking.

Bordered by Lower Manhattan to the south, Little Italy to the east and Greenwich Village to the north, the main drags, as it were, are Canal Street, the Bowery, and, most of all, Mott Street. Stalls and shop windows on these and other less-colorful streets are piled high with exotic displays of condiments and herbs, snowpeas, bean curd, shark fins, duck eggs, dried fungi, squid, and other ingredients used in the delectable cuisine, which is naturally the area's most famous attraction. But sightseers may also want to take in a visit to the Chinese Museum at 81 Mott St. (964–1542). For $1 you can view exhibits of ancient Chinese coins and costumes, deities, and dragons. Displays of flowers, fruits, chopsticks, instruments, and incense are also presented with explanations of their history and symbolism.

If at all possible, try to visit this area during the Chinese New Year celebrations in mid- to late-February. It is then that Chinatown really preens itself for the world to see. It gets noisy because of the fireworks, but it's quite a time.

Lower East Side

The former center of New York's immigrant Jewish population is especially known these days for its astounding array of quality merchandise at heavily discounted prices. Delancey, Grand, and Orchard sts. are the focal points of the area, and on Sunday mornings they are packed with bargain hunters. The most popular items are couture clothing, handbags, and linen goods. The name of the game here is haggling—never accept anything for the price offered, for you are expected to bargain! Whatever you do, don't forget to top off your stay with a visit to Ratner's, 138 Delancey St. (677–5588). This strictly Kosher dairy restaurant is great for blintzes, lox (smoked salmon), herring salad, and whitefish.

Little Italy

Cross Canal Street at Mott or Mulberry and it's like crossing into another country—this time, Italy. Centered on Grand, Mulberry, and

Mott streets, Little Italy is where many of the Italian immigrants settled in the early 1900s. Today, that cultural flavor remains in the multitude of restaurants and old-style Italian groceries. Ferrara's, 195 Grand St. (226–1650), is the best-known coffee and pastry shop, but dozens of similar eateries abound, most of which don't have the long lines you'll encounter on summer nights at Ferrara's. (Our favorite: Cafe Biondo, 141 Mulberry St.; 226–9285. The chocolate cheesecake is a knockout here.)

You'll also find plenty of Italian restaurants, clam bars, imported food shops, and cafes. Two of the more famous clam bars are Umberto's, 129 Mulberry St. (431–7545), and Vincent's, 119 Mulberry St. (226–8133). Beware, though—with the exception of these and a few other old standbys like Luna, 112 Mulberry St. (226–8657), prices in Little Italy are much higher than in Chinatown or the lower East Side. You'll have no trouble spotting the new generation of fancified restaurants here, with their smoked-glass windows, highly polished wood, and tuxedoed waiters. Expect to pay for the trimmings—or better yet, stick to the taste of old Little Italy (see the Restaurant listings in the *Practical Information* section for other Little Italy suggestions).

A fun time for sampling Little Italy's fare, if you can take the dense crowds, is during the Feast of San Gennaro, held in early September. The whole of Mulberry St., from Canal north, is turned into a carnival, with food stands hawking calzone, sausage and pepper heroes, and zeppole. Games of "skill and chance" provide diversion as you inch your way between the outdoor stands.

Soho

Soho consists roughly of the blocks between Canal and Houston sts. (hence, SoHo, or South of Houston), mostly west of Broadway (not to be confused with West Broadway, which is actually the main thoroughfare of the area).

Soho is a once-bleak neighborhood of warehouses which has become the premier center for new art and, to some extent, avant garde fashion. You'll see strollers ranging from middle class families to dressed down, all-in-black punks. The neighborhood is also interesting for its legions of cast iron buildings; in fact, the entire area is designated a landmark district. Most of the cast iron structures are of architectural but not historical significance.

Walkers will love the area not only for its architectural points, but for its sometimes outrageous, sometimes quite pretty boutiques. And gallery-hopping, especially along Prince, Spring, and Broome sts., is a favorite weekend afternoon pastime. Some galleries of particular note are the Dyanesen (122 Spring St.) for its incredible collection of Erté sculptures; Leo Castelli (420 West Broadway) for its uncanny knack of spotting talent; and Vorpal (465 West Broadway), known for its stock of prints by M. C. Escher.

Soho especially comes alive on Sundays. Joining the loft-living residents are the "bridge and tunnel crowd"—the folks pouring in from New Jersey and the "other boroughs" to brunch and shop.

Greenwich Village

The Village, as it is more familiarly known, is constantly subdividing. Whatever preconceived notions you have of Greenwich Village, you'll find verification in your travels. The East Village is a mecca for punk-rock clubs and the newest art scene. One of the city's bigger universities, Cooper Union, a Polish–Ukrainian community, many Indian restaurants (East Sixth St.), a Hell's Angels community—and much besides—contribute to the diversity.

The West Village is much more serene, and is where the old bohemians congregated. Highlighted by twisting, tree-lined streets of 19th-century brownstones, this portion of the Village is home to much of the city's gay population and to numerous small restaurants, playhouses, and antique shops. Walking along Hudson St., which runs roughly north–south, and turning onto side streets such as St. Luke's, Barrow, Grove, and Perry, is most rewarding. Literary giants such as Thomas Wolfe, O. Henry, and Mark Twain all made the West Village their home at one time or another.

The twain meet, so to speak, at Washington Square Park. In the past, the park was used as a burial place for plague victims and unfortunates who were forced to pay a visit to the gallows. On any weekend, the park is now filled with various amateur performing artists putting on free shows of song, dance, mime, and magic. On the Labor Day and Memorial Day weekends, the perimeter of the park is given over to a large outdoor arts festival, where professional painters and sculptors try to sell their works.

Fairs are a big part of the Village. In the summer, any number of streets will throw block parties and crafts festivals. The biggest one is the Festa Italiana at Carmine and Bleecker sts., held in July. In October, the Village throws a giant Halloween party, which culminates in a Mardi Gras-like parade that features all manner of natives in all manner of costumes.

More than any other neighborhood of the city, the Village is made for walking. One major promenade is Eighth St., very crowded and urban and now sadly lacking in the specialty record and book shops that once made it a mecca for bohemians from all over the world. Hudson St., Seventh Ave. South and Greenwich Ave. are more leisurely, with lots of sidewalk cafes, and Bleecker and Macdougal streets hold many of the Village's jazz clubs and Italian coffeehouses. Much of the West Village still carries an Italian flavor, as evidenced by the restaurants, food shops, and bakeries.

Beginning Your Tour: Washington Square

Washington Square is a microcosm of what the Village has to offer. The park and arch are indicative of the neighborhood's history; the row houses off to the side remind us of the area's literary heritage; the bustling New York University "campus" that has engulfed much of the surrounding area epitomizes Village life today. The beauty of the area

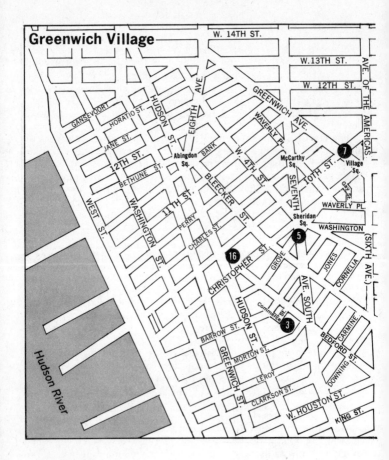

Greenwich Village

Points of Interest

1) Astor Place Theater
2) Bottom Line
3) Cherry Lane Theater
4) Circle in the Square Theater
5) Circle Repertory
6) Cooper Union
7) Jefferson Market Library
8) The New Museum/The New School (branch)
9) The New School for Social Research
10) New York University
11) Palladium
12) Players Theater
13) Provincetown Playhouse
14) Public Theater (Papp)
15) Sullivan St. Playhouse
16) Theater De Lys
17) Village Gate

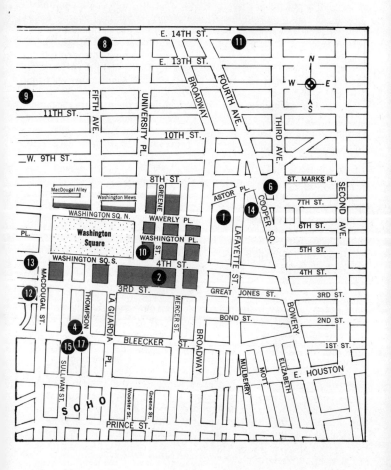

is that all segments work so well together to form one community. Among the sites and landmarks to observe are:

• Washington Arch. Built in 1889, the arch was designed by Stanford White to commemorate the 100th anniversary of George Washington's inauguration. Now it serves as a gleaming introduction to Fifth Ave. In days gone by, traffic used to pass through the arch—not so any more. At Christmastime, the arch serves as a canopy over the Village yuletide tree.

• New York University (NYU). Surrounding the park are the buildings of the largest university in New York and, student-wise, the largest in the country. Of particular interest is the Bobst Library, a 12-story structure designed by architect Philip Johnson. Its dizzying black-and-white diamond floor and strands of staircases can be seen from the park through a front wall of glass. The Grey Art Gallery, at diagonal from the library, plays host to a continually changing group of art exhibits.

• Greek Revival Row Houses. NYU also occupies a number of the lovely row houses lining Washington Square North; the university maintains its administrative offices there. In the past the houses, which date back to the 1830s, were home for some of America's most famous writers. Edith Wharton lived in the old Boorman house on the northeast corner of the square, a setting which inspired her novel *The Age of Innocence.* Novelist John Dos Passos wrote and Norman Rockwell painted at No. 3. Henry James was born just east of square. One of the row houses was the setting for *Washington Square.*

• Other literary landmarks. Spreading your scope slightly west and east of the park will bring you in contact with some other Village landmarks, including still more writers' homes. The Greenwich Hotel at Thompson and Bleecker sts., is where Theodore Dreiser stayed. James Fenimore Cooper lived at 145 Bleecker. Edgar Allan Poe lived at 85 West Third St. On the south side of the park stands Judson Hall, where John Reed wrote the articles which would later appear in *Ten Days That Shook the World.* Mark Twain lived at 14 West 10th St. On the same block, Sinclair Lewis resided at No. 37 and Hart Crane at No. 54. Thomas Wolfe lived around the corner at the Albert Hotel on University Pl. and 11th St. while teaching at NYU. And way over in the West Village, Edna St. Vincent Millay lived in the narrowest house in the city, 75½ Bedford St.

• Grace Church. This lovely white Episcopalian church on Broadway and 10th St. is an early creation of architect James Renwick, the designer of the more well-known St. Patrick's Cathedral.

• Jefferson Market Courthouse. This odd assemblage of architectural styles at Sixth Ave. and West 9th St. is currently serving as a branch of the New York Public Library. Built in 1877 and designed in part by Calvert Vaux, the co-architect of Central Park, this castle-like building was once used as a courthouse. Its clock tower also was used as the neighborhood fire lookout.

The East Village

St. Mark's Pl. is the main promenade of the East Village. It is a stretch between First and Third aves., the extension of East 8th St., and

along it you'll see one or two emporiums that frankly proclaim themselves "head shops," a reminder that just a few years ago this street was
one of New York's major outposts of the drug culture. (A remainder
of this subculture does still exist.) This is another area of the city where
old-time, immigrant families and the young, free-living newcomers are
learning to coexist.

On St. Mark's and along Second Ave. are many second-hand clothing shops, including the one popularized in the movie *Desperately
Seeking Susan,* boutiques with jewelry and leather goods, record stores,
and a popular moviehouse attracting buffs with a regular program of
classics. There are also Ukrainian, Thai, Japanese, Kosher, Indian, and
Russian restaurants, almost all of them inexpensive and catering mostly to local clientele. Stop for people-watching as well as a hearty, cheap,
stick-to-the-ribs meal 24 hours a day at the Kiev, 117 Second Ave.,
674–4040.

Still further east, along avenues A and B, in particular, is where the
latest wave of galleries is popping up, along with dance clubs that open
and close with great irregularity (most are not properly licensed). This
badly decayed area is not for people traveling solo unless they're cab-
bing to and from a specific place.

Midtown

For our purposes, midtown constitutes the area between 14th and
59th Sts., which takes in a host of residential and industrial neighborhoods. You should note, though, that when businesspeople speak of
"midtown" they are generally referring to the area from 34th to 57th
streets between Third Ave. and Broadway. This is the heart of the
non-financial business world, including advertising, publishing, fashion, and many industries. The Jacob K. Javits Convention Center
stretches from 36th to 40th streets, with the main entrance on Eleventh
Avenue. Among the individual neighborhoods within the broader defi-
nition of midtown are:

• The Flatiron District, centered on the landmark 1902 triangular
building of the same name at the corner of Broadway and 23rd St.

• The flower district, on Sixth Avenue, from 22nd to 27th Sts.

• The fur and garment districts, in the West 20s and 30s. Watch out
for those coat racks.

• Spanish Restaurant Row, 23rd Street, from Seventh to Eighth
Avenues.

• Chelsea, the warehouse and residential neighborhood, in the West
20s.

• Gramercy Park, one of the city's loveliest and most unspoiled
areas, in the East 20s and centering on a park to which only the
residents in the houses surrounding it have keys.

• Kips Bay and Murray Hill, residential neighborhoods in the East
30s.

• Herald Square, at Sixth Avenue and 34th St., the bustling center
of retail commerce, with Macy's, Herald Plaza, and, nearby, Altman's,
the Empire State Building, and the J. Pierpont Morgan Library.

- Hell's Kitchen, Ninth and Tenth aves. in the upper 30s and 40s—increasingly popular for very pleasant and affordable dining in the Broadway vicinity.
- Times Square, literally 42nd St. and Broadway, but generally taking in the area from 42nd to 53rd St., with its flashing lights, "street people" and Broadway theaters.
- The Diamond District, West 47th St., between Sixth and Seventh Aves. Jewelers galore.
- Little Brazil, on West 46th St., between Fifth and Sixth aves. There's even a fall festival sponsored by the half-dozen Brazilian restaurants on the block.
- Grand Central, centering on Grand Central Terminal at Park Avenue and 42nd St. and, at Lexington, the Art Deco classic Chrysler Building.
- Rockefeller Center, the soaring complex in the West 50s that includes Radio City Music Hall as well as sprawling office buildings connected by underground walkways and shopping promenades.
- Tudor City-Turtle Bay, serene and secluded residential areas in the East 40s and 50s.

Some of these are more interesting than others, and chances are you will want to breeze through certain areas whether they be the crowds of office workers milling around Grand Central or the legions of workers pulling dress racks down Seventh Avenue in the 30s. Other areas, such as Gramercy Park, Tudor City, and some of the "vest-pocket" parks squeezed between office buildings give the welcome gift of quiet and breathing room. You'll need to find a resting place sooner or later, because midtown offers a surprising wealth of sightseeing opportunities:

Chelsea Area

- Theodore Roosevelt Birthplace, 28 E. 20th St.; 260–1616; the birthplace of the 25th president is now a National Historic Site. It is a fine example of a typical wealthy Victorian home. The furnishings, including the scratchy horsehair chair Roosevelt later recalled in his memoirs, are unchanged. The home and an adjourning museum collection of the relics Roosevelt picked up in his travels are open to the public weekdays. Admission is $1 for adults, seniors and children free.
- Chelsea Hotel, 222 West 23 St. This largely residential hotel made national headlines a few years back when punk rocker Sid Vicious murdered his girlfriend there. But the lovely hotel has a much gentler past. Still a living symbol of the area's attractiveness to writers, the Chelsea has hosted such authors as Thomas Wolfe, who wrote his later books in Room 829, and Dylan Thomas, who died in Room 205. Mark Twain and O. Henry were also frequent guests. The building, with its Victorian Gothic wrought iron balconies, turrets, and chimney stacks, has been designated a National Historic Landmark.

Shopping Fever: Herald Square

Herald Square, between the fur and garment districts, is a shoppers' paradise—the block-square Macy's being its crown. The area is also one incredible mass of traffic and humanity. There are, however, some additional sights to be seen.

- Empire State Building, 350 Fifth Ave. No visit to the city would be complete without a stop at this 1931 Art Deco skyscraper, once the tallest building in the world, and a self-proclaimed Eighth Wonder of the World (its one-time resident, King Kong, notwithstanding). The lobby and murals depicting the other wonders are just as beautiful as the celebrated views from the 86th and 102nd floors. At night, the exterior of the building's top floors are lighted in a variety of colors, depending on the season. It's red, white, and blue for Independence Day; orange for Halloween; and blue and white for Hanukkah, etc. The observation deck (736–3100) is open from 9:30 A.M. to midnight, and costs $3.25 for adults, $1.75 for children.

- Madison Square Garden Center. This is the third location for this entertainment/sports complex. Now at Seventh Avenue and 33 Street (564–4400), the center includes the 20,000-seat Madison Square Garden, for large rock concerts, the circus, and Knicks and Rangers games; the smaller Felt Forum, for lesser rock groups, public events, and boxing; and a highly popular 48-lane bowling alley. The entire center connects with the terminus of Penn Station.

42nd Street: New York's Busiest Street

42nd Street offers everything—from the "Great White Way" to Art Deco skyscrapers, from the massive New York Public Library to the huge Grand Central Terminal. Start your tour with a slight detour to pay homage to New York's golden literary period at the Algonquin Hotel.

- Algonquin Hotel. 59 West 44 St. The place where New York's literary giants of the '20s and '30s gathered to outwit each other. Enjoy drinks surrounded by James Thurber cartoons and dine in the plush, maroon setting where the likes of Dorothy Parker, Robert Benchley, Alexander Wolcott, George Kaufman, and Edna Ferber held court at the "roundtable." As befits the atmosphere, a jacket is required at all times in the dining room. The neighboring side streets are also lined with many other "men's clubs" of this sort, though most today admit women as well. Among them: the Harvard and Princeton clubs.

- Times Square. From the Algonquin, it's two blocks west to the middle of the "Great White Way," the neon-lighted strip that serves as the theatrical and film center of the city. It is here where most "Broadway" theaters are located—few on Broadway itself, and west of Ninth Avenue a number of lively "off-Broadway" theaters have sprung up—as well as dozens of moviehouses (some of them x-rated), night-clubs, and hotels.

- New York Public Library. This gorgeous Beaux Arts structure on Fifth Avenue between 40th and 42nd sts. is the largest research branch

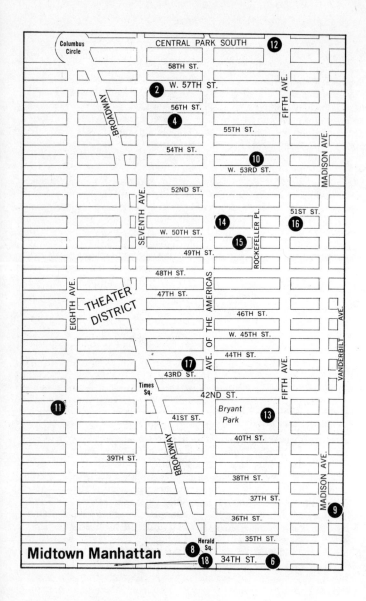

Midtown Manhattan

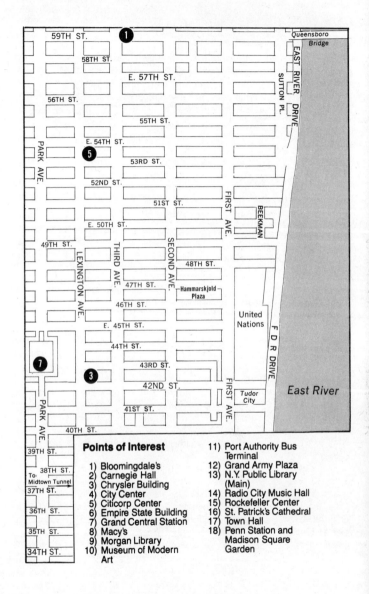

Points of Interest

1) Bloomingdale's
2) Carnegie Hall
3) Chrysler Building
4) City Center
5) Citicorp Center
6) Empire State Building
7) Grand Central Station
8) Macy's
9) Morgan Library
10) Museum of Modern Art
11) Port Authority Bus Terminal
12) Grand Army Plaza
13) N.Y. Public Library (Main)
14) Radio City Music Hall
15) Rockefeller Center
16) St. Patrick's Cathedral
17) Town Hall
18) Penn Station and Madison Square Garden

of the city's library system, and one of the five largest libraries in the world. Countless books load the shelves, with entire rooms dedicated to individual subjects. The library is also noted for the many comprehensive and well-received free exhibitions.

The building sits on the former site of the Croton Reservoir. In 1899, the reservoir was demolished to make way for the library and Bryant Park. Newly refurbished—and quite attractive—Bryant Park is behind the library, providing open markets and public seating, particularly popular for picnic luncheons and live concerts in summer. Many New Yorkers still prefer sitting on the steps of the building, between the guardian lions, dubbed "Patience" and "Fortitude" by Mayor Fiorello La Guardia. (The groan-inducing pun, "reading-between-the-lions," has often been heard in reference to this scene.) Free tours of the huge library meet Mondays through Saturdays at 11 A.M. and 2 P.M. in the main lobby.

• Grand Central Terminal. 42nd St. and Park Ave. Now in its final phase of restoration, this once-magnificent Beaux Arts train terminal still has its moments. Turn your eyes up—to the vaulted ceiling, which is a beautiful tribute to the starry skies. Once thousands of lights blinked down, but they too have vanished. The building stands on the spot occupied by a former station, built in 1871; the current structure was completed in 1913. Hungry sightseers will also want to stop by the Oyster Bar in the lower level. This restaurant sits in a spectacular setting underneath some of the magnificent vaulting of the building. Free tours of the entire station meet Wednesdays at 12:30 P.M., under the big Kodak advertisement.

• Chrysler Building (42nd St. and Lexington). New York's other major Art Deco skyscraper, the Chrysler Building is in many ways much more beautiful than the Empire State Building. Its gleaming silver spire (lit a glowing white in the evening) is a midtown beacon. If you look closely enough, you'll see that each setback represents a stylized motor motif and the fourth setback flares out into a gargoyle bearing the not-so-coincidental shape of a 1929 Chrysler radiator cap! The elegant lobby is topped off with a ceiling mural which is one of the largest in the world. Con Edison has its Conservation Center here—a free, hands-on exhibit on saving energy. Open Tuesdays–Saturdays, 10 A.M.–5:30 P.M.

• Daily News Building. 220 East 42nd St. Home to one of New York's three daily newspapers, this building is one of a number of magnificent Raymond Hood Art Deco structures found in the city. A 1958 addition on the eastern side cleverly follows the lines of the original. Inside, the showpiece lobby features the world's largest indoor globe. This revolving, highly detailed sphere also shows the distances and sizes of the solar system's planets in relation to the earth. The lobby floor has lines pointing in the direction of the world's major cities, with their relative distance from New York indicated. Meteorological instruments give weather conditions around the world.

• United Nations (UN). Turning west onto First Ave. from 42nd St. will bring you to the world's diplomatic center, the United Nations (754–7710). The complex consists of the skyscraper Secretariat Building and the low, domed General Assembly. It was constructed between

1947 and 1953 by an international team of architects (although it is Le Corbusier who has left his stamp on the whole project).

The outside gardens are graciously inviting, and inside the Assembly building works of art from all nations are displayed. These include sculptures, craft items, and tapestries. Guided tours are $4.50 for adults, $2.50 for children. Free tickets to sessions are also distributed to those who would rather see the proceedings at their own pace, though many areas are not accessible to the public except by tour.

Outside of the UN, the areas slightly south and north along First and Second aves. comprise some of the toniest residential neighborhoods in the city. Tudor City on 40th–43rd sts., between First and Second, is a complex of Tudor-style apartment houses facing a secluded park with its back to the UN, which at the time the apartments were built was the site of slaughterhouses. Farther up Second Ave., on 48th and 49th sts., is Turtle Bay, another lovely apartment retreat. Beekman Place in the low 50s is a newer exclusive neighborhood—also a very pleasant strolling ground.

Vest Pocket Parks and Atriums

Weary visitors will find that the sidewalks of midtown are filled with welcome and unexpected pleasures—both indoors and out. As a result of tradeoffs between developers and government, many skyscrapers now provide "public space" in return for the additional air space they occupy. Many of these newer buildings have chosen to do so in interesting, lovely and charming ways.

The nicest of the midtown "vest pocket" parks—small, secluded areas sandwiched between large office buildings—is the one adjoining the International Paper Plaza Building at Sixth Ave. between 45th and 46th sts. This area of shaded tables, water courses, and multi-layered sections is an open, gracious retreat from the city. During the summer, top-notch bands of all kinds give free concerts at lunchtime. Plums, a gourmet take-out restaurant in the northeast corner of the park, provides the perfect culinary complement to the setting with its salads, quiches, patés, and fancy sandwiches.

Many of the indoor atriums offer their own specialities. The Philip Morris Building (42nd St. and Park Ave.) contains exhibits from the Whitney Museum; the Ford Foundation Building (42nd St. between First and Second Aves.) provides a beautiful 10-story glass greenhouse of lush foliage; the Crystal Pavilion (50th St. and Third Ave.) goes to the other extreme in its brash, modern interior of aluminum and neon, as does the Park Avenue Atrium (45th St. and Park Ave.), with its gliding glass elevators and Christmaslike lighting.

The IBM Atrium (57th St. and Madison Ave.) and the AT&T Building (56th St. and Madison) offer contrasting settings for tired sightseers to rest their weary feet. IBM offers a sparse, rather clinical space of bamboo trees and benches (plus a wonderful art and science gallery with changing exhibitions); AT & T provides an outdoor seating area of delicate wrought iron chairs and tables placed beneath the soaring Roman style arches of the skyscrapers.

The 10 or so blocks of Fifth Avenue leading up to Central Park at 59th Street are home to some of the world's most renowned shops. Inside the Trump Tower at 56th Street—certainly the most unique atrium in the city because of its many expensive shops—are more than a dozen luxury palaces where only the richest of the rich dare to do more than window shop. Also, along Fifth nearby are Gucci for clothing, Mark Cross for leather goods and accessories, F.A.O. Schwarz for wonderful toys, and Tiffany's and Cartier (among others) for jewelry.

The New "Ladies' Mile"

In the early part of this century that appellation went to lower Sixth Avenue, where block after block of department stores lined the street. Today, Fifth Avenue boasts a similar status; indeed many of Sixth-Avenue stores moved "uptown," literally and figuratively, to Fifth. These include B. Altman's at 34th St., Lord & Taylor at 39th St., Saks Fifth Avenue at 49th St., and Bergdorf Goodman at 57th St. Around Christmas and Hanukkah, this promenade reaches its full glory, as the stores present the city with a gift of window displays outside and glittering decorations inside.

On 57th St. are Henri Bendel (between Fifth and Sixth aves.) and Bonwit Teller (between Fifth and Madison aves.). This stretch of 57th St. also houses other exclusive shops and art galleries and is one of the more pleasant commercial strips of Manhattan.

Fifth Avenue: A Wealth of Sightseeing

Fifth Avenue also plays host to two of New York's greatest sights: St. Patrick's Cathedral and Rockefeller Center, along with numerous other worthwhile attractions:

• St. Patrick's Cathedral, Fifth Ave. and 50th St. This soaring French Gothic structure designed by James Renwick is more stunning than ever after a recent facelift. Based on the design of Cologne Cathedral in Germany, this seat of the New York City Roman Catholic diocese was built between 1858 and 1906. The cathedral's white marble and stone towers rise 330 feet.

• Rockefeller Center, Fifth Ave. and 48th St. A combination of Art Deco and modern skyscrapers is spread out along Fifth Ave. between 47th and 50th sts. as far west as Seventh Ave.—all interconnected via an underground passageway almost two miles long. Along the way, you'll run into 19 buildings with 30 restaurants and several drugstores, bookstores, banks, movie theaters, subways, and a post office.

Of the stops you'll want to make, number one on your list should be the glorious Raymond Hood RCA Building at 30 Rockefeller Plaza. This 70-story building is now being enhanced by floodlighting at night. Before walking through its doors on Sixth Ave., look up to admire the Works Progress Administration murals above the entrance. Throughout the buildings are many more murals and sculptures.

Unlike many such complexes, Rockefeller Center has real uniformity. That continuity extends even to the rooftops of many of the buildings, which feature landscaped gardens. Back on the ground are more special touches. The Channel Gardens—six formal beds of ever-changing seasonal plantings stretching from Fifth Ave. to the Lower Plaza—are one of the center's major draws. The 10 foliage shows start in the spring with the Easter display of thousands of lilies and continue to the end of the year with the giant Christmas tree. The tree-lighting ceremony in early December is one of the most fun-filled New York events, but expect lots and lots of people! The tree stands on the border of the Lower Plaza ice skating rink, which on a weekend, looks like a scene out of Hans Christian Andersen. In warmer weather the rink gives way to outdoor dining.

30 Rock, as it is familiarly known, is headquarters for NBC Television and its affiliated companies. Tours of the NBC studios (664–4000) are available for $5.50.

• Radio City Music Hall, Sixth Ave. at 50th St., deserves its own tour, really, which can be had for $3.95 (757–3100). The landmark Art Deco masterpiece is the home of the world famous Rockettes chorus line. If you're in New York around Christmas, Easter, or the summer, be sure and check out the seasonal spectacle at the Music Hall—it is a spectacle, not necessarily tasteful, but unlike anything else you've ever seen and always perfect for the family. The auditorium is also used for rock and pop concerts.

• New York Experience, McGraw Hill Building, 48th St. and Sixth Ave.; 869–0345. As New York's "longest running movie," the New York Experience is a must for all visitors. A multi-media extravaganza detailing the past and present of the Big Apple, it is an excellent introduction to what the city is all about. Lots of fun, too!

• St. Thomas Church, Fifth Ave. and 53rd St. Up the block from St. Patrick's, this simple, lovely French Gothic building is a fine example of the city's church architecture, as well as a wonderful retreat from busy Fifth Avenue. Its boys' choir is justly renowned.

Central Park

In a way, no place is more typical and yet atypical of New York than the 130-year-old Central Park. Running from 59th Street (also known as Central Park South) to 110th Street between Fifth Avenue and Central Park West, the park is a microcosm of the city. Everyone comes to Central Park, from the rich who live along its southern borders to the poor of its northern neighborhoods. But, more importantly, the park is an escape from borders and boundaries, noise, dirt, and high-rises. There are spots in the middle of the park where it is impossible to believe you are in the midst of a metropolis. Near the edges of the park, though, where most people can be found, a special kind of beauty also exists. The surrounding skyline of luxury hotels on the south and expensive apartments on the east and west makes for a thrilling vista.

The park is much more than acres of hills, fields, trees, and rocks. The Central Park Zoo (due to reopen in 1988 after major reconstruction) is over to the east, in the 60s. The Delacorte Theater, with free summertime Shakespeare and other productions, is in the middle of the park in the low 80s. Also, in the summer, the Great Lawn is the scene of free New York Philharmonic and Metropolitan Opera concerts under the stars. (Note: if nothing is going on in the park, it's safest to stay out of it after dark.) The newly added Strawberry Fields Garden of Peace, near the West 72nd Street entrance, is a tribute to John Lennon; it contains thousands of rocks and plants contributed from every nation in the world (ironically, except the U.S.). The white and black marble "Imagine" mosaic is a gift from Italy.

Beautiful though it is for strollers, the park belongs to the more active population as well. Boats and bicycles can be rented at the 72nd Street Boathouse; horseback riders, joggers, and skaters have found a permanent home here, too. If you prefer to sit back and relax, horse-drawn hansom cabs lining Central Park South will be happy to serve you. It'll cost you a bit ($20 for the first half hour, $5 each 15 minutes after that) but it's another one of those New York experiences you might want to take home with you.

Upper West Side

Central Park effectively divides the upper West Side and the upper East Side. Away from the noise and confusion of midtown, both areas are fine places for strolling and browsing. Each retains its distinctive characteristics and those who can afford to live on either end do so for their opposing personalities. The stereotype has it that East-siders are traditional and old money. That's borne out by the profusion of fashion showrooms, antique stores, and art galleries lining Madison Avenue.

West-siders are supposed to be lively but chic and nouveau riche. The proof is in the boutiques, novelty stores, and nouvelle cuisine restaurants on Columbus Avenue. Museum lovers are on both sides of the park—the American Museum of Natural History straddles the west side; the east side is famous for its Museum Mile, which includes the Metropolitan Museum of Art, Guggenheim Museum, and nearly a dozen others. As for the upper West Side sights:

• Lincoln Center. The performing arts center of New York, at 64th Street and Broadway, is a series of low, connected white buildings housing the major resident orchestras, dance, and opera companies of New York. Designed by a cooperative of architects (including Philip Johnson; Skidmore, Owings & Merrill; and Eero Saarinen) overseen by Wallace K. Harrison (who played the same role in the UN complex) in the mid-'60s, the project is brilliantly illuminated in the evening. The Metropolitan Opera, with its stunning red staircase, cut crystal chandeliers, and enormous Marc Chagall tapestries peering out the front windows is the standout. Facing the Opera House, you'll find the New York State Theater to the left, Avery Fisher Hall to the right, and the Vivian Beaumont Theater to the right rear. The glistening fountain at the center of the plaza and lovely Damrosch Park (with free concerts in the summer) to the rear on the left are delightful.

• The Dakota. New York's first apartment house, this building at 72nd Street and Central Park West is so-named because at the time of its erection it was so far away from the center of things. The setting for the movie *Rosemary's Baby,* the Gothic edifice is a New York legend and home to many celebrities.

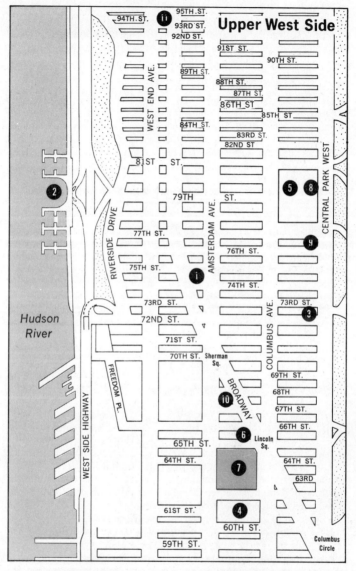

Upper West Side

Hudson River

Points of Interest

1) Beacon Theater
2) Boat Basin
3) The Dakota
4) Fordham University
5) Hayden Planetarium
6) Juilliard School
7) Lincoln Center for the Performing Arts
8) Museum of Natural History
9) New-York Historical Society
10) Merkin Hall (Goodman House)
11) Symphony Space

- Riverside Park. Running along the western edge of Manhattan from 72nd Street up through Harlem, this varied park still plays brides-maid to Central Park. Yet, to West Side residents it is a real favorite. Laid out in a more predictable fashion, it is nonetheless well-suited for strolling. A boat basin and theater-in-the-round at 79th Street serve as points of interest.

- Columbus Avenue. This is the new singles scene of Manhattan, having moved from the upper East Side. Here there are numerous popular hangouts where people wait in line for a chance to stand six deep at the bar. Dozens of restaurants have sidewalk cafes in the summer. Count on a crowd, though, even in the dead of winter on a Saturday night at 2 A.M. Strolling is best between 72nd and 86th streets.

- Amsterdam Avenue. Amsterdam is in the throes of gentrification; fashionable new restaurants (some even quite reasonable!) are popping up and helping put a new face on what has been a tenement district for quite some time. The center of the revitalization process is between 79th and 86th streets.

- Upper Broadway (north of 72nd Street) is where upper West Siders shop for groceries, bagels, gourmet foods, and household goods. If you can, get yourself up to Zabar's, at 81st Street, on Saturday around 4 P.M. or 10 P.M. You won't believe that you're seeing hundreds of people on different lines waiting an hour or more for a quarter pound of lox, some pasta with spinach sauce, or some special cheese.

- Cathedral of St. John the Divine, Amsterdam Avenue and 112th St.; 316–7540. When finished, it will be the largest Gothic cathedral in the world, although when it was begun in 1892 it was designed in the Romanesque style. Even now it is certainly stupendous. The nave seems to run forever and the glorious vaulting looks as if it continues right into the clouds. The building is architecturally astounding both inside and out. The central pillar consists of a statue of St. John, and the bronze doors leading to the center portal were created by the same Frenchman who cast the Statue of Liberty. The site contains a Museum of Religious Art, Biblical Garden, and 13 acres of landscaped grounds.

- Columbia University, Broadway and 116th St. Situated above the neighborhood of Morningside Heights, Columbia University is a unique urban campus. Founded in 1754, Columbia has gradually ex-panded its grounds until reaching its current territorial stretch of eight blocks. The campus is centered around a square of Federal style build-ings, including the Low Memorial Library.

- Riverside Church, Riverside Dr. and 122nd St.; 222–5900. Anoth-er fine example of Gothic architecture. The church has a 400-foot bell tower with the world's largest carillon—78 bells. The tower is open Mondays through Saturdays, 11 A.M.–3 P.M.; Sundays, 12:30–4 P.M.

- General Grant National Memorial, Riverside Dr. and 122nd St.; 666–1640. "So who is buried in Grant's Tomb, anyway?" The question should be, "Who *are* buried . . . ," as this granite monument contains the sarcophagi of the Civil War hero and 18th president Ulysses S. Grant and his wife, along with military memorabilia.

- The Cloisters in Fort Tryon Park is a branch of the Metropolitan Museum. It houses the medieval art collection of the museum, and is set high above the streets on hills overlooking the Hudson River. (See *Museums* for details.)

Harlem: A Neighborhood Comes Alive

For years the neighborhood of New York's black population, Harlem—which runs from 96th through 178th streets between the Harlem and Hudson rivers—has an illustrious past. During the 1930s and 1940s it was the star of the jazz and blues music scene. Recently, with the reopening of the legendary Apollo Theater, the area is regaining some of its former status. Harlem has also served as a mecca for America's most important black literary voices, including Ralph Ellison, James Baldwin, and Langston Hughes. The building at 103 West 135 Street, a white neoclassic structure designed by McKim, Meade, and White, now houses the Schomburg Center For Research in Black Culture and Museum (427–7201).

Landmarks include the Graveyard of Revolutionary Heroes and the line of rowhouses known as Strivers Row. The row is actually four rows of attached Georgian brownstone, brick, and Italianate houses on 138th and 139th streets, between Seventh and Eighth avenues. Northwest from the row and up the hill sits Hamilton Grange, the house where Alexander Hamilton lived the later part of his life. Open to the public, this building was moved to its current spot on Convent Avenue in 1899. The Morris Jumel Mansion (161th Street) is the oldest private residence remaining in Manhattan. Built in 1765, this Georgian structure was Washington's headquarters during the Revolutionary War.

Restaurants in the area include The Terrace at Columbia University's Butler Hall (400 West 119th St.), providing sweeping vistas of Upper Manhattan and New Jersey from 20 stories up and serving first class French cuisine; and Sylvia's (328 Lenox Ave., between 126th and 127th streets), a legendary ribs and down-home eatery.

While Harlem is known to many only by the movies either made in it or about it, caution is advised. It is not the type of region for leisurely ambling.

Upper East Side

The Upper East Side is not as replete with sights—it is primarily residential. The main thoroughfares, however, Park, Madison, and Fifth avenues, are striking boulevards for strolling and shopping. Park Avenue, with its garden mall down the center, is home to some of New York's wealthiest families. And Madison Avenue is unsurpassed for exclusive shopping—antique stores, art galleries, and haute couture emporiums line the avenue from the 60s through the 80s. The upper stretch of Fifth Avenue, between 82nd and 105th streets, is known as "Museum Mile," with 10 of the city's best-known museums located there. At bustling 86th Street is the hub of Yorkville, a predominantly German neighborhood filled with gourmet food shops, restaurants, and bakeries. Also noteworthy are:

• Temple Emanu-El. This awesome building at 65th St. and Fifth Ave. is the largest synagogue of modern times. The architecture is an

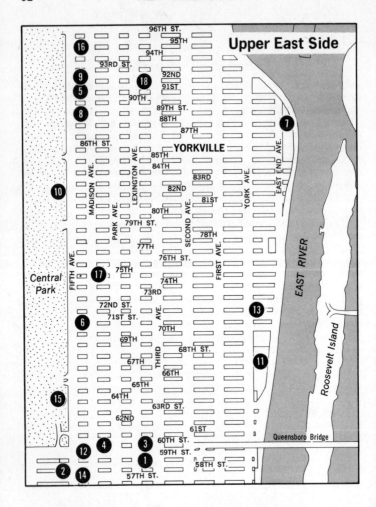

Upper East Side

Points of Interest

1) Alexander's
2) Bergdorf Goodman
3) Bloomingdale's
4) Christie's
5) Cooper-Hewitt Museum
6) Frick Collection
7) Gracie Mansion
   (Mayor's residence)
8) Guggenheim Museum

9) Jewish Museum
10) Metropolitan Museum of Art
11) Rockefeller University
12) F.A.O. Schwarz
13) Sotheby Parke Bernet
14) Tiffany
15) Central Park Zoo
16) International Center
    of Photography
17) Whitney Museum
18) YM-YWHA

eye-catching combination of Romanesque, Byzantine, and Middle Eastern elements. Many of the city's important religious leaders— Jewish and non-Jewish—have spoken here.

• Gracie Mansion, 86th St. and the FDR Drive. This lovely home on the East River dates back to 1799 and is the New York City mayor's private address during his term.

The Outer Boroughs

Although Manhattan is undoubtedly the center of New York City, visitors shouldn't feel that they should limit their sightseeing to that borough. If you have the time, the Bronx, Brooklyn, Queens, and Staten Island merit visiting for a variety of reasons, not least of all that they will offer a more typical view of what life is like for most New Yorkers on a day-to-day basis. All four so-called "outer boroughs" (even the people who live in them refer to Manhattan as "the city") are easily accessible via public transportation. Indeed, some sights, such as the Bronx Zoo, are almost mandatory stops on any New York City itinerary.

The Bronx boasts some of the most beautiful grounds in the city, including the New York Botanical Gardens and the wealthy neighborhood of Riverdale. Brooklyn is the land of brownstones and waterfront views. In Queens, middle class neighborhoods predominate, as do small green lawns. Likewise, Staten Island might as well be the "country" as far as many New Yorkers are concerned. The gateway between New York and New Jersey, Staten Island is dotted with private homes, beaches, and shopping malls.

The Bronx Bombers, Zoos, and Gardens

The Bronx lies north of Manhattan, and a trip to any of the major Bronx attractions should take only a half hour from midtown by public transportation. Not only does the borough boast the zoo, the Botanical Gardens, and the New York Yankees baseball team, but its recreational facilities include acres of beaches, golf courses, marinas, and parks, as well as museums and historical places. Among the highlights are:

• Bronx Zoo, Fordham Rd. and Bronx River Pkwy. Arguably the greatest zoo in the world, it keeps getting better and better. Animals are left to roam free in natural settings, and grouped according to habitat. There are special rides, such as the Bengali Express monorail and the Skyfari cable car. Plan to spend the better part of a day—and get there early if the weather's good on a summer weekend; the zoo can get quite zoo-y.

• Yankee Stadium, 161st St. and River Ave. The many-times world champion Yankees play ball at the refurbished "House That Ruth Built."

• New York Botanical Gardens, Southern Blvd. and Fordham Rd.; 220–8700. 250 astounding acres of flowers, trees, shrubs and forests. Open daily 8 A.M.–7 P.M. Free. A highlight is the Enid A. Haupt Conservatory, an elaborate landmark Crystal Palace housing jungles, deserts, forests, and seasonal displays. Open Tuesdays–Sundays, 10 A.M.–4 P.M. Adults, $2.50; children $1.25.

• Van Cortlandt Park, entrance at 242 St. Almost two square miles of swimming, horseback riding, picnicking, and just plain lazing. Free concerts and theater in the summer.

• Wave Hill Conservatory, 249 St. and Independence Ave.; 549–2055. This remarkable 28-acre estate is filled with greenhouses and formal gardens, as well as the added treat of scenic Hudson River vistas. Open daily, 10 A.M.–4:30 P.M. Greenhouses are open 10 A.M.–noon and 2–4 P.M.

• Van Cortlandt Mansion, 246 St. and Broadway in Van Cortlandt Park; 543–3344. This home of one of New York's wealthiest families was built in 1758. During the American Revolution it served as the headquarters for both British and Colonial troops and, yes, George Washington slept here on a number of occasions. Undergoing renovations in mid-1987, the mansion was scheduled to reopen in early 1988.

• Bartow-Pell Mansion, Shore Rd. in Pelham Bay Park; 885–1461. Built between 1836 and 1842, this mansion is an excellent example of the Greek Revival style. It is furnished with authentic period pieces. Open Wednesdays, Saturdays, and Sundays, noon–4 P.M. Adults, $1; children, free.

• Bronx Museum of the Arts, Grand Concourse and 161st St.; 681–6001. Located in the landmark Bronx County Building, this museum displays contemporary art. Open Mondays–Thursdays, and Saturdays, 10 A.M.–4:30 P.M.; Sundays 11 A.M.–4:30 P.M. Admission $1.50.

• Edgar Allan Poe Cottage, Grand Concourse and Kingsbridge Rd.; 881–8900. The last home of one of America's great poets, and the site where he wrote the mournful "Annabel Lee" and "The Bells." An audiovisual presentation documents Poe's miserable final years. Open Wednesdays–Fridays, Sundays, 1 P.M.–5 P.M.; Saturdays, 10 A.M.–4 P.M. Admission $1.

• Fordham University, Fordham Rd. and Third Ave.; 579–2000. This beautiful campus features a stunning array of Gothic architecture and some lovely chapel buildings.

• Lehman College Center For The Performing Arts, Bedford Park Blvd. West; 960–8833. The first major entertainment center in the Bronx, the complex (a concert hall, two theaters, and a recital hall) has played host to Itzhak Perlman, Marcel Marceau, Dizzy Gillespie, and the New York Philharmonic. Call for schedules.

• Museum of Bronx History, Bainbridge Ave. and 208th St.; 881–8900. Displays detailing the borough's contributions to America. Crafts demonstrations, free concerts, and outdoor art shows are also frequently given. Open Saturdays, 10 A.M.–4 P.M.; Sundays, 1 P.M.–5 P.M. Adults, $1; children, free.

• Woodlawn Cemetery, Jerome and Bainbridge aves.; 652–2100. This 125-year-old cemetery is the final resting place of F. W. Woolworth, Bat Masterson, George M. Cohan, Duke Ellington, and Admiral David Farragut. Open daily 9 A.M.–4:30 P.M. Free.

Two neighborhoods you might want to explore in the Bronx are City Island and Belmont. City Island is a nautical island where you can sniff the sea air, rent a boat, and visit the City Island Nautical Museum (190 Fordham St. and City Island Ave.). The Little Italy of the Bronx, Belmont centers on Arthur Ave., a virtual open air market of taste treats. The Enrico Fermi Library at East 186th and Hughes Sts. (933–6410) is renowned for its extensive collection of Italian-American research materials.

Self-guides to the Bronx Heritage trail (881–8900) are available for a comprehensive day of sightseeing. Stops include the Bronx Heritage Center, Museum of Bronx History, Valentine-Varian House, Edgar Allan Poe Cottage, and Van Cortlandt Mansion.

Brooklyn

Brooklyn would be the fourth-largest city in the nation if it were not a borough of New York City. The borough is really on Long Island and consists of a series of ethnic communities, including Williamsburg, seat of the Hasidic community; Greenpoint, a Polish center; and on the fringes of Park Slope, Jamaican and Dominican neighborhoods.

This is also a borough of fantastic brownstones, limestones, and rowhouses, many built in the mid- to late-19th century, and of Victorian neighborhoods that grew up in the early 1900s. Brooklyn Heights, at the foot of the Brooklyn Bridge and directly across the East River from lower Manhattan (a motor launch operates during some months), has long been popular among literary folk—Thomas Wolfe and Norman Mailer among them—for its village-like atmosphere and proximity to Manhattan.

The Promenade over the Brooklyn-Queens Expressway offers idyllic views of the Manhattan skyline. Similar neighborhoods deeper into Brooklyn have been revitalized in recent years, beginning with Park Slope, which is on the west side of Prospect Park, but including smaller communities such as Cobble Hill and Carroll Gardens.

In neighborhoods such as these you'll still see small, family-run shops that have been around for generations—butcher shops, bakeries, hardware outlets, and the like—right alongside newer boutiques catering to the young professionals who buy and renovate the three- to five-story houses along these tree-lined streets. Some of the mansions along Prospect Park, for example, might have sold for $75,000–$100,000 in the mid-1970s; today they command as much as ten times that amount. When exploring Brooklyn, take time to note:

• The Brooklyn Bridge, north of the Promenade at the foot of Fulton Street and west of Cadman Plaza. This well-loved bridge serves both figuratively and literally as an introduction to the borough. A special path is open for walkers, joggers, and bicyclists, and on a clear day it's a thrilling place to be.

• Brooklyn Academy of Music, 30 Lafayette Ave. Affectionately known as BAM, the center is respected across the country for both its classical and avant-garde programs. Its Next Wave Festival each fall is particularly renowned for presenting internationally acclaimed dance, theater, and "performance" art.

• Prospect Park. Designed by the team of Vaux and Olmstead, who were responsible for Central Park, Prospect Park includes a Quaker cemetery, a lake, a zoo, and simply spectacular open spaces. A bandshell at 9th Street and Prospect Park West is home to a Celebrate Brooklyn festival each summer that offers everything from blue grass to chamber music, African dance to punk rock, while the Picnic House near 3rd Street is used for indoor concerts, exhibits, and other events. Particularly popular is the park's restored boathouse. Also within the park: The Lefferts Homestead, a Dutch colonial farmhouse built in 1776 which originally stood on nearby Flatbush Avenue and is now a museum; and the Litchfield Villa, now the Brooklyn Park Headquarters, built in 1857.

• Grand Army Plaza, on Flatbush Avenue at the junction of Prospect Park West and Eastern Parkway. Reminiscent of the Arc de Triomphe in Paris, the Plaza's center is the Soldiers and Sailors Monument. At times you can climb this arch for a magnificent view of Brooklyn and Manhattan; the Plaza is at the northern entrance to Prospect Park.

• Brooklyn Botanic Garden. Main gate on Eastern Pkwy. a few blocks east of Flatbush Ave. 50 acres of flora, including the dazzling Cranford Rose Garden, an herb garden, and a Japanese garden. The latter is the scene of an annual cherry blossom festival in the spring (the cherry blossom grove itself is in an adjacent part of the garden).

• Brooklyn Museum, Eastern Pkwy. on the northeast corner of the Botanic Garden. The seventh-largest museum in America. (See main museum listings in *Practical Information* below.)

• Near-Eastern Bazaar, along Atlantic Ave. between Court and Henry sts. Middle Eastern foods, publications, clothing. Dine in the numerous restaurants—most family-owned—or pick up a dozen different types of olives at one of the shops.

• Brooklyn Children's Museum, 145 Brooklyn Ave. in Brower Park; 718–735–4400. An innovative underground amusement park filled with science and technology exhibits. Open Mondays, Wednesdays, Fridays, 2–5 P.M.; Thursdays to 8 P.M.; Saturdays and Sundays, and New York City Public School holidays, 10 A.M.–5 P.M.

• Beachfront Brooklyn provides the city with most of its most famous beaches. These include the legendary Coney Island, which is making a bit of a comeback these days. While at Coney Island, you'll want to check out the rides, the Aquarium (see *Practical Information* below), and the Nathan's hot dogs! Other beaches on the peninsula include Brighton (the neighborhood here is termed "Little Odessa By The Sea," since it's the settling ground of many Russian immigrants) and Manhattan beaches.

Queens: Aerial Gateway to the City

When you get off your plane at Kennedy International Airport or La Guardia Airport, you're in the borough of Queens. Physically the largest of the five boroughs, Queens also boasts nearly as much parklands as the other four combined. Like Brooklyn, the borough is on Long Island. More than just another borough, Queens is a series of small towns, and civic pride runs high. (Natives say they live in Astoria or Ridgewood, not Queens.) Once known as a "bedroom community"

—i.e., one of neat little houses whose owners commuted to Manhattan to work—the county is gradually becoming a center of industry. Queens is also a haven for sports fans (one baseball stadium, two world-renowned tennis stadiums, and two racetracks) and movie buffs (the Astoria Motion Picture Studios are here). Best of all, the borough has some of the most beautiful neighborhoods in the city—such as the garden city of Forest Hills; Whitestone, with its glittering bridge; and the surrounding well-to-do northern Queens communities of Douglaston, Bayside, and Little Neck. Let's look first at the sporting attractions:

• Shea Stadium, 126 St. and Roosevelt Ave., Flushing. Home to the New York Mets baseball team. Call 718–507–8499 for ticket prices and schedules.

• United States Tennis Association National Tennis Center, across the street from Shea Stadium, in Flushing Meadow Park; home to the U.S. Open and Davis Cup tennis championships.

• West Side Tennis Club, One Tennis Pl. (Burns and Dartmouth sts., 69th and 70th aves.), Forest Hills. Located in the beautiful enclave of Forest Hills, this former home of the U.S. Open is now used primarily for charity and celebrity games.

• Belmont Park, Elmont, right across the Queens border in Nassau County; the horseracing track where the Triple Crown Belmont Stakes is run.

• Aqueduct Racetrack, Rockaway Blvd. and 108th St., Ozone Park. The largest racetrack in the United States.

Other attractions include:

• Astoria Motion Picture Studios and Museum of the Moving Image, 34–31 35th St., Astoria; 718–784–4520. This once-active movie studio (the Marx Brothers filmed here) is again being used by moviemakers. Visitors will be interested in gallery exhibits detailing the history of the studio and motion pictures in general. Exhibits open to the public only on Fridays and Saturdays from 6:30 P.M., with lectures and films offered later in the evening.

• Bowne House, 37–01 Bowne St., Flushing; 718–359–0528. Built in 1661, this "shrine to religious freedom," has 17th- and 18th-century furnishings. Open Tuesdays, Saturdays, and Sundays, 2:30–4:30 P.M. Adults $1; children, 25¢.

• Project Studio One, 46–01 21st St., Long Island City; 718–784–2082. A former school (built in 1892), this space has been transformed into a center for art exhibits sponsored by the Institute For Art and Urban Resources. Open Wednesdays–Sundays, noon–6 P.M. Admission $1.

• Queens County Farm Museum, 73–50 Little Neck Pkwy., Floral Park; 718–347–3276. This farm, which dates to 1772, is the only remaining working farm of its era. Open Saturdays, 10 A.M.–4 P.M.; opens Sundays at 1 P.M. Admission is $2 for adults, $1 for children.

• Queens Museum, North Wing of the New York City Building in Flushing Meadow; 718–592–2405. Located in a building which served as the headquarters of the UN from 1946 to 1950, the museum features a fascinating 15,000-square-foot scale model of New York City. Open

Tuesdays–Saturdays, 10 A.M.–5 P.M.; opens Sundays at 1 P.M. Adults, $1; children, free.

- Flushing Meadow, Flushing; 718–699–4209. A swamp turned oasis, the park was the site of the magnificent 1939 World's Fair. Many of the fair's futuristic buildings still stand (although most have fallen into shameful disrepair). A second World's Fair was held here in 1964. Of special interest in the park are the Hall of Science (718–669–0675), a hands-on museum of technology, and the Children's Zoo (718–699–7239), which allows youngsters to touch and feed animals.
- Jamaica Bay Wildlife Refuge, Crossbay Blvd. between Broad Channel and Howard Beach, Rockaways, 718–474–0613. Birdwatchers and animal lovers will love this grassy marsh. Free admission.

Staten Island

Staten Island is New York's most neglected borough. The island was discovered by Giovanni da Verrazano in 1524 (hence the Verrazano-Narrows Bridge which connects Staten Island and Brooklyn). Henry David Thoreau and Ralph Waldo Emerson often stayed here, and Giuseppe Garibaldi, the Italian patriot, took refuge here. The most popular way to reach the borough these days is via the Staten Island Ferry, a half-hour ride from downtown Manhattan. Attractions include:

- Jacques Marchais Center of Tibetan Art, 338 Lighthouse Ave.; 718–987–3478. Founded in 1946, this surprising museum contains the largest collection of Tibetan art in the Western Hemisphere, all housed in two stone buildings reminiscent of Tibetan monasteries. Art from Japan, India, China, Southeast Asia, and Nepal is also included. Open Wednesdays–Sundays, 1–5 P.M. April–November. Adults, $2.50; children, $1.
- Richmondtown Restoration, 441 Clarks Ave.; 718–351–1611. These 96 acres of land constitute an outdoor museum of 26 buildings dating from the 17th through the 19th centuries. Along with viewing the interiors of 11 of these buildings, visitors may also see demonstrations of early American trades and crafts. Open Wednesdays–Fridays, 10 A.M.–5 P.M.; Saturdays and Sundays opens at 1 P.M. Adults, $2; children, $1.
- Snug Harbor Cultural Center, 914 Richmond Terr.; 718–448–2500. This National Historic Landmark has been cited as among the finest examples of Greek Revival architecture in the country. Now used for concerts and arts exhibits, the center also includes a retirement home for sailors. Eighty acres of grounds, including the Staten Island Botanical Garden (718–273–8200), are open free to the public, from dawn to dusk. The newly relocated Staten Island Children's Museum (718–273–2060), a wonderful participatory museum, is now open here as well.
- Staten Island Zoo, 614 Broadway; 718–442–3100. Also a real treat for kids, this zoo boasts one of the best reptile collections in the country, with more rattlesnakes than anyplace else. A nursing area and a new aquarium also come with the territory, as does a special children's

zoo. Open daily 10 A.M.–4:45 P.M. (Children's Zoo closes at 4 P.M.) Admission is $1, free on Wednesdays.

PRACTICAL INFORMATION FOR
NEW YORK CITY

WHEN TO GO. New York City offers everything all year round. This is a city that's alive 24 hours a day, 365 days a year. Be prepared for temperature extremes at all times. Fall and spring may be most pleasant for strolling and sightseeing. July and August are invariably very hot and humid; days when the temperature plummets to the teens in the winter are not uncommon. You'll also run into cool, dry days in summer when a sweater is necessary, especially by the waterfront, and occasional 60-degree days in the dead of winter. The theaters, museums, parks, historic sights, harbors, clubs, restaurants, and hotels of New York keep the same pace all year round.

HOW TO GET THERE. The budget-minded coming to the city from distant points should check on the availability of flights into *Newark Airport* on *Continental, New York Air,* and other discount carriers. Newark is less hectic than *La Guardia* or *Kennedy,* and is easily accessible. New Jersey Transit Authority buses shuttle you to the Port Authority (Eighth Ave. and 42nd St.) in Manhattan. Other buses are available for other points in the city.

Flights on these regularly scheduled airlines are as reliable as those on better known airlines, even if you sometimes have to pay extra to check your baggage or for a snack. From Newark, *Olympic Bus Lines* operates to downtown's World Trade Center and to the east side of Manhattan. *Carey* buses from La Guardia and Kennedy bring passengers to the Grand Central vicinity, 42nd St. and Lexington Ave., or at one of three midtown hotels—Marriott Marquis, Times Square; New York Hilton, Rockefeller Center; and Sheraton City Squire, 700 Seventh Ave. A combination bus-and-subway ride called *Train to the Plane* to and from Kennedy is another alternative. While it can be somewhat faster than the bus, it does require switching between vehicles and the trains are not coordinated with the buses, so there may be a wait—or several waits. The advantage is that the train makes a handful of convenient stops in Manhattan along Sixth Avenue.

Fares for all of the above are in the $5–$8 range, and the rides are at least as fast as, and often quicker than, a cab. **Cabs** between Newark or Kennedy and Manhattan will run in excess of $25; $12–$15 between La Guardia and midtown Manhattan. If you do use a cab, be sure the meter is running—never accept "special deals." The dispatchers at Kennedy and La Guardia can also advise you about how much the fare to your destination should be. Remember, though, that waiting time in heavy traffic adds up on the taxi meter, and getting stuck in one of New York's monumental tie-ups can be costly. No one can predict the jams ahead.

Buses coming from distant points terminate at the Port Authority Bus Terminal. From here you can switch to a subway—the Eighth Avenue IND line is right downstairs. One block east is the Times Square station of the IRT Seventh Avenue line, and a shuttle train will take you from there to the IRT

Lexington Avenue line for access to the east side of the island. Cabs are available if you're burdened with baggage, but don't let anyone take your luggage or offer to hail a cab for you—they will either disappear with your bags or demand an excessive tip for the chore.

Trains terminate at one of two terminals: *Grand Central* or *Penn Station.* Both offer ready access to the subway system. (For details about the subway, see "How To Get Around" below.)

Among the major **highways** used to reach New York are I–80 (from the west) and I–95 (from the north and south); also, the New York Thruway from the north. The Verrazano-Narrows Bridge connects Staten Island and Brooklyn, with the Brooklyn-Queens Expressway leading to the Brooklyn-Battery Tunnel and lower Manhattan.

TELEPHONES. Public phones cost 25¢ for a three-minute local call. The area code for Manhattan and the Bronx is 212; for Queens, Brooklyn, and Staten Island, it is 718. A call between the two areas is a local call, but you must dial "1," then the area code, and then the number. When calling from Brooklyn or Staten Island you must first dial area code "718." Calling to some distant points in the city costs more than 25¢; a recording will advise you if additional coins are needed.

Emergency Telephone Numbers. Dial "911" from any pay phone to get centralized police, fire, and ambulance assistance. This is a free call.

ACCOMMODATIONS. Don't come to the Big Apple without advance reservations. Given the number of conventions and tourists that come to town, finding lodging at the last minute can be difficult. Even if rooms are available, the likelihood of getting a low rate is nil; the number of such rooms at any hotel is limited, and usually reserved for those booking well ahead. You'll do best if you can time your trip around a weekend, when excellent package deals are available. Consult a travel agent about such arrangements or write the *New York Convention and Visitors Bureau,* Two Columbus Circle, New York, NY 10019, for its *Tour Package Directory,* a complete list including days, prices, frills, and conditions. Some hotels allow for a Thursday night arrival or a Monday morning departure at the lower rates.

Prices will also vary according to the extras that are thrown in—fancy brunches, newspapers (the Sunday *New York Times* is a traditional way to spend the morning), welcoming cocktails, dinner, discount coupons, limousine service to the theater or financial district, etc. Obviously, the more such items included in the package, the higher the price, though sometimes this can still work out to be cheaper than doing the same things on your own.

More formally organized tours may include theater or concert tickets, some meals, sightseeing, and other attractions. Our suggestion is to do such things on your own, mostly to get a better impression of what the city is about.

Another possibility for reduced rates is to check if your company gets a corporate discount for its employees, or if a social or religious group to which you belong operates tours. Members of airline frequent fliers clubs are sometimes entitled to discounts at certain chains.

Both regular rates and package rates change frequently, depending on the season and how busy the major hotels are. Price wars erupt every so often, though a rule of thumb is that a double room with private bath in a good tourist hotel will run at least $100 a night. Singles aren't much less. As a reference point, the best rooms, with views of the skyline or Central Park, in deluxe or super deluxe hotels typically go for more than twice that amount. Many of the top hotels—the Helmsley Palace, for example—also offer packages, though the rates hardly fall into the budget category.

Bed-and-breakfasts are a widely popular alternative throughout the United States offering room and breakfast to visitors in hosted or unhosted apartments. In New York the choices are rather limited, but there is one service that offers relatively inexpensive, clean rooms, or even entire apartments, complete with a hospitable native to provide the special insights peculiar to residents. *Urban Ventures,* Box 426, New York, NY 10024; 212–594–5650, offers double rooms beginning at $45 per night and apartments beginning at $65. They also arrange thematic tours for groups of four or more. Call well in advance of your planned visit. They get booked up early.

Because of the unique nature and diversity of New York City hotels, we have tried to add a little extra detail to our general categories, and advise you to give consideration to geographic location as well as price and appointments. Getting around the city is time-consuming and expensive; thus, a few extra dollars per night to be in the area in which you plan to spend most of your time are probably well spent.

We've categorized our selection of New York City's hotels based on price. Exact prices are generally misleading; most major properties change their room rates every eight to 12 months. The city's best lodgings are grouped into four price categories: *Super Deluxe,* over $250 per night; *Deluxe,* $200–$250; *Luxury,* $150–$200; and *Expensive,* under $150. A fifth section, *Motels, Chains, and Simple but Practical,* describes serviceable places to rest your weary body at night but with little in the way of individuality or special services. These establishments offer rooms for under $150, sometimes well under. All our categories refer to a quality double room for two people. There is an occupancy tax of $2 included in the room rate, and a 13¼ percent city and state sales tax will be added to the bill.

Since high prices are not always good indicators of impeccable service, beautiful decor, or delicious cuisine, we suggest you use our brief write-ups as a gauge for finding the type of place at which you wish to stay. For example, it would be unwise to expect the same level of service and ambience from a top flight convention hotel like the Marriott Marquis and a smaller luxury property like Morgans, although they both appear in the *Deluxe* category. Likewise, if you enjoy the hustle and bustle of a big city with lots of bright lights and activity you'll probably be happier at the Grand Hyatt than you would at the residentially situated Carlyle.

As we've already said, what follows is only a selection. There are, to be sure, many more hotels in this vast city, particularly in the *Expensive* category (and below!). However, we have only listed lodgings that are in good parts of town. If we wouldn't feel comfortable leaving or returning to our hotel after dark, then you won't find it within these pages.

If you don't care where you sleep, the New York Convention and Visitors Bureau says there are always some rooms available somewhere, and they'll help you find one. Unfortunately, their office closes at 6 P.M., so they are little help for late arrivals.

All telephone numbers for Manhattan hotels in this listing are area code 212.

Super Deluxe

The Carlyle. 35 E. 76th St.; 744–1600. Located in one of the city's poshest residential areas, close to The Metropolitan and Whitney Museums, among many others. Elegant dining.

Helmsley Palace. 455 Madison Ave. at 50th St.; 888–1624. Constructed above and around the 1855 Renaissance-style Villard Houses, this hotel is extravagantly rich-looking and located just behind St. Patrick's Cathedral. Central to the best of Fifth Avenue shopping and all midtown businesses.

Park Lane. 36 Central Park South; 371–4000. A relatively new addition to the list of classic hotels on the southern boundary of Central Park, it ranks right alongside the others for dignity and service.

Parker Meridien. 118 W. 57th St.; 245–5000. Unique features here include a health club, rooftop pool, and squash courts. Close to Carnegie Hall and the Russian Tea Room.

Pierre. 61st St. and Fifth Ave.; 940–8100. This elegant hotel, which opened in 1930, is about half residential. Its beautiful Regency restaurant is a favorite for dining.

Plaza Athenée, 37 E. 64 St.; 734–9100. Patterned after its Paris namesake, this is a small luxury hotel priding itself on individualized attention.

Ritz-Carlton. 112 Central Park South; 757–1900. This has quickly become one of the city's most prestigious hotels. Understated opulence with an emphasis on service. Attracts an international clientele.

St. Regis-Sheraton. Fifth Ave. and 55th St.; 753–4500. The ultimate in Old World wealth and rococo elegance.

Stanhope. Fifth Ave. at 81st St.; 288–5800. Particularly gracious, the hotels offers some fine cuisine, an elegant atmosphere, and classic service.

Westin Plaza. Fifth Ave. and 59th St.; 759–3000. The grandest hotel in the city remains the most imposing and beautiful place to stay in New York, so long as you have one of the renovated rooms—preferably overlooking Central Park. An enclave of tradition and elegance in the old European manner.

Deluxe

Berkshire Place. 21 E. 52nd St.; 753–5800. A local favorite for its Rendezvous restaurant and bar. Rooms here are simple and modern.

Drake Suissôtel. 440 Park Ave.; 421–0900. After a major 1987 restoration this well-located hotel retains its tasteful ambience and pleasant surroundings.

Grand Hyatt New York. Park Ave. and 42nd St.; 883–1234. This renovated palace is done with lavish amounts of brass, glass, chrome, and marble, and is situated above Grand Central Terminal.

Helmsley. 212 E. 42nd St.; 490–8900. Sleekly modern, the newly renamed Helmsley (it used to be called the Harley) is close to the United Nations, but caters to the business executive.

Inter-Continental. 111 E. 48th St.; 755–5900. Extremely pleasant and gracious. Restored to its orginal 1920s grandeur as part of a recent renovation.

Marriott Marquis. Broadway between 45 and 46 streets.; 398–1900, 800–228–9290. A spectacular hotel, and part of the effort to rejuvenate Times Square, the Marriott's 1,800 rooms clearly intend to provoke gasps. They succeed.

Marriott's Essex House. 160 Central Park South; 247–0300. Park Avenue has the reputation, but Central Park South has the view, and this is probably as attractive a location as can be found in the city. This is one of the largest on hotel row.

Morgans. 237 Madison Ave.; 686–0300. A discreet hotel on discreet Madison Avenue. Small and simple, but very chic. Expensive at regular rates, but a reasonable $85 weekend rate is offered. 140 rooms

New York Hilton. 1335 Ave. of the Americas; 586–7000. The Hilton name has become synonymous with large, fancy, modern, and impersonal hotels—this one is no exception.

Regency. Park Ave. at 61st St.; 759–4100. French tapestries, Italian marble, floors, gilt mirrors—that's the level of elegance found here.

Sheraton-Russell. 45 Park Ave. at 37th St.; 685–7676. A little removed from the heart of the city, the hotel offers a calmness that contrasts with the trials of city life. Some rooms with fireplaces.

Sherry-Netherland. 781 Fifth Ave.; 355–2800. Although less well-known than its neighbors, the Plaza and the Pierre, the Sherry-Netherland is a distinguished hotel with a grandeur all its own. Sedate, elegant atmosphere.

UN Plaza. 1 UN Plaza at 44th St. and First Ave.; 355–3400. This ultramodern tower across from the UN is jazzy and sometimes garish, but everything's here, including some duplex suites. Very good weekend packages.

Vista International. 3 World Trade Center; 938–9100. Located in the heart of the financial district, this sparkling edifice is an outstanding hotel in all ways, including its superior American Harvest restaurant.

Waldorf-Astoria. 301 Park Ave. at 50th St.; 355–3000. The Waldorf seems to improve with age. The most renowned of American hotels, a mere mention of its name conjures images of luxury.

Westbury. 15 E. 69th St.; 535-2000. Located in a superior neighborhood for boutique fans, museum-goers, and gallery browsers, this is one of the better hotels in the city, with grand furnishings and comfortable rooms.

Luxury

Algonquin. 59 W. 44th St.; 840–6800. A must for the literary-minded (it is still the hangout for the *New Yorker* magazine's editorial staff), and perfect for theater-goers. The rooms are ever so slightly tattered, but there's a feeling of old world tradition here that is unique among New York hostelries.

Dorset. 30 W. 54th St.; 247–7300. One of the lesser-known of New York's top stopping places, it offers a quiet, traditional air and is located near the Museum of Modern Art.

Elysée. 60 E. 54th St.; 753–1066. This small hotel elegantly tucked away between Madison and Park avenues is particularly attentive to details.

Golden Tulip Barbizon. Lexington Ave. and 63 St., 838–5700, 800–223–1020. A remodeling of the famous Barbizon Hotel For Women, the transformation makes for an elegant, modern addition to New York's hotels.

Kitano. 66 Park Ave. at 38th St.; 685–0022. New York's only Japanese owned and operated hotel is a peaceful retreat featuring an excellent and beautifully done Japanese restaurant.

Lombardy. 111 E. 56th St.; 753–8600. This ultra-smart hotel allows you to stay in grand surroundings in a fine location.

Mayflower. 61st St. and Central Park West; 265–0060. Excellent views of Central Park, away from the hotel clutter on the park's south end, and at half the cost. Walking distance to Carnegie Hall and Lincoln Center.

Novotel. 226 W. 52nd St.; 315–0100. A glittering 500-room emporium with several lounges and restaurants at the north end of the theater district.

Omni Park Central. Seventh Ave. and 56th St.; 247–8000. A bustling lobby belies the quiet, luxurious rooms upstairs. Ideally located.

Expensive

Gorham. 136 W. 55th St.; 245–1800. Within walking distance of Carnegie Hall and Lincoln Center. Rooms are fairly large and all have kitchenettes.

Gramercy Park. 2 Lexington Ave.; 475–4320. A little out of the way but situated in one of the city's most untouched neighborhoods. Rooms looking out onto the private park are especially pleasant.

Milford Plaza. 270 W. 45th St.; 869–3600. In the heart of the theater district, package deals often run half the official rate. Very popular for tourist groups.

New York Penta. 401 Seventh Ave. at 33rd St.; 736–5000. A huge, busy hotel located across the street from Madison Square Garden and Penn Station, and near much shopping.

Roosevelt. 45 E. 45th St.; 661–9600. Convenient mid-town location and elegant rooms make this hotel a good bargain.

Sheraton Centre. 811 Seventh Ave.; 581–1000. Five restaurants and a good location (heart of the theater district) make up for what this hotel lacks in warmth.

Shoreham. 33 W. 55th St.; 247–6700. Spartan hotel located off stylish Fifth Avenue. Nearby are St. Patrick's Cathedral, Rockfeller Center, Carnegie Hall. Excellent value.

Tudor. 304 E. 42nd St.; 986–8800. Gracious hotel with small rooms, which you might expect at these rates. Near the UN, and a convenient crosstown bus stops right outside the door.

Warwick. 65 W. 54th St.; 247–2700. Large, straightforward rooms—no frills, but convenient. A favorite in the music industry.

Motels, Chains, and Simple but Practical

Best Western Skyline Motor Inn. 725 Tenth Ave. at 50th St.; 586–3400. One of the first real motels built in New York offers comfort and proximity to the theater district. Be careful, however, in this area late at night.

Beverly. Lexington Ave. at 50th St.; 753–2700. Quiet, club-like hotel located near Museum of Modern Art and Rockefeller Center.

Chelsea. 222 W. 23rd St.; 243–3700. Long a home to literary talent, the hotel today is more than a little strange—and not for everyone.

Empire. 63rd St. and Broadway; 265–7400. Across the street from Lincoln Center and popular for tour groups. Clean, simple accommodations.

Howard Johnson's Motor Lodge. Eighth Avenue between 51st and 52nd streets; 581–4100. Right in the middle of the theater district and a few blocks from "Restaurant Row."

Times Square. 255 W. 43rd St.; 354–7900. This hotel advertises itself as "no-frills" accommodations and that it is—but the rooms are clean, if a bit small.

* * *

We cannot sufficiently stress checking for special weekend, tourist, or corporate rates—even at the best hotels. The St. Moritz, Essex House, Plaza, UN Plaza, Vista, Grand Hyatt, and other deluxe hotels may well be affordable under the right circumstances. The large, impersonal, convention hotels such as the Hilton, Sheraton Centre, and Penta can be inexpensive.

For those on an especially low budget, the many YMCAs and YWCAs, while not always the bastions of cleanliness you might expect, offer very inexpensive rooms for under $50. These, too, require reservations. Locations are at 356 W. 34th St., 760–5850; 5 W. 63rd St., 787–4400; 224 E. 47th St., 755–2410; and 215 W. 23rd St., 741–9226.

THE OUTER BOROUGHS

Most of the hotels outside of Manhattan are grouped around the city's two major airports, LaGuardia and Kennedy in Queens. Mostly, they are convenient for overnight stops. **Hilton Inn** at Kennedy, 718–322–8700; **Holiday Inn** at La Guardia, 718–898–1225 and **Marriott** at Kennedy, 718–659–6000 all offer attractive rooms for under $125.

HOW TO GET AROUND. For all the fear and loathing the New York **subway** system inspires, it is still the fastest, most economical way to get around the city. Used judiciously—which is to say by staying in designated areas for late-night passengers and avoiding loiterers no matter what their entreaties may be—the subways are also reasonably safe. Keep wallets in inside pockets, purses securely closed, and don't expose jewelry such as gold chains. At night, ride in a center car, where the conductor is located.

For directions on what train (or bus) to take to your destination, call 330–1234. This information hotline is available 24 hours a day, though if you're calling from a pay phone be prepared with plenty of change—you'll probably have to wait a while for an operator to answer your question. Asking at a token booth during uncrowded periods might be a better idea. In any case, you should certainly try to get your hands on a subway and bus map through your hotel, at a token booth, or at the Convention and Visitors Bureau. A rather handy folding, laminated, subway and street-finder map is also on sale at many card shops and book stores: it is easier to cope with than the full subway map.

The fare at this writing is $1, and passengers must purchase tokens that are inserted at turnstiles. You should buy several tokens in advance, as lines can be incredibly long during rush hours. Transfers from one train to another are usually free within the subway system, with no formal "transfer" needed, though the lines intersect only at certain points. Local and express trains on the same line run parallel.

Subway tokens are also good on **buses,** which also accept $1 in coins. Buses are a good bet for very short distances during the day, after the business day is over, or on weekends. During high traffic times, they move at a snail's pace, though this is improving somewhat on avenues with special bus lanes. Bus routes, however, are even more confusing than the interlocking subway lines. Only one free transfer is given per passenger, and the buses for which they are good (going east-west if the trip started on a north-south route, or vice versa) are listed on the transfer ticket. Transfers must be requested when the fare is paid. Riders not using tokens must have exact change.

Cab fares start at $1.15 for the first eighth of a mile, and increase by 15¢ each additional eighth of a mile. Cabs can be hailed at any curb, though it is illegal for them to stop in the middle of the street. It is next to impossible to get a cab during rush hours or when the weather is bad. Placing yourself strategically near the closest hotel is an old New York trick—and a good bet. At theaters and airports many drivers will solicit passengers for private limousines or car services. If you are inclined to take advantage of their services, be sure to negotiate a price before you get in the car. Generally these vehicles have no meters and the drivers will try to get as much as they can. The *Yellow Pages* also lists a number of private services, and in these cases you can get a price quote over the phone.

The best bet, of course, is seeing New York **on foot.** It is the most leisurely pace for sightseeing, the least expensive, and in some instances, the fastest. By concentrating on distinct neighborhoods or areas and using the subway to travel between the more distant points on your itinerary, you won't need to use public transportation much at all.

HINTS TO THE MOTORIST. There are signs along certain main avenues in Manhattan that say, "Don't Even Think of Parking Here." If your vehicle is parked there, it will be towed away. Whatever form of transportation you prefer, don't expect to drive around Manhattan for sightseeing. With very few exceptions, you simply can't park on the street in midtown, and the cost of parking is prohibitive—as much as $25 for two hours on the upper East Side or in the garment district. If you are driving into town, park the car in a lot on the far West Side, say on Tenth Avenue in the 40's, where the daily rate will be $5–$8. But forget about driving from sight to sight—traffic moves very slowly.

When you do park on the street, be sure to lock all doors and don't leave anything tempting in the car or trunk. Hotels that have parking will charge from $15 and up for overnight storage. Pay the extra amount for the hotel or another indoor garage if your vehicle has a radio and/or tape player in it. These disappear especially rapidly when cars are parked on the street or in open lots, which is why you'll see some cars with signs in the windows proclaiming "No radio!"

Above all, be reminded that the signs warning "TOWAWAY ZONE" mean what they say.

TOURIST INFORMATION. Write the New York State Division of Tourism, One Commerce Plaza, Albany, NY 12245, for copies of the latest brochures on the city and/or state. When calling from out of state, the number is 800–342–3810; in the city the number is 309–0400. The New York Convention and Visitors Bureau, on the ground floor of the former Huntington Hartford Museum at Columbus Circle (59th St. and Eighth Ave.) is convenient for questions about New York City. The bureau can be reached by phone at 397–8222 or visited in person Monday–Friday, 9 A.M.–6 P.M.; weekends and holidays, 10 A.M.–6 P.M.

Best listings for current entertainment, museum shows, sports schedules, and the like are the weekly magazines *New York* and *The New Yorker,* the weekly newspaper *Village Voice,* the Sunday Arts and Leisure and Listings sections of the *New York Times,* and the Friday editions of the *New York Post* and *Daily News.*

SENIOR CITIZEN AND STUDENT DISCOUNTS. Both senior citizens and students should carry proof of their respective status. Seniors travel on the buses and subways for half price during non-rush hours, can attend movies (including many first-run houses) for $2 or so in the afternoons, and along with students, frequently get discounts on museum admissions. Seniors might also wish to have their travel agents check on possible discounts at hotels, though this is rare in New York.

HINTS TO THE DISABLED. Most buses have hydraulic lifts for the wheelchair-bound, while many busy crosswalks have cutaway curbs. That's the good news. The bad news is that the subway system is almost completely inaccessible to those in wheelchairs since few stations have elevators. If you can afford them, taxis are a reliable way of getting around. Drivers are generally considerate and helpful to handicapped passengers. Once at your destination, you may be pleasantly surprised. New York abounds with modern buildings and most are accessible to those in wheelchairs. The same goes for most public buildings—many of which have been recently outfitted to be accessible. The big museums offer sign language interpretations of tours, while theaters are often outfitted with infrared systems to aid the hearing impaired.

Access To The World: A Travel Guide For The Handicapped, by Louise Weiss, is an outstanding book covering all aspects of travel for anyone with health or medical problems. It generally features extensive listings and suggestions on everything from availability of special diets to wheelchair accessibility all over the world. Handicapped visitors to New York will appreciate such little known information as theater discounts available to them through the Schubert Organization. Published by Henry Holt & Co., the book can be ordered through your local bookstore. (Holt will not accept orders from individuals.)

Tours specially designed for the handicapped generally parallel those of the non-handicapped traveler, but at a more leisurely pace. For a complete list of tour operators who arrange such travel, write to the Society For the Advancement of *Travel for the Handicapped,* 26 Court St., Brooklyn, NY 11242 (718–858–5483).

 FREE EVENTS. Most major museums have designated days and/or hours when admission charges are dropped (mainly Tuesday evenings), and some smaller museums and historic sites are always free *(Museum of the City of New York, Grant's Tomb).* Art lovers will also want to pay a visit to the free *Washington Square Outdoor Art Exhibit,* held each spring and fall for two weekends either side of Memorial Day and Labor Day. Hundreds of artists exhibit their work (for sale) along the Greenwich Village streets surrounding Washington Square Park.

In the summer, street fairs galore invite strolling. These are free, although the aromas wafting from vendors hawking bean sprout pancakes, zeppole, sausage and pepper heroes, barbecued chicken wings, shish kebab, and the like will no doubt entice you into spending something. Check the weekend newspapers beginning in mid-May for street fair specifics: the kickoff is the *Ninth Avenue Food Festival,* which is probably also the most interesting, foodwise. Others of particular note are the *52nd Street Fair* (for free entertainment), the May-June *Feast of Saint Anthony* in Greenwich Village, and the September *San Gennaro Festival* in Little Italy.

Parades make their way through the city streets all year long, marking various national, ethnic, and patriotic figures and events. The biggest of them all is Macy's annual *Thanksgiving Day Parade,* from West 77th Street and Central Park West to the giant department store at 34th Street and Broadway. This is the one with helium-filled balloons of cartoon characters and the first seasonal appearance of Santa Claus himself.

The performing arts are outdoors—and free—in the summer, with the *New York Philharmonic* performing in city parks in June and July, followed by the *Metropolitan Opera* in August. Bring a blanket, some pillows, and a picnic, then get ready to share the evening with some 100,000 or so other fans who'll start gathering in front of the stage by noon for an 8 P.M. performance!

Shakespeare is also free in Central Park at the *Delacorte Theater.* Tickets are distributed on the day of the performance only, and are necessary since seating is limited. The crowds start arriving early here, too, in anticipation of ticket distribution at 6 P.M. Best to bring a picnic and dine al fresco right outside the theater.

Jazzmobile takes live jazz to various neighborhoods, and you'll run into more free jazz when the *Kool Jazz Festival* hits town in July (the same goes for the August Dewar's *Greenwich Village Jazz Festival*). Free jazz concerts are also given at the South Street Seaport and at the 9th Street bandshell in Brooklyn's Prospect Park. The Seaport has entertainers roaming the area's streets during the summer; and the *Celebrate Brooklyn* festival at the bandshell offers a wide range of performing arts throughout the summer.

The days around July 4 are special throughout the city. The highlight is the *Macy's fireworks display* over the East River, but many other such displays are given in Manhattan and the boroughs. Check the papers for details on these and other Independence Day celebrations.

TOURS AND SIGHTSEEING. A general tour is always a good idea in an unfamiliar city. It can help orient you and give you a quick feel for what you want to pursue. Probably the best of the lot, available spring through fall, is not through the city streets but on the surrounding waterways: the *Circle Line* around Manhattan. Boats leave frequently throughout the day from the Hudson River pier at the foot of West 42nd Street. The narrated ride takes about 2½ hours and costs $12 for adults, $6 for children. As for bus tours, *Grayline* (397–2600), *Short Line* (354–5122), and *Manhattan Sightseeing* (869–5005) offer various options. We recommend a basic two-hour morning tour; anything you want to cover in detail will require a visit on your own.

Free or inexpensive *walking tours* set out all year long in New York—urban park rangers take visitors through the city's parks, historical or architectural societies sponsor special lecture walks, and self-guided tours through such attractions as the New York Stock Exchange (20 Broad St.; 623–5167; open Mondays–Fridays, 10 A.M.–4 P.M.) are available.

The city's major attractions also offer their own *guided tours.* Call the UN at 754–7710, Rockefeller Center at 489–2947, Radio City Music Hall at 757–3100, Lincoln Center at 877–1800, or check their listings under the *Exploring New York Section* of this book. Theater fans will also be interested in *Backstage On Broadway* tours. Call 575–8065 for details on the many tours offering insights into the various Broadway hits.

PARKS AND GARDENS. First-time visitors to New York are invariably amazed that so many green areas can be found. Brownstone neighborhoods such as Greenwich Village, Chelsea, Gramercy Park, the upper West Side, and others in Manhattan and the other boroughs have beautiful tree-lined blocks. And the city's parks offer thousands of acres of rolling green meadows. (See *Outer Boroughs* section above.)

Central Park is the most famous, and despite all the tales of crime in the park, it is a fine place to visit either during the day or when a special event is taking place on summer evenings. On the west side of town north of 72nd Street is *Riverside Park,* with a marina at 79th Street. This is a less-populated park, frequented by those living along Riverside Drive and West End Avenue.

You'll also see many so-called vest-pocket parks all over; out-of-towners may laugh at the notion of these little patches, usually with potted trees, artificial waterfalls, and the like, as being "parks," but they offer New Yorkers pleasant places to relax at lunchtime when the weather permits.

BEACHES. You'll have to go to the outer boroughs to get some sand between your toes. The most famous is no doubt *Coney Island* (take the IND subway's B, D, F, M, N, or QB line). Although the beach is a mere shadow of its former glory, and not an area for wandering in the evenings, daytime by the water is fine. *Astroland Amusement Park* is right along the shore, but may soon be razed for reconstruction.

The other major beach within city limits is in the *Rockaways*—a peninsula that juts out into the Atlantic. *Jacob Riis Park* is the most popular, with plenty of sports fields and playgrounds. Easiest access is to take the IRT subway's No. 2 or 3 line to Flatbush Avenue: a Green Line bus ($1) from here will take you directly to the beach.

Not too far from the city on Long Island is *Jones Beach*—probably the most crowded of all, so get there early. Easiest route is by bus from the Port Authority Bus Terminal (Eighth Ave. and 42nd St.; $5 each way); alternately there is a Long Island Rail Road–bus combination that can be even faster for $8.50 roundtrip, $5 one-way. (For additional information see the *Long Island* section of this book.)

 ZOOS. Nothing in these parts rivals the Bronx Zoo, Fordham Rd. and Southern Blvd. (367–1010), with its natural habitat environments, snazzy Skyfari cablecar, and Bengali Express monorail. Hours: 10 A.M.–5 P.M. (5:30 P.M. Sundays and holidays; 4:30 P.M. November through January). Admission is free Tuesdays, Wednesdays, and Thursdays; $3.75 for adults, $1.50 for children other times. Senior citizens are always admitted free. The children's zoo and rides are extra. The zoo can be reached via the IRT No 2 or 5 trains to the East Tremont Ave. stop or by car at the intesection of the Pelham and Bronx River parkways. There are also small zoos in *Central Park* and *Prospect Park,* though these are under ongoing renovation as this is written. For seafaring creatures, the *New York Aquarium,* Surf Ave. at West 8th St., near Brooklyn's Coney Island (718–266–8500), is the place to go. The aquarium can be reached via the IND "F" or BMT "M" trains to the West 8th St. Station.

 PARTICIPANT SPORTS. Habitual **joggers** need not fear having to give up their favorite exercise when they venture into Manhattan. In fact, jogging is probably the number one participant sport in the city. Although you're welcome to do your stuff in the streets of midtown, you'd be much better off taking to the city's many parks. Areas most frequented include the roads in and around Central, Riverside, and Washington Square parks.

The parks are also great for **biking, horseback riding,** and even **rowing.** Bikes can be rented for about $3 per hour; check the Yellow Pages for centrally located outlets. For a little bit of country in the city, horseback riding is an unexpected pleasure. Manhattan offers the *Claremont Stable* (175 W. 89th St., 724–5100), and there are stables in other boroughs. Hourly rates are usually between $20 and $25. Row-boating is a real summertime release, and you'll find all you need at the Central Park Lake, just north of 72nd St. The *Loeb Boathouse* rents rowboats at $6 per hour. Here, as in all rental cases, a deposit is required.

Bowling alleys and **ice skating** rinks can be found in the Yellow Pages. **Racquetball** and **tennis** are increasingly fashionable energy outlets, but most health club chains such as the *New York Health and Racquet Club* are open to members only. The beautiful *Wall St. Racquet Club* (Wall St. and East River, 952–0760), the *Village Tennis Courts* (110 University Pl., 989–2300) and the *Tennis Club* (15 Vanderbilt Ave., near Grand Central Station, 687–3841), however, all offer hourly court time to the general public. Those wishing to use outdoor tennis courts must obtain a visitor's permit. A pass is $4 and entitles the player to one hour of time on any city-run court. They can be picked up at the *Central Park Courts,* 93rd St. in the park.

Golfers can take advantage of the city's numerous public golf courses. Greens fees depend on whether you're playing on a weekday or weekend, and what time you tee off. The top fee is about $15. In Brooklyn, play at *Dyker Beach* (718–836 –9722) or *Marine Park* (718–338–7113). In Queens there are *Clearview* in

Bayside (718–229–2570), *Douglaston Park* (718–224–6566), *Forest Park* in Ridgewood (718–296–2442), and Flushing's *Kissena Park* (718–447–5686), (718–939–4594). Staten Island's courses are *Silver Lake South Shore* (718–984–0108), and *La Tourette* (718–351–1889). The Bronx offers *Mosholu-Booth* (212–822–4845), *Van Cortlandt* (212–543–4595), and *Pelham-Split Rock* (212–885–1258). There are two courses at the latter, and Split Rock may be the toughest challenge in the five boroughs.

SPECTATOR SPORTS. New York's reign as the sports town of the nation is fast coming to an end, as teams leave the city proper for nearby towns. Still, New York does boast two top baseball teams in the **Yankees** and **Mets.** The Bronx Bombers play at Yankee Stadium (293–6000), while the Mets are at Shea Stadium (718–507–8499). Yankee Stadium is most readily accessible via the IRT No. 4 and the IND D and CC subway lines to the 161st Street stop. Shea Stadium can be reached by the IRT No. 7 Flushing line to the Willets Point-Shea Stadium station or by Long Island Rail Road from Penn Station.

The **Knicks** and the **Rangers** are the city's beloved basketball and ice hockey teams playing in season at Madison Square Garden (563–8300). The Garden also hosts **boxing** and **wrestling** events and college basketball games. The **U.S. Open,** in September, is held at the USTA Tennis Center (718–592–8000) in Queens. The final race of the prestigious Triple Crown is held in June at **Belmont Raceway** (718–641–4700), just across the city line in Elmont, Long Island. The track operates from May to October. **Aqueduct,** in Queens (718–641 –4700), is the largest thoroughbred racing track in the U.S., running from October through April. **Yonkers Raceway,** for harness racing, is just beyond the city line in Westchester, while **Roosevelt Raceway** is in Westbury, Long Island. The **Jersey Meadowlands** also features a race track.

Note: The **Giants** and **Jets** football teams play at Giants Stadium (201–935–8222) in East Rutherford, New Jersey. The powerful **Islanders** hockey team is at the Nassau Coliseum (516–794–4100) in Uniondale, Long Island.

CHILDREN'S ACTIVITIES. The sites, museums, zoos, and street fairs are all perfectly suitable for children and, in fact, welcome them. The *American Museum of Natural History* is a standard children's attraction, as is the adjoining Hayden Planetarium. Although shopping is generally a bit much on young legs, no child will ever want to leave *F.A.O. Schwarz,* the giant toy store on Fifth Ave. at 58th St. Holiday time in the city is also special for children—they'll enjoy the animated windows of stores such as *B. Altman* and *Lord & Taylor* and, of course, a visit to Santa Claus at *Macy's* (but be prepared for a very, very long wait). The special holiday production at *Radio City* is always a treat, as are many other theatrical and musical events during the holidays. In fact, several theater groups offer fare especially for children, including the *Magic Towne House* (1026 Third Ave., 752–1165), the *Onstage Children's Company* (413 W. 46 St., 246–9872, September–May), and *Something Different* (First Avenue between 77th and 78th streets), an ice cream-parlor-cum-nightclub starring child performers. Also of interest, of course, is the *Ringling Bros. and Barnum & Bailey Circus,* which romps into town in the late spring. Call Madison Square Garden (563–8300) for details.

HISTORIC SITES. Start your walking tour of New York history where the city started: at the harbor. Henry Hudson sailed his ship, the *Half Moon,* into the harbor in 1609, and the area's inclusion in what Europeans called the "New World" dates from then. **Battery Park** area sites include the Shrine of Saint Elizabeth Ann Seton, the Jewish Immigrant Memorial, Verrazano Statue, Castle Clinton National Monument, Bowling Green, the U.S. Customs House, and Fraunces Tavern. To reach Battery Park, take the IRT East Side No. 6 local to Bowling Green or the IRT West Side No. 6 local to South Ferry. While at Battery Park, you will no doubt want to visit the Statue of Liberty. Lower Manhattan is also home to Wall Street, Trinity Church, the Federal Hall National Memorial, St. Paul's Chapel, and the over-commercialized but fun South Street Seaport, as well as City Hall and many city, state, and federal government buildings.

Greenwich Village history is largely literary, with the Boorman House on the northeast corner of Washington Square Park having served at various times as home to Edith Wharton, William Dean Howells, and Henry James. Other Village homes are detailed in the *Exploring* section. Architecturally, look for the Washington Square Arch in Washington Square Park, and the Jefferson Market Courthouse on Sixth Ave. at 9th St. The Theodore Roosevelt Mansion is at 28 E. 20th Street, and the Abigail Adams Smith Museum is at 421 E. 61st St. (For information on historic sites outside Manhattan, see *Outer Boroughs* section above.)

LIBRARIES. The crown jewel of the *New York Public Library* system is the main library at Fifth Avenue and 42nd St. No books are lent out here, but anyone may use its resources within the confines of the building. The library is also something of a museum. Other midtown Manhattan branches worth noting include the Mid-Manhattan Library, the main circulating library in the system, at 40th St. and Fifth Ave. The collection here emphasizes science, education, business, history, and sociology. The *Library and Museum of Performing Arts* at Lincoln Center (111 Amsterdam Ave.; the library is part of the Lincoln Center complex), offers records, printed music, and dance, film, and drama books. A special section is open by permission to qualified researchers in the arts. The *Donnell Library,* 20 W. 53rd St., is also strong on performing and fine arts, and maintains a collection of popular books in foreign languages. The *Library for the Blind and Physically Handicapped* is at 166 Ave. of the Americas.

MUSEUMS. Few cities rival New York in the quantity and quality of its museums. New York is home to some of the world's finest art museums, and it also boasts dozens of specialized museums—enough to satisfy anyone's appetites and tastes. You'll find museums devoted to fashion, theater, performing arts, dolls, fire engines, coins, architecture, photography, stamps, and even the city itself. Once a year, usually in mid-June, the stretch of Upper Fifth Avenue from 82nd to 105th streets, known as "Museum Mile," becomes a pedestrian mall. That evening, admission to the 10 museums lining the avenue is free. These include the *Metropolitan Museum of Art,* the *Guggenheim Museum,* and the *Cooper-Hewitt* mansion. In general, you'll find this area a good focal point for museum hopping, although you couldn't begin to comprehensively visit all 10 in even a weeklong stay. Midtown and the Upper West Side also offer several fine museums.

Most of the bigger museums offer "suggested admission prices"—you don't have to pay any certain amount, although one is usually "recommended." Students and seniors should also check for special discounts at museums that do have a set fee. Some museums are free on Tuesdays after 5 P.M. (For museums outside Manhattan see *Outer Boroughs* section above.)

Probably the four best-known and most popular art museums are the Metropolitan, the Whitney, the Guggenheim, and the Museum of Modern Art.

Metropolitan Museum of Art. Fifth Ave. and 82nd St.; 879–5500. Architecturally, this museum is a treat, also. The grand entrance is only one of a melange of styles, beginning with the coolly Georgian facade by Richard Morris Hunt and ending with the serenely beautiful Temple of Dendur wing designed by the firm of Roche, Dinkeloo.

The museum's collection—and reputation—rests solidly on its vast offerings of pre-20th century masterpieces (up the main staircase to the 2nd floor). In 1987, however, the museum unveiled a new wing devoted to its collection of impressive—and relatively unknown—20th century art. Adjacent to this is a new sculpture roof garden which offers spectacular views of Central Park. Other highlights include the fabulous selection of antique musical instruments, the Tiffany and other glass pieces behind the Egyptian galleries, and the ever-changing costume gallery below ground level. The recently added American wing includes a portion of Frank Lloyd Wright's prototypical ranch home, "The Little House." Adjoining this section are the lovely Japanese gardens. Open Tuesdays–Sundays, 9:30 A.M. to 5:15 P.M. and Tuesday evenings until 8:45 P.M. Suggested contribution, \$4.50; Tuesday evenings free.

The museum also maintains a medieval branch in Fort Tryon Park. The Cloisters (923–3700) is an exquisite complex constructed from the ruins of five medieval cloisters, the outdoor areas where monks used to perform morning prayers and ablutions. Also part of the collection are the famous unicorn tapestries, 12th-century Spanish frescoes, and numerous pieces and remnants of medieval churches. Contrary to many people's conceptions, this is not a monastery, only a re-creation, right down to the taped murmurings heard throughout the building. Easily accessible via the M4 bus up Madison Avenue, the beautiful museum and stunning grounds are well worth the hour trip. Open Tuesdays – Sundays, 9:30 A.M.–5:15 P.M. Adults, \$4.50; children, free.

Solomon R. Guggenheim Museum. 1071 Fifth Ave. at 88th St.; 360–3513. The museum as showpiece: when Frank Lloyd Wright unveiled the design for this creamy, spiraling building, he got what he wanted—a reaction. Today, first-time viewers are still likely to gasp upon first spying the spaceship-like exterior. Inside, the museum emphasizes 20th-century artists such as de Kooning, Ernst, and Kandinsky. Impressionist fans should also note that the museum's collection is quite good. Whatever you do—don't forget to wind your way up (or down, if you're not feeling quite that ambitious) the entire museum via ramp. Open Wednesdays–Sundays, 11 A.M.–5 P.M.; Tuesdays to 8 P.M. Adults, \$3.50; children, free. Free Tuesday evenings.

Museum of Modern Art. 11 W. 53 Street; 708–9400. Recently expanded, the museum now includes architecture and photography galleries. MOMA's strength still lies in its collection of modern art, from a few representatives of the late Impressionist works (including the huge panels of Monet's "Water Lilies") through the cubism of Picasso and the surreal works of Dali and Magritte to the pop art stylings of Lichtenstein and Warhol and the artists of the present. A quiet sculpture garden is in the back of the grounds. Special exhibits, films and lectures are almost always offered. Open daily 11 A.M.–6 P.M.; to 9 P.M. on Thursdays. Closed Wednesdays. Adults, \$5; children, free; pay what you wish Thursday evenings.

Whitney Museum of American Art. 945 Madison Ave. at 75 St.; 570–3600.
Marcel Breuer's Brutalist building is, to many, a monstrosity ruining the calm
face of Madison Avenue. Still, the museum's sunken sculpture garden and
cantilevered tiers provide a striking vista. The museum focuses on 20th-century
American painting and has the largest such collection in the world. Great
emphasis is also placed on works in other media and on alternative styles. A new
wing is currently being added to the building. Open Wednesdays–Saturdays, 11
A.M.–5 P.M.; Tuesdays, 1 P.M.–8 P.M. Sundays noon–6 P.M. Adults, $4; children,
free; free Tuesday evenings.

 ONE-OF-A-KIND MUSEUMS. If you have time, you
should also try to visit several of the following museums.
Two of these are must-sees: the American Museum of
Natural History, which almost every New York school-
child has visited—the one with the life-size dinosaur bones; and the often
overlooked Brooklyn Museum. The other three are unique to the city: the
Museum of Holography, the Museum of Broadcasting, and the Intrepid Sea-
Air-Space Museum.

American Museum of Natural History. Central Park West at 79th St.; 769–
5100. As its name implies, the museum is filled with artifacts of the earth's past
and present. You'll find representatives of every animal species, culture, and
lifeform here. And, of course, the famous dinosaur skeletons on the top floor
of the building. On the main level are the exhibits filled with incredibly lifelike
wild animals stuffed and mounted into settings of their natural habitats.

Other highlights of the collection include the giant 94-foot blue whale sus-
pended from the ceiling of the first floor Hall of Ocean Life, the 563-carat Star
of India sapphire, and an enormous 90-foot crosscut of a sequoia tree which
began growing in 550 A.D.

The building's West 77th Street facade is a stunning salmon Romanesque
Revival treatment that somehow looks museum-like in its pomposity. On the
81st Street side, you'll find the *Hayden Planetarium* (873–8828). This domed
building houses an auditorium featuring "sky shows" and laser light/rock music
spectacles (724–8700). Hours are 10 A.M.–5:45 P.M.; to 9 P.M. on Wednesdays,
Fridays, and Saturdays. Suggested contribution: $3, adults; $1.50, children; free
Friday and Saturday evenings. A separate admission is charged for the
planetarium ($3.75, adults; $2, children), though the planetarium admission
includes admission to the museum. Laser shows are held twice nightly on
Fridays and Saturdays and are $5.

Brooklyn Museum. Eastern Pkwy and Washington Ave.; 718–638–5000.
Similar in scope to the Museum of Natural History, this is the seventh-largest
museum in America. Perhaps most highly acclaimed for its world-renowned
collection of Egyptian art, the museum also has vast collections of African,
Japanese, Indonesian, and American Indian art. The real highlight here is the
wonderful selection of glass, costumes, china, and the 28 American period
rooms, ranging from Colonial days through the 20th century. Open daily, 10
A.M.–5 P.M.; closed Tuesdays. Adults, $3; children, $1.50.

Intrepid Sea-Air-Space Museum. Pier 86, Hudson River at 46th St.; 245–
2533. A U.S. Navy aircraft carrier has been transformed into a floating museum
detailing U.S. military history and technology in the air, in space, and at sea.
Exhibits are divided into five major theme halls spanning the years past and
predicting the years ahead. Open Tuesdays–Sundays, 10 A.M.–5 P.M. Adults,
$4.75; children, $2.50.

Museum of Broadcasting. 1 E. 53rd St.; 752–7684. The ever-growing collection here of old radio and television tapes and video is unsurpassed; unfortunate-

ly, the museum is rather small and waiting time can be lengthy and viewing time limited. Be forewarned that what you're most interested in is likely to be the same as everybody else; for example, a bored staffer will tell you the exact position of The Beatles performance on an Ed Sullivan tape. But for fans and media historians alike, the museum's collection is a treasure trove. Open Wednesdays–Saturdays, noon–5 P.M.; Tuesdays to 8 P.M. Adults, $3; children, $1.50.

Museum of Holography. 11 Mercer St.; 925–0526. Until recently, this was the only museum in the world devoted entirely to holography. It's still far and away the best, and as much a learning center and enthusiastic forum for lobbying on behalf of the art as a museum. Holography is the art/science of creating three-dimensional light images with laser beams. The museum features changing exhibits as well as a permanent history exhibit, a "Hol-o-Fame" of holograms of famous New Yorkers, and films, lectures, and a great bookstore. Open Tuesdays–Sundays, noon–6 P.M. Adults, $3; children, $1.75.

OTHER MAJOR MUSEUMS. Many of the other large museums of New York relate to the arts in a more general sense. Cooper-Hewitt, the Frick Collection, and the Pierpont Morgan libraries are each based on the collections of New York's grand millionaires. Still others are devoted to interior decorating, fashion design, architecture, photography and the performing arts.

American Craft Museum. 40 W. 53rd St.; 869–9422. Located in the lobby of the International Paper Company headquarters, this little museum is one of the unexpected pleasures of museum-hopping in the city. Works are exhibited by theme—tapestries, glassworks, clay, etc. Open Tuesday, 10 A.M.–8 P.M.; Wednesday–Saturday, 10 A.M.–5 P.M. Adults, $3.50; children, $1.50.

Cooper-Hewitt Museum. 2 E. 91st St.; 860–6868. The design wing of the Smithsonian Institution is housed in Andrew Carnegie's former mansion. As might be expected, the small gallery rooms are attractive in and of themselves. The collection's accent is on decorative arts of all periods and countries, with an emphasis on architecture, jewelry, and ceramics. The museum boasts the largest drawing and print collection in the U.S., and its textile department is one of the nation's most comprehensive. Outside, a landscaped garden is a tranquil escape from the surrounding city. Open Wednesdays–Saturdays, 10 A.M.–5 P.M.; Tuesdays to 9 P.M.; Sundays noon–5 P.M.; closed Mondays and holidays. Admission, $3; free, Tuesday evenings.

Fashion Institute of Technology. Seventh Ave. and 27th St.; 760–7760. Historic and contemporary designs of European and American fashions, textiles, furnishings, fashion illustrations, and photographs. Open Tuesdays–Saturdays, 10 A.M.–6 P.M.; Wednesdays to 8 P.M. Suggested donation, $2.

Frick Collection. 1 E. 70th St.; 288–0700. The Frick collection is magnificent. Set in the former private home of another New York millionaire (the Pittsburgh-born steel industrialist, Henry Clay Frick), room after glorious room is filled with some of the most famous paintings of the European masters from the 14th through 19th centuries, including works from Renoir, Rembrandt, Vermeer, Titian, El Greco, Whistler, Turner, Gainsborough, and Reynolds. The setting for such a wealth of paintings is gorgeous, as well. The glass-roofed courtyard is one of the most soothing spots in the entire city. Open Tuesdays–Saturdays, 10 A.M.–6 P.M.; open Sundays at 1 P.M. Adults, $2; $3 on Sundays; children under 10 not admitted.

International Center of Photography. 1130 Fifth Ave. at 94th St.; 860–1677. The only museum in New York devoted exclusively to photography. Housed in a Georgian-style landmark building, the exhibits are geared only to the big-time best (Cartier-Bresson, et al.). Open Wednesdays–Fridays, noon–5 P.M.; Tuesdays to 8 P.M.; Saturdays and Sundays, 11 A.M.–6 P.M. Admission, $2; free Tuesday evenings. A second branch is now open at 77 W. 45th St. Open 11 A.M.–6 P.M. weekdays; noon to 5 P.M. Saturdays. Admission, $1, adults; 50¢ students.

Library and Museum of Performing Arts. 111 Amsterdam Ave. (Lincoln Center); 870–1630. A division of the New York Public Library, this library/ museum touches upon just about every aspect of the performing arts. Exhibits include set designs, costumes, letters, posters, and a circulating collection of 30,000 Broadway cast albums. Some of the more unusual entries include Katharine Cornell's makeup kit and holographic manuscripts of Bach, Mozart, and Stravinsky. Children will love the world's largest children's library housed here, with its theater, puppet shows, and special memorabilia (like a slipper hand-embroidered by Mark Twain for child actress Elsie Leslie). Call for hours; free.

Pierpont Morgan Library. 29 E. 36th St.; 685–0008. The library's collection is housed in a Renaissance villa built in 1906 for financier J. P. Morgan. Its collection is notable for rare books and manuscripts, some of which date back to the Renaissance. Of particular interest is the Stavelot Triptych (reputedly containing fragments of the true cross), a letter from Lord Cornwallis to George Washington regarding England's surrender to the United States during the Revolutionary War, and a first edition of the Declaration of Independence, the finest of 21 existing copies. The individual rooms of the palazzo are magnificent, particularly Morgan's private study with furniture and furnishings intact, and the East Room, with its floor-to-ceiling bookcases. A number of exhibits are featured throughout the year. Open Tuesdays–Saturdays, 10:30 A.M.–5 P.M.; open Sundays at 1 P.M. Closed Mondays, Sundays in July, holidays, and the month of August. Admission, $3.

National Academy of Design. 1083 Fifth Ave. at 89th St.; 369–4880. The museum's collection, housed in the Beaux Arts mansion that was formerly the home of philanthropist Archer M. Huntington, comprises works by American artists, including Winslow Homer, Thomas Eakins, and Reginald Marsh. Open Wednesdays–Sundays, noon–5 P.M.; Tuesdays to 8 P.M. Admission, $2.50, Tuesday evenings, free.

New York Public Library. Fifth Ave. at 41st St.; 869–8089. Far more than a beautiful building with an incredible research collection, the library also supports quite a reputation as a museum. A Gutenberg Bible, early Shakespeare folios, the handwritten manuscript of Washington's farewell address, the Lenox Globe (one of the earliest globes, dating to around 1510), and numerous other rare books, manuscripts, and prints are all here. Some of the many works of art found in the building include four huge murals by Edward Laning on the second floor depicting the story of the written word from Moses and the tablets to the invention of the printing press and the gigantic "Blind Milton Dictating 'Paradise Lost' To His Daughter," located in the main stairway. The library also hosts a continuing series of exhibitions. Open Mondays–Saturdays 10 A.M.–6 P.M. Free.

Society of Illustrators Museum of American Illustration. 128 East 63rd St.; 838–2560. Located in a former carriage house owned by J. P. Morgan, this museum draws on the 1,000-piece collection of the society. Exhibits focus on the best of contemporary and historical illustrations. Open Mondays–Fridays, 10 A.M.–5 P.M.; Tuesdays to 8 P.M. Free.

Urban Center. 457 Madison Ave.; 935–3960. A series of Italian Renaissance brownstones form a palazzo called the Villard Houses; two stylish wings have been added on either side and the Helmsley Palace Hotel rises above the complex. In the left wing is the Municipal Arts Society, which puts on architectural and urban-issues exhibits during the year and maintains an excellent architecture-oriented bookstore. Open Mondays–Saturdays, 11 A.M.–5 P.M. Free.

HISTORICAL MUSEUMS. As one of the original 13 colonies and the nation's first capital, New York's contribution to the history of the United States is a rich one. The following museums recognize those aspects of the city.

Abigail Adams Smith Museum. 421 E. 61st St.; 838–6878. The museum was originally built in 1799 as a carriage house and was later converted into a residence in 1826. Abigail, daughter of President John Adams, lived here in the mid-1800s. Today the building serves as a monument to that period, with intact rooms and furnishings as well as a lovely garden. Open Mondays–Fridays, 10 A.M.–4 P.M. Adults, $2; children, free.

Federal Hall National Memorial. 26 Wall St.; 264–8711. It was near this site that George Washington delivered his inaugural address. Exhibits here include miniature paintings, snuffboxes, and documents. Open Mondays–Fridays, 9 A.M.–5 P.M. Free.

Museum of the City of New York. Fifth Ave. at 103rd St.; 534–1672. Details the story of New York from its beginnings as a small Dutch trading post to its current status as the Big Apple. Costumes, dioramas, prints, portraits, photographs, a trolley car, and period rooms are all here. This museum should be a high point of your New York stay. Open Tuesdays–Saturdays, 10 A.M.–5 P.M.; Sundays and holidays (closed Christmas and New Year's), 1 P.M. – 5 P.M. Free.

New York Historical Society. Central Park West; 873–3400. Founded in 1804, the museum showcases American art and history, with emphasis on the contributions of New York City and State. Permanent exhibitions include a comprehensive collection of paintings by the naturalist Audubon and glassworks by Tiffany, as well as antique toys, fire engines, and colonial rooms. Open Tuesdays–Saturdays, 10A.M.–5 P.M.; open Sundays at 1 P.M. Adults, $2; children 75¢; Tuesdays, pay what you wish.

South Street Seaport Museum. 207 Front St.; 669–9400. The history of New York's waterfront is detailed here through several vessels open to the public. The address is merely an information booth, since the "museum" is really the entire Seaport area. Admission to museum programs, Seaport Gallery, and vessels: adults, $4; children, $2. This fee also includes admission to three tours of the area, and two film presentations.

ETHNIC AND CULTURAL MUSEUMS. New York is home to a variety of museums for cultures as diverse and numerous as the city's population. These include:

Asia Society. 725 Park Ave. at 70th St.; 288–6400. Permanent exhibits on the Far East, including South Asian stone and bronze sculptures, a section devoted to Chinese and Korean arts, an area of Southeast Asian art, and a section housing Japanese ceramics, paintings, and wood sculptures. Open Tuesdays–Saturdays, 11 A.M.–6 P.M.; Sundays, noon–5 P.M. Adults, $2; seniors, $1.

China House Gallery. 125 E. 65th St.; 744–8181. Changing exhibits of classical Chinese art. Mondays–Fridays, 10 A.M.–5 P.M. Closed June, July, and August. Suggested contribution, $1.

El Museo del Barrio. 1230 Fifth Ave.; 831–7272. The only museum in the U.S. devoted entirely to Puerto Rican and Latin American arts and culture. Open Wednesdays–Sundays, 11 A.M.–5 P.M. Suggested contribution, $2.

Hispanic Society of America. Broadway and 155th St.; 690–0743. All of the great Spanish masters are here, from Goya to El Greco, along with displays of jewelry, sculpture, and tiles and pottery reflecting Hispanic history and culture.

Open Tuesdays–Saturdays, 10 A.M.–4:30 P.M.; Sundays, 1–4 P.M.; closed August. Free but contributions are appreciated.

Japan House. 333 E. 47th St.; 752–0824. Four yearly exhibits of Japanese arts. Open daily, 11 A.M.–5 P.M. Suggested contribution, $2.50

Jewish Museum. Fifth Ave. and 92nd St.; 860–1889. This museum is dedicated to collecting and presenting art and artifacts from 4,000 years of Jewish history. Displays include ceremonial objects, manuscripts, paintings, and sculpture. Open Mondays–Thursdays, noon–5 P.M.; Tuesdays to 8 P.M.; Sundays, 11 A.M.–6 P.M.; closed Fridays and Saturdays. 11 A.M.–3 P.M. Adults, $4.

Museum of American Folk Art. The museum is currently in the process of moving into its new building on W. 53rd between Fifth and Sixth aves. Until the move is completed (early 1989) various exhibitions from the museum's collection are being presented throughout the city on a 3-month basis. Call 481–3080 for details and information. The collection includes weathervanes, quilts, samplers, store signs, and painted and decorated furniture—all representing the rich folk heritage of this country. The museum shop, now located on 62 W. 56th St., offers handmade items, postcards, and books on folk art.

Museum of the American Indian. Broadway at 155th St.; 283–2420. The museum has the largest collection of Indian artifacts anywhere in the world. Exhibits are drawn from North, South, and Central American Indians. A wonderful collection of hides, feathers, totem poles, masks, pottery, and jewelry. Open Tuesdays–Saturdays, 10 A.M.–5 P.M.; open Sundays at 1 P.M. Admission, $2.

Studio Museum in Harlem. 144 W. 125th St.; 864–4500. Changing exhibits emphasizing works by black artists in all media. Open Wednesdays–Fridays, 10 A.M.–5 P.M.; Saturdays and Sundays, 1 P.M.–6 P.M. Adults, $1.50; children 50¢.

Ukrainian Museum. 203 Second Ave. at 12th St.; 228–0110. Located in the center of New York's Ukrainian neighborhood, this museum features costumes and folk art. Open Wednesdays–Sundays, 1 P.M.–5 P.M. Adults, $1; seniors 50¢, children under six, free.

Yeshiva University Museum. 2520 Amsterdam Ave.; 960–5390. Changing exhibits on Jewish historical and contemporary culture and arts. Open Tuesdays–Thursdays, 10:30 A.M.–5 P.M.; Sundays, noon–6 P.M. Adults, $2; children, $1.

SPECIAL-INTEREST MUSEUMS. American Numismatic Society. Broad-
way at 155th St.; 234–3130. For coin buffs—coins, metals, and decorations from all ages and all countries. Open Tuesdays–Saturdays, 9 A.M.–3 P.M.; Sundays, 1 P.M.–3 P.M. Free.

Aunt Len's Doll and Toy Museum. 6 Hamilton Terr. at 141st St.; 281–4143. Almost 5,000 dolls and accessories, plus wind-up, tin, and mechanical toys. Open Tuesdays–Sundays by appointment only. Adults, $2; children, $1.

Bible House. 1865 Broadway at 61st St.; 581–7400. Located in the headquarters of the American Bible Society, the collection features over 40,000 volumes including two leaves from a Gutenberg Bible, fragments from the Dead Sea Scrolls, and an 18-volume braille Bible. Open Mondays–Fridays, 9 A.M.–4:30 P.M. Free.

New York City Fire Museum. 278 Spring St.; 691–1303. Authentic fire fighting equipment used during the 19th and 20th centuries. The collection features hand-drawn pumpers, engines, uniforms, sliding poles, and fireboat equipment. Located, appropriately enough, in an old firehouse. Open Mondays–Fridays, 9 A.M.–4 P.M. Free.

Police Academy Museum. 235 E. 20th St.; 477–9753. This collection is the world's largest assortment of police memorabilia. Open Mondays–Fridays, 10 A.M.–2 P.M. Free.

FILM. No other city offers such a concentration of mov- iehouses as New York. And with the city cashing in on the multiplex cinemas so popular elsewhere, the number is growing. Hundreds of moviehouses can be found in Manhattan, but generally speaking most are around Times Square, the East 50s and 60s, and in Greenwich Village.

Movie tickets are higher here than in other areas of the country, with prices for first-run features currently up to $6. Reservations are usually not taken, and you should get to the movie theater at least half an hour early—more if the film is just opening or is a recently established hit. You'll be expected to wait in line to buy your ticket, and then to wait in line to get into the theater. This is especially true at night and on weekends. On a weekday, movies are often cheaper as well.

The places to go for the latest, most popular movies are Times Square and the Upper East Side—though we urge you to steer clear of the 42nd Street movie houses, no matter what's playing there. On Broadway and Seventh Avenue, and just up a few of the side streets, you're likely to find the blockbuster and action movies of the *Star Wars—Rambo* genres. The theaters stretching from 57th to 66th streets, between First and Third avenues, prefer the quieter side of Holly- wood.

New York, home of the New York Film Festival, is also vastly interested in foreign films. Your best bet for these is the *Lincoln Plaza Triplex* (Broadway and 63rd St.; 757–2280), ideally situated across the street from Lincoln Center, the home of the festival in late September. *The Plaza* (58th St. and Madison Ave.; 355–3320), *Paris* (58th St. and Fifth Ave.; 688–2013), and the *Cinema Studio* (Broadway and 66th St., also right near Lincoln Center; 877–4040) are other good outlets for foreign films.

So-called "revival houses" are popular here as well. These dozen or so theat- ers have made money out of running old and cult film classics. Several of these are in the Village: the *Bleecker Street Cinema* (Bleecker and LaGuardia Pl.; 674–2560), for old foreign films; *Theatre 80 St. Marks* (80 St. Marks Pl.; 254–7400) for strictly Hollywood classics of the 1930s and 1940s; and the *Cinema Village* (22 E. 12th St.; 924–3363) for a menu of seemingly endless repeats of Woody Allen and Beatles flicks.

Other revival houses are the *Thalia Soho* (15 Vandam St.; 675–0498), *Film Forum Two* (57 Watts St.; 431–1590), and *Carnegie Hall Cinema* (883 Seventh Ave.; 265–2520). The Thalia Soho emphasizes classics from Hollywood's golden years; the other two place the accent on art and foreign films of days gone by.

Real film fans shouldn't neglect the many museums and libraries that show rarely seen and classic movies. (See *New York Magazine's* comprehensive list- ings.) And don't overlook the number of smaller theaters offering cult films and exclusive engagements. In the Village, the *Waverly* (Sixth Ave. and Eighth St.; 929–8037) and *Eighth Street Playhouse* (52 West Eighth St.; 674–6515) serve up youth-oriented rock 'n' roll films and strange British imports. The *Film Forum* (57 Watts St.; 431–1590) and the *Public Theatre* (425 Lafayette St.; 598–7171) also offer movies that play nowhere else in the city, as does uptown's *68th Street Playhouse* (68th St. and Third Ave.; 734–0302). Finally, the grand- daddy of New York moviehouses, the *Ziegfeld Theatre* (141 W. 54th St.; 765–7600) shows exclusive engagements of first-runs and classic reissues (like *Fantasia* or *2001*).

MUSIC. New York undisputedly offers more kinds of music in more places more often than anywhere else in the world. Your only problem will be making time to fit everything in. Opera lovers will, of course, want to see a performance at the *Metropolitan Opera* and probably the *City Opera* at the New York State Theater. Classical music fans should make tracks to Carnegie Hall and Avery Fisher Hall. But many other auditoriums present the gift of music throughout the city. The sumptuous *Carnegie Hall* on West 57th St. at Seventh Ave. (247–7459) is New York's home to visiting orchestras. The building opened in 1891 with a concert conducted by Tchaikovsky, and the big names have never stopped coming back. Some pop concerts are also given here.

Lincoln Center has even more to offer. This arts complex on Broadway and 64th St. houses New York's premier resident opera, dance companies, and orchestras. *Avery Fisher Hall* (874–2424) is the home for the New York Philharmonic; *Alice Tully Hall* (362–1911) is the base for the Chamber Music Society of Lincoln Center and also hosts free concerts by the students of the Juilliard School of Music. The *Metropolitan Opera* (582–7500), located in the most beautiful of the buildings, has a season running from September through April. The *New York City Opera* (870–5570) is also based here.

Opera buffs may also want to check the schedule of the *Light Opera of Manhattan* (LOOM) at 111 E. 33rd St. (532–6180), which shows many Gilbert and Sullivan operettas. Classical music alternatives include the *Brooklyn Academy of Music* (30 Lafayette St. in Brooklyn; 718–636–4100), the nation's oldest performing arts center; and the *92nd Street Y,* Lexington Ave. and 92nd St. (427–6000), which features house and visiting orchestras and an extensive list of music and theater performances for adults and children. *Town Hall,* 123 West 43rd St. (997–1003), the famous old concert facility, has recently been refurbished and is once again offering light classics, folk music, and other fare in a gorgeous setting. Various churches also present recitals and chamber music throughout the year; check current newspaper and magazine listings for specifics.

Giving your ears a New York style treat needn't be as prohibitively expensive as you might think. The cheaper tickets to all events at Lincoln Center and Carnegie Hall can run as low as $8. Standing room tickets are also distributed just before the performance, at substantial discounts. The Bryant Park TKTS booth, 42nd Street between Fifth and Sixth avenues (382–2323), sells half-price day-of-performance tickets for music and dance events. And, of course, alternatives such as the Y are much cheaper than the big houses.

Also, during the summer the New York Philharmonic and the Metropolitan Opera stage several free evening performances in Central Park and other parks throughout the boroughs. These are wonderful events, with New Yorkers fully rising to the occasion and bringing lots of cheese, bread, wine, and candles.

DANCE. New Yorkers are forever on their toes with a wide choice of dance styles and companies. Balletomanes will find cause to celebrate at Lincoln Center's *New York City Ballet* at the New York State Theater (877–4700) under the direction of Peter Martins. Also, the *American Ballet Theatre* is at the Met (799–3100) under the direction of Mikhail Baryshnikov. It is the NYCB which, throughout December, puts on a spectacular performance of the holiday classic "The Nutcracker."

City Center, 131 W. 55th St. (246–8989), is home to the highly acclaimed Alvin Ailey Dance Group, as well as to the up-and-coming Harlem Dance Theatre and the modern stylings of the Joffrey Ballet.

The *Joyce Theatre,* 175 Eighth Ave. (242–0800) is one of the city's newer dance halls, and it has acquired quite a good reputation with its contemporary and avant garde performances. The *Brooklyn Academy of Music* hosts international dance companies in the spring and avant garde troupes in the fall.

Two other noteworthy and adventurous companies are the *Paul Taylor* and *Twyla Tharp* companies, performing at various times and places during the year. **Note:** the Bryant Park TKTS booth (382–2323) on 42nd Street between Fifth and Sixth avenues offers half price, same-day tickets for music and dance. The booth is open Tuesdays, Thursdays, and Fridays, noon–2 P.M. and 3–7 P.M.; Wednesdays and Saturdays, 11 A.M.–2 P.M. and 3–7 P.M.; Sundays, noon–6 P.M.

 STAGE. When it comes to theater, New York dominates the country and very often, depending on the quality of the season, the world. Broadway is virtually synonymous with theater to many (with the exception of Londoners who rightly take pride in their exciting theatrical scene). But theater in New York is far more than the 20 or so blockbuster musicals and mainstream dramas crowding Broadway. The so-called off-Broadway world is a viable and vital alternative, often providing more serious plays. Off-Broadway also assumes a second role, that of previewing plays which may one day make their way to the brighter lights of Broadway. The difference between off- and on-Broadway tickets is, alas, not as great as it used to be. Off-off Broadway houses, where the greatest experimentation takes place, are cheaper still, though quality is sometimes iffy, and locations are often in out-of-the-way and frequently daunting neighborhoods.

An orchestra seat to a Broadway musical goes for about $45 on a weekend evening, slightly less on weekday nights and less still on Wednesday, Saturday, and Sunday matinees; dramas are generally somewhat less expensive. The best seats for an off-Broadway production will cost you around $25.

The ever-valuable TKTS booths (at Times Square, in the World Trade Center, and in Brooklyn) make theater-going in the city a little bit easier on the pocket. These outlets have abundant quantities of half-price, day-of-performance tickets available to most of the older plays, some of the new ones in preview, and even an occasional hit. Lines at the booths tend to be very long (especially at Times Square), and so the earlier you arrive the greater your chance of getting what you want.

For matinees, the Times Square booth, at 47th St. and Broadway, opens at noon (performances are at 2 P.M. Wednesdays and Saturdays, 3 P.M. Sundays) and at 3 P.M. for evening performances (which begin at 8 P.M.). At No. 2 World Trade Center and Fulton Mall in Brooklyn, the booths open at 11 A.M. for evening performances, and tickets for matinees are available on the day before the performance. Most theaters are dark on Mondays.

Several outstanding theater companies are also in residence, often with inexpensive last minute tickets or generally low ticket prices. Joseph Papp's *Public Theatre* (425 Lafayette Pl.; 598–7100) is in a beautiful building which once housed the Astor Library. Papp has done much to revitalize the off-Broadway scene with his daring and thought-provoking productions, and some of Broadway's biggest hits have come from the Public's stages and/or workshops. *Circle in the Square* (159 Bleecker St.; 254–6330) manages to attract stars such as Al Pacino and George C. Scott to appear in its works. It is at theaters such as these that playwrights like Sam Shepard and Peter Nichols first got the attention they deserved.

As another possibility, you might also want to pay a visit to *Theater Row* on West 42nd Street between Ninth and Tenth avenues. This gentrified block has rapidly become a center of little-known but much-heralded new productions.

 SHOPPING. While most cities pride themselves on a few large shopping avenues or districts, New Yorkers know that their entire city is one vast shopping center. Neighborhoods and streets are set off not merely as store-laden areas, but as areas specializing in specific goods or services. For example, one block of 45 Street is for electronics. Or a strip of Fifth Avenue is for bookstores and some of the world's finest jewelry stores (such as *Harry Winston, Cartier, Tiffany's, Van Cleef and Arpels,* and *Fortunoff*). Or a whole neighborhood like Soho is for art galleries. Looking for a diamond ring? Try West 47th Street. If you're musically inclined, West 48th Street is filled with shops displaying instruments of all kinds.

Other streets boast broader appeal. Eighth Street in Greenwich Village is replete with funky (and punky) boutiques and shoe stores; 14th and 34th Streets are the bargain centers. Delancey, Orchard, and the surrounding streets of the Lower East Side are for incredible discounts on couture clothing. Uptown, Columbus Avenue and Broadway in the 70s are two mod and trendy strips. Madison Avenue, on the Upper East Side, is the place where the very rich go to shop for clothing, antiques, and artwork.

Although Madison and Fifth avenues are recognized around the world as home to some of the biggest, best, and most exclusive designer boutiques, it is possible to shop on any budget here. New Yorkers are proud of their ability to sniff out the best buys and to "discover" new, worthwhile places. Watch for department store holiday sales (Presidents' Day in February, Easter, Memorial Day, and throughout November and December).

All around town are stores selling "odd lots" of miscellaneous merchandise— from telephones to dishes to toys. These go by such names as Odd Lot, Job Lot, and Pushcart. But what makes New York a special shopping place is its inordinate amount of opportunities. Not only are there hundreds of book stores, but dozens that cater to a certain group of readers, from cookbooks to theater books. Not only are there many toy stores, but there's a store filled strictly with teddy bears and one flying solo with an all-kite inventory. Not only are there dozens of gourmet shops, but there are plenty of just-chocolate, just-cheese, and just-coffee stores.

The city more than holds its own when it comes to the everything-under-one-roof department stores and malls. A visit to *Macy's* (Broadway at 34th St.), the largest department store in the western world, can feed you, clothe you, and furnish your home, all in one trip. Nearby Fifth Avenue department stores also include *B. Altman's,* at 34th Street, and *Lord & Taylor,* at 39th Street. Moving north, *Saks Fifth Avenue,* at 49th Street, *Bergdorf Goodman* and *Henri Bendel* (both on 57 Street), and *Bloomingdale's* at 59th and Lexington all cater to a more upscale clientele. An inexpensive alternative, *Alexander's* (Lexington and 58th St.), offers much of the same.

As for malls, here they're bigger, splashier, and more expensive than elsewhere. Stores that wouldn't be caught setting up shop in something as unprestigious as a mall fight to get into these spaces. *Citicorp* (Lexington Ave. and 53 St.) was the first of these, and its stores include *Conran's,* a modern, fun-loving furniture outlet. Lately, such malls have sprung up with increasing speed. In the heart of Herald Square rises the new glass mall, *Herald Center.* Uptown, the ostentatious *Trump Tower* (Fifth Ave. at 56th St.) is a pink marble extravaganza. And the newest entry in the atrium wars is *The Center of Fifth* (575 Fifth

Ave.), a four-block mall of deluxe stores housed beneath a giant stained glass ceiling.

Aside from shopping streets and malls, many unique and interesting stores are spread throughout the city. These include:

- *Baccarat,* 55 E. 57th St., for beautiful crystal.
- *Barney's,* Seventh Ave. and 17th St. and *Brooks Brothers,* Madison Ave. and 44th St., both style-setters in men's clothing.
- *Caswell Massey,* at the South Street Seaport and at Lexington Ave. and 48th St., for all kinds of exquisite soaps and related products.
- *The Chess Shop,* 230 Thompson St., for chess equipment.
- *Star Magic,* Broadway and E. 4th St., for astrology, astronomy, and related goods.
- *The Strand,* Broadway and E. 12th St., for books, books, and more books (mostly used and out of print, but also reviewer's copies of new releases at half price).
- *Tower Records,* Broadway and E. 4th St. and Broadway and W. 66th St., for one of the largest selections of records in the city.

 DINING OUT. This is one of the great New York pastimes. Regardless of the neighborhood, the cuisine, or the price you want to pay, there's always someplace new and exciting to try. And for sure, there are plenty of reliable old standbys. The budget traveler can do as well as those on expense accounts in New York, particularly if he or she is just a tad adventurous. Until recently, eating ethnic was synonymous with eating cheap, except where French food was concerned. That isn't the case anymore, as some very fancy Chinese and Italian restaurants have sprouted—along with some very simple, inexpensive, bistro-like French places. In addition, many of the most expensive restaurants have inexpensive price-fixed pre- or post-theater dinner menus and reasonable lunches.

A word of caution about credit cards: many inexpensive establishments do not take them; others have a minimum amount for credit cards. Almost all of our moderate and higher-priced listings take major credit cards; the very economical places often don't. Also, New York restaurants aren't as tolerant of cashing traveler's checks as places in most other cities, so do try to carry enough cash to cover yourself. Abbreviations for credit cards, where listed, are: AE, American Express; CB, Carte Blanche; DC, Diners Club; MC, MasterCard; and V, Visa.

The price categories we use are approximate, figuring for an average three-course meal for one person at a given establishment, not including drinks and tips (usually about double the 8¼ percent sales tax). *Super Deluxe* restaurants will cost $50 and up; *Deluxe,* $35; *Expensive,* $25; *Moderate,* $15; and *Inexpensive* $15 and less. We have arranged the restaurants by general stylistic categories (steak houses, seafood), then by national or ethnic cuisine, and within that category by price.

A few notes on the major cuisines found in New York:

Chinese: Stick to Chinatown, for the atmosphere in the streets is as much a part of the meal as the food itself. Best bets for people-watching *and* food: *Hunan House* and *Peking Duck House.* Don't expect to linger, though; if that's your intention, the pricier (though still reasonable) restaurants on and around Second Avenue in the 40s—*Hunam* is the best of the lot—will have to do. Remember to order family style: three main dishes will feed four to five people.

French: "Inexpensive" and "French" are believed by many to be mutually exclusive terms. These people haven't tried *Cafe 58* or *Crepes Suzette,* where full dinners are under $20. The latter, representing the peasant tradition, is the friendlier; the former, a classic bistro, is a little haughty and slack on service, but still an outstanding value.

German: It's up to 86th Street between Second and Third Avenues for serious wienerschnitzel, sauerbraten, and the like. This is the Yorkville, or German-town, end of the city, where *Kleine Konditorei* and *Cafe Geiger* offer best values, fresh food, and *gemutlichkeit.*

Greek: It seems as though every coffee shop in the city is run by Greeks, though that's not what we refer to when discussing Greek food. The classic of the genre is the inconveniently located *Z,* but *New Acropolis* in the theater district and *Delphi* near the World Trade Center are equally worthwhile for souvlaki, moussaka, stuffed grape leaves, and baklava.

Indian: Head to Sixth Street between First and Second Avenue for a dozen or so of the cheapest restaurants in the city—cheap but with respectable menus filled with kebabs and curries. A similar string of places is on Lexington in the upper 20s. *Mitali West* in the heart of the Village and *India Pavillion West* near Carnegie Hall are a little fancier, only a little more expensive ($12–$15 per person for a meal) and quite good. Outstanding and inexpensive vegetarian Indian can be found at *Chandra Gardens* on East 86th Street.

Italian: The storefront restaurants that used to be inexpensive pasta houses are giving way to high-tech, high-price places where maitre d's in tuxedos shun anyone without a reservation or an extra $2 bread-and-butter charge. Go to the old standbys in Greenwich Village: *Monte's, Il Ponte Vecchio,* and *Rocco's.* Or make it a pizza night at *John's* or *Pizza Piazza.* In Little Italy, it's *Luna* or *Angelo's.*

Japanese: Sushi bars seem to have popped up everywhere, and many offer full dinners in the $12 range. Most also serve beef, chicken, and pork dishes as well as fish and seafood. As for sushi, order a sampler plate or à la carte; individual items usually go for $2–$4, depending on the type of fish. Anytime you eat raw foods, be sure everything is fresh. A favorite near Lincoln Center is *Dan Tempura House.*

Jewish deli: New York's delicatessens are unequalled anywhere else in the world. Corned beef, pastrami, and brisket are piled high on fresh rye bread. Share a sandwich and a side order of fries or potato salad at the *Carnegie* in midtown—one of each dish can be more than enough for two, and brings the price to within reason. Or go down to the *Second Avenue Deli* in the East Village, which is about half the price and just as good, though out of the way. Warning: plenty of sandwich shops and take-out counters call themselves deli-catessens. They are, but for serious deli, stick to our suggestions.

Kosher: Try the Second Avenue Deli; *Levana* (148 W. 67th St.; 877–8457) for fish and vegetarian dishes; *Boychiks* (19 W. 45th St.; 719–5999) for pizza, sandwiches, and quiches; *Bernstein on Essex* (135 Essex St.; 473–3900) for kosher Chinese and deli all on one menu; and *Ratner's* (138 Delancey St.; 677–5588) for dairy. Fancier spots such as *Lou G. Siegel* (209 W. 38th St.; 921–4433) and *Moshe Peking* (40 W. 37th St.) are quite expensive.

Mexican: Possibly the trendiest category, partly because it's typically inex-pensive (not at the trendy spots), partly because the restaurants tend to be colorful, and definitely because of the tequila-based drinks that are so popular. *Caramba!* in the Village and near the theater district are the innest of the in—the Village location especially for singles.

Spanish: Different from Mexican, but spicy, plentiful, and cheap, with an emphasis on fish and chicken entrees. Twenty-third Street, between Seventh and Ninth Avenues, has become a sort of Spanish Town.

AMERICAN-INTERNATIONAL

Super-Deluxe

The Four Seasons. 99 E. 52nd St.; 754–9494. One of New York's most beautiful, ambitious, and interesting restaurants. The main dining room is dominated by a shimmering pool, and you'll even spot a Picasso hanging in one of the rooms. The outside Pool Room is a little less fancy and a lot less expensive. There's a pre-dinner special available at a bargain (for here) $38.50. Closed Sundays. All major credit cards.

Windows on the World. 1 World Trade Center; 938–1111. A stunning and lavish restaurant with a wraparound view of the city from the 107th floor! The food isn't spectacular, but the experience will help you overlook that fact. The neighboring *Hors d'Oeuvrerie* offers a just-as-good view, at cheaper prices, for elegant snack food (and dancing) only. All major credit cards.

Deluxe

American Harvest. 3 World Trade Center; 938–9100. The menu at the main restaurant at the Vista Hotel is built completely on seasonal themes and features the freshest American meats, fish, and produce. Lunch weekdays only; closed Sundays. All major credit cards.

Christ Cella. 160 E. 46th St.; 697–2479. Perhaps the largest piece of roast beef around, ditto the steaks. Generally considered the best steak house in town. Closed Sundays. All major credit cards.

The Coach House. 110 Waverly Pl.; 777–0303. A glowingly handsome English inn setting where the best American dishes are served along with European classics. Open for dinner only on Saturdays; and Sundays. All major credit cards.

Rainbow Room. 30 Rockefeller Plaza; 757–9090. A classic Art Deco room dripping with chandeliers, with tables on various levels and a spectacular view of the city from the 65th floor of the RCA Building. Undergoing renovations at press time, the Rainbow Room was slated to reopen early in 1988.

21 Club. 21 W. 52nd St.; 582–7200. This favorite of the rich and powerful was recently refurbished—menu as well as decor—and passed both reviews splendidly, much to the patrons' delight.

Water Club. 500 E. 30th St.; 683–3333. With 700 seats on a converted barge, the Water Club can hardly be termed intimate. Seafood is the specialty, and there is plenty else. But, oh, what a view! All major credit cards.

Expensive

Berry's. 180 Spring St.; 226–4394. One of the first and most consistently rewarding of the Soho dining spots. Features an intimately lit Victorian dining room and a light hand in the kitchen. Closed Mondays. Major credit cards.

Cafe Un Deux Trois. 123 W. 44th St.; 354–4148. Perhaps the closest in spirit New York will ever come to a French bistro. Paper tablecloths and crayons make this a special favorite. Major credit cards.

Chelsea Place. 147 Eighth Ave.; 924–8413. From the outside, the antique store at this address gives no indication that an extremely popular restaurant is literally "through the looking glass." Food is good, if overpriced, but the setting is definitely unique. Major credit cards.

The Ginger Man. 51 W. 64th St.; 399–2358. A favorite dining spot for those entering or leaving a Lincoln Center performance. Noted for its spinach salad, steaks, and grilled fare. Major credit cards.

The Gotham Bar and Grill. 12 E. 12th St.; 620–4020. A trendy eatery with a menu that's earned critic's raves. AE, MC.

Greene Street. 101 Greene St.; 925–2415. Good food in a delightful setting—plants, catwalks, and lots of space. Live music most evenings. Major credit cards.

Hurley's Steak and Seafood. 49th St and Sixth Ave.; 765–8981. Very popular with broadcasting folk. All major credit cards.

Maxwell's Plum. 1181 First Ave. at 64th St.; 628–2100. The singles crowd has moved to Columbus Avenue, leaving Maxwell's to concentrate on its art nouveau setting and respectable menu—a genuine pre-theater bargain at $13.50. All major credit cards.

One Fifth. 1 Fifth Ave.; 260–3434. A lovely room, recreated from the ocean liner *Carolina's* dining room. Food is excellently prepared and imaginatively presented. All major credit cards.

Tavern on the Green. Central Park West at 67th St.; 873–3200. Can't be beat for the $14.50–$19.50. pre-theater dinner. A la carte, however, you pay more dearly for the admittedly spectacular setting—right in the midst of Central Park. All major credit cards.

Texarkana. 64 W. 10th St.; 254–5800. The trendiest of restaurants catering to Tex-Mex fans. AE, DC.

Moderate

Bridge Cafe. 279 Water St.; 227–3344. Near the South Street Seaport, this restaurant is well-hidden beneath the Brooklyn Bridge. The kitchen experiments with unusual combinations—a good bet for the adventurous. AE, DC.

Century Cafe. 132 W. 43rd St.; 398–1988. The Art Deco neon moviehouse sign over the bar sets the stage for this popular theater district restaurant. Skip the appetizers to leave room for the fabulous desserts. All major credit cards.

P. J. Clarke's. 915 Third Ave. at 55th St.; 759–1650. The most chic hamburger joint in town. AE, DC.

Joe Allen's. 326 W. 46th St.; 581–6464. A long-time theatrical hangout for casual food. Expect a wait for a table—or to be turned away simply because they don't know you. MC, V.

Martell's. 1469 Third Ave.; 861–6110. French farmers' sandwiches are a specialty here. All major credit cards.

Jim McMullen's. 1341 Third Ave.; 861–4700. A hangout for models, sports figures, and other beautiful folk. Good seafood and excellent steaks. AE.

Palsson's. 158 W. 72nd St.; 362–2590. Nice (if a bit stuffy) atmosphere and more than serviceable food. Cabaret upstairs. All major credit cards.

West Bank Cafe. 407 W. 42nd St.; 695–6909. Good ribs, chicken, salads, quiches. Convenient to the theater district—make sure you have reservations. AE, CB, MC, V.

Inexpensive

Elephant & Castle. 183 Prince St. and 68 Greenwich Ave.; 260–3600 and 243–1400. Very popular for burgers, omelets, and quiches. All major credit cards.

Maestro Cafe. 58 W. 65th St.; 787–5990. Attractive decor, good cuisine, and lively service. All major credit cards.

Ye Waverly Inn. 16 Bank St.; 929–4377. A Village landmark with three low-ceilinged candlelit dining rooms—two with fireplaces—and a backyard garden. All major credit cards.

STEAK HOUSES

Super Deluxe

Joe & Rose. 747 Third Ave.; 980–3985. Specials here are steaks and corned beef and cabbage. A New York phenomenon where the service and surroundings belie the prices—and the food doesn't. AE, DC, V.

The Palm. 837 Second Ave.; 687–2953. The quintessential New York steak house. If you can afford it, this is the place to go—and bring plenty of cash. Closed Sundays. All major credit cards.

Pen & Pencil. 205 E. 45th St.; 682–8660. Another steak house with an established group of supporters. In addition to grilled steaks and chops, a few Italian specialties are offered. All major credit cards.

Ponte's. 39 Desbrosses St.; 226–4621. The management here is Italian, a heritage well represented on the menu, but the specialties are large steaks and chops. Closed Sundays. All major credit cards.

The Post House. 28 E. 63rd St.; 935–2888. One of New York's newest and most comfortable steak houses. All major credit cards.

Smith and Wollensky. 201 E. 49th St.; 753–1530. Steaks, chops, roast beef, and lobsters are the basic items, with flank steak a special feature. The main dining room is clubby and formal. All major credit cards.

Uncle Sam's. 120 W. 51st St.; 757–8800. Excellent steaks and chops. All major credit cards.

Wally's Restaurant. 224 W. 49th St.; 582–0460. No frills here in decor, but great steaks, and some surprisingly good Italian entrees. Closed Sundays. All major credit cards.

Expensive

Broadway Joe's Steak House. 315 W. 46th St.; 246–6513. Well-known old-timer with an open kitchen. All major credit cards.

Le Steak. 1089 Second Ave.; 421–9072. Meats prepared lusciously in the French style. All major credit cards.

Old Homestead. 56 Ninth Ave.; 242–9040. The oldest (1865) steak house in New York, in the heart of the wholesale meat market. All major credit cards.

Moderate

Blue Mill Tavern. 50 Commerce St.; 243–7114. Tucked away amidst century-old buildings, and within walking distance of many off-Broadway theaters in Greenwich Village. AE, DC, MC, V.

Farnie's Second Avenue Steak Parlour. 311 Second Ave.; 228–9280. A neighborhood steak house that does its best to compete with its better-known and more expensive brethren. All major credit cards.

SEAFOOD

Super Deluxe

Gloucester House. 37 E. 50th St.; 755–7394. Among the most extensive—and expensive—seafood menus in the city. All major credit cards.

Deluxe

John Clancy's. 181 W. 10th St.; 242–7350. Seafood, all fresh and all excellently prepared. Broiling is done over a mesquite grill. Dinners only. All major credit cards.

Oyster Bar of the Plaza. Plaza Hotel, Fifth Ave. at 59th St.; 759–3000. Edwardian elegance combined with excellent seafood. All major credit cards.

Expensive

The Captain's Table. 860 Second Ave., 697–9538. Selections are broad and simple and the fish is fresh. AE, MC, V.

Joe's Pier 52. 163 W. 52nd St.; 245–6652. Extensive and satisfying menu of fish entrees. All major credit cards.

Marylou's. 21 W. 9th St.; 533–0012. A very handsome place on one of the Village's prettiest streets. Fish dishes are uniformly excellent. No lunch Saturdays, only brunch on Sundays. All major credit cards.

Oscar's Salt of the Sea. 1155 Third Ave.; 879–1199; also in the Citicorp Atrium; 371–2201. Stuffed lobsters are a particular specialty, but there is invariably a wait for tables. All major credit cards.

Pesca. 23 E. 22nd St.; 533–2293. A beautiful, simply appointed restaurant with an open feeling. Preparation leans to Italian and Portuguese styles. AE.

Sweet's. 2 Fulton St., South Street Seaport; 344–9189. A landmark serving excellently prepared fish considered by many to be the best in town. Closed Saturdays, Sundays, holidays. AE, MC, V.

Moderate

Claire. 156 Seventh Ave.; 255–1955. A little-known, romantic eatery where the fish specialties change each day. Prices and selection vary with market conditions. MC, V.

Dobson's. 341 Columbus Ave.; 362–0100. Best noted for seafood, the salads and burgers are more than respectable as well. Very accommodating staff, and kids are most definitely welcome. AE, MC, V.

Hobeau's. 988 Second Ave.; 421–2888. Be prepared for a wait, but also for great fish and seafood at some of the best prices in town. AE, MC, V.

Janice's Seafood Place. 570 Hudson St.; 243–4212. Seafood with fresh vegetables, handled with an Oriental flair. AE, MC, V.

Oyster Bar. Inside Grand Central Terminal; 490–6650. This shrine of seafood, located beneath the magnificent vaulting of Grand Central Terminal; offers several different kinds of oysters, clams, and crabs at any given time, plus specials including fish not often seen in New York. Closed Saturdays and Sundays. All major credit cards.

DAIRY

Inexpensive

Ratner's Dairy Restaurant. 138 Delancey St.; 677–5588. A legend in its own time for East European Jewish cooking. Try the blintzes, matzoh brei, and whatever else, an onion roll. No credit cards.

DELICATESSEN

Inexpensive

Carnegie Delicatessen. 854 Seventh Ave.; 757–2245. By far the best deli in the city. A must-see for every visitor—just remember to split portions. The sandwiches are gargantuan. Try to talk them into making you the corned beef hash. It's an experience. No credit cards.

Fine & Schapiro. 138 W. 72nd St.; 877–2874. Excellent pastrami on rye near Lincoln Center. AE.

Nathan's Famous. Broadway at 43rd St.; 382–0620. Hot dogs and french fries and don't bother with anything else. No credit cards.

Pastrami & Things. 666 Fifth Ave.; 581–6300. The pastrami sandwiches are frequent prize-winners. All major credit cards.

Second Ave. Kosher Delicatessen. 156 Second Ave.; 677–0606. Kosher deli with all the trimmings—free pickles, cole slaw, waiters who inevitably know what you want better than you do. Wonderful sandwiches far more reasonable than in midtown. No credit cards.

Stage. 834 Seventh Ave.; 245–7850. Their sandwiches are packed with meat, their rye bread superb, their appetizers tantalizing. Recently redecorated in honor of its 50th anniversary. No credit cards.

HEALTH FOOD

Inexpensive

Au Natural. 560 Third Ave., 1043 Second Ave., and other locations. Beautiful fresh salads, fruit and vegetable drinks, and some sandwiches. No credit cards.

Great American Health Bar. 35 W. 57th St., and 15 E. 40th St.; 355–5177 and 532–3232. Popular among diet-conscious shoppers and office workers. No credit cards.

Greener Pastures. 117 E. 60th St.; 832–3212. Original salads and platters; convenient to Bloomingdale's and the first-run movie houses. No credit cards.

Healthworks! 153 E. 53rd St.; 838–6221. This branch in Citicorp Center features salads, yogurts, and quiches. No credit cards.

Spring Street Natural Restaurant. 62 Spring St.; 966–0290. Rustic New England health food outpost. All major credit cards.

SOUTHERN

Inexpensive

Acme Bar & Grill. 9 Great John St.; 420–1934. Located in Lower Manhattan, this casual place serves some mean Cajun food. No credit cards.

Sylvia's. 328 Lenox Ave.; 534–9414. Located in the heart of Harlem, so taxi up there. The trip is well worth it—you'll find Sylvia's famous southern fried chicken and stuffed pork chops served with hot corn bread and authentic southern vegetables. A real treat, and very cheap. No credit cards.

Cuisine by Nationality

BRAZILIAN

Moderate

Brazilian Pavillion. 316 E. 53rd St.; 758–8129. Modern setting for fine Portuguese-Brazilian style steaks and shrimp. All major credit cards.

S.O.B.'s. 204 Varick St.; 243–4940. That's Sounds of Brazil, and you'll find the sounds in the form of live music—and some great cuisine. All major credit cards.

Via Brasil. 34 W. 46th St.; 997–1158. Located on Manhattan's Brazilian street. Grilled meats here are superb. All major credit cards.

Inexpensive

Cabana Carioca. 123 W. 45th St.; 581–8088; the second branch is up the block. Pleasant, friendly, and very reasonable. All major credit cards.

BRITISH

Expensive

Charlie Brown's Ale & Chophouse. 45th and Vanderbilt, lobby of Pan Am Building; 661–2520. Pleasant pub in a handsome setting featuring mutton chops, steak and kidney pies, and lots of ale. All major credit cards.

Moderate

Angry Squire. 216 Seventh Ave.; 242–9066. Best known for jazz duos and trios who take the bandstand around 10 P.M., the Squire turns out respectable shepherd's pie and other pub fare. All major credit cards.

Inexpensive

English Pub. 900 Seventh Ave.; 265–4360. British fare right across from Carnegie Hall. All major credit cards.

CHINESE

Expensive

Pearl's Chinese Restaurant. 38 W. 48th St.; 221–6677. Slurp up any of a selection of 12 huge soups before going on to savor the rest of the entrees. No credit cards.

Shun Lee Palace. 155 E. 55th St.; 371–8844. Cross-China food in a luxury setting. AE, MC, V.

Moderate

Fortune Garden. 1160 Third Ave.; 744–1212. The kitchen here is most successful with beef and steak dishes and turns out some interesting fish plates. All major credit cards.

HSF. 578 Second Ave.; 689–6969. The best-decorated of the smaller Chinese restaurants, this place offers excellent *dim sum* at lunch. All major credit cards.

Hunam. 845 Second Ave.; 687–7471. One of the city's best Chinese restaurants. Anyone whose Chinese eating experience has been limited to only traditional Cantonese cooking is in for a rare treat. AE, CB, DC.

Siu Lam Kung. 18 Elizabeth St.; 732–0974. Very crowded and noisy, but outstanding and often very unusual dishes. No credit cards.

Inexpensive

Empire Szechuan Gourmet. 2574 Broadway; 663–6004. Exotic Chinese food, and a great favorite in the neighborhood. No credit cards.

Hunan House. 45 Mott St.; 962–0010. Tell 'em you want it hot, and you'll get it. Typical Chinatown. AE, D.

Hunan Pan. 550 Hudson St.; 242–5566. One of the best of the many Chinese restaurants in the Village. Inventive dishes at reasonable prices. All credit cards.

Hwa Yuan Szechwan Inn. 40 East Broadway; 966–5534. A long-time favorite and that means long lines at prime dining hours. All major credit cards.

Peking Duck House. 22 Mott St.; 962–8208. This is the place that inspired a host of imitators (some by the same owner) to make Peking duck available without ordering 24 hours ahead. The dish is authentic and the presentation as exciting as the food. AE.

Say Eng Look. 5 E. Broadway; 732–0796. Our Mandarin choice is a particular favorite among Chinatown regulars. AE, MC, V.

Szechuan West. 202 Eighth Ave.; 929–3433. A new, unpretentious eatery which has become a neighborhood favorite.

CZECHOSLOVAKIAN

Moderate

Ruc. 312 E. 72nd St.; 650–1611. Specialties include duck, roast pork, and goulash. Tasty and reasonably priced. Weekdays dinner only. All major credit cards.

Vasata. 339 E. 75th St.; 650–1686. Roast duckling and goose served daily. Start off a Sunday dinner with a delicious liver dumpling soup. Closed Mondays. All major credit cards.

FRENCH

Super Deluxe

Chanterelle. 89 Grand St.; 966–6960. One of the most adventurous and interesting of the nouvelle cuisine haunts, located in a landmark Soho building. All major credit cards.

La Caravelle. 33 W. 55th St.; 586–4252. Among the top two or three French restaurants in the city. Elegant decor, top-notch wine cellar, fine food. All major credit cards.

La Cote Basque. 5 E. 55th St.; 688–6525. A totally handsome dining room, and classic cuisine. All major credit cards.

La Grenouille. 3 E. 52nd St.; 752–1495. A sublimely beautiful setting that complements a superb menu. Closed Sundays and holidays. AE, DC.

Le Chantilly. 106 E. 57th St.; 751–2931. Large, stately, classical, and pretentious—but it delivers fine fish, lamb, veal, and desserts. Closed Sundays. All major credit cards.

Le Cirque. 58 E. 65th St.; 794–9292. Plush surroundings, with haute cuisine backed by a stunning mural. Located in the Mayfair Hotel. Closed Sundays. AE, CB, DC.

Le Cygne. 55 E. 54th St., 759–5941. The best of the newer haute cuisine French restaurants offers unusual choices, including whole braised pigeon. Closed Sunday and month of August. All major credit cards.

Lutèce. 249 E. 50th St.; 752–2225. Probably the most ambitious and elaborate French food served in the United States. An unusually friendly staff adds to your enjoyment. Closed Saturdays during summer, Sundays all year. AE, CB, DC.

Deluxe

Hubert's. 102 E. 22nd St.; 673–3711. Elegant cuisine in an attractive, understated environment. AE.

La Petite Ferme. Lexington Ave. at 70th St.; 249–3272. Simple and well-prepared food in a farmhouse-like atmosphere. Dinner only Sundays. All major credit cards.

La Petite Marmite. 5 Mitchell Pl.; 826–1084. Intimate, and pleasantly situated right near the UN. Closed Sundays. All major credit cards.

La Tulipe. 104 W. 13th St.; 691–8860. Housed in the street level of a brownstone, this small trendy place offers imagination and quality. All major credit cards.

Le Perigord. 405 E. 52nd St.; 755–6244. Gratin de langoustines—crayfish in cheese sauce—is a specialty. Very formal and old world. Dinner only Saturdays; closed Sundays. All major credit cards.

The Terrace. 119th St. and Morningside Dr.; 666–9490. On the top of Columbia University's Butler Hall, with a very good view of the skyline and some fine food. Live chamber music enhances this romantic spot. Lunch Tuesdays through Fridays; dinner Tuesdays through Saturdays. All major credit cards.

Expensive

Black Sheep. 342 W. 11th St.; 242–1010. A tiny, hidden jewel almost on the Hudson waterfront. Excellent value for *prix fixe* dinners based on the price of the entree—and an outstanding (and reasonably priced) wine list. Discount for cash; all major credit cards.

Cafe des Artistes. 1 W. 67th St.; 877–3500. Amusing 1930s decor and famous murals will transport you to another time. Don't forget to try dessert here. All major credit cards.

Cafe 58. 232 E. 58th St.; 758–5665. A classic bistro offering outstanding value. All major credit cards.

La Petite Auberge. 116 Lexington Ave.; 689–5003. Pleasant inn-like surroundings, with good, standard fare. AE.

Moderate

Crepe Suzette. 363 W. 46th St., 581–9717. A little bistro that couldn't be plainer, but the food is well-prepared and the portions ample. Dinner only Sundays. All major credit cards.

Le Biarritz. 325 W. 57th St.; 757–2390. An unprepossessing restaurant with copper cookware on the walls and fine French country cooking. Closed Sundays. AE, DC, V.

Le Bistro. 827 Third Ave.; 759–5933. Small and informal, provincial in spirit. Dinner only Saturdays, closed Sundays. All major credit cards.

Le Parisien. 1004 Second Ave.; 355–0950. Simple, unpretentious and very pleasantly French. Broiled entrees work best. All major credit cards.

Madame Romain de Lyon. 29 E. 61st St.; 758–2422. Would you believe 500 different kinds of omelets? Open Saturdays to Mondays only, 11 A.M.–3 P.M. All major credit cards, with $30 minimum.

Pierre Au Tunnel. 250 W. 47th St.; 582–2166. Unusual decor resembles an actual tunnel. A familiar French menu. Closed Sundays. AE.

Inexpensive

Paris Commune. 411 Bleecker St.; 929–0509. Great Village restaurant that isn't *very* French but offers excellent breakfasts as well as lunches and dinners. AE, MC, V.

GERMAN

Moderate

Cafe Geiger. 206 E. 86th St.; 734–4428. Retail bakery in front, cafe in back. All major credit cards.

Harvey's Chelsea Restaurant. 108 W. 18th St.; 243–5644. The look of a Victorian townhouse, but specialties lean towards sauerbraten, knockwurst, and the like. AE.

Kleine Konditorei. 234 E. 86th St.; 737–7130. Simple, homey dinner with everything from steak smothered in onions to different schnitzels. AE, DC.

GREEK

Moderate

Avgerinos. Citicorp Center, 153 E. 53rd St.; 688–8828. A bit overpriced, but the setting is far more pleasant than in most Greek restaurants. All major credit cards.

New Acropolis. 767 Eighth Ave.; 581–2733. Greek specialties and very friendly. AE, DC.

Inexpensive

Z. 117 E. 15th St.; 254–0960. A favorite for years for all the standard Greek specialties, though vegetables are always overcooked and the service faster than a speeding bullet. A few outside tables in the back during summer. AE.

HAWAIIAN

Moderate

Hawaii-Kai. 1638 Broadway near 50th St.; 757–0900. Polynesian, Chinese, and American cuisine served in a touristy South Sea island setting. All major credit cards.

HUNGARIAN

Moderate

Csarda. 1477 Second Ave.; 472–2892. Bright and uncluttered with good food served tavern-style. AE.

Green Tree. 1034 Amsterdam Ave.; 864–9106. Substantial meals served up homestyle. Closed Sundays. No credit cards.

Red Tulip. 439 E. 75th St.; 734–4893. Small and crowded; live music. Closed Mondays and Tuesdays. AE.

INDIAN/BENGALI

Expensive

Nirvana. 30 Central Park South; 486–5700; also at Times Square; 486–6868. The view from the penthouse overlooking Central Park is nothing short of spectacular. Extremely romantic settings at both locales. All major credit cards.

Raga. 57 W. 48th St.; 757–3450. One of the most beautifully decorated Indian restaurants in America includes ancient musical instruments as part of its charm—and very fine cooking. All major credit cards.

Shezan. 8 W. 58th St.; 371–1414. Modern and streamlined extreme, but food is often uneven. Dinner only Saturdays; closed Sundays. All major credit cards.

Moderate

Akbar India. 475 Park Ave.; 838–1717. Tandoori items are featured in this attractive restaurant serving food from the northern part of the country. Dinner only Sundays. All major credit cards.

Annapurna. 108 Lexington Ave.; 679–1284. A quiet, gracious restaurant serving a variety of authentic Indian dishes. All major credit cards.

Nupur. 819 Second Ave.; 697–4180. Kebab and tandoori specialties in an unassuming atmosphere. AE, DC, MC, V.

Inexpensive

India Pavilion South. 33 W. 13th St.; 243–8175. A quiet, casual restaurant with standard Indian selections. The appetizers are especially delicious. Located opposite the popular Quad Movie Theater. MC, V.

Mitali. 334 E. 6th St.; 533–2508. One of two excellent family-run Indian eateries. The other, *Mitali West,* is located in the Village at 296 Bleecker St.; 989–1367 AE, MC, V.

IRISH

Moderate

Landmark Tavern. 626 Eleventh Ave.; 757–8595. A pot-bellied stove, mahogany bar, and lots of tavern fare. AE.

Tommy Makem's Irish Pavillion. 130 E. 57th St.; 759–9040. Irish contemporary art and portraits of Irish literary figures highlight this restaurant. Live Irish folk music. All major credit cards.

Rosie O'Grady's. 800 Seventh Ave.; 582–2975. Irish and continental specialties; live music nightly. All major credit cards.

ITALIAN

Deluxe

Alfredo. 240 Central Park South; 246–7050. Northern Italian specialties. Closed Sundays. All major credit cards.

Barbetta. 321 W. 46th St.; 246–9171. The most luxurious of Italian restaurants, with its 18th-century furnishings and gorgeous crystal chandelier. Northern Italian cuisine and excellent wines. Closed Sundays. All major credit cards.

Erminia. 250 E. 83rd St.; 879–4284. A mere dozen tables, but exceptional pastas, and meats seared on open wood fires. No credit cards.

Giambelli Albert. 238 Madison Ave.; 685–8727. Delicate and refined northern Italian specialties. Closed Sundays, and Saturdays during summer. All major credit cards.

Giambelli Fifth. 46 E. 50th St.; 688–2760. Good veal, fish, and pastas—but as expensive as the room is ornate. Closed Sundays. All major credit cards.

Nanni Al Valletto. 133 E. 61st St.; 838–3939. Posh Italian eatery. Closed Sundays. All major credit cards.

Romeo Salta. 30 W. 56th St.; 246–5772. This remarkable restaurant is located in a former mansion. Extraordinary pastas and veal dishes. Closed Sundays. All major credit cards.

Tre Scalini. 230 E. 58th St.; 688–6888. Flashy dining room for northern Italian cuisine. Closed Sundays. All major credit cards.

Expensive

Amalfi. 16 E. 48th St.; 758–5110. Very old and very Italian. All major credit cards.

Antolotti's. 337 E. 49th St.; 688–6767. A conventional northern Italian menu, generally well-prepared. Up the block from the UN. No lunch weekends. All major credit cards.

Bruno's. 237 E. 58th St.; 688–4190. Simple modern dining room with a country atmosphere and outstanding pasta. Dinner only Saturdays; closed Sundays. All major credit cards.

Capriccio Ristorante. 33 E. 61st St.; 759–6684. Chief among the pasta specialties here is *fuzi Angela,* though the specials of the day tend to be pleasingly exotic. Dinner only Saturday, closed Sunday. All major credit cards.

Cent'anni. 50 Carmine St., 989–9494. Crowded and plain, but the Florentine cuisine makes up for all. Dinner only. AE.

Da Silvano. 260 Sixth Ave.; 982–2343. Smartly trim storefront with excellent pasta and seafood. No credit cards.

Grotto Azzurra. 387 Broome St.; 925–8775. One of the most popular Little Italy haunts, with superior food. No credit cards.

Il Cantinori. 32 E. 10th St.; 673–6044. A Village version of the expensive Upper East Side northern Italian restaurants. Lots of fancy pastas, well done. All major credit cards.

La Strada East. 274 Third Ave.; 473–3760. Friendly, informal atmosphere for all manner of pasta, veal, and beef dishes. Dinner only weekends. All major credit cards.

Marchi's. 251 E. 31st St.; 679–2494. In an old brownstone, this place has a long-standing reputation for its unusual presentation—one many-course dinner ($23.75) which the host has prepared for you. Dinner only; no reservations on Saturdays; closed Sundays. AE.

Nanni's. 146 E. 46th St.; 697–4161. Excellent northern Italian cuisine. Closed Sundays. All major credit cards.

Parioli Romanissimo. 24 E. 81st St.; 288–2391. Small and gaudy, but terrific cannelloni and tortellini. Closed Sundays and Mondays. AE, DC.

Parma. 1404 Third Ave.; 535–3520. Plain and informal, but some of the best pasta anywhere. Dinner only. AE.

Piccolo Mondo. 1269 First Ave.; 249–3141. Very good northern Italian fare. All major credit cards.

Pirandello. 7 Washington Pl.; 260–3066. A treasure of northern Italian cooking. Service is especially friendly and attentive. Dinner only. Closed Sundays. AE.

Roma di Notte. 137 E. 55th St.; 832–1128. Appealing to the eye and the taste. AE, CB, DC.

Sal Anthony's. 55 Irving Pl.; 982–9030. Spacious restaurant offering a simply amazing tomato sauce. All major credit cards.

Salta in Bocca. 179 Madison Ave.; 684–1757. A pleasant dining room with excellent pasta. Closed Sundays. All major credit cards.

Trastevere. 309 E. 83rd St.; 734–6343. Small, intimate, and great food. AE.

Moderate

Angelina's. 41 Greenwich Ave.; 929–1255. A homey sort of place, unpretentious as far as decor and menu. AE, DC.

Beatrice Inn. 285 W.12th St.; 929–6165. A genuine family-run affair in a surprisingly decorous setting. The manicotti is outstanding and the veal, chicken, and seafood on par with far more expensive establishments. Closed Sundays. All major credit cards.

Chelsea Trattoria. 108 Eighth Ave.; 924–7786. A sleek, new restaurant specializing in Roman dishes. All major credit cards.

Forlini's. 93 Baxter St., near Canal St.; 349–6779. Red sauce cooking with finesse. All major credit cards.

Patrissy's. 98 Kenmare St., in Little Italy; 226–8509. Friendly, informal Neapolitan restaurant offering first-rate pasta. All major credit cards.

Pete's Tavern. 129 E. 18th St.; 473–7676. Nothing subtle here, but the short story writer O. Henry made it famous. The bar area is the most fun. All major credit cards.

Ponte Vecchio. 206 Thompson St.; 228–7701. An old-timer that's been unimaginatively spruced up, but the food's still great and it's always crowded and noisy. Ask for the pasta with artichokes. AE.

Rocco. 181 Thompson St.; 677–0590. Want to know what the Village and Little Italy were about in their heyday? This is the place to go. Simple, unpretentious home cooking that's always a treat—in part because the setting is so joyfully dowdy. All major credit cards.

Trattoria. 45th St. between Vanderbilt and Lexington aves.; 661–3090. Its position in the Pan Am building and its proximity to Grand Central Terminal are the major drawing cards. There's an outdoor cafe in summer in the middle of one of the most congested streets in Manhattan. Stay indoors. All major credit cards.

Inexpensive

Guido's. 511 Ninth Ave., at 39th St.; 244–9314. Hidden behind the Supreme Macaroni Company, you'll get fine family-style southern Italian cooking. Great before theater, but be sure to reserve. No credit cards.

Luna. 112 Mulberry St.; 226–8657. A holdover from Little Italy's glory days—and crowded from noon to midnight. Best value in the area, but you'll wait on line and won't be able to linger. Still, worth a visit. No credit cards.

Manganaro's. 492 Ninth Ave., near 38th St.; 947–7325. Best Italian hero sandwiches in the city. Eggplant parmigiana, mixed cold cuts, sausage and peppers. Bustling at lunch and closes at 7:30 P.M.; closed Sundays. No credit cards.

Monte's. 97 MacDougal St.; 674–9456. Nothing ever changes at Monte's, which seems to have been in the Village forever. Closed Tuesdays. No credit cards.

Perretti. 270 Columbus Ave., at 72nd St.; 362–3939. Bright, glass-enclosed neon-lit dining room popular for great pizza and satisfactory veal and seafood. Always a wait and popular for families. AE, MC, V.

Puglia's. 189 Hester St., in Little Italy; 966–6006. Go to party at camp-style tables. The food is greasy and lukewarm, but once everyone starts singing there's no stopping the reverie. No credit cards.

Umberto's Clam House. 129 Mulberry St., in Little Italy; 431–7545. Informal spot for fresh seafood till the wee hours. No credit cards.

Vincent's Clam Bar. 119 Mott St., in Little Italy; 226–8133. Home of hot and spicy tomato sauce and seafood, also till the wee hours. No credit cards.

JAPANESE

Expensive

Benihana of Tokyo. 120 E. 56th St.; 593–1627. Samurai cooking—a good show—and just as interesting are the steak and shrimp dishes. All major credit cards.

Habukai. 66 Park Ave., at 38th St.; 686–3770. Catering largely to the Japanese clientele who stay at the Hotel Kitano, in which the restaurant is located. All major credit cards.

Hatsuhana. 17 E. 48th St.; 355–3345. Generally regarded as offering the best sushi and sashimi in New York. All major credit cards.

Kitcho. 22 W. 46th St.; 575–8880. Southern Japanese cuisine in gentle, quiet surroundings. Closed Saturdays; open 5 P.M. Sundays. AE, DC.

Moderate

Japanese on Hudson. 551 Hudson St.; 691–5379. A cozy restaurant with a good sushi bar and serving the range of Japanese specialties. Wide selection of Japanese beers. All major credit cards.

Saito. 305 E. 46th St.; 759–8897. Three different areas for different specialties: tempura bar, yakitori bar, and western tables for teriyaki and sukiyaki. Closed Sundays; dinner only on Saturdays. All major credit cards.

Inexpensive

Dan Tempura House. 2018 Broadway, at 69th St.; 877–4969. Consistently satisfying sushi bar and restaurant, with deep fried ice cream for dessert. Convenient to Lincoln Center. AE.

Enka. 167 W. 45th St.; 869–5343. Unassuming, bustling theater district stronghold with a long sushi bar and other fare at tables. Closed Sundays. All major credit cards.

Fuji. 238 W. 56th St.; 245–8594. Convenient to Carnegie Hall and the theater district. All major credit cards.

JEWISH/KOSHER
(see also Delicatessen)
Expensive

Lou G. Siegel. 209 W. 38th St.; 921–4433. Authentic Jewish food prepared under rabbinical supervision. The menu has lungen and miltz stew, stuffed derma, stuffed cabbage, meats, and poultry. Closed Saturdays. All major credit cards.

Moshe Peking. 40 W. 37th St.; 594–6500. Kosher Chinese food, including Peking duck. Closed sundown Fridays to sundown Saturdays. All major credit cards.

Sammy's Roumanian Restaurant. 157 Christie St., on the Lower East Side; 673–5526. "Do you take reservations?" "For years." When you want to be overstuffed and humored by waiters who have an answer for everything. Kosher style, but not kosher. Also, don't go strolling in the area at night. AE, C, DC.

Moderate

Levana. 148 W. 67 St.; 877–8457. Fish, vegetables, pasta, and excellent cakes and Danish pastry within walking distance of Lincoln Center. Closed Friday nights through sundown Saturdays.

KOREAN
Moderate

Arirang House. 28 W. 56th St.; 581–9698. If you like spicy grilled beef and the sourest of pickles, this is for you. Darkly mysterious. All major credit cards.

Woo Lae Oak of Seoul. 77 W. 46th St.; 869–9958. Book Koki—strips of marinated beef cooked over a small fire at your table, plus pork ribs, short ribs, noodles, and all kinds of fish. AE, DC, MC, V.

MIDDLE EASTERN
Moderate

Ararat. 1076 First Ave., near 59th St.; 686–4622. Armenian cuisine in beautifully decorated restaurant. All major credit cards.

Malca's. 70th St. and First Ave.; 929–3296. The Middle Eastern tajines are the highlight from a menu offering French fare as well. All major credit cards.

RUSSIAN
Deluxe

The Russian Samovar. 256 W. 52nd. St.; 757–0168. An elegant restaurant perfect for special occasions. Dinner only on weekends; closed Mondays. All major credit cards.

Russian Tea Room. 150 W. 57th St.; 265–0947. A landmark next to Carnegie Hall. Perhaps the city's richest food, and Christmas atmosphere all year round. Borscht, blini (pancakes with caviar, among other toppings), chicken Kiev. The food isn't great, the service is poor unless you're a celebrity or a regular, but it's such an attraction in its own right it deserves at least a stop at the bar to check out the scene. All major credit cards.

SPANISH-MEXICAN

Expensive

Fonda La Paloma. 256 E. 49th St.; 421–5495. Hot and spicy Mexican dishes prepared to order and courteously served. The guacamole is without peer. Open seven days, but dinner only weekends. All major credit cards.

Victor's Cafe. 240 Columbus Ave. at 71st St.; 595–8599. Finest Cuban food in the city. The soups, fried beef with garlic and onions, and rice with seafood are delicious. Roast suckling pig on Sundays. All major credit cards.

Moderate

Cantina. 221 Columbus Ave., at 70th St.; 873–2606. Popular hangout. Try the Mexican kitchen casserole if you're very hungry. AE, MC, V.

Caramba! 918 Eighth Ave.; 245–7910; and 684 Broadway, at Third St.; 420–9817. Instantly popular and almost obnoxiously trendy addition to the singles scene. Expect to wait even with a reservation, and then have to plow through a crowd to get to your table. The food isn't great, though the drinks are. All major credit cards.

El Parador. 325 E. 34th St.; 679–6812. Small, plain restaurant that is so popular that they leave you waiting for tables even when plenty are available. But the food is unanimously praised. AE.

Inexpensive

Anita's Chili Parlor. 287 Columbus Ave., at W. 74th St.; 595–4091. Tex-Mex inside or at sidewalk tables. Standard combination plates are the way to go, or the chili, of course. AE, MC, V.

SWISS

Expensive

Chalet Suisse. 6 E. 48th St.; 355–0855. Pleasing but pricey place for fondues, onion and cheese pie, veal. Complete dinners and a la carte. No CB.

Inexpensive

La Fondue. 43 W. 55th St.; 581–0820. Fondues are the reason to dine here, though other dishes are available. Charming and casual, though crowded and rushed at lunchtime. No credit cards.

THAI

Moderate

Siam Inn. 916 Eighth Ave. near 55th St.; 974–9583. Beguiling Thai specialties presented by a gracious staff. Close to the theater district, Columbus Circle, and Carnegie Hall. Possibly the best Thai food in the city. AE, D.

Toon's. 417 Bleeker; 924–6420. An exotically decorated restaurant that serves unusual Thai dishes. But beware, the food tends to be very hot and spicy. AE, MC, V.

YUGOSLAVIAN

Moderate

Dubrovnik. 88 Madison Ave., near 29th St.; 689–7565. Interesting though limited selection of specialties such as *brudet* (a sort of chowder) and *cevapcici* (flavorful ground meat sausages). American and continental dishes fill out the menu. Dinner only Saturdays; closed Sundays. All major credit cards.

OTHER BOROUGHS

Bronx

Thwaite's Inn. *Expensive.* 536 City Island Ave.; 885–1023. Cape Cod in the Bronx—a fishing village restaurant specializing in the local catch. All major credit cards.

Mario's. *Moderate.* 2342 Arthur Ave.; 584–1188. Neapolitan family cooking served up by the Migliucci family since 1919. You can't go wrong here. All major credit cards. Valet parking. (Plenty of other Italian restaurants are within yards of Mario's; Arthur Avenue may now be the *real* Little Italy of New York.)

Brooklyn

Peter Luger. *Super Deluxe.* 178 Broadway, near Bedford Ave.; 718–387–7400. Luger is considered by many to be the city's most venerable steak house, and the limousines outside the door every night are testimony to that belief. Come by car or cab only, and have a cab called before you leave. No credit cards.

River Cafe. *Super Deluxe.* One Water St.; 718–522–5200. Nouvelle American food in a glorified barge sitting under the Brooklyn Bridge. The kitchen is uneven, but the setting, looking out on the lower Manhattan skyline, is magnificent. AE, CB, DC.

Gage and Tollner. *Deluxe.* 374 Fulton St.; 718–875–5181. The seafood menu changes with the seasons. Try the crab meat Virginia in this 1879 landmark building.

Bay Ridge Seafood Center. *Moderate.* 8618 Fourth Ave.; 718–748–2070. This is where the men and women who work at the Fulton Street Fish Market go for seafood. Be prepared for a wait. All major credit cards.

Gargiulo's. *Moderate.* 2911 W. 15th St., Coney Island; 718–266–0906. As heavy on atmosphere (a great octopus on the ceiling) and merrymaking as on solid southern Italian fare. All major credit cards.

Junior's. *Inexpensive.* Flatbush and Dekalb Aves.; 718–852–5257. Cheesecake is why you'll stop here. Go for the large breakfasts, and take home the cheesecake.

Note: Brooklyn's Atlantic Avenue and Court Street have many Middle Eastern restaurants. Most are family-owned and serve essentially the same fare. Among the best, all in the *Inexpensive* range: *Almontaser,* 218 Court St., 718–624–9267; *Moroccan Star,* 205 Atlantic Ave., 718–596–1919; and *Son of the Sheik,* 165 Atlantic Ave., 718–625–4023.

Queens

Manducati's. *Moderate.* 13–27 Jackson Ave., 718–729–4602. A Neapolitan trattoria. No credit cards.

Steinway Brauhall. *Moderate.* 28–26 Steinway St.; 718–728–9780. Hearty German food served up off Northern Blvd. near the Steinway piano factory. Closed Mondays. AE, MC.

Staten Island

Jade Island. *Inexpensive.* 2845 Richmond Ave.; 718–761–8080. Don't let the shopping center location fool you. The food is excellent and invitingly served. There's smorgasbord Mondays and Tuesdays, but the main efforts go into the Polynesian and Chinese items. All major credit cards.

BRUNCHES. Numerous restaurants offer huge weekend brunches that can carry you through the day. For about $10, you'll get breakfast-like foods such as eggs, waffles, pancakes, etc., or lunch/dinner eats like hamburgers or steak. Sometimes a free drink is included, typically champagne, mimosa, or Bloody Mary.

Many bruncheries supply music with the food—a relatively inexpensive form of entertainment as there is usually no cover charge. Among the best: the *Angry Square,* 216 Seventh Ave., 242–9066; *One Fifth,* Eighth St. and Fifth Ave., 260–3434; and *Buchbinders,* 375 Third Ave., 683–6500. The first two feature jazz, the last classical music. Many hotels, including the *Waldorf,* 49th and Park, 872–4895; *Grand Hyatt,* near Grand Central Terminal, 883–1234; and *Plaza,* 59th St. and Fifth Ave., 759–3000, also feature dining rooms that serve musical brunches in extravagant surroundings at equally extravagant prices (about $25). These should be considered for a special splurge.

 CAFES AND COFFEEHOUSES. The streets of Greenwich Village provide several opportunities for weary folk to rest and plan their day's itinerary. Many of these cafes serve a variety of coffees and pastries and will allow you to sit and daydream for as long as you wish. If you meander along Bleecker and MacDougal streets and, farther west, Greenwich Avenue, you'll find plenty of coffeehouses. Some recommendations: *Caffe Vivaldi,* on Jones St.; *Le Figaro,* at the corner of Bleecker and MacDougal streets, and *Pane e Cioccolato,* Waverly Pl. and Mercer St. *Ferrara's,* 195 Grand St., in Little Italy.

 BARS. New York is a big bar town. The city is famous for lots of neighborhood bars as well as singles haunts and celebrity hangouts. Bar hopping in the Village is easy—try University Place, Bleecker Street, and the West Village. Of particular note: *Knickerbocker Saloon,* University Pl. and 9th St., a jazz hangout catering to a slightly older crowd; *McSorley's Old Ale House,* 15 E. 7th St., one of the oldest taverns in the city, great for atmosphere, and usually jammed with college students. On the other side of the Village sits the literary pub *White Horse Tavern,* Hudson and 11th Sts., a regular haunt for Dylan Thomas and company. Another one-time literary haunt, and the city's oldest bar, is *Pete's Tavern,* Irving Pl. and 18th St., where O. Henry went to down the suds.

Among the trendiest watering holes—a restaurant, actually, but with a very active bar scene—is *The Gotham Bar and Grill,* 12 E. 12th St., an elegant space given over to quiet networking. Similarly, the spacious *Century Cafe,* 132 W. 43rd St., is a haven for the theater set. *The Saloon,* Broadway and 64th St., is known for its picture windows, its heavy-duty bar scene and for the best Buffalo chicken wings in the city. The singles scene on the Upper East Side is still swinging away. *Jim McMullen,* Third Ave. and 76th St., is named after its owner, a former model who plays host to any number of models, sports figures, and rock stars.

 NIGHTLIFE in the city is a combination of being entertained by live music, magic, or comedy, and entertaining yourself by dancing to the beat of the latest wave and keeping an eye on the omnipresent videos. For those on a budget, live acts are surprisingly affordable; the hottest dance clubs, offering only recorded music, often charge $15 and up for admission.

New York is once again the center of dance fever. Three relatively new dance emporiums reign supreme. Each is incredible both for its very existence and its indulgences. Try to visit at least one: *Limelight,* Sixth Ave. 20th St. (807–7850), *The Tunnel,* 220 12th Ave. (714–9886), or *Area,* 156 Hudson St. (226–8423). Remember, all have high admission prices and highly selective door policies—they pick and choose who gets in and who doesn't. (Tender egos beware.) If you do make it in, you'll be subject to crowded dance floors and outrageously priced drinks ($2 for a glass of water is not uncommon).

Limelight is housed in a deconsecrated church, with most of the features left unchanged. The Tunnel is a renovated train engine repair shop, long and tubular. Area is most famous for its monthly redecorations. These redecorations all have themes—suburbia, red, carnivale—and are extremely imaginative.

Still newer rivals on the dance scene include *Shout!,* 124 W. 43rd St. (869–2088), featuring all '50s and '60s dance music; *The Palladium,* 126 E. 14th St. (473–7171) is situated on the site of the old rock auditorium of the same name; and *Playboy's Empire Club,* 515 Lexington Ave. (752–3100), which features male "rabbits" along with the traditional bunnies. And, despite all of these upstarts, that old standby, *Roseland,* 239 W. 52nd St. (247–0200), is still serving up Latin and ballroom dance music, defying the wrecker's ball that periodically threatens its survival.

More sedate dancing can be found at the *Hors d'Oeuvrerie,* 1 World Trade Center (938–1111), where jazzy trios alternate with a solo pianist. The backdrop of the city below (you're on the 107th floor) is as romantic a setting as you're going to find, with the possible exception of the *Rainbow Room,* 30 Rockefeller Plaza (757–9090). At the Rainbow Room you're once again on top of the world, dancing to big bands in an extravagant Art Deco setting.

LIVE MUSIC

Quiet reveries are shared at the *Cafe Carlyle* in the Carlyle Hotel, Madison Ave. at 76th St. (744–1600). Pianist-singer Bobby Short holds court here six months of the year, with equally stylish musicians taking over during his leaves. *The Algonquin Oak Room,* 59 W. 44th St. (840–6800), is a close runner-up—a tad less haughty, and central to the theater district. Other possibilities: *Bemelman's Bar,* also at the Hotel Carlyle, and the other hotel lounges around the city.

For live rock and pop, the best known venues include the *Bottom Line,* 15 W. 4th St. (228–6300), and *The Ritz,* 119 E. 11th St. (254–2800), both for name acts. *Kenny's Castaways,* 157 Bleecker St. (473–9870) has a relaxed atmosphere for enjoying up-and-coming rock and folk acts. *S.O.B.'s,* 204 Varick St. (243–4940), is the Sounds of Brazil, and it's here where you'll find them along with a great Brazilian menu.

Two old stages new to the live scene are *Radio City,* Sixth Ave. and 50th St. (757–3100), and the *Beacon Theater,* 2124 Broadway (787–1477). Radio City is the classiest pop showcase in the country and plays host to names as varied as Diana Ross and James Taylor, Johnny Mathis and Dire Straits. Arena shows, sometimes featuring acts that have played Radio City on the same tour, will play Madison Square Garden.

Jazz buffs know, of course, that New York is home to many of the world's legendary clubs. Few of the 52nd Street and Harlem spots remain, but elsewhere there are literally dozens to choose from. The *Village Vanguard,* 178 Seventh Ave. South (255–4037), is a legend in its own time. Generally, the West Village hosts some of the better jam sessions at *Sweet Basil,* 80 Seventh Ave. South (242–1785), and *Blue Note,* 131 W. 3rd St. (475–8592), with admissions running from $8 to $18, depending on the act. *Bradley's,* 70 University Pl. (228–6440), sports a quieter atmosphere. Farther north, you might try *Fat Tuesday's,* 190 Third Ave. (533–7902). *Michael's Pub,* 211 E. 55th St. (758–2272), is a classy, surprisingly reasonable supper club where a $10 minimum on weekdays is applicable to either food or drinks and where the entertainment is consistently excellent. Woody Allen plays clarinet here on Mondays.

Some other jazz bargains: *West Boondock,* 114 Tenth Ave. (929–9645), where piano-bass duos are free with inexpensive dinners; and *West End Cafe,* 2911 Broadway at 114th St. (666–8750) where bebop and mainstream sounds prevail at low cover charges.

If you like your music on the mellow side, New York is one big cabaret. Of special appeal: *Don't Tell Mama,* 343 W. 46th St. (757–0788), *The Duplex,* 55 Grove St. (255–5438), *The Ballroom,* 253 W. 28th St. (244–3005), *Greene Street Space,* 101 Greene St. (925–2415), *Sweetwater's,* 170 Amsterdam Ave. (873–4100), and *Palsson's,* 158 W. 72nd St. (595–7400), the latter with musical revues that are often hilarious.

For country and blues, the *Lone Star Cafe,* Fifth Ave. and 13th St. (242–1664) is home to many Texans by heart. The club is often referred to as the unofficial Texas embassy in New York, but also features rock and Cajun music.

COMEDY AND MAGIC

It's always easy getting a laugh in this city, and harried New Yorkers certainly deserve one. A profusion of clubs giving over their mikes to hardworking young comedians awaits you. Among the best for atmosphere and talent: *Improvisation,* 358 W. 44th St. (765–8268), which started the whole open mike concept; *Comic Strip,* 1568 Second Ave. (861–9386); and *Comedy Cellar,* 117 Macdougal St. (254–3630). These rooms offer some of the cheapest (usually around $12), most fun-filled entertainment available. Another hilarious alternative is *Chicago City Limits,* 351 E. 74th St. (772–8707), an extremely talented sextet of improvisors. Name acts appear regularly at *Caroline's,* 332 Eighth Ave. (924–3499), and *Dangerfield's,* 1118 First Ave. (593–1640), the latter owned by comedian Rodney "I don't get no respect" Dangerfield.

For a really magical evening, you might try *Mostly Magic,* 55 Carmine St. (924–1472), which is a pleasing evening of just what it says!

LONG ISLAND

by
JOANN GRECO

To many New York City residents, "making it" means buying a house on Long Island. The "Island" represents for many a way out of the teeming jungle of the city. Living there seems to impart a certain social status. As a visitor to this narrow, 125-mile strip of land (23 miles wide at its broadest), you, too, may come to understand its magic.

You can actually see the stars out here. And smell the grass. Although urban sprawl has come to the Island, courtesy of track housing and shopping malls, the words "Long Island" still conjure a picture of large ranch houses, long driveways, individual mailboxes, backyards, and barbecues. Long Islanders *are* different—they're close to New York City, but not really of the city. They have their own railroad (the Long Island Rail Road), and their own area code (516).

Long Island is divided into two counties: Nassau and Suffolk. Nassau borders the eastern part of the Borough of Queens at points, while Suffolk reaches out farther—out into the Atlantic Ocean. More relevant to a visitor are two other lines of demarcation: the North Shore (hugging Long Island Sound, across which is Connecticut) and the South Shore (washed by the Atlantic Ocean).

The hilly North Shore is right for you if you're historically minded. Many of these small fishing villages resemble quaint New England towns and are filled with just as much history. On the other hand, the smooth, low-lying South Shore has excellent beaches, beginning with Long Beach Island and continuing straight through to Montauk Point. The middle part of the Island is primarily residential.

EXPLORING LONG ISLAND

Many individual towns on Long Island deserve a day's worth of exploring devoted just to them. Because of its lovely natural settings (no skyscrapers here!), the Island is very suitable to walking and biking tours.

The North Shore

North Shore communities are best explored on foot. The old villages and whaling towns (many settled in the mid–1600s by New Englanders of English and Dutch heritage) are of interest in and of themselves, but you'll also find many historic sites here. (See Historic Sites section of the *Practical Information* section.) For instance, Old Bethpage Village Restoration, Round Swamp Road, Old Bethpage, is a slice of living history, recreating life as it was before the Civil War.

Old Westbury Gardens and Mansion, Old Westbury Rd., are the lovely mansion and grounds of John S. Phipps and his wife. Port Jefferson, a village of many lovely houses, is a big tourist draw, from which you can take a pleasant ferry ride to Bridgeport, Conn. And Sagamore Hill is the famous estate so beloved by President Theodore Roosevelt.

Sag Harbor is known as a premier whaling village. Founded in 1707, much of this quaint town has been designated a National Historic District. During the late 1700s it was a principal whaling center and George Washington named it in 1797 as one of the two main ports of entry for the state (the other being New York City).

The entire village of Stony Brook has a nice consistency to it: the village was rebuilt in 1940 in Federal style by philanthropist Ward Melville. The lovely town merits a walking tour of its own, and there's more to see here than in many similar communities. It is home to the campus of the State University of New York at Stony Brook.

South Shore

A different type of scenery is found on the South Shore. These miles of beach towns provide excellent opportunities for bicyclists—not to mention sunbathers, swimmers, and surfers.

Southampton is known as the "playground for the rich." It is one of the oldest villages on Long Island, dating back to 1640. Now overrun by well-to-do city folk looking for a break, the area has much to offer, including a gorgeous beach.

A beautiful bike tour would start on Main Street. Proceed east through the center of the village, where you'll see many large old

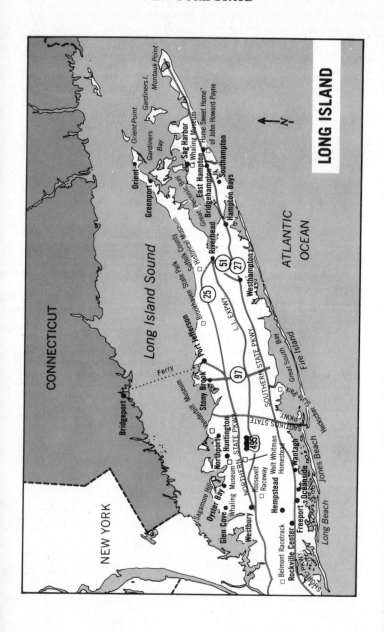

LONG ISLAND

homes. As you approach the beach, turn onto Gin Lane, following the shoreline for about two miles. You'll soon hit Agawam Lake, an oasis that makes a nice rest stop. Continue to hug the beach along Beach Road (which eventually leads to a dead end). Back up Beach Road, and turn left on Halsey Neck Road. To your left you'll see the Shinnecock Indian Reservation. Follow the road to Hill Street, and turn right to Jobs Lane, the very fashionable shopping strip. From here, it's a short ride back to the train station.

East Hampton serves as the gateway to the Atlantic, and is another mainstay of the chic. The village prides itself on its immaculate provinciality (there are many local ordinances, so beware!). The farthest east of the Hampton beaches, it provides pastoral village settings, attractive waterside vistas, and of course, terrific sunbathing.

Egypt Lane runs for about a mile and it is here that you will find many of the area's famous summer mansions. At the end of the Lane is the Maidstone Club, a lovely building of the late 1800s. Turn east through farmlands onto Further Lane. When you reach Indian Wells Road, turn right to the beach. It's a great one—rougher than the others, with many more dunes which have withstood erosion.

Montauk, the easternmost point of Long Island, is best known for its lighthouse, built in 1795 by order of George Washington. Originally, the lighthouse was situated 300 feet inland; now, due to erosion, it stands at the ocean's edge. The terrain throughout Montauk is hilly, and the sea air can be very bracing.

Whether by car, foot, or bicycle, proceed from the railroad station east about one mile to Edgewater Road. Turn left onto Edgewater and follow the road about five-and-a-half miles to the end of the peninsula, where you'll see the lighthouse. Make your way back along the same path, detouring right at West Lake Drive. Stay on the Drive for about two miles until you reach the inlet area. Here you'll see the major local industry: fishing. The neighborhood is also a nice rest stop filled with restaurants, fish dealers, and marinas. From here it's another two-and-a-half miles back to the LIRR station.

PRACTICAL INFORMATION FOR LONG ISLAND

HOW TO GET THERE. Your best bet for reaching points of interest on Long Island from New York City is by taking the *Long Island Rail Road (LIRR).* Round-trip tickets to any but the farthest points are usually under $20. Trains leave Manhattan from Penn Station, at 34 St. and Seventh Ave. For rate and schedule information, call 718–454–5477. If going by car, through Manhattan and Queens, several highways lead to various points on the Island. These include the Northern State and Southern State parkways and the Long Island Expressway (LIE). Highways you'll be using once on the Island include the Cross Island Expressway and Montauk Highway. A number of buses service the Island also, including *Greyhound, Trailways,* and *Short Line* buses. Check the information booth at the Port Authority Bus Terminal, 42nd St. and Eighth Ave.

Be forewarned when **driving** or going by **bus** to Long Island that traffic can be worse than anywhere you've ever encountered. The LIE is called the "the world's longest parking lot," and for good reason. Traffic can come to a dead halt literally for hours on end. Get early morning starts if you're headed to the beach, and try not to travel during rush hour between Manhattan and the Island. Special LIRR Jones Beach runs during the summer are an excellent alternative to driving, even though you need to take a shuttle bus from the station to the beach.

TELEPHONES. The area code for both Nassau and Suffolk counties is 516. When calling from within those counties, a local call is 25 cents. Rates, of course, vary depending on distance, length, and time you place your call.

ACCOMMODATIONS. Many of the towns featuring historical and other sights naturally provide some sort of accommodations, be they bed-and-breakfasts, inns, or motels. Rates for some of the resort towns can run as high as the best Manhattan hotels. But you'll also find an unexpected bargain or two along the way. Generally speaking, most of the following hotels stay open only during the "season"—that is, from Memorial Day to Labor Day. Those open for longer periods are so designated; cheaper rates naturally are in effect during the off-season. The price classifications for this section are for double occupancy and do not include sales tax: *Deluxe,* over $100; *Expensive,* $75–$100; *Moderate,* under $75. Unless specified, most places accept major credit cards. Abbreviations in this listing are: CB, Carte Blanche; DC, Diners Club.

AMAGANSETT

Ocean Dunes. *Moderate to Deluxe.* Box 755, Bluff Rd.; 267–3551. Private patios, pool. Open Apr.–Oct. No credit cards.

EAST HAMPTON

Hunting Inn. *Expensive to Deluxe.* 94 Main St.; 324–0410. Cafe and live entertainment.

Maidstone Arms. *Expensive to Deluxe.* 207 Main St.; 324–5006. Hotel rooms and two cottages; continental breakfast included. Weekly rates for cottages.

Dutch. *Moderate to Deluxe.* 488 Montauk Hwy.; 324–4550. Lawn games, free beach passes, private patio.

East Hampton House. *Moderate to Deluxe.* 226 Montauk Hwy.; 324–4300. Elegant accommodations.

HAMPTON BAYS

Edgewater. *Expensive.* Rampasture Rd.; 728–1020. Units with kitchens. Boating available. Weekly rates for cottages. No credit cards.

Westwind. *Moderate.* 177 W. Montauk Hwy; 728–0603. Motel rooms plus seven cottages with kitchens (and some with fireplaces). Wooded grounds. Weekly rates for cottages. No credit cards.

MONTAUK

Driftwood. *Deluxe.* Box S, Montauk Hwy.; 668–5744. Luxurious resort motel with heated pool, playground, cafe, private ocean beach, some private terraces, gardens. No credit cards.

Gurney's Inn. *Deluxe.* Old Montauk Hwy.; 668–2345. Some cottages. Box lunches available. Live entertainment, health club, whirlpool, lawn games.

Montauk Yacht Club. *Deluxe.* Star Island; 668–3100. Room service, entertainment, boutique. Open Apr.–Nov. Centrally located to tennis, golf, biking, sailing. Very expensive but elegant. No CB.

OYSTER BAY

Burt Bacharach's East Norwich Inn. *Deluxe.* Box 219, E. Norwich; 922–1500. Continental breakfast included, valet service, entertainment. $95; cottages with kitchens available. No CB.

SOUTHAMPTON

Sandpiper. *Deluxe.* Rte. 27; 283–7600. Nine cottages with kitchens; private beach on Peconic Bay. Weekly rates available.

Windward. *Deluxe.* County Rd. 39 and Hill Station Rd; 283–6100. Continental breakfast included. Tennis and golf privileges. Private patios and balconies. No DC.

Shinnecock. *Moderate to Expensive.* 240 Montauk Hwy.; 283–2406. Located near bay and ocean.

WESTBURY

Holiday Inn. *Deluxe.* 369 Old Country Rd.; 997–5000. Bar, entertainment. No CB.

Island Inn. *Deluxe.* Old Country Rd.; 288–9000. Private patios and balconies. In-room coffee and free newspaper. All credit cards.

 TOURIST AND GENERAL INFORMATION SERVICES. Contact the *Long Island Association of Commerce and Industry,* 80 Hauppauge Rd., Commack, NY 11725; *Long Island Tourism and Convention Commission,* 213 Carleton Ave., Central Islip, NY 11722; *Nassau Convention Office,* Nassau Coliseum, Uniondale, NY 11553; *Long Island State Parks,* Box 247, Babylon, NY 11702. Most individual towns also have their own chamber of commerce offices which should provide a wealth of information on the towns as well as scheduled local events.

 BEACHES, PARKS, AND GARDENS. Long Island has a plenitude of beaches and greenery. Much of the greenery comes in the form of huge, beautiful state parks, while some of the best beaches in the country can be found along the South Shore. If, after a hectic sightseeing schedule in New York City, you're ready for a little rest and recreation, Long Island is the place to go. *The Bayard-Cutting Arboretum.* Great River, on Montauk Highway (Rt. 27A); 581–1002. This park offers 690 gorgeous acres of nature trails, guided walks, and riverside meanderings.

Captree State Park. At the easternmost tip of *Robert Moses State Park* (which is located on the western end of Fire Island); 669–0449. Features untamed grassy areas and beaches.

Eisenhower Park. East Meadow; 542–4422. It covers almost 1,000 acres and has everything in the way of recreational activities, including golf, tennis, and roller skating (natural ice skating in winter). You'll also find a sit-down restaurant, two theaters, and a museum. The New York Philharmonic and other classical and pop attractions appear al fresco here in the summer.

Fire Island State Park. Along Ocean Parkway; 289–4810. This park has stunning beaches, as well as clamming, ferries, and nature walks. Fire Island itself is perhaps the most popular beach area in New York for straight and gay singles.

The Hamptons, starting with Westhampton and proceeding east to Montauk Point, feature still more outstanding beaches. The towns are all chic yet quaint, with theaters, specialty shops, restaurants, and boutiques.

Heckscher State Park. East Islip; 581–2100. Camping and picnic grounds, ballfields, a beach, and pool.

Jones Beach State Park. Wantagh; 785–1600. The largest of Long Island's parks and beaches, with over 2,400 acres and magnificent beaches, outdoor theaters and concerts, and a wonderful boardwalk. Picnic grounds, miniature golf, fishing, outdoor dancing, restaurant, cafeterias, and food stands—Jones Beach has it all, and it looks great, too.

Long Beach Island. 432–6000, smaller than Jones Beach, with a less populated beach and boardwalk—but clean and convenient to the city.

Long Island Game Farm and Zoological Park. Manorville; two miles south of Exit 70 on the LIE, 878–6644. Exotic and tame animals; oceanarium shows.

Orient Beach State Park. North Country Road, Rte. 25; 323–2440. Located on Gardiners Bay, it has beaches, fishing, and picnicking.

Planting Fields Arboretum. Oyster Bay; 922–9200. A 400-plus-acre horticultural center with nature walks, guided trails, greenhouse displays, and tours of the 75-room Tudor-style mansion of marine insurance magnate William Robertson Coe.

Robert Moses State Park, accessible via the Northern and Southern State parkways to the Robert Moses Causeway; 669–0449. Named after New York's master developer. The park features 1,000 acres of sweeping beaches and picnic grounds.

PARTICIPANT SPORTS. The various state and local parks (see *Parks* section above) invite visitors to bike, hike, horseback ride, fish, jog, and play tennis and softball. Volleyball is a popular beach sport. And boating—from sunfish to yacht—is one of the major reasons for living on the Island. Check the various shore communities on the availability of boat rentals, either for fishing parties or for sailing or cruising.

SPECTATOR SPORTS. Nassau Coliseum, Hempstead Turnpike, Uniondale; (794–9300), plays host to the New York Islanders hockey team, The New York Express indoor soccer team, and frequent wrestling matches. Roosevelt Raceway, Old Country Road, Westbury (222–2000), offers a good time for harness racing fans.

HISTORIC SITES AND HOUSES. Old Bethpage Village Restoration. Round Swamp Road, Old Bethpage; 420–5280. This restored pre-Civil War farm village includes an inn, a church, craft demonstrations, and farm activities. Access is from Exit 48 off the Long Island Expressway (LIE); Exit 39 off the Northern State Parkway; or Exit 31 off the Southern State Parkway.

Old Westbury Gardens and Mansion. Old Westbury Road, Old Westbury; 333–0048. The 18th-century Georgian-style home is a National Historic Site, and the grounds consist of 100 acres of formal gardens (including a fragrant English rose garden) as well as fields, woods, and a lake. Access via Exit 35 off the LIE; go one mile east on the service road, then one-half mile south on Old Westbury Road.

Port Jefferson and the Bridgeport Ferry. A 20-minute downhill stroll from the LIRR station in Port Jefferson (turn right as you exit). A big tourist draw of its own, Port Jeff offers many shopping and eating opportunities, including tiny indoor and outdoor malls and dock-side restaurants. The hour-and-a-half ferry ride (473–0631) to Bridgeport, Conn., is a perfect ending to a summer day. Fare is $6 to Bridgeport and $6 back ($10 for the round trip.) If you choose, you can buy a one-way ticket and return to New York City by train.

Sagamore Hill National Historic Site. Cove Neck Road, Oyster Bay; 922–4447. Former home of President Theodore Roosevelt, this estate includes a 22-room mansion with original furnishings, landscaped grounds, and a museum. Nearby is the Roosevelt Memorial Sanctuary and Trailside Museum, a 12-mile trail where Roosevelt enjoyed walking. Today, it is a bird sanctuary operated by the National Audubon Society. The site also includes the 26th president's grave.

Stony Brook Museums. Near the LIRR train station in Stony Brook; 751–0066. The complex houses the fascinating Carriage Museum with more than 100 horse-drawn vehicles, as well as a History Museum with costumes, dolls, textiles, and housewares of the past, and an Art Museum featuring 19th-century American artists. A one-room schoolhouse, blacksmith shop, and other period buildings are part of the complex. Nearby, a grist mill built in 1699 and powered by the overflow from a pond still produces cornmeal and flour.

Whaling Museum. Main Street, Sag Harbor; 725–0770. A Greek Revival edifice dating from 1845, this museum contains harpoons, scrimshaw (whalebone carvings), and other seafaring relics. Nearby is the Sag Harbor Custom House (516–941–9444), another historic landmark in this whaling village.

MUSEUMS. Many communities in Long Island have museums chronicling their development. Should you venture to these attractions—many worth a couple of hours, if not a day—you'll find yourself with plenty to do otherwise. Restaurants and shopping areas dot almost every town, as do beaches and parks. In general, the museums are close to LIRR stops. But it's best to call the attraction to make sure; or call the LIRR for information at 718–454–5477. If going by car, call your destination for detailed directions. They are listed here by community.

Amagansett. *Town Marine Museum,* Bluff Road, off Rte. 27; 267–6544. This museum concentrates on whaling, underwater archaeology, and shipwrecks.

Centerport. *Vanderbilt Museum and Planetarium,* 180 Little Neck Rd.; 757–7500. Tours of the 43-acre estate of William K. Vanderbilt, including a 24-room mansion and elaborate gardens.

Cold Spring Harbor. *Whaling Museum,* Main St., Rte. 25A; 367–3418. The biggest of the North Shore whaling museums, it contains over 400 pieces of scrimshaw (artworks carved from shells, walrus tusks, etc.). Be sure to check out the fully equipped whaleboats as well.

Cutchogue. The *Village Green;* 298–8353. A National Landmark, including *Old House* (Rte. 25), a 1649 example of English Tudor architecture; *Old Schoolhouse Museum* (Rte. 15); and the *Wickham Farmhouse,* dating from 1740 (Rte. 25). Also the *Hargrave-Vineyard* (516–734–5111) conducts winery tours.

East Meadow. *Museum in the Park,* Eisenhower Park; 542–4422. Exhibitions and reference center on Nassau County and general Long Island history.

Garden City. *Cradle of Aviation Museum,* Mitchell Field; 222–1190. Aeronautical museum housed in two hangars of a former U.S. Army Air Corps base. Includes spacecraft and aviation memorabilia. The village is particularly fashionable, with lots of boutiques and specialty shops.

Greenport. This active seaport community provides plenty of restaurants, shopping, museums and historic homes. You can sail the tall ships *Rachel* and *Ebenezer* (765–1249), visit the Museum of Childhood, and the Stirling Historical Museum (477–0720).

Hempstead. This town offers some very old churches, including St. George Episcopal Church, which was chartered in 1730 by King George II and contains a Queen Anne Bible (1706). The *Black History Museum* at 106A N. Main St. (538–2274) is another attraction.

Huntington. *Heckscher Museum,* Prime Ave. and Rte. 25A; 351–3250. American and European painting and sculpture from the 16th-century to the present. The *Powell-Jarvis House* at 434 Park Ave. (427–7045) is a 1795 homestead with period rooms intact. The *Walt Whitman House,* a state historic site at Huntington Station (427–5240), is an 1810 farmhouse which was the boyhood home of the great American poet.

Islip. *The Grange;* 567–6868. A re-creation of a Long Island farm village, with ten buildings and a working windmill.

Kings Point. U.S. Merchant Marine Academy; 773–5000. Officer's training school for the U.S. Merchant Marine and U.S. Naval Reserve. Chapel, museum, and grounds open to the public.

Manorville. Long Island Game Farm and Zoological Park, two miles south of Exit 70 on the LIE; 878–6644. Exotic and tame animals, oceanarium shows.

Riverhead. This beach town features historic landmarks dating back to the 1600s. At the *East End Arts Center Carriage House,* 133 E. Main St. (727–0900), artists-in-residence conduct workshops. The *Suffolk Historical Museum,* at 300 W. Main St. (727–2881), displays exhibits on textiles, china, crafts, whaling paraphernalia, and transportation, and details the history of Suffolk County and its people.

Water Mill. *Water Mill Museum,* Old Mill Rd.; 726–4625. Colonial crafts, tools, waterwheel, and a restored grist mill.

 RESTAURANTS. Dining on Long Island can be comparable to Manhattan in elegance, quality, service, and price. You don't have quite the selection, and most establishments, particularly in the beach areas, cater to steady clientele. Still, there are fine culinary experiences to be found. A dinner for one at a place listed as *Expensive* will cost $25 and up, with drinks, tip, and tax extra; *Moderate* means $15–$25; and *Inexpensive,* under $15. Credit card abbreviations are: AE, American Express; DC, Diners Club; MC, MasterCard; and V, Visa.

AMAGANSETT

Le Coco Beach Cafe. *Expensive.* Montauk Pkwy.; 267–8880. French nouvelle cuisine, with emphasis on local fish. Open Fridays–Sundays, May–July; seven days a week, July–September; closed October–March. All major credit cards.

Gordon's Restaurant. *Moderate–Expensive.* Main St.; 267–3010. Good continental cuisine, and an enticing dessert list. Frequented by the locals. Closed January and February; open for dinner only July and August; closed Tuesdays other months. All major credit cards.

Inn at Napeague. *Moderate–Expensive.* Continental menu, with specialties including bouillabaisse, beef Wellington, and lobster fra diavolo. Closed November–March. All major credit cards.

BETHPAGE

Hunam. *Moderate.* 3112 Hempstead Tpke.; 731–3552. Chinese entrees of leg of lamb, shrimp, whole sea bass. All major credit cards.

EAST HAMPTON

The Palm. *Expensive.* 94 Main St.; 324–0411. Located in the Hunting Inn. Sister to two Manhattan Palm restaurants specializing in steaks and seafood, and just as expensive. Closed September–May. AE, MC, V.

The Hedges. *Expensive.* 74 James Lane; 324–7100. Charming country inn, open year-round; California-style cuisine; light, summery fare. All major credit cards.

1770 House. *Expensive.* 143 Main St.; 324–1770. Continental cuisine. Closed Thursdays in summer, weekends at other times. No DC.

FIRE ISLAND

The Monster. *Moderate.* Cherry Grove, 597–6888. Eclectic menu; dancing and entertainment nightly. Open seasonally. All major credit cards.

HAMPTON BAYS

Chart Inn. *Moderate.* Shinnecock Canal; 728–1111. Outdoor cocktail deck on the water. Excellent seafood menu. Open daily in season. All major credit cards.

Indian Cove. *Moderate.* Shinnecock Canal, 728–8833. Spectacular waterside restaurant offering continental fare. Open daily July–August; weekends only fall and spring; call for winter hours. All major credit cards.

Villa Paul. *Inexpensive.* Montauk Hwy.; 728–3261. French and Italian menu. Closed Mondays off-season. AE, DC, V.

MONTAUK

Gurney's Inn. *Expensive.* Old Montauk Hwy.; 668–2345. Fresh fish and pasta entrees; Sunday brunch for $16.95. Panoramic view of the ocean. Jacket required at dinner. Open year-round. All major credit cards.

Club Terrace. *Moderate–Expensive.* Star Island; 668–3100. American/continental menu, specializing in local fish. Nightly entertainment and dancing. Closed December–February. All major credit cards.

Gosman's Dock Restaurant. *Inexpensive.* West Lake Drive; 668–9837. Casual seafood eatery on busy Lake Montauk harbor. Open seasonally. All major credit cards.

OYSTER BAY

Burt Bacharach's. *Expensive.* East Norwich; 922–0266. American/continental menu. Located in a historic 17th-century inn. Sunday brunch is offered. Open year-round. All major credit cards.

Steve's Pier I. *Expensive.* 33 Bayville Ave.; 628–2153. Elegant American/continental restaurant whose specialties include stuffed prime steak and Nova Scotia lobster. Outdoor dining on Long Island Sound. Open year-round. All major credit cards.

Canterbury Ales. *Inexpensive.* 46 Audrey Ave.; 922–3614. Pub fare in friendly atmosphere. Great sandwiches and burgers. Open year-round. All major credit cards.

PORT JEFFERSON

Bavaro's. *Moderate.* 141 W. Broadway; 928–2750. Skylit northern Italian restaurant featuring wonderful pastas. Open fire cooking adds a nice homey touch. Open year-round. All major credit cards.

Costa de Espana. *Moderate.* 9 Traders Cove; 331–5363. Elegant restaurant serving Spanish cuisine. The house specialties are the shellfish dishes. Open all year. All major credit cards.

Danford's Chowder House. *Moderate.* 25 E. Broadway; 928–5200. Waterfront seaside restaurant. Open year-round. All major credit cards.

Elk. 201 Main St.; 473–0086. *Moderate.* Specializes in Long Island duckling and seafood. Open year-round. All major credit cards.

Island Squire. *Moderate.* Middle Island; 732–2240. Continental menu emphasizing fish dishes. Open year-round. All major credit cards.

SOUTHAMPTON

Carol's. Rte. 27; 283–5001. *Expensive.* Trendy French restaurant—a must for celebrity-hunters. Charming room with pianist nightly. Open seasonally. All major credit cards.

Coast Grill. *Expensive.* Noyac Rd.; 283–2277. A swank new seafood and pasta restaurant with a California flavor. Open year-round. All major credit cards.

Balzarinis. *Moderate–Expensive.* 210 Hampton Rd.; 283–0704. Northern Italian menu, specializing in local seafood and homemade pastas. Open year-round. All major credit cards.

Herb McCarthy's Bowden Square. *Moderate–Expensive.* N. Sea Rd.; 283–2800. Interesting menu features Peconic Bay scallops, Irish smoked salmon, and filet mignon in Irish bacon. Terrace dining. Open year-round. All major credit cards.

Lobster Inn. *Moderate.* 162 Inlet Rd.; 283–9828. Seafood and steak staples. Open year-round. AE, MC, V.

Shippy's Pumpernickels East. *Moderate.* 36 Windmill La.; 283–0007. Good, homey German cuisine. Don't forget the Bavarian cream pie and Black Forest cake. Open year-round (closed Tuesdays). All major credit cards.

Sherlock Holmes Pub. *Inexpensive.* 75 Jobs Lane; 283–3311. Pub offering burgers, surf and turf, chicken, and (for something different) weiner schnitzel. Open year-round. All major credit cards.

STONY BROOK

Country House. *Expensive.* Rte. 25A and Main St.; 751–3332. Continental menu, emphasizing local seafood. Located in a historic, 1710 house—an elegant dining setting. Open year-round. All major credit cards.

Three Village Inn. *Expensive.* 150 Main St.; 751–0555. Interesting colonial homestead near the harbor, with beautiful grounds. Jacket recommended. Open year-round. All major credit cards.

UNIONDALE

Chardonnay's. *Expensive.* 101 James Dolittle Blvd; 794–3800. Located in The Long Island Marriott, this restaurant is not your typical hotel eatery. Elegant service and a gourmet menu make it special.

WESTBURY

John Peel. *Moderate–Expensive.* Old Country Rd., in the Island Inn Motel; 228–8430. Ribs and seafood. Early dinner special. English pub atmosphere with an open hearth and live entertainment. Open year-round. All major credit cards.

Giulio Cesare. *Moderate.* 18 Ellison Ave.; 334–2982. Northern Italian cuisine, uniformly excellent. Open year-round (closed Sundays). All major credit cards.

Hacienda don Pancho. *Moderate.* 535 Old Country Rd.; 333–1020. Nice selection of fiery Mexican entrees. Strolling guitarists. Open year-round. All major credit cards.

La Galleria. *Moderate.* 216 Post Ave.; 334–1160. Northern Italian menu with daily specials. Open year-round. All major credit cards.

Salisbury on the Green. *Inexpensive–Moderate.* In Eisenhower Park; 794–0880. Seafood and poultry entrees. Nice setting; early dinner special. Open year-round. All major credit cards.

Tesoro. *Inexpensive–Moderate.* 967 Old Country Rd.; 334–0022. Italian, with the emphasis on northern cuisine. Plenty of delicious pasta items. Open year-round. All major credit cards.

Wheatley Hills Tavern. *Inexpensive.* 170 Post Ave.; 333–3035. Handsome, friendly restaurant with continental entrees, especially Italian.

 CULTURE AND ENTERTAINMENT. All of the towns in the Hamptons have their own nightclubs and theaters, many of which operate only during the summer season. Another popular source of entertainment, at least when schools are in session, are the universities throughout the island. Of special note:

Bayway Performing Arts Center. 265 E. Main St., East Islip; 277–1345. Theater.

C. W. Post University Bush-Brown Concert Theatre. Northern Blvd. and Rte. 25A, Greenvale; 626–3100; live jazz and symphonic music.

Chuckles. 159 Jericho Tpke., Mineola; 746–2770. Comedy.

Circus Dance Club. Exit 33 on the Long Island Expressway, Lake Success; 829–3900. Rock dancing.

Governor's Comedy Shop. 90A Division Ave., Levittown; 731–3358. Up-and-coming comedians.

Key Largo. 135 Sunrise Hwy., West Islip; 669–2427. Live rock music.

Prism Nightclub. 8030 Jericho Tpke., Woodbury; 921–8500. Disco.

State University of New York (SUNY) at Farmingdale. 420–2104. Live comedy and music.

SUNY Stony Brook. 246–5000. College theater and big-name rock acts.

Westbury Music Fair. Exit 40 on the Long Island Expressway; 334–0800. Live pop music and musical shows, featuring big name entertainers.

HUDSON VALLEY

by
IRA MAYER

The serenity and beauty of the Hudson Valley are heightened by the region's proximity to New York City. Stretching from the Big Apple about 140 miles north to Albany, the valley—encompassing a few miles or so either side of the Hudson River—features lush foliage; historical sites dating from pre-Revolutionary times; quaint country inns; fine dining; and state parks for hiking, boating, and swimming. Whole towns such as Rhinebeck and Hurley are a step back in time, their 17th-, 18th-, and 19th-century architecture lovingly restored and maintained by families that have lived in the area through the generations—and by New York City folk who have adopted the region for weekend pursuits or even for full-time living.

Add to this the 19th- and 20th-century mansions such as the Roosevelt and Vanderbilt residences at Hyde Park; West Point Military Academy; several dozen wineries; a world-class cooking school with two dining rooms and a coffee shop open to the public; the Empire State Plaza state government office complex in Albany; overwhelming vistas of the Catskill, Berkshire, and Taconic mountain ranges; the artists' colony of Woodstock (although commercialized in recent years); and always the Hudson River, around which all these disparate elements converge.

115

The pressures of big city life recede just a few miles north of the New York City line in Westchester County. You can travel along the narrow, winding, forest-bound Taconic Parkway, with its woodchucks, squirrels, and deer roaming freely; or along the less scenic but straighter Gov. Thomas E. Dewey Thruway. Or, best of all, you can take a railroad trip right alongside the river—which is rivaled for its breathtaking views only by boat trips on the Hudson itself.

Outings from New York City

At least part of the lure of the region is its accessibility. For example, the various mid-Hudson sites make for wonderful day trips during any season from New York City, Albany, or points in between. Hyde Park, for one, is about two hours from New York, a little less from Albany. Such distances are also attractive for those seeking weekend retreats—just far enough to get away yet near enough not to require spending half the weekend in the car. The Hudson Valley is also within easy reach of southern New England; the Berkshires extend into the New York State side of the valley at the Connecticut and Massachusetts border. Similarly, you would be likely to travel through the valley from, say, Newburgh or Harriman, in order to reach the Catskills.

The matter of accessibility should not be construed by those planning an extended stay in the state as a suggestion to make the Hudson Valley a side-trip of some larger tour. That might be appropriate if the cultural offerings available summers in the Berkshires or the resort facilities peculiar to the Catskills any time of year are of special interest. But the history, architecture, culture, dining, accommodations, activities, and natural beauty of the Hudson Valley are suitable for any traveler any time of year. This is so true that if you have your heart set on a particular inn or restaurant, you'd best plan well ahead for weekend reservations. Last-minute explorers can hope for last-minute cancellations, or make use of the motels and more routine (yet often surprisingly good) restaurants that abound. Weekday meals and rooms at the most popular places are generally more freely available.

The Valley's Place in History

Accessibility is also part and parcel of the Valley's history, since the Hudson River was recognized by Henry Hudson as a gateway to northern regions in 1609. For that same reason, the river and its banks were the scene of numerous Revolutionary War battles, and there are dozens of places claiming that George Washington "slept here." Vastly improving the river's function as a major travel route—and making its impact on water transportation around the world—was the 1807 introduction of Robert Fulton's steamboat. This was followed almost 20 years later by the completion of the Erie Canal, which linked the upper Hudson at Albany with western points and the Great Lakes.

All of this activity at a point so near New York City is, of course, what gave rise to heavy settlement of the Hudson Valley. Its scenic beauty attracted a new population, albeit one with aesthetic rather than commercial or political interests, per se. The Hudson River School of

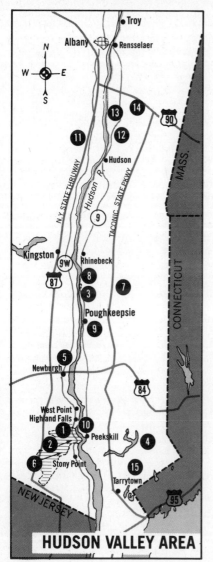

Points of Interest

1) West Point Military Academy
2) Bear Mountain State Park
3) Franklin D. Roosevelt Estate, Hyde Park
4) John Jay Homestead
5) George Washington Headquarters
6) Harriman State Park
7) Clinton House
8) Vanderbilt Mansion
9) Vassar College
10) Boscobel
11) Bronck House
12) Martin Van Buren Memorial
13) House of History
14) Shaker Museum
15) Sleepy Hollow Restorations

HUDSON VALLEY AREA

artists (Thomas Cole, Asher B. Durand, and others) is well represented in local museums and mansions, which are open to the public. Meanwhile, writers, actors, musicians, dancers, and other creative folk have long found the valley a perfect haven for living even when commuting to and from the Big Apple.

EXPLORING THE HUDSON VALLEY

For the immediate sensation of being in the country upon leaving New York City, Bear Mountain State Park can't be beat. There is skiing here in winter, with man-made snow when the weather isn't cooperative, while milder seasons call for hiking and picnicking.

West Point is where the U.S. Army has been training its officers since 1802. On the grounds are Fort Putnam, a Revolutionary War fort; a museum; several chapels; and various monuments to those who fought in the Revolutionary and Civil Wars.

Just west of Bear Mountain Park is Sterling Forest Gardens, which holds a Renaissance festival each summer with live jousting, minstrels, and other *olde* forms of entertainment. The park is open for strolling.

Also nearby is the wondrous Storm King Art Center, really a sculpture garden and museum that offers changing exhibits based on its 200-piece permanent collection.

Reliving the Revolution

The Museum Village of Orange County in Monroe, on Route 17M, starts a trip back in time with its 19th-century houses and old country store. Perhaps more meaningful, though, are the various Revolutionary War monuments in and near Newburgh. Among the sites you can also visit:

• The headquarters, near Newburgh, where George Washington formally announced the end of the war and disbanded the Continental Army.

• New Windsor Cantonment, in Vails Gate, a reconstructed army camp where Washington's men met and dined and where he worshiped, with one remaining log cabin actually built by the troops. Guides are outfitted in Revolutionary War uniforms, making this particularly colorful for children.

• The Georgian stone house headquarters of General Henry Knox, on Route 94. Tours are offered.

A detour to Washingtonville brings you to the Brotherhood Winery, at 35 North Street. This is the oldest winery in the country, and one of more than a dozen in the Hudson Valley.

New Paltz's Huguenot Houses

From Newburgh, go north on the Thruway (or on the slower but more scenic Route 9W, and then west on Route 299) to New Paltz which is a college town. The campus, part of the State University of

New York, boasts six fully restored stone houses dating back from 1692–1705 and a reconstruction of the 1717 French Church on Hugue-not Street. The Huguenot Historical Society owns and maintains these properties and conducts tours.

Also in New Paltz is the Mohonk Mountain House, a 300-room hotel built in 1870 on a 7,500-acre site. The hotel is best known for its theme weekends—mystery, chocolate, tennis, etc.—and for the wide array of activities available, including swimming, skiing, horseback riding, and hiking.

East of New Paltz, on the east bank of the Hudson, is the Vanderbilt Mansion, which we'll discuss later in conjunction with the Roosevelt Estate at Hyde Park and other mansions in the Poughkeepsie–Hyde Park area.

Kingston, Hurley, and Woodstock

The next exit up the Thruway (or you can opt for 9W) is Kingston— the starting point for a little loop that takes in Kingston, first settled in 1652, Hurley, and Woodstock. Among Kingston's historic points of interest are some 20 17th- and 18th-century Dutch houses in the Stock-ade District, the Old Dutch Church designed by Minard Lafever in 1852, and the Senate House, in which the first New York State Senate met during the brief period when Kingston served as the state capital. There is also a river cruise May–October.

Hurley is worth a brief stop if only because most of the town was constructed before 1900, with some structures dating as far back as the mid-1700s. Then backtrack a few miles on Routes 28 to Route 375, following the signs to Woodstock.

Woodstock became something of a mecca for the rock 'n' roll genera-tion in the wake of the festival of the same name—despite the fact that the festival was actually held an hour away in Bethel. But as the focus of so much attention, and as a long-popular area for musicians, artists, and literary figures, it still holds much interest.

Woodstock is so populated with tourists on summer weekends that it is difficult to find a parking space, get inside a shop, or walk on the narrow sidewalks. There is a most worthwhile theater and dance festi-val every summer, though, at the Playhouse, along with a handful of jazz and rock clubs that frequently feature name artists you wouldn't ordinarily expect to find in such small venues. The reason: they live in the town. One holdover from its legitimately artsy history: the Wood-stock Guild of Craftsmen, established in 1939, which includes galleries and a shop that feature the work of local member artists and craftspeo-ple only.

State Capital in Perspective

There is little formal sightseeing on the west bank of the Hudson between Kingston and Albany, though on clear days the Catskill Mountains can be seen to the west and the Berkshires across the river to the east.

Albany itself has been perhaps best immortalized by William Kennedy, the Pulitzer Prize-winning author of a wonderful trilogy of novels and a nonfiction work entitled *O, Albany,* set in the city and the Hudson Valley during the height of their fame from 1930–1945. Moonshine, gangsters, concrete mills, and baseball are the vehicles for Kennedy's exploration of the history and the psyche of the time. In the process of weaving his tales, the people, events, and locales take on special meaning. Similarly, for a brief but detailed overview of the monied families that settled Albany early on, and for notes on the architecture of the entire region, see Tim Mulligan's *The Hudson River Valley* (Random House; 1985).

Settled in 1614, chartered as a city in 1686, and named state capital in 1797, Albany, because it is a deep-water port, is also an international shipping center. The city's centerpiece is the Nelson A. Rockefeller Empire State Plaza, more commonly known simply as the Mall. Combining a series of office complexes with a performing arts center and public museum areas for fine arts exhibitions, the almost 100-acre Mall represents the late Governor Nelson Rockefeller's mighty effort to revive Albany's fortunes in the wake of the post-World War II exodus to suburban areas. The following suggestions are for those seeking a few highlights:

• The central plaza itself, with its trees, pools and sculptures, and the Tower Building Observatory, for the view from on high.

• The Concourse, below the plaza, exhibits contemporary works by the likes of Helen Frankenthaler, Isamu Noguchi, Louise Nevelson, Alexander Calder, and others.

• The museum features multi-media permanent displays titled *New York Metropolis, Adirondack Wilderness,* and *Upstate New York* tracing the history of those areas as far back as 4,000 years ago while inventively giving a sense of what life has been like in New York State, particularly in the 19th and 20th centuries. There are numerous transient exhibits, too, plus a fine gift shop.

• The Performing Arts Center—known somewhat fondly as "the egg," which is how you will spot it—is home to various cultural events, while the steps of the museum library serve as seating for outdoor concerts in summer.

At the far end of the Mall is the state capitol, built over a 31-year period beginning in 1867 and reflecting the design efforts of three architects—Thomas Fuller, who was removed from the project after nine years, and Leopold Eidlitz and Henry Hobson Richardson. Eidlitz was responsible for the Assembly Chamber and the Senate staircase, Richardson for the Senate chamber and the Great Western staircase. Overall, the building is a surprisingly effective combination of Italian Renaissance, Romanesque, and French Renaissance influences.

You will especially want to see the somber, rather classic-looking Senate chamber, with its mahogany walls, various marbles, granite, and stained glass windows, and the Great Western staircase. Adorning the latter are the heads of hundreds of historical and literary figures carved in stone. Guided tours are regularly scheduled. The neighborhoods around the capitol have undergone major restorations in recent years and make for a pleasant stroll, especially along the small-shop lined Lark Street.

Heading South on the East Bank

The ride out of Albany proper is via I–90. A first stop, a few miles from exit 82, should be the Shaker Museum in East Chatham. The life style of the Shakers, an 18th-century offshoot of the Quakers, was spare and simple. It is preserved and demonstrated in this village-like museum, where blacksmiths, weavers, and craftspeople ply their arts, and where displays of tools, furniture, and clothing can be found.

The countryside as you head south is particularly beautiful. Choose your route depending on interests and how leisurely you can afford to be—Routes 9 and 9G take you through the various towns along the Hudson, while the Taconic State Parkway, a bit inland to the east, is faster. The Taconic is narrow and winding for long stretches, but quite scenic.

Quite a number of mansions are here. Again, how many you visit depends on your interests. The "must-sees" are the Roosevelt estate at Hyde Park and its neighbor, the Vanderbilt mansion in the mid-Hudson region, and the Sleepy Hollow area around Tarrytown farther south. Among other stops to consider, moving north to south, are:

• Lindenwald, home of President Martin Van Buren, just south of Kinderhook. The house itself, dating back to the late 1700s, was transformed from a Federal-style mansion to an Italian-style villa in the mid-19th century and recently restored.

• Olana, just outside the city of Hudson. Built by the painter Frederic Church in 1874, this castle is filled with the artist's work and with period furniture. Outside, the castle is a startling burst of color and styles. It is situated within a 250-acre park and overlooks the Hudson.

• Clermont, a 200-year-old estate about 15 miles south of Hudson. A far more traditional house than Olana, built by the Livingston family, one of whose descendants (Robert R. Livingston) was partnered with Robert Fulton in the development of the steamboat. Fulton's *Clermont* was named after the estate. There are magnificent views, and a large state park.

• Taconic State Park. This little-known but exceptional park is right on the border of New York, Massachusetts, and Connecticut. Its star attraction is Bash Bish Falls, which can be viewed from any number of vantage points accessible by foot only. The walk on pleasant tree-covered paths is less than a half-mile from the various parking areas— and worth it at any time of year. There are also magnificent hiking trails, a bracingly cold (even in August) natural quarry for swimming, lovely shaded campsites that are booked several weeks in advance during the peak summer season, and a few cabins for rent.

• Lake Taghkanic, right off the Taconic State Parkway. A stunning lake with sand beach with a view of the Taconic range is the area's most popular for swimming, camping, boating, picnicking, softball, and just plain relaxing.

• Rhinebeck, a tiny village with a strong Colonial flavor. The Beekman Arms, an inn at the center of town, has been in continuous operation since 1766. Among its patrons of course, was George Washington. It is a pleasant place for lunch. The most popular attraction, though, is the Old Rhinebeck Aerodome, with various displays of aeronautic history. Also of note are the Delameter House, built in 1844 and now a bed-and-breakfast extension of the Beekman Arms, and the Dutch Reformed Church built in 1809. Walk or ride up some of the side streets to see some nicely restored Victorian and Colonial homes.

• The Cascade Mountain Winery, in Amenia off Route 22 (follow the signs up the side of a mountain); is a picturesque and exceedingly pleasant place to stop for a barbecue picnic consisting of local foods. The picnic is not elaborate, but everything is fresh, the setting is spectacular, and the wines quite nice. If the weather is nice you may wish to explore the vineyards.

• Mills Mansion is another Livingston family estate. The present structure was finished in 1896, features 65 rooms, and is filled with 19th-century furnishings. This is not among the best restored or maintained of the area's mansions.

• Vanderbilt Mansion. Be transported back in time to an era of grace and elegance. The building is Italian Renaissance and has been perfectly maintained as it was when the Vanderbilts lived here (among other places) at the turn of the century. The grounds, which extend right to the foot of the Hudson, are at least as spectacular as the mansion itself.

Hyde Park—Hudson's Centerpiece

Of all the magnificent architecture and spectacular landscapes to be found in the Hudson Valley, there is nothing that quite compares with the Roosevelt estate in Hyde Park. There is an overpowering sense of history here, along with good taste. In addition to the main residence, there are a library, Val-Kill (Eleanor Roosevelt's domain and residence following FDR's death), and numerous gardens, including the rose garden in which Franklin and Eleanor Roosevelt are buried.

Known properly as Springwood, the residence was purchased by Franklin Delano Roosevelt's father in 1867 and remodeled in 1915 by FDR and his mother. It is, in fact, the house in which Franklin was born. Without doubt the best guide to the estate is that written by Eleanor Roosevelt, which includes many personal reminiscences. The library, built by the Roosevelts with the specific intention of donating it to the U.S. government (as was the house), includes FDR's personal collection of literature on the Hudson Valley along with the first family's personal papers and many mementoes.

Val-Kill, which is a short ride from Springwood, comprises a stone cottage in which the Roosevelts' son John lived and a one-time furniture factory that the Roosevelts built to employ farmers during winter months. The factory was converted into Eleanor Roosevelt's residence in 1937.

Also in Hyde Park is the Culinary Institute of America (CIA), a series of magnificent buildings on a hillside overlooking the river, and widely regarded as the finest cooking school in the United States. Students enrolled in the 18-month program here must serve apprenticeships in every aspect of running a restaurant at the three restaurants owned by the school: the Escoffier, which is named for the famous French chef and serves classic haute cuisine; American Bounty, which specializes in and is the source of the nouvelle American style of cooking; and the most unusual St. Andrew's Cafe (see *Dining Out*).

Students cook the meals, serve them, act as wine stewards and maitre d's, bus tables, and wash dishes. They cannot graduate until they have done it all—but the graduates have gone on to found many outstanding restaurants in the Hudson Valley, New York City, and all around the country.

Nearby Poughkeepsie is the home of Vassar College, which offers an art gallery and a Shakespeare Garden.

The Lower Valley

The story of Boscobel's survival is almost as interesting as the house and grounds, which are magnificent. The house, which was started at the beginning of the 19th century, was moved to its present location in Garrison on Route 9D in the 1950s. Its restoration to a perfect period representation inside and out is credited to Lila Acheson Wallace, who together with her husband founded *Reader's Digest* and funded this undertaking.

Similarly extensive renovations have been undertaken on the Sleepy Hollow Restorations, three estates in or near Tarrytown that collectively take their name from the area's most legendary literary figure, Washington Irving. Sunnyside, Philipsburg Manor, and Van Cortlandt Manor make a popular weekend excursion from New York City, with various events scheduled throughout the year.

What is so impressive about the Sleepy Hollow Restorations is that they reflect three centuries of Hudson Valley life. Philipsburg, built in the late 17th century, features a working grist mill, a small private house, and a 15-minute orientation film about the estate. As you tour the grounds, the miller will encourage children to help with the chores, an added attraction for family outings. Nearby is the Old Dutch Reformed Church, also dating to the late 17th century, immortalized by Washington Irving, who is buried in the graveyard here.

Sunnyside was Irving's residence, and the embodiment of the writer's literary visions. It was enlarged from the 17th-century farmhouse he bought in 1835; there are lots of small rooms, sloping roofs, and weather vanes about, and the furnishings are much as they were when Irving lived on the estate. The grounds are also worth your while, providing unobstructed views of the river.

The main house of Van Cortlandt Manor, also built in the late 17th century, features furnishings, art, and household goods from the 1600s, 1700s, and 1800s. Of equal interest are the Ferry House, which served as an inn in the 18th century, and the magnificently planted "Long Walk" connecting the two.

Also in the vicinity is Lyndhurst, a Gothic Revival-style mansion with extensive though deteriorating greenhouses erected in the mid-1800s. The last resident of Lyndhurst was Jay Gould, the millionaire robber baron who ran the *New York World* newspaper and Western Union.

PRACTICAL INFORMATION FOR
HUDSON VALLEY

WHEN TO GO. Some Hudson Valley attractions—particularly some of the lesser known mansions in the mid-Hudson region—are closed during the winter months, but there are sights and activities available all year round. There are cross country and downhill skiing, boating, rafting, ballooning, hiking, camping, swimming, horseback riding, hang gliding, and more during appropriate seasons. There are also spring, summer, and fall boat trips and harbor festivals on and along the Hudson itself. **Fall** weekends are perhaps the most popular because of the spectacular foliage colors that blanket the area; this is also a great season for winery tours and tastings.

Winter is ideal for get-away weekends at quiet inns with big fireplaces and outstanding cuisine, for rummaging through antique shops, for exploring some of the little known local museums, and for enjoying major sites, such as the Roosevelt Estate at Hyde Park, under relatively uncrowded circumstances.

In **spring,** music, crafts, and arts festivals blossom along with the flowers, the airshows in Rhinebeck start their regular weekend schedule, and city dwellers start their searches for summer retreats in earnest.

About the only bad part of **summer** in the Hudson Valley is how arduous it is to get reservations at inns and restaurants, making impulsive weekend trips difficult (but not impossible). It's always best if you can plan ahead, but you can substitute motels for inns or bed-and-breakfasts, or you can stop at restaurants that look interesting—there are almost always some cancellations to be filled, and most establishments will go out of their way to help find space (or dinner) at a competitor whose accommodations or food they recommend.

HOW TO GET THERE. The Hudson Valley is exceptionally well served by **public transportation.** Rail and bus links are frequent, and many attractions are within walking or shuttle-bus distance of stations. Local *Metropolitan Transportation Authority (MTA)* trains and express *Amtrak* service run between New York City and Albany, leaving New York City from Grand Central Terminal. Amtrak's New Haven line and Metro North's Harlem Line serve Westchester County. *The Carefree Getaway Guide for New Yorkers,* by Theodore W. Scull (Harvard Common Press; $8.95) is filled with day-trip suggestions accessible by public transportation, with complete details and fares.

By car. Driving is best for those touring more extensively or seeking out inns and restaurants that are off the main roads. The Taconic Parkway and Thomas E. Dewey Thruway are the major north-south arteries on the east and west banks of the Hudson, respectively; the thruway is a toll road. Various state routes, such as Routes 9, 9D, 9G, 9J, 9W, and Route 22 a little farther east, run more or less parallel to the Taconic Parkway and the thruway. Bridges span the Hudson River, beginning with the George Washington Bridge at the northern edge of Manhattan (to northern New Jersey) right up to Albany. East-west routes tend be more of a back-roads nature than the north-south highways, so plan your time accordingly. In Westchester County, the New England Thruway (I–95) runs by New Rochelle and Rye and northeast to Connecticut. I–87 travels north from the Major Deegan Expressway, crossing the Hudson River via the Tappan Zee Bridge. I–684 goes north-south from White Plains, connecting with Route 22, a pretty (but slow) road that just about borders on Connecticut and Massachusetts.

By air. There are airports with local flights serving White Plains, Poughkeepsie, and Albany. From New York City, however, most air travelers will want to use Kennedy, LaGuardia, or Newark.

TELEPHONES. The area code for Columbia County, Green County, and Albany is 518; for Westchester, Rockland, Dutchess, Ulster, Putnam, and Orange counties, 914. The charge for local calls varies depending on the local telephone company, but can still be as low as five cents for three minutes in Columbia County. Similarly, check the directions on the telephone or in a local telephone directory for long distance dialing, which differ from system to system. The standard emergency telephone number throughout the Hudson Valley is 911.

ACCOMMODATIONS. Part of the weekend appeal of the Hudson Valley in recent years has been the number of inns and bed-and-breakfasts that have opened. These are highly individualistic establishments in which rooms almost always differ from one to the next, where the attitude of the owners is that of having a regular parade of guests into their "homes"—which is especially true when the inn has but one or two guest rooms. Many are owned and run by expatriate New York City folks who decided that seven-day weeks maintaining and running such hostelries were preferable to the sometimes harrowing pace of the city. Others have been purchased and restored by families long living in the area and equally interested in its revitalization.

You should understand, though, that the experience of staying at inns and bed-and-breakfasts is considerably different from that of using hotels and motels. These are very personal enterprises, usually in buildings a century and more old. Floors creak; furnishings might be genuine antiques lovingly restored, or they might be the best of the tag sales the year the inn opened. There will almost never be televisions or phones in the rooms. There may or may not be air conditioning. Menus will often be limited to a few selections served only at certain times.

These hardly seem like negatives to most travelers, but those seeking standardization or room service should stick to hotels and motels. That isn't to suggest that you shouldn't ask for what you want at an inn or bed-and-breakfast —merely that you will enjoy the experience that much more if your expectations equal what these establishments have to offer: personality, usually a porch and/or common rooms for guests to congregate, a deep love of the area and knowledge of its history, and practical familiarity with up-to-date sightseeing, dining, and other tips almost never encountered in more commercialized environments.

As might be expected, prices at inns and bed-and-breakfasts vary widely depending on the facilities, including whether there is private or shared bath, if any meals are included, whether you are traveling during peak or off-season, if it is a weekend or during the week. Many require payment in cash, or will accept a check with suitable identification. During peak seasons, many require two- or three-night minimum stays on weekends.

There are few hotels in the Hudson Valley. Most standardized accommodations are found at motels, and these are usually located within easy reach of the Taconic Parkway and the Thruway. Albany and Kingston are your best bets if you have no advance reservations and are simply looking for a place as you go. Lodging generally will range anywhere from $35 to $100 per night for a double, more if meals are included at inns.

For hostel information, see *Facts At Your Fingertips* section at the front of this book. Summer travelers may also want to check into the possibility of renting a cabin at one of the state parks in the Hudson Valley. As detailed in the *Exploring* section, Taconic State Park and Lake Taghankic are exceptionally beautiful locales for such stays. The accommodations—a sheltered step above camping—are basic, usually cots plus cooking facilities that are inexpensive and great for family or group outings.

The price classifications quoted are for double occupancy at press time, and include breakfast or other meals only as indicated: *Deluxe,* $100 and up; *Expensive,* $75–$100; *Moderate,* $50–$75; *Inexpensive,* under $50. Most hotels accept major credit cards. Those that do not are so designated.

ALBANY

Note: rates quoted are year-round averages; prices will be higher during the Saratoga racing season.

Hilton Albany. *Expensive–Deluxe.* State and Lodge Streets, 12210; 518–462–6611. Part of the Hilton chain, and offering standards in keeping with the name; downtown.

Marriott Hotel. *Expensive–Deluxe.* 189 Wolf Rd., 12205; 518–458–8444. 300 rooms, indoor and outdoor pools, sauna; airport area.

Americana Inn. *Expensive.* 660 Albany-Shaker Rd., 12211; 518–869–8100. Large motel with two indoor pools and spa with Jacuzzi; airport area.

Best Western Turf Inn. *Moderate–Expensive.* 205 Wolf Rd., 12205; 518–458–7250. 300 rooms, indoor and outdoor pools, sauna; airport area.

Quality Inn. *Moderate–Expensive.* 1–3 Watervliet Ave. Ext., 12206; 518–438–8431. 200-plus rooms, some with kitchenette. Indoor/outdoor pool.

Ramada Inn. *Moderate.* 1228 Western Ave., 12203; 518–489–2981. 200 rooms. Indoor pool, sauna; university area.

La Siesta. *Inexpensive.* 1759 Central Ave., 12205; 518–869–8471. Sixty air-conditioned rooms.

TraveLodge Albany. *Inexpensive.* 1230 Western Ave., 12203; 518–489–4423 or 800–255–3050. 75-room motel; university area.

AMENIA

Troutbeck. Leedsville Road, 12501; 914–373–8581. An executive retreat during the week, this is one of the fanciest inns in the nation. The $450 and up charged per couple per weekend includes open bar, wine, and truly first class cuisine as well as lake, year-round pool, tennis courts, and extensive gardens. Advance reservations are mandatory, and rooms—26 of the 31 have private bath—must be taken for Friday through Sunday. Meals are available to non-guests, but reservations are necessary. Near New York State wine country.

ARMONK

Ramada Inn. *Deluxe.* Rte. 22, 10504; 914–273–9090. 140 rooms in IBM territory.

BEAR MOUNTAIN STATE PARK

Bear Mountain Inn. *Moderate.* US 9W, 10911; 914–786–2731. 60 rooms, picnic grounds, outdoor pool.

CANAAN

Inn at Shaker Mill Farm. *Moderate.* Cherry Lane, 12029; 518–794–9345. Near the Shaker Museum in New York as well as the Hancock Shaker Village in Massachusetts, and convenient to both Albany and the Berkshire towns of Williamstown, Lenox, Lee, and Stockbridge, the inn borrows its decor from Shaker traditions. All 20 rooms have private bath, while the inn also features a sauna. Food is simple, and you may bring your own bottle, though wine is available. Breakfast included in rates; weekend packages available.

Berkshire Spur. *Inexpensive–Moderate.* Rte. 22 at I–90, 12029; 518–781–9998. Heated pool.

COLD SPRING

Hudson House. *Moderate.* 2 Main St., 10516; 914–265–9355. The dining room and many of the 14 guest rooms (all with private bath) look out on the Hudson and nearby West Point. The inn also features both a bar and a restaurant.

One Market Street. *Moderate.* Corner of Main Street, 10516; 914–265–3912. For true privacy, this inn offers one suite with fully stocked kitchen above the innkeepers' antique shop.

DOVER PLAINS

Old Drovers Inn. *Deluxe.* Old Drovers Inn Road, 12522; 914–832–9311. The dining room, first opened in 1750, is the inn's main claim to fame, if only because it has but three guest rooms (each with private bath). But the rooms are luxuriously outfitted with appropriate antiques and bedding. Lodging available Thursdays through Sundays only, with the entire inn closed most of December.

ELMSFORD

Holiday Inn. *Expensive.* Tarrytown Road, 10523; 914–592–5680. 150 rooms, outdoor pool.

Howard Johnson's. *Expensive.* 290 Tarrytown Rd., 10523; 914–592–8000. 100 rooms, outdoor pool, 24-hour restaurant.

FISHKILL

Holiday Inn. *Moderate.* US 9 at I–84, 12524; 914–896–6281. 150 rooms; outdoor pool AE, D, MC, V.

GARRISON

Bird & Bottle Inn. *Deluxe.* Rte. 9, 10524; 914–424–3000. Four rooms, each with private bath and four-poster or canopied bed in a building first constructed during Revolutionary War times. It has gone through several incarnations in the interim, reopening as an inn in 1940. Closed Mondays and Tuesdays, November–April. AE, MC, V.

Golden Eagle Inn. *Moderate–Expensive.* Garrison, NY 10524; 914–424–3067. *Hello Dolly* was filmed at this inn, which first opened across the river from West Point in 1840. Of the five rooms, three have private bath. Continental breakfast included. Closed February and March. AE, MC, V.

HIGH FALLS

Captain Schoonmaker's 1760 Stone House. *Moderate.* Box 37, 12440; 914–687–7946. This is the beautifully restored 1760 home of Captain Frederick Schoonmaker, plus the restored 1810 barn and carriage house. All rooms share baths with another room. Breakfast is included. No credit cards.

House On the Hill. *Moderate.* Box 86, Rte. 213, 12440; 914–687–9627. Simple, unassuming, and friendly colonial inn with three suites and one private bath. Breakfast included. No credit cards.

HILLSDALE

Swiss Hutte. *Deluxe.* Rte. 23, 12529; 518–325–3333. The setting at the foot of Catamount Mountain is what makes the Swiss Hutte so special. There are inn-like rooms in the main building, and motel-like accommodations overlooking Catamount, ponds, and gardens. Tennis courts, grass and snow skiing, and horseback riding are right at the doorstep. All 21 rooms have private bath and TV. Rates include breakfast and dinner for two in a good if not great restaurant. Closed April and mid-November–mid-December.

L'Hostellerie Bressane. *Moderate–Expensive.* Rtes. 22 and Rte. 23, 12529; 518–325–3412. There is no finer. The six rooms are quite simple, and only two have private bath. But the luxury of dining in what is one of the best restaurants outside New York City and then ambling up the stairs to sleep is an experience to be treasured. Chef Jean Morel also teaches cooking classes here during the week, with room and board (and what board!) included in the cost of the lessons. The food, is classic French with nouvelle touches. Closed March and April, Mondays in summer, and Sundays and Mondays in winter. No credit cards.

HYDE PARK

Dutch Patroon. *Inexpensive.* U.S. 9, 12538; 914–229–7141. Small motel with outdoor pool. Kitchen units available.

KINGSTON

Ramada Inn. *Moderate–Deluxe.* Rte. 28, 12401; 914–339–3900. 150 rooms, indoor pool.

Holiday Inn. *Moderate.* 503 Washington Ave. 12401; 914–338–0400. About 200 rooms, with indoor pool, whirlpool, sauna.

Howard Johnson's. *Moderate.* Rte. 28 at Thruway Exit 19, 12401; 914–338–4200. 118 rooms, indoor and outdoor pools, sauna, 24-hour coffee shop.

Sky Top. *Inexpensive–Moderate.* Rte. 28, 12401; 914–331–2900. 70 rooms, outdoor pool.

MILLBROOK

Cottonwood Inn. *Inexpensive–Moderate.* Rte. 44, 12545; 914–677–3919. A pleasant, low-priced inn not far from Poughkeepsie and Hyde Park. The 14 rooms each have private bath and TV.

NEWBURGH

Holiday Inn. *Moderate.* Rte. 17K, 12550; 914–564–9020. 120 rooms, outdoor pool.

Ramada Inn. *Moderate.* 1055 Union Ave., 12550; 914–564–4500. 125 rooms, outdoor pool.

NEW LEBANON

Valley Rest. *Inexpensive–Moderate.* Box 1135, Rte. 20, 12125; 518–794–9957. 14 motel rooms; two-day minimum stay summer weekends.

NEW PALTZ

Mohonk Mountain House. *Deluxe.* Lake Mohonk, 12561; 914–255–1000. A resort hotel with 300 rooms (250 with private baths) that has seen its better days, but which is most popular for its theme weekends. Best to go in a group and take advantage of the numerous activities available on the grounds.

Thunderbird. *Inexpensive–Moderate.* Rte. 299, 12561; 914–255–6200. 36-room motel with outdoor pool.

Ujjala's Bed and Breakfast. *Inexpensive–Moderate.* 2 Forest Glen Rd., 12561; 914–255–6360. "Unusual" is the adjective most frequently applied to both Ujjala Schwartz and her Victorian-style inn, where she practices the holistic life she lectures about at the state university. Health foods and massages are the options to the three rooms, all with shared baths. Rates include breakfast and afternoon tea. No credit cards.

NEW ROCHELLE

Sheraton Plaza Inn. *Expensive.* 1 Sheraton Plaza, 10801; 914–576–3700. About 130 rooms, outdoor pool, golf and racquetball privileges.

PORT CHESTER

Rye Town Hilton. *Deluxe.* 699 Westchester Ave., 10573; 914–939–6300. More than 450 rooms, indoor and outdoor pools, sauna, whirlpool, entertainment, tennis, golf privileges. Special weekend packages available.

POUGHKEEPSIE

Holiday Inn. *Moderate–Expensive.* Sharon Drive, 12601; 914–473–1151. 123 rooms, with outdoor pool, racquetball and health club privileges.

Po'keepsie. *Moderate.* 418 South Rd., 12601; 914–452–5453. 115 air-conditioned rooms. Outdoor pool and 24-hour coffee shop.

PURDY

Box Tree. *Deluxe.* Rtes. 116 and 22, Box 77, 10578; 914–277–3677. Noted primarily for its classic French cuisine served in an 18th-century setting, the Box Tree also has accommodations for one couple in a one-bedroom suite with wood-burning fireplace. Rates include breakfast and dinner. No credit cards.

RHINEBECK

Beekman Arms. *Moderate–Expensive.* Rte. 9, 12572; 914–876–7077. The Beekman Arms is one of the oldest inns in continuous operation in the country. It is a pleasant place, though somewhat stiff, with mediocre food. The **Delameter House** *(Moderate–Expensive)* on nearby Montgomery Street is an American Gothic building that the Arms runs as a bed-and-breakfast—and which may be the better bet. Main house, carriage house, and motel rooms available. In any case, the town is charming and a great central location for exploring the Hudson Valley mansions, with many excellent restaurants within reasonable distance (including the Culinary Institute of America).

ROSENDALE

Astoria Hotel. *Moderate.* 25 Main St., 12472; 914–658–8201. Spend a night in the 19th century a few miles outside New Paltz. The eight rooms each have private bath. Includes brunch. No credit cards.

STEPHENTOWN

Millhof Inn. *Moderate–Deluxe.* Rte. 43, 12168; 518–733–5606. A chalet-style inn with pool and air conditioning in the heart of Shaker country at the Massachusetts border. There are 11 rooms, including four suites, all with private baths. Includes continental breakfast and afternoon tea.

STONE RIDGE

Baker's Bed & Breakfast. *Moderate.* Old King's Highway, RD #2, Box 80, 12484; 914–687–9795. Five rooms sharing two baths in a restored 1760 stone house just outside High Falls and Kingston. Breakfast included. No credit cards.

TARRYTOWN

Hilton Tarrytown. *Deluxe.* 455 S. Broadway, 10591; 914–631–5700. 250 rooms, indoor and outdoor pools, whirlpool, sauna, entertainment, tennis, jogging trail, health club. Weekend packages available.

Marriott Westchester. *Expensive–Deluxe.* 670 White Plains Rd., 10591; 914–631–2200. 450 rooms, indoor/outdoor pool, whirlpool, sauna, health club.

WEST POINT

Hotel Thayer. *Moderate.* Southern Gate, U.S. Military Academy, 10996; 914–446–4731. Government-run, with 213 rooms.

WHITE PLAINS

La Reserve. *Deluxe.* 5 Barker Ave., 10601; 914–761–7700. Popular for executives on extended stays, or for luxurious seclusion. Golf, health club.

Stouffer Westchester. *Deluxe.* 80 West Red Oak Lane, 10604; 914–694–5400. Convenient to Hutchinson River Parkway and I–287, with more than 350 rooms, indoor pool, and health club.

HINTS TO THE MOTORIST. Roads are well marked, though you should be on the lookout for county and state route numbers; the numbers are sometimes the same, sometimes near each other, and when they are, go off in totally different directions. During peak tourist seasons, you may have to park a fair distance from the attraction you're visiting. During the winter, some roads in higher areas are not passable. And any time of year when there's a heavy rain, opt for the Thruway rather than the Taconic State Parkway, as the latter floods easily.

TOURIST INFORMATION. In addition to the New York State Tourist Bureau's "I Love NY" guides, which have quite a bit of information on the Hudson Valley, you may wish to contact the Hudson River Valley Association and the Hudson River Wine Council, both at 72 Main St., Cold Spring, NY 10516 (914–265–3066) for regional materials. Some of the best sources for up-to-the-minute goings on, new restaurants, tag sales, house rentals (by the week, month, and season), local movie times, and you-name-it are the free shoppers' guides published in many towns and distributed at supermarkets, gas stations, drug stores, and other establishments. Daily and weekly newspapers from Manhattan to Albany also list many goings-on for the Hudson Valley since weekend events are so popular.

SENIOR CITIZEN AND STUDENT DISCOUNTS. Since many of the attractions in the Hudson Valley are operated by the state or federal governments, there are frequent discounts for senior citizens and students. As elsewhere, proof of age or student status is usually required. Also, the outdoor music and arts festivals that run throughout the summer almost always offer reduced rate admission for seniors and students.

HINTS TO THE DISABLED. Many of the mansions in the Hudson Valley, built for private use by families in which there were apparently no physically handicapped individuals, are not very accessible to wheelchairs, though the grounds around them are. Remember, however, that many of these estates are on hillside property and may be difficult to navigate. The summer festivals tend to be accessible, some providing per diem rental of motorized wheelchairs. Some inns and/or bed and breakfasts may be accessible; best to check when making reservations.

SEASONAL EVENTS. There are fees for most of the annual fairs and festivals in the Hudson Valley, though most are quite reasonably priced. Among the most popular: Each **January,** *Ski Jumping Competitions* are held at Bear Mountain State Park. **June** brings the *Great Hudson River Revival* to Croton-On-Hudson during the third or fourth weekend in the month. Folk, blues, country, and jazz musicians are joined by craftspeople and a host of environmental groups in a two-day celebration of Hudson folklore, commerce, and history. The sloop *Clearwater,* run by a nonprofit organization dedicated to cleaning up the river and educating people in the area about ecological concerns, is usually docked nearby and sails the river throughout the summer. *Rhinebeck Crafts Fair,* fourth weekend in June (Thursday–Sunday) is probably the best crafts fair on the East Coast, with highly unusual handmade furniture and jewelry as well as sculpture, canvases, woven fabrics, dolls, and more. Get there early in the day or before the weekend to avoid the crowds. Also June is the *Imagination Celebration,* a wonderful week-long program for children at Albany's Empire State Plaza.

In mid-**July,** the *New York Renaissance Festival* gets started at Sterling Forest Gardens; weekends through Labor Day. Jousters, jesters, minstrels, clowns, and musicians stage a full-scale Renaissance revival with Olde Tyme Foodes on sale, too. **August:** *Dutchess County Fair* at the fairgrounds in Rhinebeck. Also, *Columbia County Fair* at the fairgrounds in Chatham.

September: *Harvest Festival and Crafts Fair,* Shaker Museum, Old Chatham; three weekends. Lots of apples, cider, and Shaker crafts, along with games for children. **October:** *Bear Mountain Crafts Festival,* Bear Mountain State Park, mid-month. Popular for those seeking to beat the December rush for gifts. **December:** *Christmas Festival,* Bear Mountain State Park, throughout the month. Also, candlelight tours of various Revolutionary War sites—Boscobel and nearby environs—at the end of the month.

TOURS. Almost all of the major sites in the *Historic Sites* section below feature guided and/or self-guided tours. There are also packaged bus tours to West Point, Hyde Park, and the Vanderbilt Mansion. The "I Love NY" publications list a variety of packaged tours that usually use inns for accommodations, but which are built around bicycling, ballooning, sightseeing, and other activities. For escorted tours try *Aristocrat Tours,* 8 Raymond Ave., Poughkeepsie 12603; 914–452–2130. For tours of the Woodstock Artist Colony, contact *Abigale Robin Tours,* Box 553, Woodstock 12498; 914–679–7969.

PARKS AND GARDENS. The mid-Hudson mansions offer some of the most spectacular gardens in the Northeast. Visit in particular the rose garden at the Roosevelt Estate in Hyde Park from mid-June through fall, Van Cortlandt Manor, and the Storm King Art Center. Of the state parks, Bear Mountain, Taconic State Park, Franklin D. Roosevelt, James Baird, and Lake Taghankic are all excellent for day-trips (or more) from New York City.

In summer months, there are day-liners that cruise up to Bear Mountain Park from Pier 81 at 41st St. and 12th Ave. in Manhattan (212–279–5151). A second stop is nearby West Point Military Academy. You can get off at either stop and catch the boat back later in the day, after it has turned around upriver at Poughkeepsie, or you can stay on for the round trip. Adults, $15; children, $7.50.

PARTICIPANT SPORTS. Tennis is available free at local high schools in many areas; the State Tourism Division's *I Love NY Camping* brochure lists an additional 14 commercial court sites, and some hotels and motels in Westchester County either have their own courts or have arrangements with nearby private clubs for tennis and/or golf. **Bicycling** is excellent, with rental shops in some larger towns; check the *Yellow Pages* or contact the *Lake Region Bike and Ski Club,* Box 111, Monroe, NY 10950 for Hudson Valley information. **Sailing** and **rowboating** are popular at Lake Taghankic and Franklin D. Roosevelt Park. Both have launches for privately owned sailboats, though you will need to purchase a permit at the park. **Fishing** is permitted only in designated rivers, streams, and lakes; a state permit is required. The Hudson is known for American shad, striped bass, and large and small-mouthed bass.

There are nine 18-hole and nine 9-hole **golf** courses in the Hudson Valley; the Rockland Lake North course (914–786–2701) carries championship status.

 HISTORIC SITES. The entire region is filled with the spirit, monuments, and architecture of the Revolutionary War period, as well as a wealth of estates of the nation's politically, socially, and commercially best-known families from Colonial times up to today. The *Exploring* section (above) of this chapter gives the highlights of these sites. Details are listed below. We have provided telephone numbers to facilitate calling ahead, and urge you to do so, particularly if you are traveling at other than peak tourist seasons.

Albany Institute of History and Art. 125 Washington Ave., near the capitol, Albany; 518–463–4478. The specialties here are the Hudson River School of artists, New York and American folk art, and regional furniture and silver collections. The museum is open Tuesdays–Saturdays from 10 A.M. to 4:45 P.M., and Sundays from 2 P.M. to 5 P.M. A lunch gallery is open Tuesdays–Saturdays from 11:30 A.M. to 1:30 P.M. Admission is by donation.

Boscobel. Rte. 9D, Garrison; 914–265–3638. Guided tours of this magnificently restored 19th-century house are available April–October, Wednesdays–Mondays, 9:30 A.M.–5 P.M., and in November, December, and March until 4 P.M. The house is closed Tuesdays, plus January and February, Thanksgiving and Christmas. Adults, $4; children 6–14, $2.

Cherry Hill. 523-1/2 South Pearl St., Albany; 518–434–4791. Most interesting for the lovers' triangle and murder that took place here—and for the sense of rummaging through someone's long unexplored attic while strolling through the house. Open Tuesdays–Saturdays 10 A.M.–4 P.M., and Sundays 1–4 P.M. Closed Jan. 1, Thanksgiving and the day before, and December 24, 25, and 31. Tours hourly, Tuesdays–Saturdays 10 A.M.–3 P.M., and Sundays 1–4 P.M. Admission is $3.50 adults, $3 seniors, $2 college students, and $1 children 6–17.

Clermont. 15 miles south of Hudson; 518–537–4240. A 200-year-old estate built by the descendants of Robert R. Livingston, who was a partner with Robert Fulton in the development of the steamboat. There are magnificent views and a large state park. The park is open year-round, the house from late May–October, Wednesdays–Saturdays, 10 A.M.–5 P.M., Sundays 1–5 P.M. Admission is free.

Executive Mansion. 138 Eagle St., Albany near the Mall; 518–474–2418. The governor's official residence, started in 1850, with periodic additions to the structure and a fine art collection. Can be visited by guided tour only Thursdays at 1, 2, and 3 P.M., with reservations required at least one week in advance. Admission is free.

Fort Crailo State Historic Site. Rensselaer, on the east bank of the Hudson; 518–463–8738. An 18th-century private house that also served as a fort. The house's restoration has been meticulous. Some historians claim that the song "Yankee Doodle Dandy" was composed here. Open January–March, Saturdays 10 A.M.–5 P.M. and Sundays 1–5 P.M.; April–December, Wednesdays–Saturdays 10 A.M.–5 P.M., Sundays 1–5 P.M. Admission is free.

Lindenwald. south of Kinderhook; 518–758–9689. The home of President Martin Van Buren is open from June to mid-September (phone for hours). Grounds are open daily. Admission is free.

Lyndhurst. Near Sleepy Hollow Restorations, Tarrytown; 914–631–0046. Gothic Revival-style mansion erected in mid-1800s, last occupied by Jay Gould, who ran the *New York World* newspaper and Western Union. Extensive greenhouses in sad state of disrepair. Open April–October, Tuesdays–Sundays, 10

A.M.–5 P.M., and on weekends in November and December. Adults, $5; senior citizens, $3.50; children 6–16, $2.50.

Mills Mansion. Near Amenia, off Rte. 22; 914–889–4100. Another estate of the descendants of Robert R. Livingston, this is not the best restored or maintained of the area's mansions. Open Memorial Day–Labor day weekend, Wednesdays–Saturdays, 10 A.M.–5 P.M.; Sundays, 1–5 P.M. Admission is free.

Museum Village of Orange County. Rte. 17M, Monroe; 914–782–8247. 19th-century houses and old country store. Museum open April–October, Tuesdays–Sundays, 10 A.M.–5 P.M. Adults, $4.75; senior citizens, $3.50; children 5–15, $2.75.

Nelson A. Rockefeller Empire State Plaza (The Mall). Albany. Office complexes, performing arts center, and museum areas. For tours daily of the entire mall or an on-high view from the Tower Building Observatory, call 518–474–2418. Open daily except New Year's Day, Thanksgiving, and Christmas from 9 A.M. to 4 P.M.; no admission fee. Regularly scheduled tours of the art collection in the concourse are conducted Wednesdays at 10:30 A.M. and 2:30 P.M. from the Visitors Services Office. Tours can also be arranged by appointment (518–473–7521) for other times. The mall's museum is open every day except New Year's Day, Thanksgiving and Christmas from 10 A.M. to 5 P.M.; admission free. Free guided tours of the state capitol (518–474–2418) are offered daily between 9 A.M. and 4 P.M.

New Paltz's Huguenot Houses. North of Newburgh on Thomas E. Dewey Thruway, or Rte. 9W, then west on Rte. 299, to New Paltz; 914–255–1660. Tours of these restored stone houses (1692–1705) are conducted by the Huguenot Historical Society, Memorial Day–September, Wednesdays–Sundays, 10 A.M. and 4 P.M. Appointments are recommended for large groups. Tours are tailored to your interests and the amount of time you wish to spend. Full tour: $5 adults, $4 senior citizens, $2 children 7–12.

Olana. Outside Hudson; 518–828–0135. Castle built in 1874 by the painter Frederic Church, and filled with his work and with period pieces of furniture. The 250-acre grounds overlooking the Hudson are open year round from 8 A.M. to sunset. House can be toured May–October, Wednesdays–Saturdays, 10 A.M.–5 P.M., and Sundays 1–4 P.M., earlier in the fall, and for an open house shortly before Christmas. Adults, $1; children 50 cents.

Old Rhinebeck Aerodrome, Rhinebeck; 914–758–8610. Various displays of aeronautic history and mock "air fights" Saturdays and Sundays from mid-May to October at 2:30 P.M. Adults, $6; children 6–12, $3. Exhibits are open daily 10 A.M.–5 P.M.during the season; adults, $1.50; children, $1.

Roosevelt Estate. Hyde Park; 914–229–9115. Springwood, the main residence, and the Roosevelt Library are open daily from March–November, and Thursdays–Mondays the rest of the year, 9 A.M.–5 P.M. They are closed Thanksgiving, Christmas, and New Year's Day. Val-Kill, the stone cottage that was Eleanor Roosevelt's residence, is open 9 A.M.–5 P.M. daily, April–October; Thursdays–Mondays, November and March. It is closed December, January, and February. One adult ticket is good for admission to Springwood, the library, Val-Kill, and the Vanderbilt Mansion; adults, $3.50; children and senior citizens, free. There is also an inexpensive shuttle bus between Springwood and Val-Kill.

Schuyler Mansion State Historic Site, 32 Catharine St., Albany; 518–474–3953. The Georgian-style home of Revolutionary War Major General and post-war U.S. Senator Philip John Schuyler and his wife Kitty Van Rensselaer was built in 1761, and served as the site of their daughter's wedding to Alexander Hamilton 19 years later. Although the mansion was sold out of the family early in the 19th century, New York State acquired it in 1912 in order to restore and preserve it. The design, construction, and antiques are noteworthy. Open April–December, Wednesdays–Saturdays, 10 A.M.–5 P.M.; Sundays, 1–5 P.M.; call for hours at other times of the year. The mansion is also closed most holidays, except for Memorial Day, July 4th, and Labor Day, which are popular for local sightseeing. Admission is free.

Sleepy Hollow Restorations. Three estates (Sunnyside, Philipsburgh Manor, and Van Cortlandt Manor) in or near Tarrytown that collectively take their name from the area's most legendary literary figure, Washington Irving. Write or call for specifics: Sleepy Hollow Restorations, 150 White Plains Rd., Tarrytown, 10591; 914–631–8200. The three estates are open 10 A.M.–5 P.M. daily except Thanksgiving, Christmas, and New Year's Day. Admission charged; however, ticket prices are based on how many of the sites you wish to visit. Tickets are good for six months, giving visitors the freedom to take their time and return at a later date if they don't get to see everything in one day. Picnic facilities are available at all three.

Ten Broeck Mansion. 9 Ten Broeck Place, Albany; 518–436–9826. Built in 1798. Federal on the outside, originally Georgian-style on the inside, though the layout was significantly altered in the mid-19th century. Furnishings are mostly of the Federal style. Open Tuesdays–Saturdays, 2–4 P.M., and Sundays, 1–4 P.M. Closed holidays. Admission is by donation.

Vanderbilt Mansion. Near the Roosevelt Estate, Hyde Park; 914–229–9115. Elegant Italian Renaissance mansion designed by McKim, Mead and White, maintained just as it was when the Vanderbilts lived there. Open year-round, 9 A.M.–6 P.M. in summer, to 5 P.M. rest of the year. Closed Thanksgiving, Christmas, and New Year's Day. The $2 fee for adults is also valid for the Roosevelt home and library. Children and senior citizens, free.

U.S. Military Academy. West Point, 10996; 914–938–2638. Visitors invited daily, except for Thanksgiving, Christmas, and New Year's Day, though the fort is closed during the winter. There are military parades in spring and late summer through fall. For further information contact the Visitors Information Center at the academy, open 8:30 A.M.–4:15 P.M. During the summer, there are day-liners that cruise up to the Point, as well as to Bear Mountain State Park, from Pier 81 at 41st St. and 12th Ave., in Manhattan (212–279–5151) You can get off at either stop and catch the boat later in the day, or you can stay on for the round trip. Adults, $18; senior citizens, $14; children, $9.

A few other unusual places that make pleasant afternoon excursions from New York City:

Museum of Cartoon Art. Comly Ave., Rye Brook, NY 10573; 914–939–0234. Open Tuesdays–Fridays, 10 A.M.–4 P.M.; Sundays 1–5 P.M. $1.50 for adults; 75¢ for senior citizens and children under 12.

Museum of the Hudson Highland. The Boulevard, off Rte. 218, Cornwall-on-Hudson; 914–534–7781. Open daily except July 4th, Thanksgiving, Christmas, and New Year's Day, though hours vary. Indoor exhibits and self-guiding nature trails. Admission is free.

Van Wyck Homestead Museum. Rte. 9 at I-84, Fishkill; 914–896–9560. Dutch home that served as Washington's headquarters. Open Memorial Day–Labor Day, Saturdays and Sundays, 1–5 P.M.

John Jay Homestead. Rte. 22 between Katonah and Bedford Village; 914–232–5651. Tour the home of the first Chief Justice. Open Memorial Day–Labor Day, Wednesdays–Saturdays, 10 A.M.–5 P.M. (fall: noon–5 P.M.); and Sundays, 1–5 P.M. Donations accepted.

DINING OUT. The Hudson Valley happens to abound in outstanding restaurants, but don't expect life outside Manhattan to be appreciably cheaper when it comes to first-class food. *Expensive* means $25 and above, *Moderate* means $15–$25, and *Inexpensive,* $15 and under. Abbreviations for credit cards are: AE, American Express; MC, MasterCard; V, Visa.

The most interesting dining experience to be found in the region is probably the **Culinary Institute of America (CIA)** (*Moderate*), Rte. 9, in Hyde Park. This is the nation's leading cooking school, and has three student-run restaurants. These aren't your everyday students, though, for the school has trained some of the leading proponents of nouvelle American cuisine, as well as many classically oriented French cooks, and its influence can be felt coast-to-coast.

The three restaurants: **American Bounty,** which is where you'll find the most imaginative combinations, some of which work, some of which don't, but all of which are highly original and intriguing; the **Escoffier Room,** honoring the renowned French chef and serving classic French cuisine; and the **St. Andrew's Cafe** which features a low-sodium, low-carbohydrate menu and offers guests a computer printout of what they have eaten, including a calorie count.

Weekend reservations at both American Bounty and the Escoffier Room must be made at least two to three months in advance—longer during summer and fall. The St. Andrew's Cafe is open for lunch and dinner Monday through Friday and no reservations are necessary. The entire establishment is closed when school is out. Reservations are more readily obtainable during the week, and if you have the time (to plan ahead or to go on a weekday), it is worth building a trip to the area (the Roosevelt Estate and Vanderbilt Mansion are nearby) around a meal taken at the institute. There are also tours of the school on Tuesday and Thursday afternoons. For reservations: 914–452–9600, ext. 220.

A number of Hudson Valley inns also feature restaurants so good that they are worth building a weekend around, even if you can't get a room there. **L'Hostellerie Bressane** (*Expensive*), at the junction of Rtes. 22 and 23 in Hillsdale, 518–325–3412, tops the list.

A series of small dining rooms, most with fireplaces, and a charming bar near the entrance are cozy and inviting. The food is French with nouvelle twists, and a meal is paced for enjoyment over several hours. Dinner for two will easily run $125 with a moderately priced wine, but there is a fixed price dinner on Sundays for under $20 per person that is truly a bargain. For those with the time and the inclination, there are cooking lessons during the week, with room and board (you eat what you cook) for about $400 per person. Alas, weekend reservations here are required well ahead during summer and fall.

Very close runners-up in this category of inns where dining is the central pleasure (and that are ideal for romantic getaways):

Old Drover's Inn. Dover Plains; 914–832–9311. American fare that will run about $30 per person at dinner. Closed Tuesdays and Thursdays and most of December. No credit cards.

Troutbeck. Amenia; 914–373–8581. Dinners run about $35, reservations are necessary; or stay at the inn Friday through Saturday, with all meals and alcohol included for upwards of $450 per couple. Closed to the public weekdays. All major credit cards accepted.

These are the cream of the crop, along with **DePuy Canal House,** Rte. 213 (*Expensive*), High Falls; 914–687–7700, once an inn but now run exclusively as a restaurant serving inventive American cuisine highlighted by fresh seafood, produce, and game in season. About $100 for two. Dinner served Thursdays through Sundays, as well as weekend brunches 11 A.M.–2 P.M. The Hudson Valley, however, has many moderately priced and inexpensive restaurants to choose from, as well as roadside stands where you can purchase local produce, cheese, and home-baked breads for your own picnics.

At **Random Harvest,** on Rte. 23, five miles east of the Taconic Parkway (just before Hillsdale), you can even buy the picnic basket—and then, in summer, fill it with fresh, crusty, French bread, a selection of local goat cheeses, juicy home-grown tomatoes, and just-picked strawberries and blueberries. Similarly, **Hotaling's Farm Market** on Rte. 9H just north of Claverack is an orchard where you can pick your own apples, cherries, and plums, or stock up on corn, cabbage, and in fall, pumpkins. While an immediate picnic might be the formal reason for stopping at Random Harvest or Hotaling's, it is worth taking a detour in order to bring such goodies back home. As for more traditional spots for dining, a selection is listed below.

ALBANY

Farnham's Larkin. *Moderate.* 199 Lark St.; 518–462–2400. American/continental fare; closed Sundays. All major credit cards.

Jack's Oyster House. *Moderate.* 42–44 State St. 518–465–8854. Seafood and steaks. All major credit cards.

La Serre. *Moderate.* 14 Green St.; 518–463–6056. French cuisine in 19th-century factory-turned-restaurant. Closed Sundays. All major credit cards.

L'Auberge. *Moderate.* 351 Broadway; 518–465–1111. French food in Victorian setting. Closed Sundays. AE, MC, V.

Yates Street Restaurant. *Moderate.* 492 Yates St.; 518–438–2012. Restored old neighborhood tavern, elegant atmosphere. Contemporary American cooking, creative menu. Closed Sundays. All major credit cards.

BEACON

Dutchess Manor. *Moderate.* NY 9D; 914–831–3650. Continental cuisine overlooking the Hudson. Fixed price dinner under $20 or a la carte. Closed Mondays and Tuesdays. All major credit cards.

BEARSVILLE

Bear Cafe & Little Bear. *Moderate.* 295 Tinker St. (on Rte. 212); 914–679–9427. The Bear serves American/continental fare in a spacious wood-and-plants barn, and, in summer, alongside a tranquil stream. The Little Bear specializes in Chinese food. Both are very reasonable for surprisingly superior food. Closed Wednesdays, MC, V.

CENTRAL VALLEY

Gasho of Japan. *Moderate–Expensive.* Rte. 32; 914–928–2277. The building housing the restaurant was brought over from Japan and reconstructed in traditional fashion—without nails. All food is prepared on hibachi grills, with diners sitting around communal "tables," the chef at the center. There is one small glass house available for private parties as well. Not the best Japanese food in the world, but the setting, amid beautifully manicured Japanese-style gardens, is exceptional. Reservations suggested—but be prepared for a wait on weekends. All major credit cards.

COLD SPRING

Plumbush. *Expensive.* Route 9D; 914–265–3904. Fixed price Swiss dinners in the $25–$50 range, served in small dining rooms, each featuring its own fireplace. Closed Mondays and Tuesdays in winter. All major credit cards.

GARRISON

Bird & Bottle Inn. *Expensive.* Old Albany Post Road; 914–424–3000. American and French menu with fixed price dinners at about $30 as well as a la carte. (See also *Accommodations* section.) AE, MC, V.

HIGH FALLS

Top of the Falls. *Moderate–Expensive.* Box 123, Rte. 213; 914–687–7565. Continental cuisine in a beautiful setting. Dinner daily, plus brunch on Sundays. AE, MC, V.

HILLSDALE

Swiss Hutte. *Moderate–Expensive.* Rte. 23; 518–325–3333. The Swiss pick up their influences from France and Germany—and the menu here reflects both. Restaurant looks out on Catamount Mountain. Closed April, November, and part of December. (See also *Accommodations* section.) AE, MC, V.

HYDE PARK

Springwood Inn. *Moderate.* Rte. 9; 914–229–2681. Directly across from the Roosevelt Estate. Lunch and dinner seven days a week. All major credit cards.

KINGSTON

Hillside Manor. *Inexpensive.* 240 Boulevard; 914–331–4386. Northern Italian food in a pretty setting. AE, MC, V.

MILLBROOK

Daniele's. *Moderate.* U.S. 44; 914–677–3993. Italian accented prime ribs, lobster and other hearty dishes served at lunch and dinner daily. All major credit cards.

NEW PALTZ

Dominick's. *Moderate.* 30 N. Chestnut St.; 914–255–0120. Straightforward continental fare for lunch and dinner seven days a week. All major credit cards.

Locust Tree Inn. *Inexpensive–Moderate.* 215 Huguenot St.; 914–255–7888. The setting is exceptionally pretty, looking out on a golf course. Dinner Tuesdays–Sundays; lunch Tuesdays–Fridays; Sunday brunch. All major credit cards.

DuBois Fort Restaurant. *Inexpensive.* 81 Huguenot St.; 914–255–1771. Like eating in a private home—this one having happened to have been built in 1705. The food? Potted roasts and the like. Meals run $7–$10 at dinner, about $5–$7 at lunch. No credit cards.

RHINEBECK

Beekman Arms. *Moderate.* Rte. 9; 914–876–7077. Very standard American fare for lunch, dinner, and Sunday brunch, but the setting is charming. All major credit cards.

Chez Marcel. *Moderate.* U.S. 9; 914–876–8189. Pleasant French dining. Dinner daily except Mondays; Sundays from noon. AE, D.

Schemmy's. *Inexpensive.* 19 E. Market St.; 914–876–6215. An ice cream parlor that's great for breakfast, lunch, or snacks. No credit cards.

 ARTS AND ENTERTAINMENT. Almost every small town has a **movie** theater—often a great old Art Deco theater that seats perhaps 200 people, with showings sometimes on weekends only, and almost always at regular times (7 and 9 P.M., for example). Albany's well regarded equity **theater** company, Capital Repertory, offers productions from October through May. **Dinner theaters** are also popular in the mid-Hudson area—watch for event listings in local newspapers. The **Storm King Art Center** (914–534–3115), north of Bear Mountain, is a sculpture garden and museum that is open mid-May–October, 2–5:30 P.M.; closed Tuesdays; admission, $2.

Hillsdale, Canaan, New Lebanon; and other towns along upper Rte. 22 are also considered to be in the foothills of the Berkshires and provide easy access to that area's extensive summer **arts festivals:** *Tanglewood,* summer home to the Boston Symphony Orchestra; the *Jacob's Pillow Dance Festival;* the *Stockbridge* and *Williamstown* playhouses for theater; and similar fare. Also, the northern reaches of the valley in and around Albany are close to the *Saratoga Summer Festival.* More southerly points are within reach of the outdoor festivals at Katonah and Purchase in Westchester.

 SHOPPING. The Hudson Valley can be very good for antique hunting, with shops in almost every town and city. Particularly noteworthy is Rte. 23 heading east from the junction of Rte. 22 in Hillsdale. Crafts are to be found at the *Rhinebeck Crafts Fair* in June and at the *Bear Mountain Festivals* in October and December. For upscale shopping, *White Plains* and the *Crossgates Center* outside Albany are best bets. *Woodbury Common* is a new discount shopping center located just off the New York State Thruway exit at Harriman.

THE CATSKILLS

by
IRA MAYER

The Catskills are often referred to simply as "the mountains," at least by those who approach them from New York City. The region's attraction stems largely from the popularity of several gargantuan resorts, the most famous of which are Grossinger's and the Concord, which offer everything from three meals a day (with unlimited seconds and as many selections from the menu as your stomach can handle) to golf, tennis, resident matchmakers (for young and old alike), and big name entertainers.

In their heyday from the 1930s through the 1950s, these hotels, their smaller competitors, and the bungalow communities that catered to families who preferred to do their own cooking, served as the training ground for the stand-up comics who went on to fame on radio and television, carrying with them the so-called "borscht belt" humor of the Catskills. Borscht, of course, is the Russian soup well-known to the eastern European Jews who made the Catskills their summer haven away from New York City. Other ethnic groups have long since come to adopt the Catskills as their own, too, as is apparent from the numerous festivals held in different towns each summer.

The hotels are still a major attraction of the region, even as they change with the times. Grossinger's was sold out of the family in late

1985 to developers who promised a low-calorie dining room to complement the traditional kosher cooking for which the 1,300-capacity hotel
is famous, and to build condominiums on its 800 acres. But the prom-
ises are still waiting to be kept and Grossinger's future is still uncertain.
Such shifts are emblematic of what is happening in the Catskills.

Year-Round Resort

Special interest weekends are among the most popular events, bringing younger people to the Catskills; once there, the guests discover the
natural beauty of the region. Other developers are coming in and
building up the ski areas around Hunter Mountain and Belleayre,
among others, adding night skiing, summer sports, lodges, restaurants,
and condominiums intended to turn this into a younger, year-round
resort. Even the old bungalow communities are being spruced up and
gentrified as the children who vacationed in the Catskills with their
parents in the '50s return to the area with their own families. Those new
families are taking advantage of long-time attractions such as the Catskill Game Farm, the old west Carson City, and Ice Caves Mountain.
But they are also venturing out onto the Delaware River for rafting
trips, hiking the Appalachian Trail, and otherwise exploring the more
natural sightseeing possibilities.

The Catskills, then, offer a variety of distinctive vacation opportunities. The hotels are self-contained miniature cities, with their vast
dining rooms (the Concord seats 3,000 at a time!), full facilities, day
care and babysitting services, golf courses, dancing lessons, and regular
regimen of Simon Says games. The larger hotels also offer various
theme weekends—treasure hunts, mystery games, and chocolate-lovers
along with the single meets. The smaller hotels might specialize in
horseback riding or golf or fishing, or perhaps in simply offering the
best in rest and relaxation with great views, large sitting rooms and
common areas, and individualized service.

Motels, Lodges Abound

But the Catskills are also overflowing with motels and lodges, particularly around the ski areas. Using these, or the growing number of
inns and bed-and-breakfasts, means less formal structure and a greater
likelihood of exploring on your own. You'll probably want a car if
you're touring the area, for while public transportation exists, it is
infrequent and won't give you the freedom to really roam.

The network of inns and bed-and-breakfasts is not as highly developed in the Catskills as it is in the Hudson Valley and the Berkshires,
though there are a fair number from which to choose. We anticipate
that this will increase as the Hudson Valley becomes saturated with
such establishments and as real estate in that area becomes too expensive for such endeavors. The upshot is a warning to reserve well ahead
at those places listed in the *Practical Information* section of this chapter
or to consider some of the places in "gateway" towns and cities such
as Kingston and New Paltz.

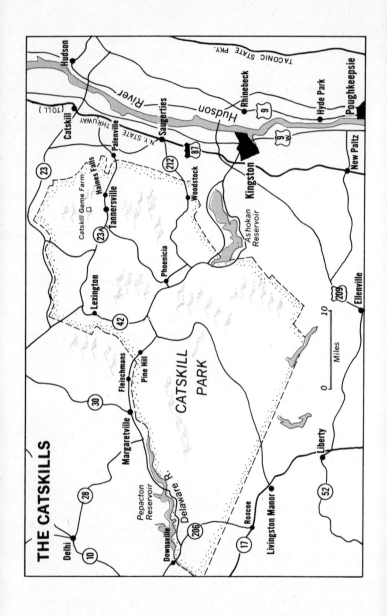

Finally, it should be noted that the Catskills are particularly well suited for all kinds of camping—trailer, tent, and backpacking. Catskill Park, the Delaware River environs, and other areas have ample sites for overnight, weekly, monthly, or seasonal stays.

EXPLORING THE CATSKILLS

Visiting the Catskills for other than a stay at the major resort hotels is a highly individual endeavor. There isn't an extensive list of historic sites, museums, or attractions in the Catskills—rather, you have a region whose natural resources seem to demand active participation. You *can* limit such activity to driving, and you will be rewarded with spectacular scenery. But even the casual walker will find plenty of suitable trails that won't be strenuous or taxing; experienced hikers, of course, have long flocked to the region.

Cross country skiing is another increasingly popular way to tour the area and so is white-water rafting. For the more adventurous, there are balloon trips and even hang-gliding. In other words, in planning a trip to the Catskills, whether for a weekend or longer, be sure to leave time for such activities. Rushing from one place to the next without stopping when a particular view catches your fancy, or without absorbing a feel for mountains that have long been favorably compared to Europe's Alps, is to miss what the Catskills have to offer.

With that caution in mind, we offer a continuous narrative route through the Catskills that essentially runs in several small loops, each highlighting a different aspect of the region: the part of Catskill Park southwest of Route 28, including the Woodland Valley; the park northeast of Route 28, covering the Hunter and Windham ski resorts, the Catskill Game Farm, and other attractions; the area along the Delaware River and down to Port Jervis; and the central Catskills hotel region around Ellenville, Liberty, and Monticello. You can certainly drive your way through most of the region in three or four days, but you would best focus on some small portion of the tour outlined. The best part of this approach is that it will leave you yearning to return, with much more to explore.

Following the Onteora Trail

We'll start at Kingston, easily accessible by the Gov. Thomas E. Dewey Thruway. (For information on Kingston and nearby High Falls and Woodstock, see the chapter on the *Hudson Valley* above.) From Kingston, follow Route 28 around the Ashokan Reservoir, which provides much of the water for New York City. As you circle the reservoir, the grandeur of the Catskills becomes evident. On the north rise The Overlook, Mount Tobias, Mount Tremper, and others. Toward the west are Mount Pleasant, Panther Mountain, Wittenberg, and, in the distance, the monarch of the peaks, Slide Mountain. Slide is the highest of the Catskills at 4,204 feet. Its summit can be reached via a short climb along a trail commencing at Winnisook Lake.

Of all the roads entering the Catskills, few offer the unspoiled natural attractions of the Onteora Trail, reaching from the Hudson Valley over the divide of the southern mountains to the east branch of the Delaware River. An ancient Indian pathway, the trail runs beside streams bordering vast forests. Soon you are alongside the Esopus Creek and in the town of Phoenicia, summer resort and trout fishing capital of the eastern slopes. The town is also the scene of annual White Water Races, held early in June. In winter, Phoenicia and nearby Fleischmanns, Shandaken, and Big Indian are ski resorts. The 668,660-acre Catskill State Park, a part of the huge Catskill Forest Preserve, stretches over this area, with over 200 miles of marked hiking trails open to the public.

Hunter—Where Skiers Meet

Hunter, a few miles north on Routes 214 and 23A, is probably the most popular of the region's ski resorts, a favorite for day and weekend trips from New York City. Many city ski shops, in fact, run package tours to Hunter that include lodging, lift tickets, breakfast, and dinner, with ski rentals available—and you'll see lines of young people outside these stores on Friday evenings, waiting for the buses that will take them on the 2½-hour ride north. Indeed, despite a lift capacity of some 14,000 people per hour, the slopes here are very crowded on winter weekends, a time when local residents would never consider skiing the nearly 40 trails that zigzag around and down the 4,050-foot (1,600-foot vertical drop) mountain.

Those with the luxury to get there during the week, however, enjoy no lift waits and pretty much continuous skiing, including nighttime, since the mountain is floodlit. With snow-making machines, the resort can help Mother Nature when necessary. Lift tickets run $29 a day for adults, $22 for children under 12, $6 for under age 5, and there are weekend, week, and season tickets available. Local telephone: 518–263–4223; toll free information service: 800–631–7811. Ski condition reports are available in New York State at 800–FOR–SNOW; elsewhere, 800–548–6648. Hunter also offers summer skiing, first introduced during the 1960s. In addition, there are Italian, German, American Indian, and Celtic festivals as well as country music and polka festivals from July through September.

Van Winkle Country

Palenville, 12 miles to the east of Hunter via Route 23A, is the legendary home of Rip Van Winkle. Heading west on 23A and then a few more miles on Route 23, is Prattsville, named after its founder, the colorful industrialist Zadock Pratt. Shortly after Pratt came to the area, he amassed a fortune from a general store and constructed his own village, building more than 100 houses for new settlers. At one point, he operated a grist mill and a hat factory, as well as the largest tannery in the Catskills. Mountain neighbors called him "the most wonderful man the country ever produced."

Determined to preserve his name for posterity, Zadock donated a public park to the village, named Pratt Rocks, and had sculptors carve in them a bust of himself, his favorite dogs and horses, a bust of his son, a coat of arms, and a settee and armchair. The tannery was destroyed by a flood, but you can still see Pratt Rocks, as well as the Zadock Pratt Museum.

Heading east again on Route 23 brings you to the Windham ski area (accessible more directly from Hunter via local road 296). Windham has 25 trails and the White Birches Ski Touring Center—about 15 miles of cross country trails. This is less crowded and attracts a somewhat tonier crowd than Hunter. For information, call 800–342–5116, or, in the immediate vicinity, 518–734–4300. A bit farther east are Cairo (pronounced KAY-row) and Catskill.

Catskill Game Farm

From here, head north on Route 32 to reach the Catskill Game Farm and its 2,000 varieties of animals and birds. Also on Route 32 is Carson City, a replica Wild West town. Catskill is also the site of the home of Thomas Cole, the founder of the so-called Hudson River School of painting. The home is now a museum, although Cole's paintings are mostly represented by illuminations rather than the canvases themselves. West of Cairo, along Route 145, is East Durham, with its Butterfly Art Museum.

Backtracking westward on Route 23 brings you to the Schoharie Reservoir and Gilboa Dam, site of a most unusual natural phenomenon. Contractors excavating for the dam found a fossilized prehistoric forest here, the oldest known in the world. Hundreds of stumps and branches having fernlike foliage were unearthed. Geologists believe that this forest grew during the Devonian period of the earth's formation, some 200 million years ago. Near the dam is an interesting exhibit of the fossilized ferns that were the ancestors of our trees today. Gilboa Dam now holds back 20 million gallons of water from Schoharie Creek, reversing its normal flow toward the Mohawk River and sending it instead southward to feed the Ashokan Reservoir.

Continuing west on Route 23 is the attractive town of Stamford, home of a Maple Sugar Museum that displays old-time maple sugar manufacturing equipment. Above the town's maple-lined streets towers Mount Utsayantha. According to legend, beautiful Utsayantha, a Mohawk princess, fell in love with a Sioux brave, but was not allowed to marry him. She leaped into a lake and drowned, and was buried on the summit of the mountain, where there is still a grave marker.

South of here, on Route 30, is Roxbury, home of naturalist-essayist-philosopher John Burroughs. The drive along this road combines entrancing scenery with historic landmarks, and Burroughs' home, Woodchuck Lodge. A short distance beyond the home is Boyhood Rock, which now has a bronze tablet inscribed with a verse from Burroughs' poem *Waiting*. A rectangular stone wall in front of the rock marks his grave, near which bubbles a spring from which he used to drink.

The Woodland Valley

Back along the Onteora Trail (Route 28), at Big Indian, a road turns left into the Woodland Valley. Woodland Creek flows beside the road, the forest is all around, and there is a public rest site at the end of the valley. From here, leading up to the highest peak, the Slide Mountain Trails begin. Of this area, John Burroughs wrote, "Of all the retreats I have found among the Catskills, there is no other that possesses quite so many charms for me as this valley. It is so wild, so quiet and has such superb mountain views." On the highest elevation, white quartz and pebbles pave the trails, the result of erosion of the rock on Slide's summit.

Slide Mountain is at about the center of Catskill Park, which is spread over four counties: Ulster, Greene, Delaware, and Sullivan. Almost all of the other notable Catskill summits are within the boundaries of the park, too, and here also begin tributaries of three rivers: the Hudson, the Delaware, and the Schoharie.

Routes 10 and 28 come together in Delhi, site of the Delaware County Historical Museum, where early farm tools and a country schoolhouse can be seen in the restored 18th-century home of Jude Gideon Frisbee. The museum is open Memorial Day through Labor Day (607–746–3849). A little to the south is Downsville, which has a covered bridge built in 1854, and from which the Pepacton Reservoir and Bear Spring Forest Preserve are accessible. Below that is Livingston Manor, site of four covered bridges, junction of the Beaver Kill and Willowemoc rivers, and one of the gateways to the southern Catskills.

Hawk's Nest Drive

There are a number of ways to approach the southern half of this region. Route 17, the Quickway, is a fast, direct drive through the Catskills, meeting the Thruway at Harriman. But the leisurely sightseer will start at Hancock and head south along Route 97, the Hawk's Nest Drive. The Drive parallels the main branch of the Delaware River, running high above the river's gorge and permitting spectacular views for almost its entire length. There are several interesting things to see, although most of them are open only during summer: The Delaware River Model Railroad Exhibit offers electric trains in action. Fort Delaware, now the Museum of the American Frontier, dramatizes life in the area between the French and Indian War and the American Revolution in its replica of a 1754 stockade. Snug Harbor is a collection of old country store furnishings and stock.

From Narrowsburg, the drive leads to Barryville, where the Delaware River White Water Canoe Regatta is staged in August, and where the Indian League of the Americas holds its annual powwow. Here also is the Eldred Preserve, a private fishing preserve and horseback riding area. From here the road moves along to Port Jervis, where three states meet. U.S.-6 and I–84 extend east into Middletown, the home of the

Orange County State Fair and the scene of an annual September Steer Roast held at the fairgrounds.

From Middletown it's a short run down the Quickway to Goshen, site of the oldest race track in America, dating back to 1838 when trotters were raced under saddle. Harness races are still held here on the afternoons of the first week in July. Nearby in a famous old stable is the Hall of Fame of the Trotter. The museum contains records, Currier and Ives prints, paintings and statues, dioramas of famous horses, and a library.

Warwick, pleasantly situated along a branch of the Wallkill River, has an interesting 1810 house with period furniture from Queen Anne to Duncan Phyfe, as well as an intriguing collection of sporting equipment, antique dolls, and flowering fruit trees. The Shingle House, a 1764 saltbox, has carriages and sleighs, plus interesting farm tools and machinery.

Monticello and the Resort Region

An alternative finish for the Hawks Nest Drive is to turn east at Callicoon onto Route 17B, which brings you into Monticello. The "Capital of the Mountains" boasts trotting races, an annual arts and crafts show on the courthouse green and Kutsher's Country Club resort. But there's a lot more in the Monticello area. Loch Sheldrake has a number of famous resorts, including Brown's and the Pines. Four trout ponds and a well-stocked 15-acre lake make for good fishing at Mountain Dale's Hey-Ru Trout Park, a private area where you don't need a license, but pay by the pound for fish caught. South Fallsburg has an outdoor art show and flea market in July, a classic car festival in September, and many fine resorts open all year.

A bit east are Ellenville, Kerhonkson, and Mohonk Lake. The area is full of trout streams and fine resorts. Ellenville, on U.S. 209, is the center of the Ulster County resort area. Another attraction is Ice Caves Moutain, 2,255 feet above sea level, with a view of five states and a host of scenic nature trails and rock formations. Ice Caves is open daily from April through November, 9 A.M. to dusk; 914–647–7989. Kerhonkson deserves mention as the site of the Merriman Dam and the Rondout Reservoir, an important part of the New York City water system. Mohonk Mountain House, an elegant resort in the Shawangunk Mountains (see *Hudson Valley* section), and nearby Lake Minnewaska, founded almost a century ago, are graced by natural wild gardens of glacier-polished rocks, delicately balanced boulders, wind-twisted pines, soft moss, mountain ferns, and bushes upon bushes of huckleberry, azalea, rhododendron, and laurel. It is a photographer's as well as a vacationer's dream come true.

PRACTICAL INFORMATION FOR THE CATSKILLS

WHEN TO GO. The Catskill resorts are a retreat all year round, with a full complement of activities indoor and out no matter what the weather is. Downhill skiing is available at Hunter Mountain so long as the temperature is cooperative—the mountain has extensive snow-making machinery; but cross-country trails at the hotels or on public grounds are more dependent on Mother Nature. Spring is pretty and generally quiet, though many people fill the kosher resorts for a week during the Jewish Passover holidays, usually in mid-April. Summer is the most bustling time, with hikers, rafters, grass skiers, and other "activists" taking to the great outdoors. Fall descends early—by late August the nights are chilly. But the fall foliage season, which can bring weekend traffic to a snarling halt, extends through early October.

HOW TO GET THERE. The most frequent **bus** service is to Monticello and Liberty, for the major hotels, or to Kingston and, in winter, Hunter Mountain. **Rail** service goes most conveniently to Poughkeepsie, Rhinecliff, Hudson, and points north via *Amtrak.* You'll need a car from there. Indeed, except for stays at the major hotels, which provide all services and activities, **driving** is the most convenient way to get around the Catskills. Among the preferred routes: the Gov. Thomas E. Dewey Thruway (I–87) runs between New York City and Albany. From the south, you can exit at Harriman for Rte. 17, known as the Quickway, which will take you directly to Monticello.

Kingston, approximately midway between New York City and Albany, is another popular gateway to the region. Those approaching from the northwest region of the state would pick up Rte. 28 at Oneonta.

TELEPHONES. The area code for most of the region is 914, though some towns to the northeast of Catskill State Park are 518, while those to the northwest could be 607. See the instructions on pay telephones for rates. Dial 911 in case of **emergency.**

ACCOMMODATIONS. Because of size alone, most Catskills visitors stay at the major resort hotels, some of which accommodate as many as 3,000 guests at a time. Rates at these hotels usually include breakfast, dinner, and often lunch as well as all activities. You pay extra only for alcohol and, sometimes, the bigger name entertainers. Rates also take into account the extent of activities and services available. Most of the resorts also have special packages for weekends and, particularly during ski or golf seasons, weekdays.

Motels are not abundant in the area, so it is important to have a reservation if you are traveling during a high traffic period—which is almost every weekend, and often on weekdays when skiing is good. Inns and bed-and-breakfasts can be found increasingly in the Catskills, but reservations well in advance are almost always a necessity. Depending on the area in which you will be spending your time, you may also be able to use lodging at gateway points such as Kingston and New Paltz.

One type of accommodation that is widely available is the campsite, though even these should be reserved ahead, if possible. The *I Love NY Camping* pamphlet from the state Tourist Bureau lists more than 5,000 sites in the Catskills alone. That pamphlet can be obtained from the State Division of Tourism, Department of Commerce, 1 Commerce Plaza, Albany, NY 12245.

Most major hotels accept credit cards, and those listed here that do not are so indicated. The rates given are based on double occupancy, and are arranged by community in the following categories: *Deluxe,* $100 and up; *Expensive,* $85–$100; *Moderate,* $45–$85; *Inexpensive,* less than $45. A few rent by the week under the American Plan, with meals included. These are so indicated.

CAIRO

Lange's Grove Side. *Moderate.* Rte. 23, 12405; 518–622–3393. 23-unit motel, outdoor pool, tennis.

Holiday House Motor Court. *Inexpensive.* Box 748, Rte. 145, 12413; 518–622–9704. Small motel with 13 units, outdoor pool. Open May–October. No credit cards.

CALLICOON

Villa Roma, *Moderate–Expensive.* RD1, 12723; 914–887–4880. A resort famous for its early Roman theme carried throughout the complex which includes 223 air-conditioned rooms plus time-sharing apartments. The resort has an indoor pool and two outdoor pools. Restaurant, entertainment and dancing.

CATSKILL

Carl's Rip Van Winkle. *Inexpensive–Moderate.* Box 45, Star Rte. 1, 12414; 518–943–3303. 30 cottages, additional motel rooms, open April–October only. Outdoor pool, some kitchen units.

Catskill Motor Lodge. *Inexpensive–Moderate.* Rte 23B, 12414; 518–943–5800. 70-plus rooms; outdoor pool; restaurant.

Red Ranch. *Inexpensive–Moderate.* Box 216, RD1, 12414; 518–678–3380. 39 room motel; outdoor pool. $30–$50 off-season, higher during ski and summer seasons.

DELHI

Buena Vista Motel. *Inexpensive.* Route 18, 13753; 607–746–2136. Standard motel with 30 rooms.

ELKA PARK

Redcoat's Return. *Moderate.* Dale Lane, Platte Clove, 12427; 518–589–9858. 14-room inn, five with bath; breakfast included. Convenient to Hunter Mountain, other ski areas. Two-night minimum winter weekends; three nights on holidays. Closed end of October to before Thanksgiving, and March–Memorial Day.

ELLENVILLE

Nevele. *Moderate–Expensive.* U.S. 209, 12428; 914–647–6000. 450 rooms; Kosher menu (breakfast and dinner included); night tennis, golf (greens fees extra), four pools, private lake, ice rink, health club, entertainment. Two-night weekend minimum.

FREEHOLD

Pleasant View Lodge. *Moderate–Expensive.* Gayhead Road, 12431; 518–634 –2523. Breakfast and dinner included. Tennis, golf (greens fees extra), health club, entertainment some nights. 130-plus units in cabins and lodges.

GREENVILLE

Greenville Arms. *Inexpensive–Moderate.* South Street, 12083; 518–966–5219. A Victorian country inn with 19 guest rooms and 13 baths. Rates include breakfast and dinner, with dinner limited to a single entree per night. Closed November 1–May 1. No credit cards.

KERHONKSON

Granit. *Deluxe.* 12446; 914–626–3141. 300 rooms; indoor and outdoor pools, tennis, golf (greens fees extra), ice rink, health club, entertainment.

KIAMESHA LAKE

Concord. *Expensive–Deluxe.* 12751; 914–794–4000. The largest of the Catskill resorts, with 1,250 rooms and dining rooms that accommodate 3,000 at a sitting. There's a registered nurse in charge of the nursery, which will take care of newborns to three-year-olds, and various programs for older children and teens. Indoor and outdoor pools, tennis, golf (greens fees extra), health club, entertainment, skiing, etc. Rates include all meals; weekly and family rates available.

LOCH SHELDRAKE

Brown's. *Moderate.* Rte. 52, 12759; 914–434–5151. It takes 17 buildings to house the 570 rooms available here. Open April–November only. Tennis, nearby golf, indoor and outdoor pools, roller rink, day camp for kids, special teen program. Kosher food. Weekly rates available.

MONTICELLO

Kutsher's Country Club. *Moderate–Expensive.* Anawana Lake Road, 12701; 914–794–6000. Medium-sized—by Catskill standards—resort with 375 rooms and all the accoutrements common to the breed, including three pools, whirlpool, summer and winter sports, entertainment, health club, and ice skating rink. Weekly rates higher during the fall Jewish holidays and lower the rest of the year.

Holiday Mountain Motor Lodge. *Moderate.* Rte. 17, Rockhill, NY 12775; 914–796–3000. 70-room motel with pool, some steambaths.

PINE HILL

Pine Hill Arms. *Inexpensive.* 12462; 914–254–9811. 35 rooms all with private bath. Weekend rate with meals available. No credit cards.

ROUND TOP

Winter Clove Inn. *Inexpensive–Moderate.* Winter Clove Rd., 12473; 518–622 –3267. Features Colonial architecture located on 400 acres. Double rooms include all meals. Tennis, nine holes of golf, bowling. 50 units in the main inn, plus motel.

Pickwick Lodge. *Inexpensive.* Winter Clove Rd., 12473; 518–662–3364. About 45 rooms, plus tennis, driving range, and private stocked fish pond. By the week only. Open Apr. 1–Nov. 1.

SHANDAKEN

Shandaken Inn. *Moderate–Expensive.* 12480; 914–688–5100. A very personal inn with 12 individually decorated guest rooms, each with private bath. Rates include breakfast and dinner. Guests are expected to stay for the weekend—the inn is closed weekdays and in April and November. No children; no credit cards.

Auberge des 4 Saison. *Inexpensive.* Rte. 42, 12480; 914–688–2223. 36 rooms (half with private bath). Unfancy inn-like accommodations in the main house, plus a chalet-style motel. Rates include breakfast and dinner.

Copper Hood. *Inexpensive.* Rte. 28, 12480; 914–688–9962. Medium-sized inn with 23 rooms. Indoor pool, sauna, tennis, canoeing. Double occupancy rates include all meals. No credit cards.

SOUTH FALLSBURG

Pines. *Moderate.* 12779; 914–434–6000. 400 rooms, three pools, indoor and outdoor tennis, skiing, roller rink, health club, entertainment.

SWAN LAKE

Stevensville Country Club. *Inexpensive.* 12783; 914–292–8000; in New York City, 212–736–1874. Indoor and outdoor pools and tennis, golf, racquetball, and handball, ice and roller skating, health club, and entertainment. Rates per person include all meals.

TANNERSVILLE

Eggery Inn. *Moderate.* County Rd. 16, 12485; 518–589–5363. 13-room (10 with private bath) bed-and-breakfast that serves dinner Saturday nights and has a panoramic view of Hunter Mountain. Weekend rates include Saturday dinner. Closed April and first two weeks of November.

Washington Irving Lodge. *Inexpensive–Moderate.* Rte. 23A, 12485; 518–589–5560. 28 rooms (five with private bath). Open July and August, and November–April plus some holiday weekends. No credit cards.

Greene Mountain View Inn. *Inexpensive.* Church and South Main Sts., 12485; 518–589–5511. Essentially a ski lodge, but open all year round. Rates include breakfast and private bath. Buffet dinners are available.

WEST KILL

Marie's Dream House. *Inexpensive–Moderate.* Rte. 42, 12492; 518–989–6565. 16 rooms, all with private bath, in lodge-style atmosphere. Rates include breakfast. Restaurant offers Austrian cuisine. No credit cards.

WINDHAM

Windham Arms. *Inexpensive.* Rte. 23, 12496; 518–734–3000. 70-room motel with tennis, golf privileges (greens fees extra), entertainment. Weekly rates available; rates for doubles include breakfast and dinner. No credit cards.

HINTS TO THE MOTORIST. During ski season, you'll want snow tires or chains—they're mandatory on many roads. You might also want to carry some rock salt, a light shovel, a brush, and maybe a can of spray defroster for opening the door lock or speeding the removal of ice from your windshield. Just remember to keep such items where you can get at them.

TOURIST INFORMATION. The various county chambers of commerce and public information offices have reams of information on resorts, activities and lodging alternatives. Try the *Delaware County Chamber of Commerce,* 56 Main St., Delhi, NY 13753 (in N.Y. 800–356–5615; in other northeast states, 800–642–4433); *Greene County Promotion Dept.,* Box 527, Catskill, NY 12414 (518–943–3223); *Sullivan County Office of Public Information,* County Government Center, Monticello, NY 12701 (914–794–3000 or toll free in N.Y. 800–882–CATS; out of state 800–343–INFO); *Ulster County Public Information Office,* County Office Building, Box 1800, Kingston, NY 12401 (914–331–9300). The region is also brimming with vineyards and wineries; for information, contact the Hudson River Region Wine Council, 72 Main St., Cold Spring, NY 10516.

SENIOR CITIZENS DISCOUNTS. Some of the resorts may offer special rates for seniors, and most will accommodate special menu needs.

HINTS TO THE DISABLED. At least parts of most of the resorts are wheelchair accessible. Check with the resort or with an agency listed in the *Facts at Your Fingertips* chapter in the front of this book.

PARKS. Much of what is known as the Catskills lies within the bounds of Catskill State Park, which includes numerous ski areas and the Ashokan and Rondout reservoirs, and borders on the Delaware River.

PARTICIPANT SPORTS. There is little you can't do in the Catskills. **Hiking** and **skiing** (downhill and cross country) are among the favorites, the latter to be found at Hunter, Windham, Belleayre, Big Indian, and elsewhere. But add some 35 **golf** courses, scores of **tennis** courts, indoor and outdoor **pools** at all of the resorts and many of the larger inns and lodges, **tobogganing, ice and roller skating, horseback riding, snowmobiles, bicycling, and boating.** If we've left anything out, ask at one of the resorts—they'll probably be able to guide you to the right place. Or get a copy of the *I Love NY Camping* booklet from the State Division of Tourism, Department of Commerce, 1 Commerce Plaza, Albany, NY 12245.

Those with a strong interest in sports can do no better than signing on at one of the resorts, given that most fees (with the occasional exception of greens and tennis fees) are included in the standard rates. Skiers can often get special packages—most advantageous during the week, of course, but worth investigating for weekends as well—that include lift tickets and/or equipment rentals. Such deals are available at lodges and inns as well as at the resorts. Those inclined toward independent sports such as bicycling won't need the full array of resort offerings.

CHILDREN'S ACTIVITIES. The *Catskill Game Farm,* 518–678–9595, and *Carson City,* 518–678–5518, both on Rte. 32 in the Catskill-Cairo area, are favorites for children. Most of the resorts have excellent programs for kids of all ages (some even have nurseries for the very young)—as well as baby sitting or baby monitoring service. (Baby monitoring is where someone goes to each room periodically to check that the child is sleeping or all right.) The resorts also usually have special wading and children's pools. Elsewhere, children might enjoy *Rip Van Winkle's home* in Palenville, 518–943–6559 and *Fort Delaware* on Rte. 97 along the Delaware, 914–252–6660.

HISTORIC SITES. The Museum of the American Frontier at Fort Delaware on Rte. 97, 914–252–6660, features a replica of a mid–18th century stockade and focuses on life between the French and Indian War and the American Revolution.

MUSEUMS. The *Zadock Pratt Museum,* Rte. 23A in Prattsville, 518–299–3395, commemorates the industrialist Zadock Pratt and his contributions to the area. The *Thomas Cole Home,* 218 Spring St., Catskill, 518–943–6533, is a museum honoring the founder of the so-called Hudson River School of painting. The home of naturalist *John Burroughs* is in Roxbury, 607–492–1756, and is sometimes open to the public; near the home is his Boyhood Rock. Delhi's *Delaware County Historical Museum,* 607–746–3849, displays early farm tools and a country schoolhouse. And the *Hall of Fame of the Trotter,* 240 Main St., Goshen, 914–294–6330, housed in an old stable, has exhibits and a library. Next door is the *Goshen Historic Track,* the oldest harness track in America.

DINING OUT. For the most part, you'll probably want to eat where you're staying in the Catskills. At the major resorts, where meals are included in the price—usually with box lunches—that's the natural way to go. A note, though, on the major resorts: some, as noted in the *Accommodations* section above, offer only kosher food under orthodox supervision. Others tend to be kosher-style. And often, quantity is equated with quality, which can be fun if you're determined to try one of everything over a three-day weekend. (We wouldn't recommend finishing everything on every plate—you'll see why.) Haute cuisine this is not; hearty and ample it is.

Most of the inns and lodges in the area serve home-style meals, either with one entree each evening or buffet style. As at the resorts, meal time becomes an opportunity for meeting people—a more intimate opportunity (albeit with less variety in people and food) at inns and lodges. Almost all of the places that offer lodging and meals will accept non-guests for dinner, but reservations are always required, whether at the resorts or at the smaller establishments. Indeed, some of the inns are more reputed for their dining than for their accommodations; these are singled out below.

Of course there are other restaurants, diners, and fast fooderies; to find them, just head for the town's main street. Generally, if fine dining is high on your list of priorities, you will have the most options in the Hudson Valley (or New York City). The places listed here will average $15–$25 per person plus drinks, taxes, and tip. Some offer children's portions at reduced rates, while ordering one course a la carte or sharing some dishes can bring the price of a meal down.

Reservations are recommended in all cases. Abbreviations for credit cards are: AE, American Express, D, Diners Club; MC, MasterCard; and V, Visa.

CATSKILL

Harbor Lights. Greene St.; 518–943–5500. Fresh seafood, with outdoor tables in summer. AE, D, MC, V.

La Rive. Old King's Road (County Rd. 47); 518–943–4888. French food in a farmhouse setting. Dinner daily except Mondays, open Sundays from 1:30 P.M. Open May–November. No credit cards.

ELKA PARK

Redcoat's Return. Dale Lane; 518–589–6379. The accent is decidedly British, but very homey. Dinner only. Closed end of October–Thanksgiving, and March–Memorial Day. AE, D, MC, V.

GLENFORD

Le Refuge du Lac. Maverick Road; 914–657–8934. French country cooking with an accent on game in season. Dinner daily.

MT. TREMPER

La Duchesse Ann. 4 Miller Rd.; 914–688–5260. Classic French, with a creperie next door. Dinner only; closed Tuesdays and Wednesdays. MC, V.

SHANDAKEN

Auberge des 4 Saisons. Route 42; 914–688–2223. Obviously French, and one of the better choices in the region. All major credit cards.

TANNERSVILLE

Chateau Belleview. Rte. 23A, between Hunter and Tannersville; 518–589–5525. Seafood prepared French style is the specialty. Dinner only; closed mid-May, mid-October. All major credit cards.

WINDHAM

La Griglia. Rte. 296; 518–734–4499. American and continental fare, specializing in fresh game. Dinner only, daily in summer, daily except Mondays in winter, and Thursdays–Sundays in spring and fall. All major credit cards.

Windham Arms. Rte. 23; 518–734–3000. Breakfast and dinner in slightly formal atmosphere. Open daily. No credit cards.

ARTS AND ENTERTAINMENT. The major resorts have big name entertainment most weekends—comedians, musical comedy stars, and pop singers are the most popular. Many also feature dancing to both live bands and records.

THE NORTH COUNTRY

by
PHILIP C. and BRIGITTE JOHNSON

The Johnsons live in Saratoga County. Phil's articles on North Country topics have appeared in such publications as Sports Illustrated, Field & Stream, Skiing, New York Alive, *and* The Conservationist. *His wife, Brigitte, has been a North Country explorer since coming to the region from her native Germany in the mid-1960s.*

Name another place in America where you can catch native brook trout for breakfast, raft down whitewater rapids at midday, attend a major stakes horse race in the afternoon, enjoy haute cuisine for dinner, hear a major symphony orchestra live in the evening, and bed down under the stars that night by a wilderness brook where you'll try for a repeat on the trout in the morning.

Stretching north from the Hudson and Mohawk rivers to the St. Lawrence and east to west from Lake Champlain to Lake Ontario, New York's North Country is one of the largest, most all-encompassing leisure/recreation areas in the United States. It includes Saratoga Springs, America's "Queen of Spas," the six-million-acre Adirondack Park featuring the largest wilderness area east of the Mississippi River, and the Champlain and St. Lawrence valleys, their once strategic waterways now popular vacation draws.

It is an area where people come to be seen, especially at Saratoga in summer, when the New York City Ballet and Philadelphia Orchestra are in residence and where the finest thoroughbreds run in August. It is also an area for those people who don't wish to be seen at all. More than one million acres of land in the Adirondacks are officially designated "forever wild" and for those who prefer the long haul, the Northville–Lake Placid Trail is a 7–10-day hike that crosses just three paved roads in 132 miles.

Accessible by Highways

Ever since the New York State Thruway was completed in the late 1940s, and especially since I–87 from Albany to the Canadian border was built in the 1960s, what was once a refuge for the rich and the determined has become easily accessible to the general public. Even so, much of the territory retains its primeval character due to the state constitution's restrictions on development in the Adirondacks.

Although the North Country is roughly twice the size of Massachusetts, there are no large cities. What population centers exist are located on the fringes: Saratoga Springs, Glens Falls, Plattsburgh, Massena, Ogdensburg, and the largest, Watertown, with some 35,000 residents. In between is rugged, lake-studded territory left behind when the last glaciers receded some 20,000 years ago. Geologically, the area is not part of the Appalachians, but rather of the Laurentian Plateau that fans out northward through Canada. The mountains provide a watershed for both the St. Lawrence and the Hudson Rivers.

The combination of harsh climate and relatively barren soil made most of the region inhospitable to settlement. Indians used it primarily for trapping, hunting, and fishing. The territory was first spotted by Europeans in 1535 when Jacques Cartier and his party looked south to the Adirondacks from Mt. Royal in what is now Montreal. The French explorer Samuel de Champlain is credited with being the first white man to visit the area, naming the beautiful lake he reached in 1609 after himself. On that trip, he earned a lasting enemy for France when he killed two Iroquois chiefs with a single shot from his harquebus. To the south, Dutch traders established an outpost at Ft. Orange (now Albany) in 1624. Apart from the occasional white trader or trapper, however, the North Country by and large remained Indian territory through most of the 18th century. The dominant tribe in the region were the Algonquins who, because they lived and hunted in the forests, were given the derisive name "Adirondacks"—bark eaters or tree eaters—by their enemy, the Iroquois.

Decisive Revolutionary Actions

The British had gained control of the Dutch-held territories in 1664, and from the early 1700s through the War of 1812 the North Country was of great strategic importance. In the French and Indian War, there were battles at Ticonderoga and at Lake George. The first American victory in the Revolution took place at Ft. Ticonderoga in 1775 and a little more than a year later, Benedict Arnold led a flotilla of ships in America's first naval battle off Valcour Island on Lake Champlain. What many historians view as the decisive action of the revolution took place in 1777 when colonial troops, irregulars, and Indian allies stopped the advance of a British army sweeping south from Canada in two battles at Saratoga. In the War of 1812, there were numerous skirmishes in the Champlain and St. Lawrence valleys and significant naval engagements on Lake Ontario and at Plattsburgh Bay.

Because the bulk of the territory was unsuited for farming, even the promise of free land with no taxes for seven years could not lure more than a handful of veterans to the area after the American Revolution. Although much of the territory had been bought by speculators in the late 18th century, the interior remained largely unexplored. It was not until 1837 that the first ascent of Mt. Marcy was reported and New Yorkers for the first time realized that Adirondack peaks were higher than those in the Catskills.

Artists, philosophers, and poets romanticized the wilderness during the period but development in most of the region in the 19th century was tied to lumber, paper, and mining industries. The unchecked consumption of raw material ravaged the land, and by the middle of the century there was already a lively debate on land use and protection. In 1885, the state legislature passed the law creating the Adirondack Forest Preserve, the basis of a century of natural resources preservation in the region.

Legislated "Forever Wild"

Much of the impetus for that legislation and the adoption 10 years later of what has become known as the "Forever Wild" statute of New York's constitution came from wealthy down-staters who did not want to see the wilderness character of their vacation area spoiled. Many of these people were introduced to the North Country through Saratoga Springs. By the time of the Civil War, this was a popular resort, the appeal of its famed mineral water baths enhanced by its gambling casinos and a sparkling new race course.

Frequented by colorful visitors such as Diamond Jim Brady and Bet-a-Million Gates, Saratoga Springs was the premier place for flash and fancy in the United States. For others of means who preferred their pleasures more subdued, it was the period for the development of the so-called Great Camps in the Adirondacks and many of the grand vacation homes in the Thousand Islands. A good rail system that had developed to support commerce also brought in tourists. This was the era of the great hotels and virtually every lake from Old Forge to Essex had its grand salon.

Indians introduced whites to the spa baths in the 18th century, and in the late 19th century, the mountain air was recognized for its curative powers. Dr. Edward L. Trudeau founded the Trudeau Sanatorium at Saranac Lake in 1885, and 10 years later, Melvil Dewey (inventor of the Dewey Decimal System) opened his famous Lake Placid Club as a refuge from the dirty air of New York City. Dewey's son Godfrey was the moving force behind the selection of Lake Placid as host for the 1932 Winter Olympics; as a result, this small Adirondack village,

Points of Interest

1) Adirondack Museum
2) Eisenhower Locks
3) Fort Drum Military Reservation
4) Ft. Ticonderoga
5) Mt. Marcy
6) Saratoga Battlefield
7) Saratoga National Historic Park
8) Thousand Islands
9) Whiteface Mountain

permanent population 2,800, has been an international winter sports capital ever since.

The region has changed considerably since World War II. Mining activity in the Adirondacks decreased sharply in the 1950s, and the lumber and paper industries declined, too. Federal investigations headed by Senator Estes Kefauver put an end to gambling in Saratoga at about the same time. While this was occurring, a modern road system was being established and cars and vacationers were becoming commonplace. The outcome has been the development of tourism as the core of the economy throughout the region.

The North Country is vast, and because of its size, natural resources, and restricted development, it will always appeal to those who appreciate the outdoors. At the same time, it is not a frontier. There are facilities and attractions enough to suit the most sophisticated adult or cantankerous child. Few places can boast such variety.

SARATOGA HISTORY

To understand Saratoga's history, think furs, fights, fun, and fast horses.

Named "Saragthogue" (Place of Swift Waters) by the Iroquois, this gateway to New York's North Country is defined by water—its boundaries by the Hudson and Mohawk Rivers, and its cachet by the mineral springs from which flows its name—"America's Queen of Spas."

The abundant water was particularly suited to the beaver, which once flourished in the area. To support European fashion demands, beaver pelts brought the best prices from 17th- and 18th-century traders who especially liked the rich, full fur from animals who had been raised on the mineral water in the Saratoga area. The natural effervescence of the water also was valued for its curative powers. According to one story, the Iroquois brought the Crown Superintendent of Indian Affairs, Sir William Johnson, to the area for the cure in 1771.

British Strategy Backfires

The visit of General Burgoyne and his British army during the American Revolution six years later did not end so comfortably. The English strategy was to split the colonies by marching an army south from Canada to meet up at Albany with another army marching north from New York City and a third force marching east through the Mohawk Valley. Things didn't work out that way. The British army in New York City instead moved to Philadelphia, and the advance from the west was stopped at Oriskany. Burgoyne was left to face the Americans alone.

The campaign had begun well. Heading south in June, Burgoyne's army of 9,000, including Loyalists, Indians, and German mercenaries, easily recaptured Ft. Ticonderoga and Skenesborough (Whitehall). Then, the trouble began. Burgoyne insisted on hauling artillery and heavy wagons (including those carrying his supply of champagne) through trackless wilderness. His transport problems were complicated by the Americans' harassing tactics, including a scorched-earth policy that left little for the British army to forage. Making things worse for the British were two ill-conceived expeditions to Bennington, Vermont, which met stiff opposition.

Battle of Saratoga

Rather than withdraw his weakened army to Ticonderoga to wait for reinforcements, Burgoyne chose to go ahead, cross the Hudson, and face the Americans who held the high grounds at Bemis Heights. The first Battle of Saratoga took place on September 19, 1777. It was a confrontation between formal European tactics and American frontier fighting with the colonists taking a tremendous toll on Burgoyne's officers, who were leading the lines of troops in the open field. The battle was officially a draw, but with dwindling manpower and supply problems, Burgoyne's situation was deteriorating.

By early October, with hopes for reinforcements fading, the British army, now numbering about 5,000, faced an American force of some 11,000 under General Horatio Gates. The second battle took place October 7 and what at first was a standoff turned into an American victory when Col. Benedict Arnold rallied the troops and carried the day. For Arnold, heroism in the North Country was old hat by then. In 1776 the flotilla he raised at Skenesborough faced the British fleet at Valcour Island on Lake Champlain and created enough havoc to delay the invasion by a year. Arnold was also instrumental in the American victory at Oriskany and in colonial successes in the first Saratoga battle.

Despite the defeat, Burgoyne's retreat was slow, he was surrounded by the Americans and forced to surrender. Many historians believe the actions leading to Burgoyne's surrender were the turning point of the war. News of the British defeat was the prod needed for the hesitant French to help the Americans openly, and soon after, the Spanish and the Dutch followed suit. This foreign aid played a major part in the eventual American victory.

Postwar Development

Saratoga's development after the war was rapid. Mills sprung up throughout the area and as the population grew, it seemed natural that services would follow. One mill owner, Gideon Putnam, opened an inn and tavern at Saratoga in 1803, marking the beginning of what would be a remarkable century for the spa. The railroad came in 1832, bringing more and more people to town, many of whom found the United States Hotel across the street from the station just right for their stay. The mineral springs and nearby Saratoga Lake with its steamboat cruises and frequent concerts were the major draws, at least until Ben Schribner came along. In 1842, he opened Saratoga's first gambling parlor.

Within a generation, gambling surpassed the baths as the number one tourist attraction. In 1863 the Saratoga Racing Association was formed, and a year later the race course was opened. By that time the United States Hotel had been joined by two others, Congress Hall and the Grand Union—the dining rooms seated more than 1,000 at one time and full verandas out front were perfect spots for guests to sport their finery.

During the 1870s, gambling reached new heights when John "Old Smoke" Morrissey, an ex-champion boxer with questionable connections, opened Saratoga's second casino right near the hotels. It set the stage for folks such as Diamond Jim Brady, who in 1896 traveled to Saratoga with 27 houseboys in tow and daily changes of jewelry. Brady's companion, the actress Lillian Russell, pedaled around Saratoga on a gold-plated bicycle.

Reform Wins Out

Inevitably, the everything-goes spirit ran into the social reform movement, and in the early years of the 20th century the social reformers won out. Richard Canfield, who by then owned the casino, objected to restrictions placed on his operation and grew so frustrated that in 1908 he closed the place down. Three years later it became part of a village park. A crackdown on bookmaking even closed the racing seasons in 1911 and 1912. But gambling, while battered, was not beaten. The track was back in 1913 and in 1919 it gained a lasting spot in sports lore when a horse named "Upset" beat the great "Man o' War." It was the first in a long series of racing upsets at the flats that earned the Saratoga track the reputation as "the graveyard of favorites."

While the sporting life was making a comeback, there were other developments as well. The Saratoga Springs Reservation was created by New York State in 1909 and the baths, eclipsed in the Golden Era and generally in bad shape, were restored. Skidmore College was founded, and Yaddo, the artists' and writers' retreat, was established.

The proliferation of the automobile made Saratoga more accessible than ever, but that development also helped end an era. People were no longer bound to town, and when the race track was closed summers during World War II, the United States Hotel never reopened. Within 10 years, the Grand Union Hotel closed, too. Gambling was under renewed attack by then and was ended in the early 1950s because of the pressure generated by the Kefauver hearings in Washington, D.C.

By the late 1950s, Saratoga was on the ropes. But in the past 25 years, it has made a remarkable comeback.

EXPLORING SARATOGA SPRINGS

Saratoga Springs is a two-season town: August, and the rest of the year. August, of course, refers to the four-week racing season at the century-old race track on Union Avenue. The best thoroughbreds in America come each summer, many for the Travers, the oldest race in the country and generally considered the "fourth leg" of the triple crown. Many of the horses were once yearlings for market at the annual

Fasig-Tipton sale, which takes place the second week of the race meet. One yearling sold for $4.6 million in 1984.

People coming to Saratoga Springs in August can expect to pay premium prices for their pleasures. A hotel room which may run $35–$50 the rest of the year will be gobbled up at three times that amount during "the flats." Menu prices soar, too. Even New York State gets into the act, raising the price at the Roosevelt and Lincoln baths from $9 to $13 for the 90-minute soak, rubdown, and rest while wrapped in warm sheets.

Culture Plays Strong Role

Today the place is alive not only in August, but 12 months a year. The catalyst for this renaissance was the development in the mid-1960s of the Saratoga Performing Arts Center (SPAC), a sparkling amphitheater on the grounds of the 2,000-acre Saratoga State Park just south of town. Today SPAC is the summer home of the New York City Ballet, the Philadelphia Orchestra, the New York City Opera, a procession of concerts featuring popular performers ranging from the Grateful Dead to Willie Nelson to Tina Turner, and the Newport Jazz Festival in July. With the arts and thoroughbreds, could activities such as polo and parties be far away? Of course not. World class polo is played in town in August and the schedule of parties is a century-old tradition. The annual Whitney bash on the eve of the Whitney Stakes keeps society columns filled for weeks.

At about the time the Performing Arts Center was being built, I-87, the Aridondack Northway, was being completed. As a result, Saratoga Springs has become part bedroom community for the Albany area. That has meant an influx of young professionals to the area and the impact has been substantial. The residential areas in town have been gentrified with many of the fine old homes restored. A walk through the downtown area today is a pleasant stroll. Broadway, is spruced up from the casino (now the historical museum) and Congress Park at the south end to the new Ramada Renaissance Hotel and Conference Center at the north end. The downtown is characterized by small shops and boutiques plus an exceptional number of fine restaurants. On one 50-yard stretch along Phila Street off Broadway, there are five restaurants all worth trying, plus the legendary Caffe Lena, which features young folk artists. Don McLean was an unknown performing there in the early 1970s.

Tribute to Racing

While the thoroughbred track is open in August only, the National Museum of Racing and Thoroughbred Hall of Fame across Union Avenue is open year round. Just a bit farther along is the artists' and writers' retreat, Yaddo. The grounds of the 400-acre estate, including the beautifully sculptured gardens, are open to the public. Continuing east out of town is the road to Saratoga Lake. Although Saratoga Lake no longer has the sparkle and activity of a century ago, it still attracts sportsmen remains an exceptional fishing spot.

With all the attention given the flat track, sometimes overlooked is the Saratoga Harness Track less than a mile to the south. The harness track is a clean, first-rate facility with an attractive clubhouse overlooking the course that serves good meals. Racing is held during several months of the year, including mid-winter.

The Saratoga State Park nearby is more than the Performing Arts Center and the baths. It also features an excellent 18-hole golf course, tennis courts, and a Victorian swimming pool with its Greek revival colonnade. All are open to the public. The Gideon Putnam Hotel is also on the park property, and is a grand dame of a place. The Gideon's popular Sunday brunch can be particularly enjoyable in winter when combined with cross country skiing on the park grounds. Also on the grounds, but at the other end of the Avenue of the Pines is a quarter-mile speed skating oval, a busy spot for training and regular competitions in winter.

Tour Starts at Track

A Saratoga visitor should do "the route" at least once on an August day. It begins at 7 A.M. with breakfast at the track. Choose the terrace if possible so you can keep an eye on the field and the people. The clubhouse some mornings will attract more than 1,000 diners, so get there early. For breakfast, be sure to order a melon, one of those from the Hand farm in nearby Greenwich which ripens in August and around track time has become a tradition with Saratoga folk. If you finish in time, take a tour of the back stretch for a close look at the horses and horsemen.

From the track walk down Union Avenue and Circular Street past the Victorian homes to the downtown. A whole host of stops can be made there, including Congress Park with its Canfield Casino, now a museum. A handy pocket guide and tourist map published by the Chamber of Commerce is widely available. Don't miss the Regent Street Antique Center, an old theater on Regent Street which is home base for 25 antique dealers. For a break, try one of Saratoga's famous front porches. The one upstairs at the restored Adelphi Hotel on Broadway is an excellent choice for people-watching.

Racing at the flats starts at 1:30 P.M., with the 9-race card running until about 6 P.M. Since we're in dress or tie-and-jacket on this trip, the extra dollar for a clubhouse ticket gives us access to all facilities.

After the races, celebrate success or tear up tickets at the Spuyten Duyvil, followed by dinner at Siro's, two spots closeby that, like the track, operate only in August. After dinner, wind down over a glass of Saratoga mineral water by the piano bar at the Ash Grove Inn, just west of town on Rte. 9N. The day hasn't been cheap, but as Edna Ferber said in her novel *Saratoga Trunk,* "There is nothing like it in the whole country."

Historic Sites

There are other spots of particular interest in the Saratoga area. A must is the Saratoga Battlefield in Stillwater–Schuylerville, eight miles to the east on Rtes. 4 and 32. Maintained and staffed by the National Park Service and featuring an interpretive center and the period Schuyler House nearby, it offers a fascinating look back on the events and participants in the Battle of Saratoga. The entire area is filled with the history of the period. For instance, Whitehall, 30 miles farther north on Rtes. 4 and 22 is where Benedict Arnold launched the ships of America's first flotilla and sailed off on Lake Champlain to battle the British at Valcour in 1776. The "Birthplace of the American Navy" is celebrated in town at the Skenesborough Museum.

Water of another sort was crucial to 19th-century development at the southern end of the county, 15 miles from Saratoga Springs. The Erie Canal made the Mohawk River passable to east-west commerce in 1825. Some of the original locks remain at Vischer Ferry in an area that is also a nature preserve. For a look at the canal today, an interesting spot is "the flight," five adjacent locks that bring boats around Cohoes Falls and into the system at Waterford, the town where the Mohawk and Hudson rivers meet. For years the Hudson River as it passed through the Saratoga area and on south flooded the countryside each spring. In 1931, the Sacandaga Reservoir was completed and water flow in the Hudson was controlled. Today, the 29-mile reservoir is a first-rate summer recreation area that boasts the largest northern pike ever caught in North America, a 46-pounder. Today, releases of water from the reservoir provide exciting whitewater rafting all summer long on the Sacandaga River where it runs into the Hudson at the town of Hadley, 15 miles north of Saratoga Springs on Rte. 9N.

ADIRONDACKS HISTORY

Artists, philosophers, and poets extolled its virtues, but the first person to popularize the Adirondacks was the Boston minister and temperance lecturer William H. H. Murray, author of the 1869 book *Adventures in the Wilderness.* It was in the bookstores no more than a few weeks when the rush to the North Country began. Not only did Murray publicize the place as refreshment for the body and spirit ("The air which you there inhale is such as can be found only in high mountain regions, pure, rarified and bracing.") but he also gave explicit instructions on how to get there and what to bring along. "Adirondack" Murray later voiced doubts about the incursion of civilized activity into his beloved wilderness, but by then, and in large part due to his efforts, the Adirondacks had become fashionable for city people who wanted to get away from it all.

Until the 19th century, the Adirondacks was a place for transients; Indians, soldiers, trappers, and loggers. During the French and Indian Wars and the American Revolution, the fighting in the region, while crucial to the outcome of both conflicts, was confined to the Champlain Valley. The wilderness interior made for good spy routes, but little else. However the Adirondacks were valuable as a bargaining chip. The colonists, in return for assistance against the British, promised to honor the Oneida Iroquois claim to some 4½ million acres in the region. The

Oneidas agreed to the deal, but then received less than a penny an acre when New York appropriated the land right after the war. The state, in need of money shortly thereafter, turned around and sold the land for 8 cents an acre to Alexander McComb in 1791. What McComb and other speculators guessed was that the region would be a part of the young country's westward expansion.

Beaver Trapping Exploited

But unlike the Appalachians where this was the pattern, it didn't happen in the Adirondacks. Those who attempted to settle were, as historian Alfred Donaldson noted, "overwhelmed by the odds of arctic climate, barren soil, and virtual isolation." Even trapping became inhospitable as European demand thinned out the beaver population so much that by 1830 only 300 of the animals were estimated to be left in the state.

As over-trapping cost the trapper his business in New York, similar excess by lumbermen in Maine brought development of a major new industry to the Adirondacks in the 19th century. As early as 1806, the New York legislature declared some waterways as "public highways," permitting lumbermen to cut deep in the woods, sending the logs down streams into the Hudson River and on to the mills at Glens Falls. With the completion of the Champlain Canal in 1824, markets in Canada were opened and a year later the west became reachable via the new Erie Canal. The canals brought new commercial opportunities. But settlers now passed directly to the fertile plains in the west, ending the land rush dreams of the original Adirondack speculators.

Effects of Lumbering

Lumbermen roamed free in the Adirondacks, buying up cheap land, logging it heavily, then abandoning it to the state for taxes. Trees were consumed for lumber, for paper, and for charcoal to fuel the kilns at the mines which had sprung up throughout the Adirondacks. Geologists had originally hoped to find gold, silver, or coal in the region, but what they found instead was high-quality iron ore. Deforestation was the price of supporting these mines, at least until coal and better rail operations helped reduce consumption after 1860. Inevitably, those whose livelihood depended upon lumbering clashed with those who valued the wilderness.

Ebenezer Emmons, on assignment from the New York State Legislature in 1837, was the first person to catalogue the interior of the region, giving the mountains the name "Adirondacks" in the process. Given the spirit of westward expansion throughout the country, many people were surprised to discover for the first time that such a wilderness still existed in the Northeast. The discovery was especially welcome, because at this time Thoreau and others were reacting against the industrial revolution.

"Grand Parks" Plan Boosted

In 1864, an editorial in the *New York Times* called for the Adirondacks to become "grand parks" which "in spite of all the din and the dust of furnaces and foundries . . . will furnish abundant seclusion for all time to come." Enter Verplank Colvin, member of a prominent New York family and an ardent believer in maintaining the wilderness character of the North Country. While serving as superintendent of a state topographical survey of the Adirondacks, he frequently called for the establishment of a preserve on the model of California's Yosemite. In the end, those concerned with the watershed and forest management, those inspired by the creation of Yellowstone National Park, and those who just wanted their own share of the wilderness protected were successful.

In 1885, the Adirondack Forest Preserve governing state land was established. The so-called "blue line" setting the boundaries of the Adirondacks region was presented in 1891, and a year later the Adirondack Park—state and private land—was established by law. In 1894, an article was added to the state constitution—the "forever wild" clause protecting New York's wilderness areas from further encroachment.

Artists', Writers' Impressions

The wilderness character of the Adirondacks had many patrons. The prominent artist Charles Cromwell Ingham was with the Emmons party in 1837 and painted the *Great Adirondacks Pass*. Ralph Waldo Emerson's poem "The Adirondacks" was based on an expedition he and a group of notables made to Philosophers' Camp on Follensby Pond in 1858. Seneca Ray Stoddard documented the times and places with his photography. James Fenimore Cooper's *Last of the Mohicans* featured Ft. William Henry at Lake George and a cavern hideout under the falls at Glens Falls. Later, Theodore Dreiser's *An American Tragedy* was based on a murder at Big Moose. Edward Zane Carroll Judson, too, spent time in the Adirondacks, churning out his potboiler novels under the nom-de-plume Ned Buntline. Robert Louis Stevenson was a reluctant visitor as a patient at the Trudeau Sanatorium in Saranac. He didn't like it much, noting to a friend that in the winter of 1888 the "mercury in the thermometer curls into the bulb like a hibernating bear." He left for Samoa that spring.

The best that could be said for early Adirondack roads was "they were a valuable substitute for a swamp." Thus, the coming of the railroads in the late 19th century opened the area to easy travel for the first time. It was the era of the great camps, collections of buildings constructed of local materials in remote places. These refuges for wealthy families were rustic but elegant. In time came the land-owning clubs, and the great hotels as more and more people sought to share the wilderness. The Adirondack Mountain Club was formed by outdoorsmen in 1922 and ritualized thereafter was the climb of the 46 high peaks, those mountains then believed to be 4,000 feet or higher.

Olympics Bring Renown

The 1930s brought new attention to the area when Godfrey Dewey, son of Lake Placid Club founder Melvil Dewey convinced the International Olympic Committee to hold the 1932 Winter Games at Lake Placid. He then convinced New York State to invest the funds to make the games possible. The Olympics focused wide attention on the Adirondacks in winter and served as the foundation on which the winter sports and recreation activity was built in the region.

The mining industry in the North Country flourished as late as the 1950s, but with the exception of garnet mining operations at North Creek, it has almost disappeared today. Lumbering activity is no longer a staple of the economy. What is left is what the Adirondacks started with: wilderness character and natural beauty.

EXPLORING THE ADIRONDACKS

The Adirondacks comprises 2,300 lakes and ponds, 1,200 miles of rivers, 30,000 miles of streams, and some 100 peaks with of greater than 3,400 feet. But it is not the wilderness that strikes most first-timers who come north on the main route into the region, I–87, the Adirondack Northway.

The gateway to the Adirondacks is the Glens Falls–Lake George area, where attractions of nature share billing with the creations of man. Glens Falls flourished in the heyday of lumbering. Today, the log floats are gone but some of the timber-based industry remains in this small city, which, because of its neat white houses and otherwise prim appearance, has been called "Hometown, U.S.A." It has minor league professional baseball and hockey teams; the Hyde Collection, an outstanding gallery featuring works by Rembrandt and Rubens; an annual hot air balloon festival that each fall attracts a skyful of colorful floaters to the area; and the 25-year-old Lake George Opera Festival, which performs regularly in summer. In winter, some of the finest cross country ski competition in the East takes place on the city's lighted tracks in Crandall Park. Route 9 between Glens Falls and Lake George is an 8-mile long commercial strip that includes all forms of dining, lodging, and shopping, plus an amusement park, "The Great Escape."

America's "Lake Como"

Lake George, a beautiful 32-mile long, island-studded waterway, has been called the "Lake Como of America." Its south basin gets heavy use from June through August, while the wider, deeper north basin has less traffic, reflecting the more modest development at that end of the lake. The main tourist center is Lake George Village at the southern tip. Ft. William Henry, which played an important role in the French and Indian War, is there and has been restored. There are a host of commercial attractions in the village, including the Adirondack Adventure, a 35-minute multi-media slide show of the region. The *Minne-Ha-Ha,* the *Mohican,* and the *Ticonderoga* are steamships offering lake cruises, and you can rent your own boat nearby. The public "Million Dollar Beach" is just east of the boat dock. Lake George Village is compact enough so that everything is within walking distance.

North from Lake George, Route 9N follows the shoreline past a host of lakeside motels and restaurants up through Diamond Point and the village of Bolton Landing. New at Bolton is the spectacular renovation of the Sagamore Hotel, a facility built in 1883 and, after years of sitting idle, restored and reopened in 1985 as the Omni International Resort and Conference Center. On an island connected to the village by a causeway, the hotel opens to a beautiful vista looking south over the lake. A true resort with first class lodging, first class dining, and first class amenities, there is nothing else like it in the region.

Continuing north, Route 9N skirts Tongue Mountain, best known as home to most if not all the rattlesnake population in New York State. The route takes you through the largest village in the north basin, Hague, then on to Ticonderoga, where Lake George meets Lake Champlain.

Historic Fort Restored

Because of the strategic importance of the location to and from Canada, Ft. Ticonderoga (then called Carillon) was built by the French in 1756. It was taken by the British in the French and Indian War and then twice changed hands in the American Revolution. Owned by the Pell family of New York since the early 19th century, this fort has been painstakingly restored over the last 100 years and is open to the public throughout the summer. Other strategic military sites at Mt. Hope and Mt. Defiance, plus the Ticonderoga ferry that crosses Lake Champlain, give visitors a great look at the surrounding territory.

Continuing to the north on Route 9N, there is now a National Historic Landmark at Crown Point where a fort controlled the Lake Champlain narrows in the 18th century. Next to the site is a bridge across Lake Champlain to Vermont. In the village of Crown Point, there is an interesting detour three miles inland to the settlement of Ironville and the Penfield Homestead, where an electromagnet was used for the first time as a power source in an industrial process. This is a well-preserved small country settlement, a good spot for a picnic. Along the same back road is the Essex County Fish Hatchery, where fingerling trout are raised in tanks near a pool where 10-pounders swim. If the urge to fish for a trout in the wild proves irresistible, you can try Put's Creek, which flows alongside the road.

Route 9N winds north through the old iron ore shipping village of Port Henry and the pleasant lakeshore community of Westport, and then swings west toward the interior of the Adirondacks. To continue north through the Champlain Valley, take Route 22 through Essex, where there is a ferry to Vermont, and on to Willsboro, a town on the Boquet River. There, biologists have tried to establish a run of Atlantic salmon from Lake Champlain and have created a fish ladder at the falls in the center of town. Some fish come upstream in the spring, but the best time to see salmon tackle the trip is in early October. There is a viewing window at the fish ladder.

Throughout the trip north from Lake George, Route 9 has woven a companion track to 9N. Travelers electing Route 9, the original north-south main road before I–87, will find spots of interest at the Natural Stone Bridge and Caves two miles north of Pottersville and the Adirondack Center Museum with its colonial garden at Elizabethtown. Along that route also is a fine, free public beach in the village of Schroon Lake.

Routes 9N and 9 crisscross at Elizabethtown, and 9N from Keene through Ausable Forks is one of the most scenic auto routes in the region.

Chasm Inspires Awe

Perhaps the best-known natural attraction in the region is Ausable Chasm, just north of Keeseville, where Routes 9, 9N, and 22 join again. First opened to tourists in 1870, this is where the Ausable River has cut a chasm several hundred feet deep and over a mile and a half in length. There are walkways along the way and a ride down the rapids at the end.

The largest city in the Champlain Valley is Plattsburgh, today home of a major airbase. In the War of 1812, the city was important strategically, and the Kent Delord House used by the British as a headquarters during the Battle of Plattsburgh Bay in 1814 has been restored and is open year round to the public. At Plattsburgh, too, is the tour ship *Juniper,* which sails Lake Champlain mid-May–September. The last settlement north is Rouses Point, home of the ruins of "Ft. Blunder," originally called Ft. Montgomery before it was discovered that a part of the fort had been built on Canadian soil.

The Champlain Valley is the only good farming territory in the Adirondacks, and a trip timed to coincide with apple season in the fall can be a special treat. The lake itself is the largest body of fresh water in the United States other than the Great Lakes. It is 133 miles long and encompasses 490 square miles (including islands); 322 square miles in Vermont, 151 in New York, and 17 in Canada. It is connected to the St. Lawrence River by the Richelieu Canal and to the Hudson River via the Champlain Canal. Although during the Ice Age it drained into the Hudson, Lake Champlain now drains north into the St. Lawrence. In 120,000 years, it is expected to turn and flow south again.

Champlain's Own "Nessie"

As befits a body of water this size, Lake Champlain has its own "monster." Reports of "Chaousarou" date back to Indian times, and Samuel de Champlain wrote of a creature of which "the point of the snout is like that of a hog" on his 1609 expedition. Modern sightings of "Champ" center around the Port Henry area, but like its Loch Ness counterpart, the evidence to back up such reports is skimpy.

From the valley to the lakes and mountains is not a long haul in the Adirondacks. There are three principal routes into the heart of the park: Route 28, which can be picked up in the east off Route 9 from the Warrensburgh exit of I–87 near Lake George, or from the west at Utica and north to Old Forge; Route 30 north from the Amsterdam exit of the New York State Thruway or south from Canada; and the Olympic Route, Route 73, just west of I–87 exit 30 to Lake Placid.

Route 28 north from Warrensburgh follows the Hudson River into the interior of the Adirondacks. The village of North Creek was once the railhead for the area, which prospered from lumbering and mining. Today, the Barton Mines at North River is still the world's leading producer of industrial garnet. The Hudson River here is a mountain stream and North Creek is the home of one of the nation's oldest whitewater derbies. Kayaks, canoes, and assorted other crafts head downstream to Riparius on the first weekend in May each year.

Hudson Lures Rafters

The river in recent years has also become a major tourist attraction. More than 25,000 people took the five-hour whitewater rafting trip from Indian Lake to North Creek last year. These wilderness runs are from ice-out in early April to early June, and there is a September schedule too. North Creek was also one of the earliest downhill ski sites in the U.S., with a tow in place in the early 1930s. Trains carrying as many as 1,500 skiers were pulling into town on Friday nights in 1937. Today the skiing centers on state-owned Gore Mountain, three miles outside of town. Gore's lifts include a four-passenger gondola, which also operates for sightseers in the summer and fall.

At Indian Lake, Route 28 meets Route 30, the major route north along the Sacandaga River. From Indian Lake, both routes continue together to Blue Mountain Lake, the divide between streams that flow north to the St. Lawrence and those that flow south to the Hudson.

Blue Mountain Lake is home to the Adirondack Museum, considered by professionals to be one of the finest regional museums in the United States. Located right on Routes 28 and 30, the museum's tiered concrete parking area is disconcerting at first glance. Despite this decidedly non-wilderness touch, the museum lives up to its excellent reputation. On the grounds are 20 exhibit buildings organized thematically, and it is a matchless source for Adirondacks information.

The museum was begun in 1955 and has among its extensive regional transportation collection an exceptional array of Adirondack guideboats. These boats, perhaps the Adirondacks' most distinctive creation, are canoe-shaped, but are fitted for oars. Generally from 13 to 17 feet long, they are sturdy enough to carry as many as three people with full gear, but are at the same time intended to be light enough to be handled by one person. The heyday of guideboat building in the central Adirondacks was the late 19th–early 20th century. Boats of the same design and construction built by area craftsmen today cost several thousand dollars.

Canoe Excursions

Far more common than the guideboat today is the canoe, and the central and northern Adirondack areas offer some of the best touring around. Like the Northville–Lake Placid hiking route that goes through this area, canoeing the Fulton Chain of Lakes to Saranac Lake is a 7–10-day back-country excursion. The most common starting point for the trip is Old Forge, a tourist village 30 miles west of Blue Mountain Lake on Route 28. (Old Forge also has one of the highest annual snowfalls in the state and is a popular spot for snowmobilers.) The route includes both lake and river paddling, and there are several portages along the way but no difficult whitewater. For those with less time or inclination, there are several spots in the area where a seaplane can be hired for a look at the territory from above.

People continuing north on Route 30 to Tupper Lake and beyond will come upon the St. Regis area, another attractive spot for canoers. Because many of these waterways are off the beaten path, there is excellent fishing, too.

At Long Lake, 10 miles north of Blue Mountain Lake, Route 28N splits off from Route 30 and goes east through Newcomb, the geographical center of the Adirondacks, but a town better known for the black bears that scavenge in the town landfill each evening.

Few "Great Camps" Survive

Newcomb also is the location of Camp Santanioni (the Indian pronunciation of St. Anthony) one of the "great camps" in the region, now in poor condition. A few of the remaining great camps are still privately owned. Some, like Camp Sagamore at Raquette Lake and Camp Minnowbrook at Blue Mountain Lake, are conference centers. A handful, are open to guests. Although not a great camp, the feel of that era is particularly evident at the Elk Lake Lodge, located between Newcomb and North Hudson. This 12,000-acre preserve includes two lakes and will take just 50 guests at a time.

The best entry point to the High Peaks area of the Adirondacks is I–87 exit 30. The 28 miles from the intersection of Route 9 and 73 just west of the exit to the village of Lake Placid is one of the most attractive auto routes in a region that claims many attractive roads. The Chapel Pond section to Keene Valley and the Cascades area between Keene and Lake Placid offer some of the most rugged terrain in the area, with steep climbs and sheer cliffs to test the most experienced rock climbers in summer and fall and ice climbers in winter. There are plenty of well-marked hiking areas here, and Route 73 is the prime access point to most of the High Peaks, including Mt. Marcy, at 5,344 feet the highest point in New York State. Both the east and west branches of the Ausable River flow alongside portions of the road, offering fishermen easy access to some of the most celebrated trout waters in the country.

Two-Time Olympic Site

As host to the 1932 Olympics, Lake Placid gained a leg up in winter sports facilities. Now having hosted the 1980 games, the area can boast some of the most modern facilities in the world. At Mt. Van Hoevenberg off Route 73, six miles east of the village, is the only refrigerated luge and bobsled track in the United States, and in the same complex are world class cross country ski trails and a biathlon facility.

Closer to Lake Placid on Route 73 is Intervale, the 70- and 90-meter ski-jump hill. There is practically year-round competition with warm weather jumping done on plastic mats. The 90-meter ski tower has an observation tower at the top and the high peaks vista there is one of the most popular tourist attractions in the region. Eight miles north of the village is Whiteface Mountain, where the alpine events in the 1980 games were held.

In order to guarantee a good base for those events, an extensive snow-making system was installed at Whiteface. What made the system possible is the west branch of the Ausable River which flows by the foot of the mountain. Just two miles upstream, the river passes through High Falls Gorge, a natural chasm that is open for visitors from late May through mid-October. Whiteface Mountain's chairlift is also open in summer, and the mountain is the only high peak that has a road to the top—the Whiteface Memorial Highway, which starts in Wilmington. At the top, there is an elevator to the mountain peak where a weather observation tower is staffed by the Atmospheric Science Research Center of the State University of New York. In summer, the ASRC holds a popular weekly science lecture series at its Whiteface headquarters off the mountain highway. The handsome log building there was made from trees felled in a famous "blowdown" that destroyed half a million acres of timber in the high peaks in 1950.

The village of Lake Placid is very small for an international sports capital. What most visitors see is a one-street commercial area overlooking Mirror Lake. There are a wide variety of accommodations, restaurants, and shops in town, but the arena where the U.S. hockey team won the gold medal in the 1980 games remains the focal point for most tourists. It is located on Main Street, with the 1932 arena on one side and the Lake Placid High School on the other.

The area has been a summer resort for nearly a century now, dating back to the founding of the Lake Placid Club in 1895. Today, with modern facilities extending the winter sports season into spring and the growing popularity of fall foliage visits, Lake Placid is becoming a year-round tourist community. And there is more than sports and shopping. The Lake Placid Center for the Arts maintains a year-round program as well as a regional crafts center. Of historical interest near Intervale is the John Brown Farm, home of the 19th-century abolitionist, who came to the area in the 1850s to run a farm for runaway slaves.

Saranac's Mountain Air

To complete the loop through the park, head west from Lake Placid on Route 86 to Saranac Lake. Home to the Trudeau Sanatorium, (now the Trudeau Institute) since 1885, Saranac has long been heralded for the curative power of its mountain air. Always popular in summer, it also has a century-old off-season fling with its annual Winter Carnival best known for the large-scale ice sculptures constructed on Lake Flower. An interesting side trip north on Route 86 is Onchiota, the smallest hamlet in the Adirondacks. Here is the Six Nations Indian Museum, where the stories about Iroquois history and culture make the trip worthwhile.

Water and wilderness are what makes the Adirondacks popular. These are the same elements that appeal to what, without question, can be a trip spoiler first class—the black fly. Fortunately for visitors and residents alike, the black fly season runs only some six weeks, from about early May to mid-June. Anyone planning to stray from the asphalt in the region during that period should do so only after a drenching in heavy-duty insect repellent.

The Adirondacks cover some 9,375 square miles, about 38 percent of which is owned by New York State. This region of lakes, streams, mountains, and wilderness is within a day's drive of approximately 60 million people.

SEAWAY HISTORY

What the Indians called "The River Without End" was named St. Lawrence by the French explorer Jacques Cartier who saw it first on that saint's birthday. So significant is the St. Lawrence to waterborn trade, it has been designated America's "Fourth Coast."

Although a French missionary had used the area as a base from which to convert Indians to Christianity as early as 1748, it was not until after the War of 1812 that the Seaway–Thousand Islands area began to develop significantly. Trade with Canada, the foundation of the area's commerce, was officially cut off with the passage of the U.S. Embargo Act of 1807, and when war broke out five years later, those along the river—the border of British territory—felt especially vulnerable. The fear was not unfounded. One of the first naval engagements of the war was fought at Sackets Harbor near the mouth of the St. Lawrence, and in February 1813, a force of British soldiers and Canadian militia marched across the frozen river and captured Ft. Oswegatchie (which after the war would become Ogdensburg).

After the War of 1812 ended, the area attracted substantial numbers of New Englanders and refugees from the Napoleonic Wars. One refugee, Count Pierre Real, built a house in Cape Vincent for Napoleon in anticipation of the emperor's escape from St. Helena.

In the 19th century the principal products of the area were potash, lumber, and farm produce, especially dairy products. Ogdensburg, the oldest settlement in the area, is the only deep water port on the river, so it became an important seaport community. Alexandria Bay did a good business in the period as a fueling stop for steamships. Both Clayton and Sackets Harbor successfully converted shipbuilding activities from war to peacetime. Much of the early growth, however, slowed as the river's importance in the east-west trade dropped after the Erie Canal was completed in 1825 and railroads and other overland trade routes were developed shortly thereafter.

Tourism Creates New Economy

While the railroads may have hurt the Seaway–Thousand Islands commerce, the tracks eventually brought tourists to the area. By the 1870s, the tourism had created a whole new economy for the region, particularly the Thousand Islands. Grand hotels and elegant private homes were built. The grandest of them all was the ill-fated Boldt Castle on Heart Island at Alexandria Bay. There in 1900, George Boldt, a Prussian immigrant who had made a fortune developing New York's Waldorf-Astoria and other luxury hotels, began construction of what was to be a six-story castle-mansion with more than 120 rooms. In all, the 11-building, $2.5 million project was to include dredging the island's shoreline into the shape of a heart. It was intended as a monument to Boldt's wife Louise, but when she died suddenly in 1904, all work was stopped. Boldt never visited the island again and the project was abandoned.

The era of the grand hotels ended with the Great Depression, but by then the great highway construction boom had already begun. In 1938, President Franklin D. Roosevelt was on hand for the dedication of the Thousand Islands International Bridge linking Canada to the U.S. in a series of five spans covering seven miles. After World War II, the area grew in popularity with visitors from both sides of the border. One group that favors the area is fishermen. The largest muskellunge ever landed in the U.S., a 69-lb., 15-oz. giant, was caught in the St. Lawrence by Arthur Lawton in 1957. More recently the area has been celebrated for its bass fishing.

While the natural beauty of more than 1,800 islands has carried the economy of the Thousand Islands, more important downriver has been the effect of the St. Lawrence Seaway. Since the completion of that project in 1959, the Atlantic Ocean has been linked for shipping with the headwaters of the Great Lakes, 2,342 miles to the west.

EXPLORING THE SEAWAY

Stretching across the rim of New York State from Plattsburgh to the beginning of the St. Lawrence at Lake Ontario, the North Country's north is a rolling plain where the Adirondacks level out to the river valley.

Route 11 is the main road from Lake Champlain west, and a worthwhile early stop is at Chateaugay for the spectacular 120-foot waterfall at High Falls Park. There is a children's area and picnic spot. Nearby is a state fish hatchery and recreation park. Several miles farther on is Malone, home to Ballard Mill, an interesting arts and crafts center. Route 37 from Malone goes north to the Canadian border, then west along the seaway and into the Thousand Islands area. Routes 37 and 11 eventually meet again at Watertown, so there is opportunity to travel the territory on either the inland or seaway route, or to make a full loop without retracing the route.

West on Route 11 following the valley route, you come to Potsdam, a college town of 10,000 on the Raquette River. Clarkson College of Technology and the State University of New York at Potsdam with its famous Crane School of Music are here. If you include the student population at St. Lawrence University and the State Agricultural and Technical College in nearby Canton, there are some 12,000 students gathered in an otherwise rural eight-mile area. Also in the area and growing in recent years is an Amish population. It is not uncommon to see the characteristic horse-drawn carriages on roads around hamlets such as Raymondville, Norwood, and Rensselaerville Falls.

North Country's Largest City

At the western end of Route 11 is Watertown, now the largest city in the north country with 35,000 people, and soon to become much larger. Just to the east of the city is the Fort Drum Military Reservation, long a temporary training ground for the U.S. Army but recently named the home of the reactivated 10th Mountain Light Infantry Division. The influx of soldiers into the area is expected to boost the population by some 90,000 within the next decade.

Up to now, Watertown has been known as the place where Frank Woolworth first sold merchandise, and for endless snowstorms that sweep in from Lake Ontario. One thing that snowfall does is feed the Black River, which flows through town and offers some exciting whitewater rafting all summer long. In the Watertown area and worth a sidetrip are the Natural Bridge Caverns, 15 miles east of town on Route 3. There the visitor can get a full briefing on the natural history of the area while on an underground boat ride on the subterranean Indian River.

Five miles due west of Watertown is Sackets Harbor, headquarters for the U.S. Army of the Northern Frontier and the Navy of the Great Lakes during the War of 1812. Two battles at Sackets Harbor during that war are marked at the Old Union Hotel, now a visitors' center and museum, and at the battlefield, now a state historic site.

Thousand Island Trail

Route 12E north from Watertown takes the traveler to Cape Vincent at the start of the St. Lawrence River. The Tibbits Point Lighthouse there is a landmark. This is the beginning of the scenic Thousand Island Trail and for a change of pace before heading downriver, take the only international ferry in New York State over to Wolfe Island on the Canadian side of the midriver border. This is great territory to tour by boat and there are cruises and rentals available throughout the region. This is also one of the finest areas for bass, pike, and musky fishing in the U.S.

Heading east on Route 12, the next stop is Clayton. A must on any tour is the Thousand Island Shipyard Museum with its large collection of antique boats. Also in Clayton is the Old Town Hall Museum which includes the Muskellunge Hall of Fame and is the site for Riverbarge Theatre productions in summer.From Clayton (or from Alexandria Bay) you can cruise through the Thousand Islands. There are actually some 1,800 islands in the area and about the time you have become accustomed to viewing the fine homes and cozy grounds, invariably you will round a point and come up on an ocean-bound cargo vessel, a reminder that the neighborhood is also a main route for international commerce.

Bridge Link to Canada

Between Clayton and Alexandria Bay is Collins Landing, where the Thousand Islands International Bridge island-hops seven miles to Canada. This toll bridge offers a great view of the island-dotted seaway.

Alexandria Bay is the most developed tourist village in the region. No one should leave this area without a boat tour of the nearby islands, which includes Heart Island, site of Boldt Castle. Since being taken over by the Thousand Island Bridge Authority in the late 1970s, Boldt Castle has undergone major preservation work and the stop is worthwhile. Alexandria Bay in 1980 was the site for the national championship of the Bass Anglers Sportmens Society (BASS).

As you move east, Route 12 through the Thousand Islands merges with Route 37 heading down the Seaway to Ogdensburg. This is the oldest settlement in the area and its custom house, built in 1809, is the oldest active federal building in the U.S. Ogdensburg also boasts a museum of national significance, the Frederic Remington Art Museum with over 200 Remington works on display. This artist of the American West was born in nearby Canton, and in this building where his widow lived from 1909 to 1918, Remington's studio has been recreated and his memorabilia is on display along with his paintings, sculptures, and drawings. You can also cross into Canada here via the Ogdensburg-Prescott International Bridge, the most direct route from New York to Ottawa.

National Recreation Trail

In 1980, the state legislature established a New York State Seaway Trail, which, in 1983, was also designated a National Recreation Trail. The 454-mile trek begins at the Seaway International Bridge at Rooseveltown, just east of Massena, where the St. Lawrence River ceases to be the U.S.-Canadian border. Massena is home to Alcoa Aluminum, the largest employer in the region, but it is more widely known as the home of the St. Lawrence Seaway.

Six miles east of town are the Eisenhower locks that, when completed in the 1950s, permitted oceangoing ships to pass from the Atlantic into the Great Lakes. Ships as long as 733 feet and as wide as 73 feet can move through the locks, and there is a viewing deck for spectators to watch operations. At Barnhart Island, you can see the Moses-Saunders Power Dam, a joint American-Canadian hydroelectric project with a visitors' center atop the dam. Also on Barnhart Island is Robert Moses State Park with a beach and picnic area. Massena is the final stop on the loop through the St. Lawrence Valley.

Like in the rest of the region, tourism is a major part of the economic well-being, so there tends to be a little of something for everyone. It is an area that by and large requires a car to explore, but distances are not so great that long stretches behind the wheel are required. If you travel the area by boat, there are numerous marinas on both the American and Canadian sides of the river plus some campsites accessible by water only.

 SIGHTSEEING CHECKLIST. Here is a baker's dozen of activities that can serve as an introduction to the visitor opportunities in New York's North Country. In fact, for many of these places, you should consider going out of your way if you have to. More information on most of these entries will be found in the *Practical Information* section below.

Saratoga State Park. Where else in the world can you play a round of golf, enjoy a mineral spring bath and massage, have an excellent meal, attend a major orchestra concert, and sleep in a luxury hotel room, all within easy walking distance?

Saratoga Springs. The village of Diamond Jim Brady and Bet-a-Million-Gates today is an upscale community featuring a downtown of nice shops and fine restaurants, elegant restored Victorian homes, good museums, and in August, the finest thoroughbred horse racing in the world.

Saratoga Battlefield. The United States might still be the colonies if the Continental Army hadn't stopped the British here in 1777. Now a national historic site.

Cruising Lake George. Whether you like the village or not, the lake is one of the prettiest in North America. There are cruises to fit the time you have available.

Ft. Ticonderoga. Meticulously restored 1750s fort, captured by Ethan Allen in 1775 for the first American victory of the Revolution.

Whitewater Rafting. An exciting spring, summer, and fall adventure through some beautiful wilderness territory.

The High Peaks. Whether you hike or simply take a look from the chairlift at Whiteface or the ski jump tower at Lake Placid, the view is extraordinary.

Lake Placid. The smallest place to host an Olympics and one of only three places (others are St. Moritz and Innsbruck) to do it twice. Don't miss a visit to the arena where the U.S. hockey team won the gold medal in 1980.

Adirondack Museum, Blue Mountain Lake. No better place to get an understanding of the history and development of the region. This is considered one of the finest regional museums in the United States.

Eisenhower Locks, Massena. The completion of these locks in the late 1950s permitted the linkage of the Atlantic Ocean with the Great Lakes, earning the St. Lawrence area the designation as "America's fourth seacoast."

Wilderness. If you can't try a hike, arrange for one of the many planes-for-hire to fly you over the vast, lake-dotted wilderness areas in the Adirondacks.

Ausable Chasm. A remarkable outdoor lesson in the natural history of the region.

Thousand Islands. A unique mixture of tourist shops, elegant homes, excellent sport fishing, and international cargo vessels all together in the same neighborhood.

PRACTICAL INFORMATION FOR
THE NORTH COUNTRY

HOW TO GET THERE. Most people coming to the North Country come by **car.** The primary route from the south, east, and north is I–87, the Adirondack Northway, a modern four-lane divided highway that runs from Albany up through the eastern Adirondacks to the Canadian border. The first exit after I–87 crosses the Mohawk River is No. 8. Saratoga Springs is exit 13, 14, and 15. Lake George Village is exit 21 and 22. Lake Placid is exit 30 and 34 and Plattsburgh is exit 37, 38, 39, and 40.

From the west, I–81, a four-lane divided highway north from the New York State Thruway at Syracuse, is the most direct route to Watertown and the Thousand Islands. (It can be a treacherous route in winter.) To reach the interior of the Adirondacks, the best routes are Route 28 from Route 9 and I–87 exit 23 in the east, and from the west via Route 12 and the New York State Thruway at Utica. Route 30, which runs north-south through the Adirondacks, can be joined at the Amsterdam exit of the New York State Thruway and at the Kensington-Trout River border crossing from Route 138 southwest from Montreal.

From Canada's MacDonald-Cartier Autoroute, which runs east-west along the border, there are bridges to the Thousand Islands–Seaway area on the American side at Rooseveltown near Massena, at Ogdensburg, and at Collins Landing between Clayton and Alexandria Bay. There are bridges across Lake Champlain from Vermont at Rouses Point, at Crown Point, and at Ticonderoga. There are also car and passenger ferries from Vermont at Cumberland Head (Plattsburgh), Pt. Kent, Essex, and Ticonderoga. Route 4 from Vermont to Whitehall and Glens Falls is an attractive road into the area, as is Route 22 north from the Massachusetts-New York border.

By Bus. *Greyhound* and *Trailways* service the region and there are many charter tours available, especially to Saratoga in summer.

By Train. *Amtrak's Adirondack* runs once a day both north and south between New York City and Montreal. The portion of the trip along the west shore of Lake Champlain is very picturesque. North Country stops are Saratoga Springs, Ft. Edward, Whitehall, Ticonderoga, Pt. Henry, Westport (some shuttle service to Lake Placid), Willsboro, Pt. Kent, Plattsburgh, and Rouses Point.

By Air. The larger airports servicing the region are at Montreal, Albany, and Syracuse. Commercial service in the region is provided by *Piedmont Commuter* flying to Saranac Lake, Plattsburgh, Massena, Ogdensburg, and Watertown. There is air charter service and private aircraft accommodations available throughout the area. Only some lakes are open to seaplanes. To check which ones, call the *Adirondack Park Agency* in Ray Brook, 518–891–4050.

HOW TO GET AROUND. Because most of the area is so sparsely settled and there is so little public transportation, almost the only way to get around the region is by **automobile.** Be careful to watch your gas gauge, particularly in the central Adirondacks at night. Most stations are closed by dinnertime, especially September through May. Increasingly popular these days is **bicycle** touring. The Thousand Islands–Seaway area is relatively flat. Try the National Heritage Trail that begins at Massena and follows the waterways across northern New York. *Jefferson County Circle Tour* guide is available from 1000 Islands International Council, Box 400, Alexandria Bay, NY 13607. The Saratoga area through the Champlain Valley is gentle terrain, but the Adirondacks region is a calorie- and muscle-burner. For help planning a tour, check the *American Bicycle Atlas,* available from American Youth Hostels, 1332 I Street, NW, Suite 800, Washington, D.C., 202–783–6161, or contact the *New York Department of Parks, Recreation and Historic Preservation,* Albany, NY 12238, 518–474–0456, for its brochure *North Country Bike Routes.* For a specially designed trip that can include canoeing too, contact the *Raquette River Bike & Boat Co., Inc.* in Tupper Lake, 518–359–3228; *Adirondack Bicycle Touring* in Lake Placid, 518–523–3764; and *Mountainaire Adventures, Inc.* on Rte. 28 in Weavertown, west of I–87 exit 25 at Chestertown, 518–251–2194.

You can **canoe** through the entire region, including the long haul of Revolutionary days from the head of Lake Champlain south to the confluence of the Hudson and Mohawk Rivers in Waterford. Those looking for a long canoe trip with more wilderness flavor can try the Fulton Chain, 90 miles from Old Forge to Saranac Lake.

On Foot. The Adirondacks offer the widest range of hiking opportunities in the east, ranging from a leisurely wilderness stroll to the 132-mile trek lasting a week or more from Northville at Sacandaga Lake to Lake Placid. That legendary trail, which is not for beginners, crosses just three paved roads along the way. For the committed, tackle the Adirondack High Peaks. These are the 46 highest peaks (most over 4,000 feet) in the Adirondacks. There have been more than 1,800 certified "46ers" since the Adirondack Mountain Club began keeping records in 1936. ADK, as it is known, publishes far and away the best guides to the area. Hiking books by Barbara McMartin and Bruce Wadsworth are particularly well respected, but all ADK publications are excellent. The *Guide to Adirondack Trails* series is very detailed, and compact for easy packing.

While the Adirondacks contain more than a million acres that have been officially designated "wilderness," trails are well marked and the prudent hiker will keep an eye out for the circular color-coded trail markers nailed to trees.

There are year-round hikers in the area, but first-timers and those not fully at home in the woods should consider September hiking. This avoids the summer bugs and heat and the late-autumn deer hunters and cold. Since New York's trout season in most spots remains open through the month, pack fishing gear for an introduction to an Adirondack native, the brook trout.

TELEPHONES. From Albany north to the Canadian border, the area code in most of the North Country is 518. However, the Thousand Islands and portions of the western Adirondacks are in the 315 zone. Those in the latter area are indicated in the directory listings here. The cost of a local call from a public pay phone is 25¢. Since 1985, private pay telephones have been legal in New York. Some of these work on payment-only after the party being called has answered, and there are no refunds for busy signals or no answer if you deposit when dialing. Check the instructions on the pay telephone you are using before depositing money. Calls to and from Canada require only the proper area code.

HOTELS AND MOTELS. The livelihood of the North Country depends upon satisfying visitors, so by and large, accommodations throughout the region are excellent. Summer—from July 4th through Labor Day—is the high season and many of the choicer spots, particularly the old lodges, are booked a year in advance. A promising recent development is the restoration of several older country inns, with most of the projects turning into year-round operations as fall and winter tourism in the area grows. Fall foliage season, late September–early October, has become a time to reserve well ahead, and to be safe, school holiday periods—Christmas and Washington's Birthday—and special local event dates require advance booking, too. Prices are based on double occupancy, European Plan (room only) unless otherwise noted: *Deluxe,* over $75 per night; *Expensive,* $55–$75; *Moderate,* $35–$55; *Inexpensive,* under $35. Since prices may vary considerably according to season, be sure to confirm before booking.

We've begun our listing in the southeast corner of North Country in the Saratoga (Washington County) area, north to the Lake George area, farther north to the Champlain Valley, then westward to the Central Adirondacks and Olympic areas, and ending at the Canadian border in the Thousand Islands–Seaway area. Unless specified, the area code for all telephone numbers is 518.

SARATOGA AND WASHINGTON COUNTY

Deluxe

Gideon Putnam Hotel and Conference Center. Saratoga State Park, Saratoga Springs; 584–3000. Victorian elegance; 132 rooms and suites; excellent dining; mineral baths, outdoor pool. Fishing, golf, tennis nearby; cross country skiing on grounds. Open all year. No pets.

Expensive

Adelphi Hotel, 365 Broadway, Saratoga Springs; 587–4688. A Victorian inn that combines old and new; 21 rooms and suites. Two-night minimum required on holidays and weekends during racing season. Full bar service. No pets. Open May–November.

Best Western Playmore Farms, RD 5, S. Broadway, Saratoga Springs; 584–2350, 800–528–1234. 30 rooms, kitchen facilities, cottages, TV, outdoor pool. Senior citizens group discounts.

Ramada Renaissance Hotel. 534 Broadway, Saratoga Springs; 584–4000, 800–228–9898. 190 air-conditioned rooms with TV; kitchen facilities available. Indoor pool, fishing, golf, tennis, skiing, boating nearby.

Moderate

Burgoyne Motor Inn. 220 Broad St., Schuylerville; 695–3282. 11 air-conditioned rooms, TV, coffee shop, breakfast only.

Carriage House. 178 Broadway, Saratoga Springs; 584–4220. 10 air-conditioned kitchen units with refrigerator, cable TV. Family, weekly, senior citizens, and ski rates. Crib free, cot $5.

Community Motel. 248 S. Broadway, Saratoga Springs; 584–6666. 42 air-conditioned rooms. Family, weekly rates off-season; cable TV, in-room movies, free coffee. Some in-room steam baths.

Grand Union. 92 Broadway, Saratoga Springs; 584–9000. Pleasant rooms. Crib free, cot $3–$5. Cable TV, pool, wading pool, lifeguard, lawn games.

Holiday Inn. Broadway and Circular St., Saratoga Springs; 584–4550. 150 air-conditioned units, suites. Dining room, cocktails, coin laundry, heated pool.

Saratoga Downtowner. 413 Broadway, Saratoga Springs; 584–6336. Small motel with 28 air-conditioned units. Dining room, cocktails, coin laundry, heated pool.

Springs. 165 Broadway, Saratoga Springs; 584–6336. Small motel with 28 air-conditioned rooms. Weekly rates available; children under 12 free; crib free, cot $3. Free coffee in rooms. Pool.

Turf & Spa Motel. 140 Broadway, Saratoga Springs; 584–2550. 42 air-conditioned rooms; TV. Outdoor pool, fishing, golf, tennis, skiing nearby.

Washington Inn. S. Broadway, Saratoga Springs; 584–9807. 20 rooms with private bath, two with kitchenettes; no TV, no phones. One-week minimum stay during racing season. Well-trained pets permitted. Open July–August.

Inexpensive

Empress Motel. 173 Broad St., Schuylerville; 695–3231. 12 air-conditioned units, some with shower. Coffee shop open during July and August.

The Kimberly. 158 S. Broadway, Saratoga Springs; 584–9006. Eight rooms, six with private bath, all with TV. No phones. Open all year.

Town House Motor Inn. 56 N. Park St., Cambridge; 677–5524. 12 units, one efficiency; cable TV; restaurant nearby.

LAKE GEORGE AREA

Deluxe

Sagamore. Causeway, Bolton Landing; 644–9400, 900–228–2121. Historic Adirondack retreat on private island. Magnificently restored landmark, luxurious lakeside cottages, hotel rooms, and suites. Four restaurants, cocktail lounges, nightclub. Indoor, outdoor pools. Private beach; 18-hole championship golf course; four tennis courts, two indoor. Children's recreational programs. Health spa, jogging track. No pets.

Expensive

Alpine Village. Lake Shore Dr., Lake George Village; 668–2193. Eight cozy rooms in lodge; 12 rooms in cabins. Weekly, family rates available in informal, friendly atmosphere. Crib, cots available. Family-style meals, snack bar, bar. Playground, tennis, private beach with boats, waterskiing; ice skating, sleigh rides, cross-country skiing. No pets.

Best Western of Lake George. Lake Shore Dr., Lake George Village; 668–5701. 48 elegant air-conditioned rooms. Youngsters under 17 free. Cable TV, pool, playground.

Blenheim on the Lake. Lake Shore Dr., Lake George Village; 668–5580. Five large, high-ceilinged rooms in stone house built in 1895 overlooking lake. No TV or phones; no pets. Open mid-June to Labor Day.

Canoe Island Lodge. Lake Shore Dr., Diamond Point; 668–9611. Rustic atmosphere on private island, with 30 units in cottages; 18 rooms in two-story lodges. Cable TV in some rooms. Barbecues, box lunches available. Cafe. Free transportation to bus depot. Sand beach, boats, canoes, dockage.

Dunham's Bay Lodge. Rte. 9L, Lake George Village; 656–9242. 50 rooms with TV; full meal and bar service. Marina with private sand beach. No phones; no pets. Open May–October.

Fort William Henry Motel. Canada St., Lake George Village; 668–3081. On lake, 99 rooms, three-day minimum stay during holidays. Under 12 free, crib free, cot $5. Cable TV, indoor pool, poolside service, sauna, whirlpool.

Georgian Motel. 384 Canada St., Lake George Village; 668–5401. 167 rooms, suites, many rooms with lake view. Cable TV. Fine dining in Georgian Cafe. Pool with poolside service, private beach with dockage, paddleboats.

Hidden Valley Ranch. I–87 exit 21, just west of Rte. 9N, Box 228, Lake Luzerne; 696–2431. 100 rooms in 15 lodges, weekly, family rates, three-day minimum during holidays, crib, cot free. Rustic western decor, situated in wooded area on Lake Vanare. Two pools, one indoor. Buffet weekly, box lunches, snack bar, gift shop. Cafe, entertainment, dancing. Exercise course, fitness trail. Tennis, snowmobiling, 15-mile cross country ski trails, horse-drawn sleigh rides.

Holiday Inn. Rte. 9, Box 231, Lake George Village; 668–5781. Modern rooms, bridal suites. Under 18 free. Cable TV, coin laundry. Two pools, one indoor, wading pool, sauna, poolside service, playground. Dinner theater, bar. Bicycle and snowmobile trails and rentals.

Howard Johnson's. Aviation Rd., Glens Falls; 793–4173. 121 air-conditioned rooms, suites. Under 18 free, crib, cot free. Cable TV, indoor pool, whirlpool. Dining in the Blacksmith Shop, bar. No pets. Open all year.

Lake Crest Motel. 366 Canada St., Lake George Village; 668–3374. Beautiful rooms overlooking lake. Cable TV, heated pool, private sand beach with dock, paddleboats. No pets. Open April–Oct. 1.

Melody Manor. Six miles north of I–87 exit 22, Bolton Landing; 644–9750. Pleasant resort-type motel with 40 air-conditioned rooms. Three-day minimum stay in July and August, children over three years old only during those months. Pool, tennis, putting green, private sand beach with boats, dockage. Open June–September.

O'Connor's Resort Cottages. Lake Shore Dr., Lake George Village; 668–3367. 32 two- and three-bedroom kitchen cottages, suites, studio apartments. Crib free. Cable TV. Playground, miniature golf, wooded grounds, private beach. No pets.

Queensbury. 88 Ridge St., Glens Falls; 792–1121. 143 air-conditioned rooms. Under 18 free, crib, cot $6. Cable TV. Fine dining in the Garden in the Park. Bar, gift shop, barbershop. YM–YWCA facilities available. Open all year.

Ramada Inn. Rte. 9N, Box 351, Lake George Village; 668–3131. Modern air-conditioned rooms, suites, crib free, cot $8. Cable TV, indoor pool, whirlpool. Bar, entertainment, dancing weekends during off-season. Tennis, golf nearby. No pets.

Roaring Brook Ranch and Tennis Resort. Luzerne Rd., Lake George Village; 688–5767. 118 air-conditioned rooms. Modified American Plan, various rates during high season and holiday weekends, crib, cot free. Three pools, one indoor, poolside service, saunas. Cafe, cookouts in summer, bar. Children's programs in summer. Golf privileges, five tennis courts, pro in season, waterskiing. Free bus to depot and houses of worship. No pets. Open mid-May–mid-October.

Sheraton Glens Falls Inn. Aviation Rd., Glens Falls; 793–7701. 110 air-conditioned rooms, four kitchenettes, under 17 free, crib, cot $10. Cable TV, free coffee in rooms. Bar, entertainment, dancing summer weekends. Playground. Free bus transportation to airport and bus depot. Open year-round.

Still Bay Resort. Box 569, Lake Shore Dr., Lake George Village; 668–2584. Lovely rooms, kitchenettes, kitchen units on lakeshore. Crib, cot, $5. Cable TV, play area. Private beach with boats, dock. No pets, no credit cards. Open May–October.

Surfside Motel. 400 Canada St., Lake George Village; 668–2442. Seven two-bedroom units, seven efficiencies. Restaurant, heated pool, playground, beach with dock, fishing. No pets.

Tahoe Beach Club and Resort. Lake Shore Dr., Lake George Village; 668–5711. 73 air-conditioned units on terraced, lakefront grounds. Heated pool, cable TV. 150-foot sand beach, rental boats, fee for dock, fishing. Open May–October.

Tea Island Motel. Lake Shore Dr., Lake George Village; 668–2776. Lovely rooms, kitchenettes, and one two-bedroom kitchen cottage. Crib free, cable TV, playground, private beach with boats, dockage. No pets. Open May–October.

Tiki Motor Inn. Canada St., Lake George Village; 668–5744. 90 rooms, under 18 free, crib, cot free. Cable TV, bar, entertainment. Outdoor pool. Open mid-May–mid-October.

Moderate

Bayfront Housekeeping Cottages. Lake Shore Dr., Lake George Village; 668–2658. Rustic setting on lake, with six kitchen units in motel, six kitchen cottages. Beach, boats, dockage, waterskiing instruction. No pets, no credit cards. Open mid-May–mid-October.

Bonnie View Resort. Lake Shore Dr., Bolton Landing; 644–5591, 644–3611. Rooms and 1–3 bedroom and kitchen cottages. Free coffee in motel rooms, cable TV. Playground, tennis, private beach. Open mid-May–September.

Colonial Manor Inn. Box 528, Lake George Village; 668–4884. 35 motel rooms, 9 cottages, 11 two-bedroom cottages. Under 12 free in motel. Senior citizen rates during off-season. Crib free, cable TV, pool, playground. No pets.

Graycourt. Lake George Rd., Glens Falls; 792–0223. 25 motel rooms, five cottages. Crib, cot $5. Free coffee in rooms. Cable TV, heated pool, playground. Open May–October.

The Hayes House. 7161 Lake Shore Dr., Bolton Landing; 644–5941. Cape Cod cottage from the 1920s. Three rooms, each with private bath. No phones, TV only in common room. Picnic lunches available. Children under 12 not accepted, no pets. Open year round.

Juliana. Lake Shore Dr., Diamond Point; 668–5191. Lovely rooms, kitchenettes, and kitchen cottages. Crib, cot available. Cable TV, pool, playground, private sand beach with boats, aquabikes. Open May–September.

Merrill Magee House, Warrensburg; 623–2449. Beautiful 19th-century house with three rooms sharing bath. Breakfast, no TV or telephones. Lovely candlelit dining room and cozy tavern. Hiking, golf, boating, and canoe access, skiing nearby. No pets.

Split Rail Motel. Lake Shore Dr., Diamond Point; 668–2259. Ten units in motel, ten kitchen cottages, free coffee, cable TV. Heated pool, playground, private beach with boats, dockage. No pets. Open May–mid-October.

Treasure Cove. Lake Shore Dr., Diamond Point; 668–5334. 23 air-conditioned rooms, one cottage with kitchen. Crib, cot available, free coffee, cable TV. Pool, playground, beach with boats, dockage. Open May–November.

Victorian Village. Lake Shore Dr., Bolton Landing; 644–9401. 33 rooms, three-day minimum stay late June–Labor Day. Cable TV, tennis, private sand beach with boats, canoes, dockage. Open mid-April–October.

Inexpensive

Briar Dell Motel. Box 123, Lake Shore Dr., Lake George Village; 668–4819. Pleasant motel rooms and 16 cabins. Lakefront location, TV. Private beach with boats, dockage. Open May–October.

Country Road Lodge. 12 Hickory Hill Rd., Warrensburg; 623–2207. Five rooms with semi-private baths. Family style meals, breakfast in summer only, dinner in winter. Children accepted only when part of group of eight. No TV or telephones, no pets, no credit cards.

King George Motor Inn. Lake George Rd., Lake George Village; 668–2507. 56 units, weekly rates available, senior citizens discount. Coffee shop, breakfast buffet, pool, playground. Open May–October.

Pine Point Cottages. 3205 Lake Ave., Lake Luzerne; 696–3015. Motel rooms, 10 cottages on Lake Vanare, weekly rates. TV, playground, private beach with boats, waterbikes, free transportation to bus depot, airport.

CHAMPLAIN VALLEY

Moderate

Grand Prix Motor Lodge. 44 N. Ausable St., Keeseville, two miles east of I–87 exit 34; 834–7126. 16 air-conditioned units, cable TV, outdoor pool. No pets. Open mid-May–mid-October.

Holiday Inn, Plattsburgh, one mile west of I–87 exit 37; 561–5000. 102 air-conditioned rooms, under 20 free, senior citizens discount, crib free, cot $5. Dining room, cocktails, cable TV, heated pool.

Howard Johnson's. Plattsburgh, I–87 exit 37; 561–7750. Situated in new shopping center, 96 air-conditioned rooms, under 12 free, crib free, cot $5, senior citizens discount. Restaurant and coffee shop, cable TV, coin laundry, indoor pool with poolside service.

Inn on the Library Lawn. Corner of Main and Washington Sts., Westport; 962–8666. 20 rooms (10 in annex). Freshly baked goods served as part of full breakfast each morning. Free transportation to train, bus depots. Golf, tennis, cross country skiing, ice fishing, and snowmobiling nearby. New ownership in 1987.

Travellers Motor Inn. Junction of I–87 (exit 37) and Rte. 3, Plattsburgh; 563–0222. Modern air-conditioned units; senior citizens discount. Complimentary coffee, donuts, restaurant adjacent, satellite cable TV. No pets.

Valcour Lodge. Rte. 9 South, Plattsburgh; 563–3518. On Lake Champlain, access by boat. 16 rustic cabins at site of first major naval engagement of Revolutionary War. Weekly, monthly rental. Fine dining room, piano bar. No pets. Open late April–mid-October.

Inexpensive

American International. One mile north on Rte. 74 from Rte. 22, Ticonderoga; 585–7353. 30 air-conditioned units, family rates. Free coffee in rooms, TV, pool. Open late May–mid-October.

Pioneer Motel. Rte. 9N, Plattsburgh; 563–3050. Rustic log construction with 23 rooms, crib, cot $4. Breakfast available, TV, lakeshore privileges. Open year-round.

Westport Hotel, Westport; 962–4501. Century-old inn furnished in early American, with 12 guest rooms, six with private bath. Breakfast, lunch, and dinner served. Outdoor dining in summer.

Windows on the Bay, 444 Margaret St., Plattsburgh; 563–9574. On Lake Champlain, 17 units, cable TV. No pets.

CENTRAL ADIRONDACKS

Deluxe

The Point, Upper Saranac Lake; 891–5674. Exclusive retreat where driving instructions are sent on request after advance reservations are made. The ultimate in country inns with Adirondack Great Camp ambience, owned by William Avery Rockefeller in the 1930s. Ten guest rooms, each with private bath, most with fireplace. American plan with excellent cuisine. No TV, no phones in rooms, no pets, American Express only. Water sports in summer, cross country skiing in winter. New ownership since fall 1986.

Expensive

The Balsam House. Friends Lake Rd., Chestertown, (I–87 exit 23 to Warrensburg); 494–2828. Beautifully restored inn built in 1865, with 20 uniquely decorated rooms, some with phones. Gourmet restaurant (MAP), open to the public. No TV, no pets. Beach on Friends Lake for swimming, boating; tennis, hiking guides, snowmobiling, skiing nearby.

Elk Lake Lodge. I–87 exit 29 to Elk Lake; 532–7613. Extraordinary wilderness lodge on 12,000-acre private preserve in the high peaks area, with no more than 50 guests at a time. Main lodge has six rooms; seven cottages accommodate 2–12 persons. Full-American Plan with meals in main lodge dining room overlooking lake. Trout and salmon fishing on two private lakes and stream, assigned area for hunting in season, 40 miles of maintained hiking trails.

Friends Lake Inn. Friends Lake Rd., Chestertown, I–87 exit 25; 494–4751. A completely restored 1860s inn with 14 rooms, 7 with private bath. Modified American Plan, with European Plan available. Fine restaurant open to public. Beach nearby, hiking, cross country skiing on premises, downhill nearby, group hayrides, skating parties available. No pets.

The Hedges, Blue Mountain Lake; 352–7325. Informal atmosphere, rustic setting in wooded area on lakeshore. 13 rooms in two lodges and 13 cottages. Family, weekly rates, crib, cot free, additional person is half rate. Box lunches, no room service, no phones in rooms. Tennis, playground, hiking trails, sand beach with boats, canoes. No pets, no credit cards. Open late June–mid-October.

Hemlock Hall, Blue Mountain Lake; 352–7706. Lovely 1895 country inn in secluded lakeside setting, with 9 rooms in lodge and 10 kitchenettes in cottages. Family rates, crib free. Modified American plan available. Playground, private sand beach with boats, canoes, sailboats. No pets, no credit cards. Open mid-May–mid-October.

Highwinds Inn. Gore Mountain Rd., North River; 251–3760, or 251–3435. Mountain retreat, four spacious rooms each with outstanding view of the Siamese wilderness area. Tennis court, three trout-stocked ponds, private hiking trails through 1,600 acres of woods and meadows. Horseback riding and whitewater rafting nearby. Breakfast and dinner included in lodging rate. No pets. No credit cards. Open all year except November and June.

Woods Lodge. East St., Schroon Lake Village; 532–7529. Beautiful, quiet setting overlooking Schroon Lake, with 14 lovely rooms in inn, four kitchen apartments, four cottages. Crib, cot $5, free morning coffee, no meals. Tennis, private sand beach with boats available. No pets, no credit cards. Open mid-May –mid-October.

Moderate

Black Mountain Ski Lodge. Star Rte., North Creek, 4 miles west of junction of Rte. 28; 251–2800. 25 rooms, family, weekly, skiing, and hiking rates December–May; package rates April–May; crib, cot $5. Dining room, wine and beer, TV, pool, skiing nearby. No pets.

Cold River Ranch Lodge. Eight miles east of Tupper Lake on Rte. 3; 359–7559. An authentic turn-of-the-century Adirondack lodge with six bedrooms, shared baths. Informal atmosphere; home-style cooking, American Plan. Caters to outdoor enthusiasts. Horseback riding, cross country skiing trails on premises. No pets.

Country Club. Rte. 28, Box 625, Old Forge; 315–369–6340. 17 rooms, weekly rates, crib free, cot $3, free coffee in rooms. Pool, tennis, playground, 18-hole golf privileges.

Covewood Lodge. NY–28, five miles east of Big Moose Rd. Eagle Bay; 315–357–3041. Rustic lodge with three two-bedroom apartments with kitchen, 18 cottages with kitchen and fireplace, crib, cot free. Located in middle of a wildlife sanctuary on Big Moose Lake, dock, water-skiing instruction available. TV, playground. Transportation to airport, rail, and bus depots.

Dun Roamin Cabins. Rte. 9, 2 miles north of Schroon Lake Village; 532–7277. Nine well-maintained cabins, six kitchenettes, crib, cot free. Fireplace in some cabins, cable TV. Various boats, water-skiing instruction available, skiing nearby.

Forge. Rte. 28, Old Forge; 315–369–3313. 61 rooms, crib, cot $3; TV, in-room movies, heated pool. Near public beach with boats, boat trips, tennis, golf privileges.

Garnet Hill Lodge. Rte. 28, 11½ miles from intersection with Rte. 8, North River; 251–2821. An old Adirondack lodge in the mountains overlooking Thirteenth Lake. Pleasant and relaxing atmosphere featuring home-baked goods. 26 rooms, various meal plans available, senior citizens rates, family, weekly, ski rates, rafting package. Dining room with Saturday night smorgasbord, room service. Tennis, fishing guides available, stocked lake, ski rentals. Free transportation to bus depot.

Holl's Inn. Rte. 28, Inlet; 315–357–2941, 733–2748. Summer resort on 1,800 feet of lakefront. 47 rooms with private bath. American Plan dining room overlooks Fourth Lake. Outdoor activities include hiking with trail lunches, golf, tennis, water sports. No pets, no credit cards. Open July 4th–Labor Day.

Irondequoit Club Inn. Old Piseco Rd., Piseco; 518–548–5500. Ten rooms in main lodge, three housekeeping cottages. Dining room in main lodge. Private beach, tennis, canoe, rowboat and sailboat rentals. No pets. Open all year.

Long Lake. Boat Landing Rd., Long Lake; 624–2613. Eight motel rooms, eight cottages, four kitchenettes, crib, cot $4; coffee in rooms, cable TV, private sand beach.

Inexpensive

Blue Spruce. Main St., Old Forge; 315–369–3817. 12 rooms, crib free, cot $4. TV, pool, tennis privileges, cross country, skiing, snowmobile trails nearby.

Davis. Rte. 9, south of Schroon Lake Village; 532–7583. Overlooks Schroon Lake, 20 motel rooms, four kitchenettes, 10 kitchen cottages. Family, weekly rates, crib, cot $5. Cable TV, heated pool, playground, swimming, boats.

Hansen's Adirondack Lodge. South Shore Rd., Lake Pleasant; 548–3697. Restored century-old house with four guest rooms, shared bath. Rates include full breakfast. No TV, no phones, no pets, no credit cards.

19th Green, Old Forge; 315–369–3575. 13 air-conditioned rooms, crib $5, cot $10, free coffee, TV. Cross country skiing, snowmobile trails nearby. No room phones, no pets.

Norridgewook III, Beaver River; 315–376–6200. Opened in 1911 and operated by same family since. Fully equipped cabins to accommodate 30 guests. Access by boat or snowmobile only. State boat launch at Stillwater Reservoir General Store, north of Old Forge. Boat taxi service available. Located in recreation area, caters to lovers of outdoors and sports. Rustic main lodge with dining room (American Plan) and bar, trail lunches available. Weekly rates.

Pine Terrace Motel & Tennis Club. Moody Rd., Tupper Lake; 359–9258. 18 cottage units, five kitchenettes, overlooking lake, mountains. Family, weekly, tennis rates, crib, cot available. Cable TV, pool, lighted tennis courts, boat dock. Open May–October.

Red Top Inn. Moody Rd., Tupper Lake; 359–9209. 20 units with four modest cottages, overlooking Big Tupper Lake. Restaurant, TV, golf and ski package plans available, pool, fishing, beach, boat ramp.

Sandy Point, Long Lake; 624–3871. 11 units, seven kitchenettes, crib, cot $4. Free coffee, cable TV, sauna, private sand beach with boats, dockage. No pets. Open May–October.

Shaheen's. 310 Park St., Tupper Lake; 359–3384. 35 rooms, 17 air-conditioned. Family rates in units for up to six. Crib free, cot $5. Free coffee in rooms, cable TV, playground. No pets.

Shore Enough. Echo Lake, Rte. 9, Pottersville; 494–9910. Low-key family cottage colony with education center, nature, and outdoor activities for adults and children.

Sunset Park. De Mars Blvd., Tupper Lake; 359–3995. Lovely rooms, some kitchenettes, crib, cot $4; free coffee, cable TV. Private sand beach with dock for small boats.

Timerlock. Indian Lake; 648–5494. Rustic family resort with no electricity in 25 cabins, some with private bath. Three meals served daily on lodge's porch overlooking Indian Lake. Horseback riding and tennis on premises, sailboats, canoes, kayaks, windsurfers on lake. Open June–Labor Day.

Valhaus. Peaceful Valley Rd. and Rte. 28, North Creek; 251–2700. 12 rooms, weekly package rates, TV, free coffee. Half mile to Gore Mountain Ski Center access road, rafting nearby.

Wawbeek Mountain House, Tupper Lake; 359–3777. Authentic Adirondack lodge with six rooms, eight efficiency cabins. Beautiful setting overlooking lake. Guideboat tour packages, beach with boats, fishing, hiking, tennis courts. Open summers only.

OLYMPIC AREA

Deluxe

Hilton. Mirror Lake Dr., Lake Placid; 523–4411. 178 modern, air-conditioned rooms in five-story structure. Restaurant, bar. Under 18 free, crib, cot $6, ski plan and off-season weekend rates. Two indoor pools with poolside service, whirlpool, rowboats, paddleboats, sailboats.

Expensive

Adirondack Inn. 217 Main St., Lake Placid; 523–2424. Beautiful rooms and suites overlooking lake, crib, cot $6, under 6 free, ski plan. Restaurant, coffee shop, cocktail lounge. Two pools, one indoor, sauna, playground, tennis, beach.

Best Western Golden Arrow. 150 Main St., Lake Placid; 523–3353. 74 air-conditioned rooms, studios, suites, under 12 free, crib, cot $5. Fine restaurant and bar. Indoor pool, health club, racquetball. Private beach on Mirror Lake with boats, canoes.

Holiday Inn. Olympic Dr., Lake Placid; 523–2556. On hilltop overlooking lake, with 182 air-conditioned rooms. Under 12 and crib free, cot $10, ski and weekend rates. Restaurant, bar, heated pool with poolside service. Tennis, rowboats, racquetball, health club.

Howard Johnson's. Saranac Ave., Lake Placid; 523–9555. 92 rooms, under 12 and crib free, cot $6, ski rate plan. Restaurant and bar, indoor pool and whirlpool, coin laundry, tennis, boat dockage.

Lake Placid Manor. Whiteface Inn Rd., Lake Placid; 523–2573. Rustic elegance on the lake, view of Whiteface Mountain, with 38 rooms in 10 lodges and cottages. Crib, cot $5. Restaurant and bar, playground, private beach with own boats, swimming, water skiing, and fishing. Hunting, tennis, and golf, all winter sports facilities nearby.

Mirror Lake Inn. 35 Mirror Lake Dr., Lake Placid; 523–2544. Colonial decor in 72 air-conditioned rooms in inn; penthouse terrace rooms with cathedral ceilings, lakeshore cottages. Under 11 free, crib free, cot $5. Ski, golf, weekend, and honeymoon rates. Gourmet restaurant, heated pool, health club. Playground, private beach with sailing, boating, and windsurfing instruction and rentals.

Ramada Inn. 12 Saranac Ave., Lake Placid; 523–2587. 90 air-conditioned rooms, under 18 free, crib free, cot $10. Ski, golf packages. Restaurant and bar, two pools, one indoor, whirlpool.

Wildwood. 88 Saranac Ave., Lake Placid; 523–2624. 23 air-conditioned rooms, 10 cottages with kitchen, under 12 free, crib free, cot $5. Free coffee in rooms, heated pool, health club. Playground, beach with boats, canoes. Airport transportation.

Moderate

Alpine Motor Lodge. Wilmington Rd., Lake Placid; 523–2180. Neat, clean rooms in two-story inn, cot $4. Restaurant features German specialties. Outdoor pool. Walking distance to shops.

Art Devlin's Olympic Motor Inn. 350 Main St., Lake Placid; 523–3700. 40 air-conditioned rooms, crib free, cot $4, ski package. Pool, playground, transportation to airport, bus depot.

High Valley, Wilmington; 946–2355. 20 rooms, 12 with air-conditioning, crib, cot $4. Heated pool, playground. Wooded grounds extend to Ausable River, with excellent fishing. Closed mid-March–mid-June and mid-October–mid-December.

Holiday Lodge. Wilmington; 946–2251. 27 air-conditioned rooms, crib free, cot $4, weekly, ski rates available. Restaurant, bar, heated pool.

Hungry Trout, Wilmington; 946–2217. On Ausable River, 10 air-conditioned rooms, crib, cot $5. Ski, fishing packages, fishing guides available. Restaurant and bar, pool, playground.

Interlaken Lodge. 15 Interlaken Ave., Lake Placid; 523–3180. Victorian setting and relaxing atmosphere with 12 guest rooms. MAP, but breakfast-only plan available. Extra charge for children 2–12 sharing room with parents, crib $5. Packaged for golf, skiing, bicycling, and canoeing can be arranged. Dining room featuring continental and American cuisine, bar. No pets.

Lake Side. 27 Lake Flower Ave., Saranac Lake; 891–4333. 22 rooms, 14 with air conditioning, crib $1, cot $2. Heated pool, beach with boats, patio overlooks lake.

Ledge Rock, Placid Rd., Wilmington; 946–2302. 18 rooms, under 18 free, crib, cot $3. Coffee available in rooms heated pool, playground. Overlooks Whiteface Mountain Ski Center. Open Memorial Day–mid-October.

Hotel Saranac of Paul Smith's College. 101 Main St., Saranac Lake; 891–2200. 92 rooms in refurbished hotel first opened in 1927, with original lobby preserved—replica of the foyer in the Danvanzati Palace of Florence, Italy. Restaurant is college-operated training facility, bar, gift shop.

Stagecoach Inn. Old Military Rd., Lake Placid; 523–9474. Gabled two-story stone and wood building dating back to 1833. Once owned by Melvil Dewey, inventor of the Dewey Decimal System. Six rooms, two with private bath. Full breakfast included in rates. No pets, no credit cards.

Whiteface Chalet. Springfield Road, Wilmington; 946–2207. 18 rooms, family rates except on holidays, weekly, ski rates, crib free, cot $4. Restaurant, bar, heated pool in summer, playground, tennis, hiking. Airport, train, bus depot transportation.

Whiteface Resort Golf and Country Club. Whiteface Inn Rd., Lake Placid; 523–2551; for groups, 523–3872. Lovely rooms in cottages and lakeside cabins, each with private bath. Restaurant and bar, heated pool, children's pool. Playground, tennis, 18-hole golf course, cross country trails.

Inexpensive

Adirondack Loj. Box 867, Lake Placid; 523–3441. Rustic high-mountain bunkbed hostel with two large and four small bunkrooms and four double rooms, each with shared bath, three cabins, with guest supplying own sleeping and cooking gear. No pets.

The Bark Eater. Alstead Mill Road, Keene; 576–2221. Seven rooms with shared baths. Complimentary baked goods for breakfast. Warm, woodsy atmosphere. For those who want to hike for a week with a guide or ski from inn to inn, special meals-included package tours are available.

Deer's Head Inn. Rte. 9N, I–87 exit 31, Elizabethtown; 873–9995. Oldest Adirondack hotel, in operation since 1818, has six guest rooms, four with private bath. Early American decor. Three separate dining rooms. Golf and tennis nearby.

Shulte's. Cascade Rd., Lake Placid; 523–3532. Alpine decor in 16 air-conditioned rooms, 15 kitchen cabins. Family rates, crib free, cot $4. Heated pool, playground.

Woodruff. I–87 exit 30, Keene; 576–4551. 19 units, three with kitchen, weekly, ski, and fishing plan rates, crib, cot free, heated pool, playground.

THOUSAND ISLANDS–SEAWAY

Deluxe

Bonnie Castle Resort. Holland St., Alexandria Bay; 315–482–4511. Overlooks St. Lawrence River and famed Boldt Castle; 100 air-conditioned rooms, all with wet bar, refrigerator, balcony. Some suites have Jacuzzis. Excellent restaurant. Nightclub with entertainment. Outdoor pool, tennis course, marina.

Expensive

Capt. Thompson's Motor Lodge. James St. on St. Lawrence River, Alexandria Bay; 315–482–9961. 117 air-conditioned rooms, each additional person $5, free coffee in rooms, under 12 free. TV, pool, wading pool, boat dockage, no pets.

Edgewood Resort. Edgewood Rd. on St. Lawrence River, Alexandria Bay; 315–482–9922. Extensive grounds on riverfront, with 160 rooms, most air-conditioned, $4 charge per extra person, crib, cot free, under 6 free. Fine restaurant, box lunches provided, bar, entertainment, dancing, gift shop. Poolside service, playground, boat dockage.

Pine Tree Point Club. 1 mile northeast of Alexandria Bay; 315–482–9911. Lovely air-conditioned rooms in lodge and chalets, under 12 free, crib $5, cot $7.50. Fine restaurant with room service, box lunches, bar, entertainment, dancing, pool. Golf privileges, dock with launching ramp. No pets.

Riveredge Resort. 17 Holland St., Alexandria Bay; 315–482–9917. 82 air-conditioned rooms on Seaway, extra person $5, crib free, TV. Dining room serving all meals, pool, whirlpool. Private boat dockage. Open late April–October.

Thousand Island Club. On Wellesley Island in St. Lawrence River; 315–482–2551. 55 air-conditioned rooms, suites, family rates, additional person $5. Outstanding restaurant, bar with entertainment, dancing, gift shop, pool. Tennis, 18-hole professional golf course. Shuttle boat service. No pets.

Moderate

Alexandria Motel. 122 Church St., Alexandria Bay; 315–482–2515. 38 air-conditioned units with TV, weekly rates available. Coffee shop, pool, playground. Open mid-May–mid-October.

Arsenal Street Motel. 1165 Arsenal St., Watertown; 315–788–3760. Lovely air-conditioned units with cable TV, most with phones, one two-bedroom unit. Opposite restaurant.

Bertrand's Motel. 229 James St., Clayton; 315–686–3641. 27 air-conditioned units, one two-bedroom unit, four efficiencies. Discount for senior citizens. Rental refrigerator, cable TV, pool. No pets. Open April–December.

Best Western University Inn. East Main Street, Canton; 315–386–8522. Adjacent to St. Lawrence University, with 75 air-conditioned rooms, under 12 free, extra person $7, crib, cot available. Restaurant with room service, gift shop, pool, golf pro.

Fair Wind Lodge. RD 12-E, Clayton; 315–686–5251. On St. Lawrence Seaway, with 10 rooms in lodge, eight two-person cottages, crib free, cot $4. Heated pool. Open mid-May–mid-October.

Flander's Inn. West Orvis and Main sts., Massena; 315–769–2441. 140 units in four-story building with elevator, under 12 free, crib free, cot $8. Cafe, TV, barber, beauty shop. No pets.

Holiday Inn. 300 Washington St., Watertown; 315–782–8000. 172 air-conditioned rooms in three-story elevator building, under 19 free, extra person $5, crib free, cot $5. Dining room with room service, poolside service, bar with entertainment, dancing. Valet service, barber, beauty shop.

Ledges Resort. Alexandria Bay; 315–482–9334. 24 rooms, nine with air-conditioning; crib, cot $5. Pool, free private dockage, water skiing, adjacent to golf, tennis. No pets. Open early May–mid-October.

Meadow View. RD 2, Massena; 315–764–0246. Lovely air-conditioned units with cable TV, crib $2, family rates, pool, playground.

Nomad. RD 2, Rte. 11, Potsdam; 315–265–6700. 18 air-conditioned rooms; extra person $4–$8. Breakfast available, playground, no pets.

North Star. Rte.–12, Alexandria Bay; 315–482–9332. 18 air-conditioned rooms with TV, crib $2, cot $5. Care, pool, playground, putting green, boat launch, dockage. No pets.

Norton. Rte. 56N, Potsdam; 315–265–4640. Ten air-conditioned units with cable TV, family rates, crib, cot $6. Breakfast available, pool, no pets.

Quality Inn. 1190 Arsenal St., Watertown; 315–788–6800. 96 air-conditioned units with cable TV, extra person $5; senior citizens discount. Restaurant with coffee shop, coin laundry, heated pool.

Quality Inn–Gran View. Riverside Dr., Ogdensburg; 315–393–4550. Overlooking St. Lawrence River, with 48 air-conditioned rooms, additional person $6, under 16 free, crib free, cot $6. Senior citizen rates and weekend plans. Restaurant, bar with entertainment, dancing, pool, dockage.

Ramada Inn. 6300 Arsenal St., Watertown; 315–788–0700. 146 air-conditioned units with cable TV, extra person $6, senior citizens discount. Dining room, cocktails, heated pool, 20 steam baths. Ski trails, airport transportation, no pets.

Riverfront Inn. Riverside Dr., Ogdensburg; 315–393–3730. Overlooks river, 20 air-conditioned units with cable TV, crib fee, cot $5. Complimentary continental breakfast. Pool, playground, 18-hole golf privileges, boats, dockage. No pets.

Torchlite. On Wellesley Island in St. Lawrence River; 315–482–3550. Two-story structure with 18 air-conditioned units, eight kitchenettes; additional person $10, senior citizen rates, weekly golf, fishing rates. Free coffee, continental breakfast. Free dockage for boats, guides available for Seaway cruises. No pets. Open mid-May to mid-October.

Inexpensive

Alta. Riverside Dr., Ogdensburg; 315–393–6860. 20 air-conditioned units with cable TV, 14 kitchenettes, under 12 free, weekly rates, crib, cot $5, heated pool.

Best Western Crossroads. Rte. 11, Moira; 529–7372. 43 air-conditioned rooms with cable TV, crib, cot $6. Restaurant, gift shop, barber, bowling alleys, heated pool.

Bob's. RD 2, Massena; 315–769–9497. 32 air-conditioned rooms with TV, free coffee, weekly rates in off-season, crib free, cot $4. Seaway entrance nearby. No pets.

Davidson's. Black River Rd., Watertown; 315–782–3861. Near Fort Drum, with 20 air-conditioned rooms, crib free, cot $4, heated pool, cable TV. No pets.

Four Seasons. West Main St., Malone; 483–3490. Attractive rooms with cable TV, in-room movies. Additional person $5. Free continental breakfast, pool, no pets.

Hotis. RD 5, Watertown; 315–788–4460. 23 air-conditioned units with TV, additional person $5, crib free, free coffee, family, weekly rates off-season, pool.

New Parrott. Outer Washington St., Watertown; 315–788–5080. 25 rooms with cable TV, most air conditioned, family rates off-season, crib, cot $4, indoor pool.

Nite 'N Gale. Rte. 56, Massena; 315–769–2401. 20 air-conditioned rooms with cable TV, crib free, cot $4. Breakfast served Mondays–Saturdays; pool, playground. No pets.

The View. Rte. 11, Malone; 483–0500. 34 rooms with cable TV, crib, cot $3, heated pool, playground.

Village. Maple St., Massena; 315–769–3561. 29 air-conditioned rooms, three kitchenettes; additional person $3, crib, cot $3.

 BED-AND-BREAKFASTS. North Country bed-and-breakfast hosts range from full-time farmers to empty-nest villagers, and the places from Victorian mansions to unique Adirondack lodges. The breakfasts are usually continental, and some feature home-baked goods. Rates for accommodations vary widely. Don't automatically assume that a B & B will be inexpensive, especially in July and August. If you are traveling with children, be sure to check on extra person charges. Special rates may be available for longer stays, and because the operator is usually the owner, there is a good opportunity for a briefing on what to do—and what to avoid—in that area. Reservations well ahead of time are strongly advised, particularly in summer. Off-season, however, the situation becomes more fluid and even some lodges that normally work on a full American Plan may accept a bed and breakfast arrangement before July and after Labor Day.

For listings of bed-and-breakfast places in the Adirondacks and Lake Champlain regions, contact the *North Country B & B Reservation Service,* Box 238, Lake Placid, NY 12946, 518–523–3739. In the Lake George area, contact the *Warren County Tourism Office,* Municipal Center, Lake George, NY 12845, 518–761–6366. In the Saratoga area, contact the *Saratoga Chamber of Commerce,* 494 Broadway, Saratoga Springs, Ny 12866, 518–584–3255. For information in the Thousand Islands–Seaway area, contact the *1000 Islands International Council,* Box 400, Alexandria Bay, NY 13607, 315–482–2520.

TOURIST INFORMATION. The New York State Department of Commerce has been involved in the "I Love New York" tourism program since the mid-1970s and now publishes an excellent series of travelers' guides. The best general publication is the *I Love N.Y. Travel Guide & Vacation Packages* booklet that, by region, provides both general visitor information and specific attractions by location. It's a "must," especially for first-time visitors, and it's free. As part of the same program, the state publishes more specific guides on topics such as fishing and camping, and also a quarterly events calendar. To get these publications or information on any other travel topic, contact Division of Tourism, New York State Department of Commerce, One Commerce Plaza, Albany, NY 12245, 1–800–CALL–NYS. In the North Country, the department also maintains a tourism office on Main Street in Lake Placid, 518–523–2412. Three other agencies that provide regional tourism information in the North Country are the *1000 Islands International Council,* Box 400, Alexandria Bay, NY 13607, 800–547–5263 (in NY), 800–847–5263 (elsewhere in the continental US), the *Olympic Regional Development Authority,* Olympic Center, Lake Placid, NY 12946, 518–523–1655, and the *Central Adirondack Association,* Tourist Information Center, Old Forge, NY 13420, 315–369–6983. Throughout the North Country, information is available from both local chambers of commerce and county tourism boards. For instance, for Saratoga information, you can contact both the *Greater Saratoga Chamber of Commerce,* 494 Broadway, Saratoga Springs, NY 12866, 518–584–3255, or the Saratoga County Promotion Director, 40 McMaster Street, Ballston Spa, NY 12020, 518–885–5381.

There are visitor information centers at Rtes. 29 and 30 in Vail Mills near Gloversville; between I–87 exits 9 and 10 north in Clifton Park, exits 17 and 18 north in Glens Falls, exit 32 south of Essex and between exits 40 and 41 south approaching Plattsburgh. On I–81 in the Thousand Islands area, there is an information center at exit 505, Alexandria Bay and on I–81 north, just past Exit 49. There are also information centers on Rte. 37 near Massena at both the Eisenhower Lock and the Visitors' Center at the Moses-Saunders Power Dam east of Massena, and at the Bridge Authority Plaza in Ogdensburg. In addition, many villages maintain their own information booths in July and August. These are almost always staffed by local volunteers who often can offer the kind of information no published guide covers.

CURRENCY. Canadian currency will be accepted at a discount throughout most of the region. Other foreign currencies could present a problem for the visitor, so conversion to American traveler's checks before arrival is advised. Because of the proximity to Quebec, many signs in the area say "nous parlons français." Finding local people who can help in translating other languages is not as easy, although there is a significant first-generation German population in the Lake Placid area.

DRIVING. The speed limit on the interstates and most highways is 55 miles per hour, and state police use radar. When driving at night, be particularly wary of deer on the highway.

TOURS. No matter where you visit in the North Country, from May through September, there is a **boat tour** nearby that is worth a try. Here is a sampler. In the Mohawk River, the *Nightingale II* has sightseeing tours, some including dinner, leaving from the Rte. 9 bridge, south of Saratoga Springs, 273–8878. On Lake George the steamship company operates three tour boats with one-hour to all-day sails from its docks in the village, 668–5777. On Lake Champlain, the *Juniper* sails from Plattsburgh around Valcour Island both days and evenings, 561–8970. While in the Champlain Valley, the ferries between New York and Vermont are a good way to see the lake. Especially pretty is the trip from Essex.

Other ferry locations are Ticonderoga, Pt. Kent (to Burlington) and Cumberland Head (Plattsburgh). Times and rates are available from the *Lake Champlain Transportation Company,* 802–864–9804. In the Thousand Islands, there are guided tours leaving regularly from Alexandria Bay—*Empire Boat Lines,* 315–482–9351, and *Uncle Sam Tours,* 315–482–2611—and from Clayton—*1000 Islands Seaway Cruises,* 315–686–3511, featuring stops at Boldt Castle. At Cape Vincent, you can take the region's only ferry to Canada. In the interior of the region, there are summer boat tours of Lake Placid, 523–8155, Saranac Lake, 891–3806, the Fulton Chain at Old Forge, 315–369–6473, and Blue Mountain Lake, 352–7351.

Back on land, Saratoga, in addition to its self-guided walking tour, offers a two-hour guided **bus tour** in July and August, 584–3255. In Lake Placid there is a guided tour of the Olympic venues, 523–4431, or you can take a **self-guided tour** that includes a ride up the Whiteface Mountain chairlift, 523–1655.

Within easy reach are four spots of special natural historic interest: *Ausable Chasm* on Rte. 9N south of Plattsburgh, 834–7454; *High Falls Gorge,* Rte. 86 in Wilmington between Whiteface Mountain and Lake Placid, 946–2278; *Natural Stone Bridge and Caves,* Rte. 9 north of I–87 exit 25 at Pottersville, 494–2283; and the *Barton Mines* outside North Creek, 251–2706. All four have tour programs in the summer months.

For **foliage** enthusiasts, the season starts in early September in the northern Adirondacks and generally runs through Columbus Day. I–87 between Lake George and Keeseville is an attractive route into the region. Other scenic highways that make for fine foliage trips include Rte. 73, from Rte. 9 off I–87 exit 30, to Lake Placid; the Blue Ridge Road from I–87 exit 29 to Newcomb; Rte. 30 from Northville to Lake Pleasant; Rte. 28 from Blue Mountain Lake to Alder Creek; Rte. 28 from Warrensburg to Indian Lake; Rte. 8 from Brant Lake to Rt. 30; Rte. 9N from Elizabethtown to Lake Placid, and Rte. 86 from Jay to Lake Placid via Wilmington.

SPECIAL-INTEREST SIGHTSEEING. For military history buffs, the North Country is of special interest. An easy tour of Revolutionary War sites would begin at the *Saratoga Battlefield* in Schuylerville, then north on Rtes. 4 and 32 to Whitehall, where the Skenesborough Museum marks the birthplace of the American Navy. North again, Rte. 22 along the east side of Lake George brings the visitor to *Ticonderoga.* The fort at Ticonderoga and the nearby batteries at Mt. Defiance and Mt. Hope guarded the key Lake Champlain–Lake George connector, while farther north on Rte. 9N, the state history site at Crown Point marks the spot of the fort overlooking the strategic Lake Champlain narrows section. This area was also crucial in the French and Indian wars, and two places readers of James Fennimore Cooper's *Last of the Mohicans* will recall are *Ft. William Henry* at Lake George (the 1936 Randolph Scott film is regularly featured at the fort) and the falls at Glens Falls, where Hawkeye and his party hid from the Hurons in a cavern. War of 1812 buffs will seek out the region's most northerly areas of interest, ranging from Plattsburgh, which the British occupied in 1814, to Sackets Harbor, which was headquarters to both the U.S. Army of the Northern Frontier and the Navy of the Great Lakes.

People in Saratoga during racing season may enjoy a behind-the-scenes look into the stables area. Regular tours are run from the flat track in the early mornings, while tours at the harness track can be arranged by calling 584–2110. Combine these activities with visits to the *National Museum of Racing and Thoroughbred Hall of Fame* on Union Ave., 584–0400, and the *Harness Hall of Fame* on Jefferson St., 587–4210.

The region features two waterways that were crucial to economic development. To see how the falls at Cohoes were bypassed to connect the Hudson and Mohawk rivers, the five lock "flight" at Waterford is an interesting stop. There are original canal locks in the *Vischer Ferry Nature* preserve west of the "flight" at Clifton Park. At the other end of the North Country, it was the locks at Massena and the creation of Lake St. Lawrence that permitted shipping from the Great Lakes to reach the Atlantic. The *Eisenhower Lock* and the nearby *Moses-Saunders Power Dam* are good spots to visit.

An interesting perspective on the region is from the **air.** There are sightseeing flights of the Thousand Islands–Seaway area from the Massena airport, High Peaks flights from the Lake Placid airport; seaplane tours of the Central Adirondacks wilderness areas from several locations along Rtes. 28 and 30 from Inlet to Long Lake to Wells; and perhaps most unusual of all, hot air **balloon tours** of the Adirondack foothills, leaving from Glens Falls, 793–6342.

STATE PARKS. When you think of state parks and the North Country, consider first that the *Adirondack Park* is larger than any park in the United States outside Alaska. Covering more than 6,000,000 acres, it is larger than Yosemite or Yellowstone. For that matter, it is also larger than the State of Massachusetts. At the other end of the spectrum is *Saratoga State Park.* In place of wilderness, it offers mineral spring baths with hot towels and massage, a luxury hotel, and a modern amphitheater that each year hosts an outstanding series of cultural events and prominent stars.

In between, there is every kind of park the visitor could want, including more than 250 North Country campgrounds, some 70 of which are operated by New York State. At least 10 of those can be reached only by boat. Most of the state campgrounds open in May and close in September. Reservations can be made up to 60 days in advance for the Memorial Day–Labor Day period, and available sites for July and August are taken quickly. However, the state will not reserve all its spaces and does leave spots open on a daily first-come, first-served basis. You must be at least 18 to reserve a state campsite. Reservation policies vary, so for a full listing of parks, their facilities, and how to make reservations, contact the *New York State Department of Parks, Recreation and Historic Preservation,* Albany, NY 12238, 518–474–0456.

Private campgrounds in the North Country that are open all year include the *Pine Grove* in Stratford, 315–429–3662; *Adirondack Loj* east of Lake Placid 518–523–3441; the *Lake Placid Whiteface Mountain KOA* in Wilmington, 518–946–7878; *High Falls Park* in Chateaugay, 518–497–3156; *Whispering Woods* in Long Lake, 518–624–5121; *Singing Waters* on Rte. 28 south of Old Forge, 518–369–6618; *Natural Bridge KOA* on Rte. 3 east of Watertown, 315–644–4880, and *Camp-a-Lot* in Pottersville, I–87 exit 26, 518–494–3692. The *Welles-*

ley Island state park campground near Alexandria Bay, 315–482–2722, is also open year round.

For those considering winter camping, be prepared for very cold weather, high winds, and heavy snow that can sweep quickly through the North Country. Also know the signs of frostbite and hypothermia. From mid-May through late June, the problem is of a different sort. The North Country, and the wilderness Adirondacks in particular, is home to the black fly. With careful dressing and cover-to-cover heavy-duty bug dope, you may duel the black fly to a draw. Fortunately, the black fly season generally ends by late June.

 RECOMMENDED READING. By far the richest collection of writing about the North Country focuses on the Adirondacks, dating back to William H. H. Murray's 1869 classic *Adventures in the Wilderness* that first popularized the region. Other books of note include William Chapman White's 1967 history *Adirondack Country;* Paul Jamieson's *Adirondack Reader,* a collection of stories and essays; and Frank Graham's *The Adirondack Park: a Political History,* a well written account on the who, what, and why of the establishment of the forest preserve. There are also two exceptional photo books on the Adirondacks, one by Clyde Smith and an album by Nathan Farb, produced to coincide with the Forest Preserve Centennial in 1985.

There is also *The Adirondack Guide* which bills itself as "an almanac of essential information and assorted trivia." Published by the Sagamore Institute in Raquette Lake, it is a matchless collection of regionalia. The best magazine of the area is *Adirondack Life,* published since 1970, now a bi-monthly and generally available on newsstands.

For the outdoors person, all publications of the Adirondack Mountain Club (ADK) should be considered authoritative.

For a lively history of 19th-century Saratoga, try George Waller's *Saratoga: Saga of an Impious Era. Lake Champlain, Key to Liberty* by Ralph Nading Hill traces development there from the French explorers up through the 19th century. Adrian Ten Cate's *The Pictorial History of the Thousand Islands* offers the best view of that region.

Daily newspapers in the region are published in Saratoga Springs, Glens Falls, Plattsburgh, Watertown, Ogdensburg, and Saranac Lake.

 SEASONAL EVENTS. The North Country calendar of events is a full one. Here's a sampling of annual activities. **Winter** is a carnival time in the North Country, and the oldest winter carnival in the country is held at Saranac Lake the second weekend in February. The ice sculptures on Lake Flower are worth the trip alone, 518–891–1990. Other winter carnivals are held at Lake George, Tupper Lake, Canton, Speculator, Raquette Lake, and Hague. Watertown celebrates its well-documented claim as "Snowtown USA" with festivities in early February. For specific events and dates contact *I Love N.Y. Tourism Office,* 90 Main Street, Lake Placid, NY 12946, 518–523–2412. At Lake Placid's Olympic facilities there are a full range of winter sports competitions, many at the national championship and international levels. For current listings, contact the *Olympic Regional Development Authority,* Olympic Center, Lake Placid, NY 12946, 518–523–1655.

Spring features a cluster of events the first weekend in May. At North Creek is the *Hudson River Whitewater Derby,* an annual event since 1958. In Saratoga, the annual *St. Clements Horse Show* is also that weekend, as is the lively *Caroline Street Block Party* downtown, 584–3255. On May 6, the chimney swifts return to the village of Northville, and the last Sunday in May, the annual **bed race** is held on the Main Street of Bolton Landing on Lake George. May is also the month for the annual Adirondack Folk Singing and Storytelling Festival at the Sagamore Lodge and Conference Center in Raquette Lake, 315–354–5311. On the second Sunday in June, the most grueling event of the year takes place: the eight-mile **road race** straight up Whiteface Mountain from Wilmington. Also in June, the *New York State Fiddlers' Contest* is held the third weekend at Old Forge; and under the heading of "If you can't beat them, lets have a party anyway," there is the *Black Fly Festival* at Inlet on Rte. 28 the first weekend in June, 315–369–6145.

In **summer** throughout the region there are flea markets, arts and crafts shows, and antique shows. The annual **guide boat/canoe race and marathon** is held at Tupper Lake in late June, 518–359–2507; and about the same time in Lake Placid is the annual *I Love N.Y. Horse Show,* 523–2445. On July 4th there are parades in Jay and in Schroon Lake, and the annual ski jump competition is held at Intervale just outside Lake Placid. The weeklong *Seaway Festival* is held in Ogdensburg in July 315–393–3620; and on the second weekend in the month, there are *Woodsmen's Days,* at Tupper Lake, 518–359–2507; a *French Festival* at Cape Vincent, 315–482–2520; and the *Mayor's Cup* sailing races on Lake Champlain at Plattsburgh, 518–563–1000. August features include the *Festival of North Country Folklife* at Massena, 315–379–3525; and the annual *Antique Boat Show* at Clayton, 315–686–4104. Summer is the time for country fairs in the region, with 10 scheduled from mid-July through late August.

Fall events include the colorful *Hot Air Balloon Festival* at Glens Falls in late September, 518–761–6366; an annual competition among members of the *Muzzle Loading Association* the third weekend in September at Ft. Ticonderoga; and on Columbus Day weekend, a townwide street sale billed as the "World's largest garage sale" in Warrensburg and an *Oktoberfest* and parade at North Creek and the Gore Mountain Ski Center.

The New York State Department of Commerce publishes a quarterly calendar of special events. To receive copies, contact the department's *Division of Tourism,* One Commerce Plaza, Albany, NY 12244, 800–CALL–NYS. Full calendars of events are also available through chambers of commerce and county promotion offices throughout the North Country.

PARTICIPANT SPORTS. Everyone in the North Country is a sportsman of some sort, or at least so it seems. The reason is that the ingredients for outdoor activities are so close at hand as to be almost unavoidable. Apart from the ever-present opportunities for hiking and swimming, perhaps the most popular activity in the region is **fishing.** Brook trout and lake trout are native to the area and bass migrated into the North Country with the opening of the Erie Canal. The largest northern pike ever caught in North America, a 46-pounder, was taken in the Sacandaga Reservoir in 1940, and the largest muskellunge, 69 lbs 15 oz, was caught in the St. Lawrence River in 1957. The St. Lawrence is today considered one of the finest bass waters in the U.S., having hosted the annual *Bass Anglers Sportsmen Society (BASS) Classic* in 1980. Lake Champlain, Lake George, Saratoga Lake, and the Mohawk River are excellent fishing waters, but good catches are possible just about anywhere in the region. For example, there are 407 trout ponds in the Adirondacks. The State Department of Environmental Conservation (DEC) maintains fishing hotlines in its regional offices. In the southern and eastern areas of the North Country, the number is 518–623–3682; in the northern area, 518–891–5413; and in the western are 315–782–2663.

Hunting. DEC also manages hunting in New York. Largely a fall activity, bear hunting begins in late September and is done mostly in the Central Adirondacks. The regular deer hunting season runs from late October through early December, and while it is popular throughout the region, the larger takes are from the lowlands, with St. Lawrence County generally the most productive area. Reestablished in the area just a few years ago, the wild turkey is rapidly becoming popular with hunters, particularly in Washington County, east of Lake George. Contact DEC for hunting and fishing license information. Licenses are available at sports shops throughout the region.

Whitewater rafting. Growing in popularity is whitewater rafting, particularly the run from Indian Lake to North Creek on the Upper Hudson River (*Hudson River Rafting Co.,* 518–696–2964), the Black River Route at Watertown (*Adirondack River Outfitters,* 315–788–1311), and, for the most adventurous, along the Big Moose River near Old Forge (*Adirondack River Outfitters,* 315–369–3525). For tubing, try the Sacandaga River along Rte. 30 from Wells to Hope Valley, a leisurely route, or, for more action, the lower section of the Sacandaga between Stewarts Dam and the town of Hadley on Rte. 9N, west of Lake George.

Canoeing is also a popular sport throughout the North Country. There are a variety of opportunities for competition, including the *Hudson Whitewater Derby* in North Creek each May, one of the oldest events in the county, and the races at Tupper Lake and Saranac Lake each summer.

Running. Runners will find the North Country very appealing, and there are road races held regularly throughout the region, most of which can be entered the day of the run. Among the most pleasant spots to run is along the Avenue of the Pines in Saratoga's State Park, and around Mirror Lake in Lake Placid. Popular road races in the area are the *Saratoga Battlefield 15K* in September; the *Fort-to-Fort Run* between Crown Point and Ticonderoga, also in September; the *Lake Placid Marathon* in the fall, and the *Flaming Leaves 10K* in North Creek, held in conjunction with the Oktoberfest there. The toughest race of the lot is in June, an eight-miler from Wilmington straight uphill to the summit of Whiteface Mountain.

There are **golf** courses throughout the area, with the Lake Placid Club and the new Sagamore golf course at Bolton Landing the most challenging. Many clubs and lodges have **tennis** courts. Among the best free facilities are seven courts at Schroon Lake Village.

The North Country has not been developed for **winter sports** to the extent of Vermont and New Hampshire, due in large part to the restrictions covering the rugged Adirondack areas. However, excellent facilities exist in the region, especially in the Lake Placid area.

Alpine Skiing. There are five "major" (more than 1,000 feet of vertical drop) ski areas in the North Country, including *Whiteface Mountain* in Wilmington, site of the 1980 Winter Olympic Alpine events. The other large areas are *Big Tupper,* just south of Tupper Lake; *Gore Mountain* in North Creek; *Hickory Ski Center,* just west of Warrensburg; and *West Mountain,* west of I–87 exit 18 at Glens Falls. For less expansive and generally less expensive skiing, there are several smaller areas in the region: *McCauley Mountain* at Old Forge; *Oak Mountain* at Speculator; and in the south, *Alpine Meadows Ski Area* at Corinth; *Royal Mountain* at Caroga Lake; and *Willard Mountain* at Easton.

Cross country skiing is widely enjoyed. Some of the more popular spots where there are first rate trails and good grooming include *Saratoga State Park, Crandall Park* in Glens Falls; *Barkeater Lodge* in Keene; *Mt. Van Hoevenberg,* site of the 1980 Winter Olympic Nordic races; *Cold River Ranch,* east of Tupper Lake; *Garnet Hill Lodge* in North River; *Cunningham's Ski Barn* in North

Creek; *Lapland Lake Nordic Ski Center* at Benson off Rte. 30 north of North-ville; *Nature Center,* Wellesley Island; *Wiley Nature Center,* Watertown.

Snowmobiling is popular throughout the region, although *Old Forge,* with over 500 miles of marked trails, can claim to be the center of activity. For regulations and maps contact the New York State Department of Environmental Conservation at 50 Wolf Road, Albany, NY 12233, or local chambers of commerce.

Skating. The *Olympic Arena,* where the U.S. hockey team won the gold medal in 1980, offers some public ice skating, and the quarter-mile speed-skating oval next door, where Eric Heiden won his five Olympic gold medals, is open to the public, too. There are ice rinks at Glens Falls, Plattsburgh, Saranac Lake, Potsdam, and Canton, plus numerous other rinks and pond and lake skating throughout the region. Speed-skating enthusiasts, novice to expert, will enjoy fraternity and competition at the oval track in Saratoga State Park.

Bobsledding is not for everyone, but the only place you can discover how it suits you is at Mt. Van Hoevenberg near Lake Placid, where a ride down from the halfway point costs $7.50. A far tamer slide is the toboggan ramp onto Mirror Lake in Lake Placid.

For a solid introduction to some of the participation activities, the *Sagamore Lodge and Conference Center* in Raquette Lake, 315–354–5303, and the *Adirondack Mountain Club* in Glens Falls, 518–793–7737, offer excellent instructional programs.

 SPECTATOR SPORTS. By far the most popular spectator sport in the region takes place over a four-week period in August at Saratoga. There, the best *thoroughbreds* in the country **race** at the 100-year-old flat track. Because of the stiff competition under stringent rules, Saratoga is often called the "graveyard of champions." The highlight of the annual meet comes on the third Saturday—*Travers Day.* The Travers, the nation's oldest stakes race, is considered by race fans as the "fourth leg of the Triple Crown," and over the years it has been tough on favorites. Man o' War was beaten for the only time there by a horse named Upset, and more recently, Secretariat suffered his only loss there too. Saratoga in racing season also hosts world class **polo** competition. Less than a mile from the flat track is *Saratoga Harness,* billed as the "fastest half mile track in the country." The harness track has racing dates throughout the year, including mid-winter when the glass-enclosed grandstand is especially welcome.

There is an American League **hockey** team in Glens Falls and major intercollegiate hockey is played by Clarkson in Potsdam and St. Lawrence University in Canton.

Because of its facilities and aggressive management by the *Olympic Regional Development Authority (ORDA),* Lake Placid continues to host international winter sports competition, including World Cup, North American, and U.S. championships in alpine and Nordic **skiing, biathlon, ski jumping, bobsled, luge,** and **speed skating.** There are frequent hockey matches and figure skating competitions in the Olympic Arena, too. For information, contact the Olympic Regional Development Authority, Olympic Center, Lake Placid, NY 12946, 518–523–1655.

Two of the more unusual spectator sports in the region are the Adirondack hot air **balloon** races at Glens Falls in late September, and dog sled racing at Saranac Lake in January.

For an offbeat summer activity, watch the **ski jumping** on plastic mats at the Intervale site at Lake Placid. There is jumping competition on July 4, in August, and on Columbus Day weekend.

 CHILDREN'S ACTIVITIES. Children who enjoy (or who are likely to enjoy) the outdoors will love the North Country. It is an exceptional place for families to explore together. Hiking, biking, boating, camping, and fishing are all readily available, and lodges throughout the area have listings of local activities. In the Adirondacks in particular, there are plenty of activities that aren't available back home.

Although not for toddlers, **whitewater rafting** trips on the upper Hudson and Black rivers have thrills aplenty, and with expert guides are a safe adventure. Teenagers will enjoy it. Try the Sacandaga at Hadley-Lake Luzerne in July and August for an introduction to whitewater. A couple of trial **hikes** gentle enough to start the kids off would be *Mt. Severance* in Schroon Lake and *Mt. Jo* from Adirondack Loj near Lake Placid. **Canoeing** in the Raquette River area or the St. Regis area north of Tupper Lake are good introductions to the wilderness, with the likelihood that the party will spot some wildlife—deer, beaver, and perhaps a mink—along the route.

To make the wilderness adventure as full as possible for both children and adults, consider hiring a guide for the trip. There is a colorful history to Adirondack guiding, dating back to the early 19th century. For information, contact the *New York State Outdoor Guides Association,* Box 4337, Albany, NY 12204.

At the *Adirondacks Lakes Center for the Arts* in Blue Mountain Lake, there are **puppet shows,** 518–352–7715. For an interesting look at how maple syrup is made, try Cornell University's Uihlein Research Extension Field Station at Lake Placid in July and August, 518–523–9337.

In Watertown, there is the *See Tech Center* on the second floor of the State Office Building 315–788–1340, and in nearby Sackets Harbor, *Old McDonald's Farm* features a tractor hayride. On the **farming** theme also is the *Miner Institute* two miles west of Chazy near plattsburgh on Rte. 191; 518–846–8020/7217, open daily until 6 P.M. year-round.

Horseback touring at **dude ranches** such as *Roaring Brook, Sit 'N Bull,* and *Rydin-Hi* in the Lake George area are child-pleasers, too. *The Painted Pony Ranch* at Lake Luzerne has a **rodeo** every Friday and features overnight horseback camping trips. For backwoods riding, try the Cold River Ranch east of Tupper Lake.

In winter, **ski centers** in the area offer instruction tailored for youngsters and *Whiteface Mountain* in Wilmington and *Gore Mountain* in North Creek have excellent base lodge day care facilities. To get the youngsters on downhill skis without a lift charge, try *Dynamite Hill* on Rte. 8 at Chestertown. There is a tow-rope, and it's a good spot to introduce a child to the slopes.

The 18th-century history of the region is animated at Ft. William Henry in Lake George and Ft. Ticonderoga. Both feature regularly scheduled period military drills and parades. If you are in the Champlain Valley in early fall, everyone will enjoy an apple-picking stop at any one of several "pick-your-own" farms in the Ticonderoga–Crown Point area.

Of interest to children, and free, are the **fish hatcheries** in the area. The largest is located at Saranac Inn near Saranac Lake. Others are at Crown Point, Warrensburg, and Cape Vincent. Not a hatchery, but fascinating if you hit it at the right time in the fall, is the fish ladder at Willsboro where salmon go around the falls and up the Boquet River. There is a viewing window at the falls, which are in the center of town.

Mid-July to August is **county fair** time in the North Country, and there are 10 fairs each year in the region. Young children in particular will enjoy the farm animals.

Amusement-theme parks in the region are located along I–87 at exits 19, 21, 29, and 39; at Caroga Lake; Old Forge; and at Wilmington.

 MUSEUMS AND HISTORIC SITES. Practically every town in the North Country has a historical society that will enable visitors interested in local history to find an outlet for curiosity and study. Museums and galleries range from repositories of artifacts, curios, handicrafts, and memorabilia to exhibits of genuine artistic endeavor. Most are free and open only during the summer months. They are listed here by community as well as by area. Unless otherwise specified, telephone numbers are area code 518.

SARATOGA AREA

Saratoga Springs. *Historical Society of Saratoga Springs Museum and Walworth Memorial Museum/Casino.* Congress Park; 584–6920. Former gambling casino with exhibition highlighting 19th-century Saratoga. Open daily June–October; Wednesday–Sunday P.M. only. November–May. Adults, $2; senior citizens and students, $1.50.

National Museum of Racing and Thoroughbred Hall of Fame. Union Avenue; 584–0400. Horseracing paintings, trophies, and memorabilia. Open seven days a week June 15–September 15; Monday–Friday and Saturday P.M. remainder of year. Free.

Ballston Spa. *National Bottle Museum.* In Verbeck House, 20 Church Ave.; 885–7589. Features antique bottles, jars, stoneware, and related items; research library on bottle collecting. Early June–Labor Day, daily 10 A.M.–4 P.M. Donation, $1.

Schuylerville. *Saratoga National Historical Park.* Rtes. 4 and 32; 664–9821. Visitors' Center with film and walking/driving tour of Revolutionary War battlefield. Open daily April–November. One week pass costs $3 per car.

General Philip Schuyler House. Rte. 4; 695–3664. 18th-century "country home" near Saratoga battlefield. Open daily mid-June–early September; fall and spring, weekends only; closed winter. Free.

Whitehall. *Skenesborough Museum.* Rtes. 4 and 22; 499–0754. Exhibits mark launching place of first American naval vessels to see combat in American Revolution. Open daily, June–Labor Day. Admission by donation.

ADIRONDACKS

Blue Mountain Lake. *Adirondack Museum.* Rte. 28N; 352–7311. Exceptional regional museum with 20 buildings devoted to history and culture of the Adirondacks. A must for those interested in the region. Open daily June 15–Oct. 15. Adults, $6; senior citizens, $5; children 7–15, $3.75.

Caroga. *Caroga Historical Museum.* Rtes. 29A and 10, London Bridge Rd., Caroga Lake; 835–4400. Cobbler shop, general store, small community artifacts, some crafts. Open Tuesday–Sunday, July–September. Free.

Crown Point. *National Historic Landmark,* Rtes. 9N and 22; 597–3666. Visitors' center at site of 18th-century French and British fort. Open late May–late October, Wednesday–Sunday. Free.

Penfield Homestead Museum. four miles west of Crown Point, in hamlet of Ironville; 597–3804. Quaint 19th-century settlement once a center for iron mining. Good spot for picnic. Open Tuesday–Sunday mid-May to mid-October. Free.

Elizabethtown. *Adirondack Center Museum–Colonial Garden.* Rte. 9; 873–6466. Emphasis on early Adirondack artifacts. Colonial garden in rear. Open daily May 15–October 15. Free.

Glens Falls. *Chapman Historical Museum.* 348 Glen St. (Rte. 9); 793–2826. Late 19th-century home featuring local history exhibits and extensive photo library. Open Tuesday–Saturday afternoons; closed January. Free.

Tupper's Early American & Farm Museum. 10 miles north I–87 exit 20, then 10 miles north on Rte. 149 to Copeland Pond Rd. at W. Fort Ann; 792–6058. Parklike collection of early American buildings, covered bridge, waterwheels, and wagons. Nature trails. Open dawn–dusk daily, June–October. Free.

Lake Placid. *John Brown Farm.* 1 mile south of Rte. 73 near Intervale ski jumps; 523–3900. Home and burial site of famous abolitionist who operated farm/refuge for runaway slaves. Museum open Wednesday–Sunday May–late October. Free.

Lake Placid/North Elba Museum and Country Store. Off Rte. 73 in converted train station; 523–3551. Local history items, including some Olympic artifacts. Open Wednesdays–Sundays afternoons, June–October. Free.

Onchiota. *Six Nations Indian Museum.* 6 miles north of Saranac Lake; 891–0769. Iroquois relics and folklore; exhibits and lectures. Open daily Memorial Day–Labor Day.

Plattsburgh. *Kent-Delord House Museum.* 17 Cumberland Ave.; 561–1035. 1799 home commandeered by British as headquarters during 1814 Battle of Plattsburgh. Guided tours, Tuesdays–Saturdays at 10 A.M., 1 P.M., and 3 P.M. Adults, $2; senior citizens, $1; children 12 and under, 50¢.

Raquette Lake. *Camp Sagamore.* 4 miles south of Rte. 28 at Raquette Lake Village; 315–354–5311. Adirondack Great Camp built in 1897 by Albert Vanderbilt; now a conference center. Guided tours with slide show. Open July–August, weekends; fall, Sundays. Call for times and rates.

Saranac Lake. *Robert Louis Stevenson Memorial Cottage.* 11 Stevenson La.; 891–4480. Adirondack retreat of famed author includes letters and first editions. Open Tuesdays–Sundays, July 1–September 15. Adults, $1; children 12 and under, 50¢.

Ticonderoga. *Ft. Ticonderoga Museum;* 585–2821. Carefully restored fort first built by the French in 1755. Excellent collection of 18th-century weapons plus regular military drills and parades. Open daily mid-May–mid-October. Adults, $5; senior citizens, $4.50; children 10–13, $3; children 9 and under, free.

THOUSAND ISLANDS – SEAWAY

Clayton. *Thousand Islands Shipyard Museum;* 315–686–4104. Fine collection of antique boats and items on river history. Open daily, June–Labor Day; Thursday–Monday in May and September–October. Adults, $3; senior citizens, $2; children 7–17, $1.

Massena. *Massena History Center and Museum;* 315–769–8511. Local history from 1802. Open year round, Mondays–Fridays afternoons. Free.

Sackets Harbor. *Battlefield.* Rte. 3; 315–646–3634. Site of two battles in War of 1812. Former Union Hotel is visitors' center. Open Tuesdays–Sundays, June–Labor Day. Free.

CULTURAL EVENTS AND PLACES. Despite its rugged appearance and despite much of its area being designated "forever wild," the North Country offers a delightful potpourri of cultural activities and sites, ranging from classical music and ballet to lecture series and art displays. Settings may be a modern auditorium, a rustic building, or outdoors—almost always with a backdrop of mountains, lakes, or both. The cultural events and places listed here are by area and community. Unless otherwise specified, telephone numbers are area code 518.

SARATOGA AREA

Saratoga Springs. *Saratoga Performing Arts Center;* 587–3300, 584–9330. A steady program of first rate arts activities from June to September. The calendar includes the New York City Ballet in July, the Philadelphia Orchestra, in August, modern dance, theater, chamber concerts, and special events such as the Kool Jazz Festival and popular music concerts. Clearly the performing arts capital of the region in summer.

The National Museum of Dance. Rte. 9, in the remodeled Washington Bath House in Saratoga Spa State Park; 584–2230. This institution, the only of its kind in the country, had its inaugural season in the summer of 1987. Open Tuesday to Saturday 10 A.M.–5 P.M., Sundays 12–4 P.M.; after mid-September Thursday to Saturday 10 A.M.–5 P.M., Sundays 12–4 P.M. Closed Dec. 20 through May. Admission charged.

ADIRONDACKS

Blue Mountain Lake. *Adirondack Lakes Center for the Arts.* Rtes. 28 and 30; 352–7715. Concerts, theater, arts and crafts in summer. Center open year round.

Adirondack Museum. Rtes. 28 and 30; 532–7311. This excellent museum has a fine collection of paintings of the region plus Adirondack crafts. Also "Mondays at the Museum" lecture series July–August. Open daily June 15–October 15.

Glens Falls. *Hyde Collection.* 161 Warren St.; 792–1761. The best general fine arts collection in the region includes works by Rembrandt, Rubens, and Degas. Tuesdays, Wednesdays, Fridays–Sundays, afternoons, all year.

Lake George Opera Festival. Aviation Rd.; I–87 exit 19, between Glens Falls and Lake George; 793–6642. July and August performances, including Sunday evening opera cruises on Lake George. Professional company since 1961.

Lake Luzerne. *Luzerne Chamber Music Festival.* Rte. 9N west of Lake George; 696–2771. Ensemble concerts by members of the Philadelphia Orchestra. July and August.

Lake Placid. *Lake Placid Center for the Arts.* Rte. 86; 523–2512. Summer program includes theater, concerts, and films. Art gallery year round.

Adirondacks Environmental Lecture series at Adirondack Loj; 523–3441. Sponsored by Adirondack Mountain Club. Wednesdays and Sundays evenings, July and August.

Old Forge. *Community Arts Center.* Rte. 28. Art exhibits, crafts programs, theater productions, films. Residency programs in painting and photo journalism. Open daily 9 A.M.–5 P.M., July–August; Wednesdays–Sundays afternoons, spring and fall.

Plattsburgh. *Rockwell Kent Gallery.* SUNY at Plattsburgh Gallery; 564–2121. Most complete collection of American artist's work, including paintings, drawings, and prints. Open year round Tuedays–Fridays, 11 A.M.–4 P.M. Free. Part of full cultural events program at college.

Saranac Lake. *Pendragon Theater.* 518–891–1854.

Schroon Lake. *Boathouse Concerts;* 532–7675. Waterfront chamber music series. Sunday evenings, July–August.

Seagle Colony. Rte. 9, south of village, right on Charley Hill Road; 532–7675. Summer retreat for musical theater professionals who present three productions July–August.

Ticonderoga. *Festival Guild.* Montcalm St.; 585–6716. Concerts on the green July–August.

Westport. *Depot Theater.* 4 miles east of I–87 exit 31, at Westport train depot; 962–4449. Summer theater and recitals program. Memorial Day–Labor Day.

Wilmington. *Whiteface Lecture Series.* West of Wilmington on Whiteface Mtn. Highway to Atmospheric Sciences Research Center Rd.; 946–7191. Excellent Tuesday evening series of lectures on Adirondack science topics preceded by in-depth weather briefing by senior staff of this meteorological research center.

THOUSAND ISLANDS–SEAWAY

Clayton. *Thousand Islands Museum Crafts School;* 315–686–4123. Courses in pottery, textiles, jewelry-making, painting. July–August. Also, there is the *River Barge Production Theater* performing in the Town Hall, 315–686–3566.

Malone. *Ballard Mill.* S. Williams St. by Salmon River; 483–0909. Restored mill now serves as an arts and crafts center; shops too. Open daily. Free.

Ogdensburg. *Remington Arts Museum.* State and Washington Sts.; 315–393–2425. Largest collection of paintings, bronze sculptures and drawings by Frederic Remington, the best artist of the American West. A must-see. Open year round 10 A.M.–5 P.M., Mondays–Saturdays; Sundays, 1–5 P.M., June–September.

Potsdam. *Music Theatre North.* SUNY at Potsdam; 315–267–2251. Summer program of musicals at college known for its Crane School of Music. Also on campus is well regarded Brainerd Hall Art Gallery. Call for program and events.

 BEACHES. You are never far from fresh-water swimming in the North Country, for there are more than 50 public beaches in the region. Some of the better known facilities are at *Moreau State Park* near Saratoga; *Lake George Village, Schroon Lake, Plattsburgh, Robert Moses State Park* near Massena, and *Mirror Lake* at Lake Placid. Unless you have a strong tolerance to cold water, swimming is a July–August activity in this region.

 SHOPPING. The North Country is not a place people come for a shopping binge, but should the urge strike, there are some unusual stores in the region.

Some 90 percent of the world's industrial garnet is mined at the *Barton Mines,* Rte. 28, 251–2706, outside North Creek. There are regular tours of the Barton site, plus a gift shop which offers some one-of-a-kind garnet jewelry items.

For mountaineering geer, try *Eastern Mountain Sports* in Lake Placid or the *Mountaineer* on Rte. 73 in Keene Valley. For the best in fly fishing tackle—and advice on where to use it—visit *Francis Betters'* shop on Rte. 86 in Wilmington. Betters is credited with developing the Ausable Wuff, a well known trout-taker in Adirondack streams.

There are shopping centers in the cities around the perimeter of the region and one stretch of Rte. 9 from Glen Falls to Lake George is particularly interesting for its name brand outlet shops. But as you move to the interior where the population is scattered, the general store is the center for shopping. Two of the more interesting ones are *Hoss' Country Corner* at the intersection of Rtes. 28N and 30 at Long Lake, and *The Old Forge Hardware* in Old Forge, "the Adirondack's most general store." For pricy shopping, the *Adirondack Store* on Rte. 86 west of Lake Placid has an unusual collection of regional items and a mail order catalogue.

There are craftspeople throughout the region. A sampling of the better known includes the *Jay Crafts Center,* Rte. 9N in Jay; the *North Country Craft Co-op,* Rtes. 9 and 22 in Westport; Adirondack boat builder *Carl Hathaway* in Saranac Lake; *Green's* custom snow shoes in Broadalbin (for demonstrations, call ahead, 883–3703); *Blue Mountain Designs, Crafts,* Rtes. 28N and 30, Blue Mountain Lake; *The Banjo Shop,* musical instruments, Rte. 28 in Old Forge, and *Heitz' Rustic* furniture, Rte. 28, between North Creek and Indian Lake. The Lake Placid Center for the Arts, Rte. 86 west of the village, now includes the *North Country Crafts Center,* a gallery and store featuring the work of regional artists.

For more idle browsing of the sort requiring several small shops, Saratoga Springs and Lake Placid are the best bets. Both have a streetful, most one-of-a-kinds. In Saratoga Springs you can fuel your stroll with a stop at *Mrs. London's* on Phila Street. A calorie jolter along Main Street in Lake Placid is *Helmut's* strudel. Unusual shopping opportunities are limited in Saranac Lake, but try it anyway for an excuse to sample the baked goods at the *Yum Yum Tree.* For those with a sweet tooth, don't leave the High Peaks area without a container of locally produced maple syrup.

Bookstores throughout the North Country have regional works as well as standard fare, but two that specialize in area titles are *With Pipe and Book,* Main Street, Lake Placid, and *Wildwood* on Rte. 28 in Old Forge.

 DINING OUT. The Saratoga area is clearly the North Country's cuisine capital, with a long list of excellent restaurants. There are fine dining spots elsewhere in the region, most notably in some of the country inns, and always worth a try for the adventure alone is Hotel Saranac in Saranac Lake, which culinary arts students from Paul Smith's College use as a laboratory-classroom. The emphasis in most North Country restaurants is on straightforward presentation and ample portions. Breakfasts tend to be especially large, perhaps a legacy of the lumbering days when men in the field camps regularly consumed a dozen or more eggs in the morning to get themselves through until dinner. Prices noted are for an average three-course dinner for one person; beverages, tax, and tip are extra. *Expensive,* more than $20; *Moderate,* $12.50 to $20; and *Inexpensive,* less the $12.50. Prices are based on peak season—summer months and holidays.

As in our listing of hotels, we've begun the restaurant listing with the Saratoga area, followed by the Lake George area, Champlain Valley, Central Adirondacks, the Olympic area, and ending in the Thousand Islands–Seaway area. Unless specified, the area code for all telephone numbers is 518.

SARATOGA AND WASHINGTON COUNTY

Expensive

The Chateau Fleur de Lys. Rte. 22, North Granville; 642–1511. In a Victorian mansion with five guest rooms. Owner-chef's specialties include veal, sweetbreads, frog legs. Special children's menu.

Cock 'n Bull. Parkis Mills Rd., off Rte. 147, Galway; 882–6962. Tucked away in the smallest incorporated village in New York State, this converted barn offers daily chalkboard specials, including pheasant, quail, and game, according to season. Standard menu selections include prime ribs of beef, cock 'n bull kabob, fresh seafood. Dinners daily; open for lunch June–August.

Donovan's. Rte 146 and Plank Rd., Clifton Park; 383–2294. Specializes in hickory-smoked barbecued ribs and chicken. No children's menu.

The Elms. Rte. 9 in Malta; 587–2277. Fine Italian cuisine with veal dishes a specialty, along with homemade pastas.

Ertha's Kitchen. Phila St., Saratoga Springs; 583–0602. Outstanding blackboard menu changes daily. Dinner only.

Gideon Putnam. Saratoga Spa 584–3000. Elegant American dining, with the Sunday brunch a worthwhile treat.

Mrs. London's Bake Shop and Tea Room. 33 Phila St., Saratoga Springs; 584–6633. This patisserie-cafe serves breakfast and lunch; specialties include pastries, teas, coffees. Open June–August.

Sam's Place. Rte. 9, Malta; 587–5943. Italian cuisine in unusual, converted diner setting (don't let the outside fool you). Distinctively good food, especially the squid and other seafood and pasta dishes.

Ye Olde Wishing Well. Rte. 9, 5 miles north of Saratoga Springs; 584–7640. American cuisine specialties served in 1823 farmhouse. Baking done on premises. Children's plates. Reservation a must in summer.

Moderate

Chez Pierre. Rte. 9, Gansvoort; 793–3350. Family-operated restaurant since 1963 with French cuisine. Specialties include veal Oscar, tournedos Henri, turtle soup, and shrimp bisque. Cold soups especially popular in summer. Home-baked pastries; children's plates.

Lillian's Restaurant. 430 Broadway, Saratoga Springs; 587–7766. Lunch favorites here are gourmet burgers and crock of soup with half sandwich. Dinner menu offers seafood, beef, and chicken dishes. Typical yuppie atmosphere.

Old Dater Tavern. Farm to Market Road, Clifton Park; 877–7225. 200-year-old tavern with five small dining rooms, specializing in veal, chicken, and seafood. All breads, desserts, soups, and salad dressings homemade. No children's menu; craft shops upstairs.

The Olde Bryan Inn. 123 Maple Ave., Saratoga Springs; 587–2990. Historic tavern with three fireplaces; building dates to 1773. Light dining, including salads, sandwiches, omelets, and burgers.

Spa Brauhaus. East High St., Ballston Spa; 885–4311. Solid German cooking. Open year round.

Top Notch Tavern. Three miles west of Galway village center off Rte. 147; 842–8915. Prime rib portions up to 32 ounces. Open year-round; closed Mondays.

Union Coach House. 139 Union Ave., Saratoga Springs; 584–6440. Stuffed pork chops and chicken Kiev are favorites here. Dinner year round except January, when restaurant is closed; lunch served summers.

Wallie's. 56 Main St., Greenwich; 692–7823. Specializing in prime rib and seafood, large portions. Homemade baked goodies; children's plates.

Inexpensive

Cliff's Country Inn. Rte. 9P, Saratoga Lake; 584–9791. Decidedly unfancy, but steak lovers don't care when Cliff delivers a 20-ounce prime piece of beef for about $10. Prime rib even bigger on weekends. Closed Tuesdays. No credit cards.

Hattie's Chicken Shack. 45 Phila St., Saratoga Springs; 584–4790. Don't miss Hattie's for the best southern fried chicken in these parts. Reservations a must in summer.

Mother Goldsmith's. 43 Phila St., Saratoga Springs. Mother's rib eye steak platter is a favorite among residents.

Stewart's. Headquartered in Saratoga but located throughout the area and into the Adirondacks, these convenience stores serve good ice cream and—at most shops—inexpensive deli sandwiches. Open early morning to late evening, year-round.

LAKE GEORGE AREA

Expensive

The Georgian. 384 Canada St., Lake George Village; 668–5401. Pleasant setting overlooking lake offers continental menu, with specialties including roast Long Island duckling, sauteed filet of tenderloin. Home baked goodies. Outdoor dining for lunch in summer. Bar, children's menu.

Log Jam. Rtes. 9 and 149, Lake George Village; 798–1155. Traditional American fare, such as steaks, fresh seafood, prime rib, in rustic decor. Home-made breads and salad bar. Light menu and children's plates also offered.

Merrill Magee House. 2 Hudson St., Warrensburg; 623–2449. Charming 19th-century inn serving lunch and dinner in two small dining rooms illuminated by candlelight. Specialties include beef Wellington, tournedos, and New York strip steak; sinful desserts baked on premises.

Montcalm South. Lake George Village; 793–6601. Continental, American menu with specialties including red snapper, veal Oscar, prime rib. Homemade baked goods. Children's plates; senior citizen rates on Sundays. Bar and valet parking.

Red Coach Grill. Lake George Rd., Glens Falls; 793–4455. Traditional American menu includes prime rib, veal dishes, roast duck, bountiful salad bar, homemade breads and pastries. Children's plates. Valet parking.

The Sagamore. Causeway in Bolton Landing; 644–9400. Resort complex on private island has a choice of dining areas. The Trillium is the formal dining room; the Sagamore Dining Room offers a fixed price haute cuisine menu. Reservations and jackets are required for dinner in both. The hotel's less formal dining area is called Mr. Brown's Cafe. Van Winkles is a nightclub in the hotel.

Moderate

Algonquin Bar and Restaurant. Lake Shore Dr., Bolton Landing; 644–9442. Popular spot in summer, due in part to access by boat. Restaurant and bar overlook lake. Full menu includes veal specialties, seafood, burgers, and sandwiches.

Ashley's. Lake Shore Dr., Bolton Landing; 644–3484. Casual atmosphere, with specialties including steaks, seafood, veal, and—in season—saddle of venison.

Bavarian House. Lake Shore Dr., Lake George Village; 668–2476. Family-operated establishment for over 25 years, specializing in German dishes. Children's menu. Open May–October.

Blacksmith Shop. Aviation Rd., Glens Falls; 792–4550. Steak, steak, and only steak—plus salad bar and children's portions—at this popular spot.

Garden in the Park. In Queensbury Hotel, 99 Ridge St., Glens Falls; 792–1121. American cuisine, with seasonal menu including steak and seafood dishes. Homemade baked goods; luscious desserts. Leisurely brunch on Sundays.

Manor Inn Restaurant. Lake Shore Dr., Bolton Landing; 644–9750. Northern Italian, German, and seafood specialties served in casual, pleasant atmosphere. Children's menu. Docking space for boats. Open mid-May–mid-October.

Inexpensive

Coach House. Lake Shore Dr., Diamond Point; 668–2498. American fare includes light dining and children's portions; scrumptious desserts. Open Memorial Day–Labor Day.

CHAMPLAIN VALLEY

Expensive

Valcour Lodge. Lakeshore Rd., Plattsburgh; 563–3518. Lakeside dining includes French specialties, along with steaks and seafood. Homemade baked goods; children's menu; Sunday brunch. Reservation recommended. Limited docking, boat mooring. Open Memorial Day–Labor Day.

Moderate

Anthony's Restaurant. Upper Cornelia Street, Plattsburgh; 561–6420. Attractive split-level dining room serves continental cuisine plus fresh seafood, steaks. Cocktail lounge; children's menu.

Ausable Chasm Inn. Rte. 9, 3 miles north of Keeseville; 543–6576. Historic stone building dates back to 1876. Specialties are stuffed pork chops with inn's special dressing, homemade soups, seafood, prime ribs.

Bayview Restaurant and Lounge. I–87 exit 33, Willsboro; 963–4177. Overlooks Farrell Bay of Lake Champlain; 150 feet of boat dockage. Specialties include prime rib; veal, and seafood, plus unusual spinach linguine with red clam sauce.

D & H Restaurant. Bridge Street Station, Plattsburgh; 561–1973. Historic railroad building, built in 1886. Two levels of dining, each with a view of Lake Champlain. Serves prime rib, steaks, seafood, veal dishes, homemade pasta. Sunday brunch.

Indian Kettles. Rte. 9 N, Hague (7 miles south of Ticonderoga); 543–6576. Rustic restaurant overlooking Lake George. Steak and prime ribs are weekend specialties, preceded by fish bake on Fridays. Docking facilities. Open May–October.

Old Dock House. Essex, adjacent to the ferry landing; 963–4232. Recently restored. Outdoor grill and waterside dining. Docking for boats. Open mid-May–mid-October.

Royal Savage Inn. Lakeshore Rd., Plattsburgh; 561–5140. Early American setting in converted hay barn. Baked stuffed shrimp are surpassed only by tempting homemade desserts. Children's plates; gift shop on the premises.

Westport Hotel. 153 Pleasant St., Westport; 962–4501. Casual atmosphere, with veal a specialty and vegetable platters available. Desserts prepared on premises; champagne brunch on Sundays.

Westport Yacht Club Restaurant. Old Arsenal Rd., 962–8777. Gracious lakeside dining on Lake Champlain, serving charbroiled prime meats, live lobsters from the tank. Limited docking for boaters. Open May–October.

Windows on the Bay. Rte. 9, north of downtown Plattsburgh; 563–9574. Overlooking Lake Champlain. Serving traditional American fare: fresh fish, chicken, and steak. Children's menu; Sunday brunch.

Inexpensive

Gene's. Rtes. 9N and 22, Port Henry; 546–7722. A take-out spot serving hamburgers, french fries, and the best hot dogs in the North Country. Try their

"Michigan Hots" with meat sauce and onions. Gene's has been in business since 1948.

Thatcher's Old School House. Rtes. 9N and 22, 2 miles north of Ticonderoga; 585–4044. Converted century-old schoolhouse with classrooms converted into dining rooms. American menu with daily specials. Family style service available in summer.

CENTRAL ADIRONDACKS

Expensive

The Balsam House. Friends Lake Rd., Chestertown; 494–2828. Elegant dining in a beautifully restored inn built in 1865. Lunch served on the front porch; Sunday brunch in glass-enclosed atrium; main dining room has candlelight, flowers, and classical music. European chef's specialties include rack of lamb, duckling chambertin, braised sweetbreads, and Adirondack trout. Sunset cocktail cruise on Friends Lake available.

Friends Lake Inn. Friends Lake Rd., Chestertown; 494–4251. Nicely restored 1860 country inn, reflecting that ambience in the dining room. Daily selections may include snapper en papillote, beef Wellington, or poached salmon with dill hollandaise. Tempting desserts are prepared on the premises.

Highwinds Inn. Gore Mountain Road, 5 miles west (and up) from North River; 251–3760 and 251–3435. Dining room seats 20 with guests given first preference. Innkeepers shop for and prepare excellent meals. One sitting nightly. Blackboard menu. Open all year except November and June.

Rene's. White Schoolhouse Road, Chestertown; 494–2904. Casual dining in converted 1917 farmhouse. All items are fresh, homemade European fare, including German and Italian dishes and French desserts. Delicious ice cream is also homemade. Reservations recommended on weekends. Closed Mondays.

Moderate

Big Moose Inn. On Rte. 28, Big Moose, at Big Moose Lake; 315–357–2042. Off-the-beaten-path establishment that specializes in prime rib, veal, and lamb dishes. Outdoor dining in summer. Homemade baked goods, cocktail lounge with fireplace. Closed Columbus Day–Christmas and end of March–Memorial Day.

Bruin Haven. Rte. 30, Sabael, 5 miles south of Indian Lake; 648–5450. Continental cuisine with favorites such as roast pork with sauerkraut, black diamond steak marinated with fresh herbs and seasonings. Two candlelit dining rooms; casual decor with European atmosphere. Open May–October.

Garnet Hill Lodge. Thirteenth Lake Rd. North River, north of North Creek via Rte. 28; 251–2821. Mountaintop lodge known for cross country skiing and fine food, especially the $11.50 Saturday evening buffet featuring roast beef and fish, often a salmon. No credit cards.

Glenmore Motel. Glenmore Road, Big Moose; 315–357–4891. Rustic atmosphere in this dining room featuring four specialties: king crab claws, prime rib, veal parmigiana, and veal Oscar, plus large salad bar. Closed Tuesdays in summer.

Old Mill. Old Forge; 315–369–3662. Converted gristmill with traditional American menu includes steaks and seafood. Lunch on the terrace in summer months. Homebaked breads. Closed in November.

Rocky Point. Rte. 28, Inlet; 315–357–3751. Continental cuisine, with different menu each day. Children's plates. Bar, entertainment, dancing, view of Lake Fourth. Reservations, jacket required.

OLYMPIC AREA

Expensive

Charcoal Pit. Rte. 86 near Cold Brook Plaza, Lake Placid; 523–3050. Fine American fare served in rustic atmosphere with fireplace. Veal Francaise or veal Normandy may be prepared en flambé at tableside. Roast duckling also a favorite. Children's menu available.

Frederick's. Signal Hill, Lake Placid; 523–2310. Gourmet dining overlooking beautiful Lake Placid. Tournedos Rossini is a specialty. A seafood platter for two combines lobster, scallops, Alaskan crab, and shrimp scampi. Also favored are seafood coquille and veal scallopine; tempting dessert cart.

Interlaken Restaurant. 15 Interlaken Ave., Lake Placid; 523–3180. Dine in a distinctive European atmosphere here, with gourmet menu featuring Swiss and French dishes.

Lake Placid Hilton. Saranac Avenue, Lake Placid; 523–4411. Dining room of this hotel offers breathtaking view of the lake and mountains. Outdoor terrace dining in summer months. Menu offers seafood, beef, poultry, and veal dishes.

Mirror Lake Inn. 35 Mirror Lake Dr., Lake Placid; 523–2544. Home-baked bread and diverse salad bar accompany fresh seafood and veal dishes here. Top off a meal with homemade Adirondack maple nut sundae with pure maple syrup, or homemade fudge brownie à la mode. Children's plates available.

Steak and Stinger. 15 Cascade Road, Lake Placid; 523–0027. Despite its name, not only steaks served in this rustic establishment. Continental and American menu also features veal Oscar, shrimp scampi, and chateaubriand.

Woodshed. 237 Main St., Lake Placid; 523–9470. Much improved in recent years. The back room, called Lindsey's, is especially good.

Moderate

Alpine Cellar. Wilmington Rd., Lake Placid; 523–2180. Excellent German cuisine and atmosphere. Specialties include sauerbraten, Alpine schnitzel, and rouladen, along with homemade breads. Children's plate. Dinners only.

Cascade Inn Restaurant. Cascade Rd. and Rte. 73, Lake Placid; 523–2130. Hearty American dishes, including Delmonico steak; nightly specials. Children's portions available. Dinner all year; lunches summer only.

Hotel Saranac of Paul Smith's College. 101 Main St., Saranac Lake; 891–2200. Fine dining in the hotel's Regis Room. Light meals served in the Boathouse Lounge, including popular steak sandwich. Special inexpensive buffet Thursday nights. Elaborate Sunday brunch. The Bake Shoppe features fresh baked goods daily.

Jimmy's. Main Street, Lake Placid; 523–2353. Diverse selection of steaks, seafood, chicken, and veal dishes served at this lakeside place, popular with locals.

Villa Vespa. Saranac Ave., Lake Placid; 523–9959. The town's favorite "nice little Italian restaurant" featuring homemade pastas; fresh seafood daily; unique salad bar. Special pizzas and menu for children.

Inexpensive

Artist's Cafe. Main St., Lake Placid; 523–9493. Enclosed deck dining overlooking Mirror Lake. Among the favorites are 16-ounce T-bone steak, surf and turf, and steamed shrimp. Children's menu.

Casa del Sol. Rte. 86 east of Saranac Lake (no phone). Yes, there is a Mexican restaurant in the Adirondacks, and this is a favorite among locals. Chili and other traditional Mexican dishes can be tempered to the desired degree of spiciness.

Deer's Head Inn. Rte. 9N, Elizabethtown; 873–9995. The oldest inn in operation in the Adirondacks (since 1818), it reflects German-Swiss influence, with sauerbraten and homemade dumplings a specialty, along with home-baked pies. Children's menu.

Potluck. Main St., Lake Placid; 523–3106. Specialty foods served in attractive delicatessen setting include hefty sandwiches on hearty breads and pasta salads.

Purdy's Elm Tree Inn. Keene; 576–9769. A local landmark. Purdy Burger is the best in the region.

THOUSAND ISLANDS–SEAWAY

Expensive

Bonnie Castle Manor. Holland Street, Alexandria Bay; 315–482–2000. Beautiful St. Lawrence River view from this pleasant place serving continental dishes of prime rib of beef, seafood, and veal. Home-baked goods. Cocktail bar; entertainment and dancing in evenings.

Cavallario's Steak and Seafood House. 24 Church St., Alexandria Bay; 315–482–9867. The name says it all for this steakhouse a la Italiana, with other traditional American dishes to choose from. Home-baked goods; children's menu. Reservations recommended.

Crown 'N' Feather. 1200 Arsenal St., Watertown; 315–788–1850. Motif is 18th-century British pub, specializing in prime ribs, clams casino, and veal marsala. Children's plates; hefty Sunday brunch.

De Fazio's Towne House. Oak and Lincoln Sts., Waddington, 16 miles west of Massena on Rte. 37; 315–388–7772. Fine Italian dishes, along with prime ribs; salad cart at table; baking on premises.

The Ship. 29 James St., Alexandria Bay; 315–482–9500. Of course, the decor is nautical at this not-all-seafood house which also serves good veal dishes and other American fare. Closed November–March.

Thousand Island Club, Wellesley Island; 315–482–3550. Striking view of the St. Lawrence from this non-private club serving traditional American fare and featuring entertainment and dancing in evenings. Outdoor dining during summer. Closed November–May.

Village Inn. Maple Street Rd., Massena; 315–769–6910. Veal dishes, prime ribs, and seafood are the standouts at this pleasant inn, which is closed on Tuesdays. Reservations recommended.

Moderate

Benny's Steak House. 1050 Arsenal St., Watertown; 315–788–4110. A not-all-steak house, which has other traditional American and Italian dishes on its menu. Thursday–Saturday evenings, there's also entertainment and dancing.

Crossroads. Rte. 11, 11 miles west of Moira; 529–7372. Try their prime ribs roasted in English ale, or the roast duckling, or various seafood dishes. End up with homemade ice cream. Sunday brunch; children's plates.

The Golden Lion Restaurant. 1116 Arsenal St., Watertown; 315–782–1440. Relaxed atmosphere, with traditional American fare. Cocktail lounge; entertainment in evenings. Sunday brunch; children's plates.

Gran-View. Riverside Dr., Ogdensburg; 315–393–4550. Formal decor in this fine spot overlooking the St. Lawrence. Continental and Italian menu with homemade pastas. Sunday brunch; children's plates.

Half-Way Chalet. Rte. 12E, 7 miles west of Clayton; 315–654–2123. Typical American fare: steak, prime ribs, salad bar, homemade pastries. Children's menu. Entertainment Saturday evenings. Closed Mondays and Tuesdays, October–April.

Maxfield's. 5–7 Market St., Potsdam; 315–265–3796. Homey is the atmosphere here, what with the plants and wicker furniture. The food: veal, chicken, ribs; fresh seafood every day.

Pine Tree Point. One mile northeast of NY12, Alexandria Bay; 315–482–9911. Continental menu, with specialties including Gaspé salmon, prime ribs, and veal dishes. Home-baked goods; children's plate. Entertainment, dancing. Reservations advised. Closed mid-October–mid-May.

Tardelli's. 141 Market St., Potsdam; 315–265–0948. Rather good wine cellar at this Italian establishment featuring homemade pastas as well as American dishes. Children's plate. Reservations recommended.

Thousand Islands Inn. 335 Riverside Dr., Clayton; 315–686–3030. On the St. Lawrence riverfront, this attractive inn specializes in prime ribs, with extensive salad bar, home-baked pastries. Closed mid-October–mid-May.

Viola. 209 Center St., Massena; 315–764–0329. Family-operated Italian establishment since 1947 featuring homemade pastas, along with steak and veal dishes. Closed Mondays.

WILDERNESS. Because of the vast areas of unspoiled territory, the Adirondacks are a special place, not just for those who live there but for those who visit as well. More than 1,000,000 acres in the 6,000,000-acre *Adirondack Park* are officially designated as wilderness, and the entire region is protected under the state law. The largest of the 15 wilderness areas in the Adirondacks is also the best known, the High Peaks area from the vicinity of Rte. 73 near Keene to Long Lake and the Raquette River. In that area, which covers some 230,000 acres, there are 238 miles of foot trails and just one mile of public road.

The *Adirondack Mountain Club* (ADK), founded in 1922, is a leader in promoting wilderness appreciation in and continuous use of the region. It publishes an excellent series of guides and maps with detailed information on various hiking trails and canoe routes in the region. It also operates Adirondack Loj near Lake Placid and Johns Brook Lodge near Keene Valley, both excellent starting points for trips into the High Peaks. ADK has 27 local chapters and is headquartered at 172 Ridge Street, Glens Falls, NY 12801, 793-7737.

In the 19th century, visitors who ventured into the wilderness generally went in the company of an Adirondack guide. There is renewed interest in **guiding** today, and requirements for a license in New York State recently have been stiffened. The use of a guide, particularly on the first trip into a region, is a good way to get maximum exposure to all the pleasures of the wilderness without some of the pitfalls. A listing of guides can be obtained from the *New York State Outdoor Guides Association,* Box 4337, Albany 12204; from the *New York State Department of Environmental Conservation,* 50 Wolf Road, Albany 12233; or from DEC regional headquarters in Ray Brook, NY 12977, 891–1370, or Watertown, NY 13601, 315–782–0100.

In the wilderness, the tree cover reflects elevation. The lower altitudes are heavily forested, with spruce and balsam being the most common trees. As you go higher, hardwoods such as red maple and yellow birch become more common and sugar maples and beech are plentiful. This is characteristic of the Adirondacks up to the 2,500-foot elevation. Above that height, the spruces and balsam dominate again up to tree line at 4,300–4,900 feet. There are 10 Adirondack peaks in the alpine zone above 4,900 feet.

Recently, efforts have begun to reintroduce the bald eagle into the North Country. Rare, but established in the region and sometimes mistaken for an eagle, is the osprey. It is black, not brown, but is almost the same size as the eagle and shares the same habitat. Two other birds that rate close watching if spotted are the common loon (which is not common—there are less than 500 in the region) with its black head and distinctive mournful cry, and the great blue heron, a sky, long-legged bird most often seen on wilderness lakes or ponds along shallow points and mud flats.

Animals common in the area are the white-tailed deer, beaver, otter, muskrat, porcupine, fisher, raccoon, red and gray fox, squirrel, chipmunk, and mink. There are estimated to be some 3,600 black bears in the Adirondacks, many of which have become accustomed to feeding on garbage at area landfills. If you camp in the wilderness, don't store food in your tent, on the ground, or even in your car. Hang it from a rope at least 15 feet above ground.

Because they are vulnerable to a disease born by deer, there is no native moose population in New York State. There are a few bobcats in the region. There have been no wolves for more than a century but there is an increasing population of coyotes and, through interbreeding, coydogs.

Lake trout are native to the Adirondacks, but require deep cold lake water to survive. Brook trout, also native, are much more widely distributed. There are some 350 ponds stocked by the state with brookies and many more where the population is self sustaining. Spring, before black fly season, and September are the best months for brook trout fishing. Even if visibly clear, drinking the water directly from streams should be avoided if possible due to a parasite known as Giardia, which causes a sometimes severe intestinal illness known as "beaver fever."

The black fly season runs from approximately mid-May through late June, and even the most savvy mountain veterans find these insects troublesome. There are rattlesnakes in the Adirondacks but almost all are in the Tongue Mountain area near Lake George.

While the favored wilderness hiking is in the High Peaks, the favored back country canoeing is in the Fulton Chain from Old Forge to Tupper and Saranac lakes and the St. Regis canoe area in the northwest Adirondacks.

There are lodges that by location or inclination allow guests to take maximum advantage of the wilderness setting. Three of note are the Elk Lake Lodge, 532–7616, four miles west of I-87 exit 29 (maximum 50 guests on 12,000 acres of land that includes two lakes); the Cold River Ranch, 359–7559, east of Tupper Lake on Rte. 3 at Coreys (six guest rooms, backwoods, horseback camping); and Norridgewock III, 315–357–2444, at Beaver River (maximum 30 guests, boat access only).

For those interested in developing or improving wilderness skills, training programs are run by the Adirondack Mountain Club and by the *Sagamore Lodge and Conference Center,* Raquette Lake, NY 13436, 315–354–5303, as part of its "Adirondack Bound" series.

 NIGHTLIFE. The nightlife in the North Country centers in the resort areas in summer. Lake George Village is headquarters for the born-to-boogie set and for local dude ranches. *Roaring Brook* and *Hidden Valley* on Lake Luzerne Road have been popular with singles for years. *The Sagamore,* in Bolton Landing, has a nightclub for an upscale evening out. In Lake Placid, *Mud Puddles* attracts a young crowd, while *The Cottage* on Mirror Lake draws both locals and visitors, especially early in the evening when the hors d'oeuvres are served. *The Hilton* in town has entertainment regularly. In Alexandria Bay, *Bonnie Castle* is among the spots offering entertainment. Potsdam and Platts-burgh have activities into the wee hours and somewhere nearby, wherever you may be in the area, there will always be a country-and-western band doing "done me wrong" songs. But for the most part, the lights go out early in the North Country.

NIAGARA FALLS–
BUFFALO AREA

by
DEBORAH WILLIAMS

Deborah Williams is a former reporter and editor for the late Buffalo
Courier Express—*the same newspaper, she points out, that was Mark
Twain's alma mater. Her travel articles have appeared in a number of
magazines and newspapers.*

The first recorded "tourist" to lay unbelieving eyes on Niagara Falls
was Father Louis Hennepin. Ever since that cold December day in
1678, it has been a world-class attraction.

It is, as always, an awesome spectacle: a 184-foot-high cataract of
thundering water, surrounded by towering clouds of mist and spray.
For generations, Niagara Falls has been the stuff of romance. If the
vaunted honeymoon connection has become a cliche these days, the
lure that made it so has not. Millions of visitors stop here each year
to witness one of the world's most impressive natural phenomena. They
line the promenade opposite, gape from the deck of a boat below, peer
out from the caves behind, ogle from a helicopter above—drinking in
the vista from every conceivable angle.

"Niagara Falls! By what mysterious power is it that millions and millions are drawn from all parts of the world to gaze upon Niagara Falls? . . . It calls up the indefinite past," said President Abraham Lincoln.

Writers have long struggled to capture the immensity of the Falls. Thomas Moore, the Irish poet, wrote after his visit: "It is impossible by pen or pencil to convey even a faint idea of their magnificence. . . . We must have new combinations of language to describe the Falls of Niagara."

Taming the Falls

The Falls are part of the border between the United States and Canada, the longest unfortified border in the world. The American and Bridal Veil Falls are in New York, and the Horseshoe Falls are on the Canadian side in Ontario. There is an impressive 3,175 feet of waterfall. The falls were the birthplace of alternating electric current and they drive the largest hydroelectric development in the Western world.

The honeymoon connection began in 1803 when the first honeymooners arrived. They were rich newlyweds from Baltimore—Jerome Bonaparte, kin to the French emperor, and his bride, daughter of a wealthy merchant—on a grand tour of the Northeast. They stayed for a week. By the mid-1800s, honeymoons at Niagara had become quite the rage. They were a definite status symbol for young couples, and the tradition continues today.

With the arrival of steamships in 1820, the Erie Canal in 1825, and the railroad in 1840, the town was accessible to millions of tourists who wanted to see the legendary falls. Since 1860, the falls have been lit at night. The spectacle of lights playing on the water and mist has a special attraction for visitors.

Daredevils Take the Plunge

The waters also lured a special breed of daredevil. The first stuntster, Sam Patch, survived two dives from Goat Island into the turbulent waters below the Falls. Then in 1859 and 1860, tightrope walker Jean François Gravelet, the great Blondin, thrilled onlookers as he walked, danced, rode a bike, and even carried his terrified manager on a high wire across the falls. The first person to go over in a barrel was a schoolteacher, Mrs. Annie Edson Taylor, in 1901. Others followed, though not all as successfully as Mrs. Taylor. Such stunts are now illegal but nothing stops the determined stunter. During 1985 two more daredevils survived a plunge over the falls.

It's hard to believe it wasn't always so, but unrestricted viewing of Niagara Falls did not begin until 1885. "Free Niagara!" was the rallying cry in the 1870s as a group of dedicated Americans led by landscape architect Frederick Law Olmsted and artist Frederic E. Church set out to extricate the falls from the clutches of profit-hungry landowners.

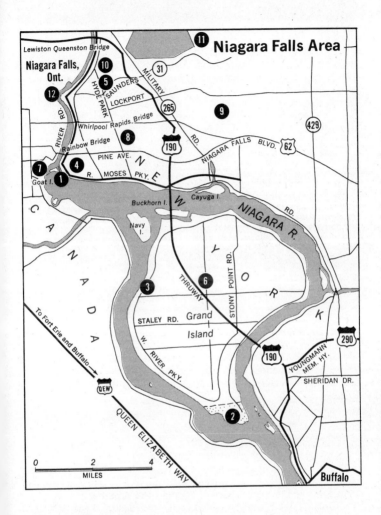

Niagara Falls Area

Points of Interest (Niagara Falls)

1) American Falls
2) Beaver Island State Park
3) Big Six Mile Creek Marine State Park
4) Convention Center
5) Devils Hole State Park
6) Fantasy Island

7) Horseshoe Falls
8) Hyde Park Stadium
9) Niagara Falls International Airport
10) Niagara University
11) Tuscarora Indian Reservation
12) Whirlpool State Park

First State Park in Nation

The land around the falls had become one of the most vulgar tourist traps anywhere, with visitors having to pay for the privilege of seeing the cataracts through peepholes in the fences. The campaign resulted in the establishment on July 15, 1885, of the nation's first state park, embracing 435 acres of land along the American Falls. The Canadians followed with similar action around their portion of the cataract, and the protection of the Falls was assured. The park's creation affirmed the premise that the nation's natural treasures belong to everyone.

Carnival Atmosphere

Of course, the commercialism did not disappear. On the contrary, even a casual visitor sees an abundance of souvenir shops, T-shirt emporia, chain motels, oddity museums, and fast-food eateries.

At Clifton Hill on the Canadian side, where the carnival atmosphere is strongest, there are museums dedicated to Houdini, sports heroes, Ripley's "Believe It or Not," and the *Guinness Book of World Records,* not to mention a Louis Tussaud wax museum.

Several sightseeing towers stand as sentries over the falls, and a cable car carries visitors across the Niagara rapids. On the American side, the city has been undergoing a massive urban renewal program designed to change the face of downtown Niagara.

The water that flows over the falls drains four Great Lakes: Superior, Michigan, Huron, and Erie, into the fifth, Ontario, at a rate of 700,000 gallons per second during the summer. It fluctuates with the seasons and although the river never completely freezes in winter, an ice bridge does form below the falls—a bridge that can grow to 150 feet thick and two miles long.

Falls Turned Off

On March 29, 1848, a strange silence fell in the city. The roar of the falls had stopped. Huge chunks of ice had formed a dam in the river, stopping the flow of water and leaving the falls dry. This lasted for two days until the dam broke and water began to flow again.

On June 12, 1969, the Falls—actually just the American Falls were turned off again, this time by humans. Water was rerouted to the Horseshoe Falls to enable engineers to survey the American Falls and the rocks below to help prevent further erosion. Some 185,000 tons of rock had fallen from Prospect Point. By December, the falls were turned back on and they have been flowing since.

Geologists say Niagara Falls began 12,000 years ago, seven miles north of its present location at what is now the village of Lewiston. Artpark, the only state park in the nation devoted to visual and performing arts, was opened in Lewiston in 1974. It occupies a site where Indians, French, British, and Americans fought for control of the strategically important Niagara River.

The Falls continue to creep steadily upstream at the rate of 1–2 feet a year, even though the erosion rate has been reduced by the diversion of water into hydroelectric plants. At the present rate it will be some 130,000 years before the majestic Falls are reduced to an impressive rapids in the area of what is now Buffalo, 20 miles to the south.

Buffalo: "Beautiful River"

Buffalo is the state's second largest city and an important port at the head of the Niagara River where Lake Erie empties into the river. There never have been any buffalo in Buffalo, and even the look-alikes at the Buffalo Zoo, one of the country's oldest, are bison. The most popular theory about the origin of the city's name comes from a mispronunciation of the French words, *beau fleuve,* or "beautiful river."

Its location on Lake Erie makes Buffalo prey to "lake-effect" snowsqualls, making the city one of the snowiest in the country. But the lake also acts as a gigantic air conditioner during the summer. Days are warm, but not hot, and nights are cool and ideal for sleeping. In keeping with the lakeside location, the city is home to the nation's only inland naval park.

Buffalo is "smalltown" when compared with the glamorous New York City, but the state's second city has its own style and a surprisingly rich ethnic, cultural, and architectural diversity as well as a variety of year-round spectator and participatory sports. It has been home to U.S. Presidents Millard Fillmore and Grover Cleveland and such writers as Mark Twain, F. Scott Fitzgerald, and Taylor Caldwell.

The theater district is thriving and the once-neglected waterfront has been undergoing a renaissance. Allentown, the city's Greenwich Village, is the nation's largest historic preservation district and is full of renovated 19th-century homes, boutiques, antique shops, and restaurants. The city can be dubbed a college town with 18 educational facilities of higher learning. The State University of New York at Buffalo is the largest university in the state.

PRACTICAL INFORMATION FOR
THE NIAGARA FALLS–BUFFALO AREA

HOW TO GET THERE. By Air. Greater Buffalo International Airport is the primary air entry for the Buffalo–Niagara Falls area. The Niagara Falls Airport handles military and charter planes. Buffalo's airport is served by *USAir, American, Eastern, United, Republic, Northwest, Continental, Piedmont, Mall, Brockway,* and *Skywalker.*

By Bus. *Niagara Scenic Bus Lines, Inc.* (648–1500, 282–7755), operates shuttle service between the Buffalo airport and major hotels in Niagara Falls. The shuttle runs from 7 A.M. to 8:30 P.M. and takes about an hour each way. Fare is $8. *Greyhound,* 181 Ellicott St., 855–7511, operates from the Ellicott Street Bus Terminal in Buffalo and provides intercity transportation. Greyhound also operates from the Niagara Falls Transportation Center, 4th and Niagara Sts., Niagara Falls.

By Train. Amtrak has two connecting stations in Buffalo: 75 Exchange Street, downtown, 856–2075, and 55 Dick Rd., Cheektowaga, south of the airport, 683–8440. The Amtrak station in Niagara Falls is at Hyde Park Blvd. and Lockport Rd., 285–4224. Outside the area, call the toll-free Amtrak number, 800–877–7245.

By Car. Access from the east and south is primarily via I–90, the New York State Thruway. An expressway spur, I–190, leads from I–90 at Buffalo and goes across Grand Island to Niagara Falls. I–190 skirts the eastern and northern portions of the city and has interchanges with major streets in downtown Buffalo. From the north, Rtes. 104 and 18 tie in with I–190.

Approaches from the west are via a number of highways in Canada, including the Queen Elizabeth Way with three bridges funneling traffic stateside: the Rainbow Bridge in the southwest of the city; the Whirlpool Rapids Bridge just below Whirlpool State Park; and the Lewiston–Queenston Bridge, Lewiston, connecting the northern terminus of I–190 with Canada's Hwy. 405. Entering the Buffalo area from the south are U.S. 219 from Springville and Rte.–400 from South Wales. Both join I–90.

 TELEPHONES. The area code for Niagara Falls, Buffalo, and western New York is 716. Information (directory assistance) is 555–1212. An operator will assist you on person-to-person, credit-card, and collect calls if you dial "0" first. From outside the area, directory information can be obtained by dialing (716) 555–1212. Dial (800) 555–1212, directory information for toll-free 800 numbers, to see if there is an 800 number for the business you want to reach. A call from a pay phone is 25¢. Long distance rates apply between Niagara Falls and Buffalo.

 HOTELS AND MOTELS in the Niagara Falls and Buffalo area primarily fall into the category of major hotel chains and lower priced motels. In Niagara Falls, high season prices apply from Memorial Day through Labor Day. Elsewhere, prices remain the same throughout the year. Hotels and motels tend to be moderately priced, especially in comparison with New York City. Occupancy tax in Niagara Falls is 3 percent and in Buffalo it is 5 percent, plus 7 percent sales tax in Niagara Falls and 8 percent in Buffalo.

Hotel rates are based on double occupancy. Categories determined by price are: *Deluxe,* $80–$100; *Expensive,* $60–$79; *Moderate,* $50–$59; *Inexpensive,* $40–$49; and *Basic Budget,* under $40.

BUFFALO AIRPORT AREA

Deluxe

The Ramada Renaissance. 4243 Genesee St.; 634–2300. 275 units. Family plan. Two pools, one indoor, saunas, exercise room, movies, dining room, entertainment, nightclub, disco.

Expensive

The Sheraton Inn–Buffalo East. 2040 Walden Ave.; 681–2400. 300 units. Family plan. Indoor pool in tropical garden, saunas, exercise room, dining room, entertainment, cocktail lounge, pets.

Inexpensive

Airways Hotel. 4230 Genesee St.; 632–8400. 150 units. Family Plan. Pool, dining room, cocktail lounge.

Basic Budget

Days Inn. 4345 Genesee St.; 631–0800. 130 units. Family plan, pool, dining room.

Luxury Budget Inn. 4630 Genesee St.; 631–8966. 84 units. Family plan, restaurant adjacent, pets $3 additional.

BUFFALO AREA

Deluxe

Buffalo Marriott. 1340 Millersport Hwy.; 689–6900. Indoor/outdoor pool, sauna, whirlpool, entertainment, dining room, cocktail lounge, popular with local clientele.

Expensive

Asa Ransom House. 10529 Main St.; 759–2315. This is a picture perfect country inn. Original parts of the building date back to the early 19th century. Restaurant and Tap Room. No smoking in four bedrooms; no credit cards; closed Fridays, and Saturdays.

Buffalo Hilton at the Waterfront. Church and Terrace sts.; 845–5100. 500 units. Family plan, indoor pool, health club, indoor tennis and racquetball courts, jogging track, squash courts, dining room, coffee shop, entertainment, disco, pets with $100 deposit.

Hyatt Regency Buffalo. 2 Fountain Plaza; 856–1234. 401 units. Family plan. Built from a historic office building with a three-story glass atrium overlooking Main St. It combines the best of the new and old. Indoor pool, exercise room, dining room, coffee shop, entertainment, cocktail lounge.

Ramada Inn. 6643 Transit Rd.; 634–2700. 123 units. Family plan, pool, playground, dining room, cocktail lounge.

Moderate

Best Western Inn–Downtown. 510 Delaware Ave.; 886–8333. 61 units. Family plan. In the heart of the theater district.

Holiday Inn–Amherst. 1881 Niagara Falls Blvd.; 691–8181. 202 units. Family plan, pool, dining room, cocktail lounge, entertainment, pets.

Holiday Inn–Cheektowaga. Rossler and Dingens Sts.; 896–2900. 118 units. Family plan, pool, dining room, cocktail lounge, pets.

Holiday Inn–Downtown. 620 Delaware Ave.; 886–2121. 168 units. Family plan, pool, dining room, entertainment, cocktail lounge, pets.

Lord Amherst Motor Hotel. 5000 Main St.; 839–2200. 100 units. Family plan, pool, restaurant, coffee shop, cocktail lounge, pets.

The Roycroft Inn. 40 S. Grove St., East Aurora; 652–9030. 12 units. Listed on the National Register of Historic Places, the inn was built in 1903 by Elbert Hubbard, the founder of the Roycroft Movement. It is in the middle of a complex of ten buildings on the Roycroft campus which are used for crafts and art studios, print shops, gift shops, museums. Dining room and English-style pub. At press time the inn and restaurant were undergoing renovation and expansion.

Inexpensive

The Lenox Hotel. 140 North St.; 884–1700. 220 units. Family plan, kitchenettes, restaurant.

Basic Budget

Buffalo TraveLodge. 984 Main St.; 882–2200. 69 units. Family plan, pets, restaurant adjacent.

New Towne House Hotel. 999 Main St.; 884–2160. 90 units. Family plan, 16 efficiencies, pool, dining room.

Red Roof Inn. 42 Flint Rd.; 689–7474. 109 units. Family plan.

University Manor Motel. 3612 Main St.; 837–3344. 40 units, 7 efficiencies.

The Williamsville Inn. 5447 Main St.; 634–1111. 99 units. Family plan, dining room, entertainment, cocktail lounge.

NIAGARA FALLS

The price ratings are for the summer high season. During the rest of the year rates are at least $10 per room less. In a number of hotels and motels there are three seasons, the high summer season, the shoulder season during early fall and late spring, and the winter season.

Deluxe

Holiday Inn Downtown at the Falls. 114 Buffalo St.; 285–2521. 194 units. Family plan, indoor pool, saunas, exercise room, dining room, cocktail lounge, pets.

Niagara Hilton. Third St. and Mall; 285–3361. 396 units; some with views of the Falls. Indoor pool, health club, dining room, coffee shop, cocktail lounge, adjoins Wintergarden, tropical indoor garden.

Radisson Inn—Niagara Falls USA. 240 Rainbow Blvd.; 282–1212. 224 units. Indoor pool, lobby overlooks Wintergarden, cocktail lounge, two restaurants.

Expensive

The Hotel Niagara. 201 Rainbow Blvd.; 285–9321. 220 units. Family plan, dining room, cocktail lounge.

Howard Johnson's Motor Lodge. 454 Main St.; 285–5261. 75 units. Family plan, indoor pool, sauna, restaurant, cocktail lounge.

Quality Inn Intown. 443 Main St.; 284–8801. 166 units. Family plan, pool, restaurant.

Ramada Inn. 401 Buffalo Ave.; 285–2541. 193 units. Family plan, pool, dining room, cocktail lounge, pets.

TraveLodge. 200 Rainbow Blvd.; 285–8366. 49 units. Family plan.

Basic Budget

Coachman Motel. 523 Third St.; 285–2295. 18 units, refrigerators.

NIAGARA FALLS AREA

Deluxe

Holiday Inn Resort & Conference Center. 100 Whitehaven Rd., Grand Island; 773–1111. 265 units. Family plan, indoor and outdoor pools, saunas, exercise room, dock, fishing, ski trails, ice skating, rental bikes, golf, dining room, coffee shop, cocktail lounge, pets.

Expensive

Best Western Red Jacket Inn. 7001 Buffalo Ave.; 283–7612. 150 units. Family plan, pool, dock, fishing, dining room, cocktail lounge.

Howard Johnson's Motor Lodge–East. 6505 Niagara Falls Blvd.; 283–8791. 84 units. Family plan, pool, restaurant, cocktail lounge, pets.

Inexpensive

Beacon Motel. 9900 Niagara Falls Blvd.; 297–3647. 10 units; restaurant adjacent.

Bit-O-Paris Motel. 9890 Niagara Falls Blvd.; 297–1710. 15 units; pool.

Basic Budget

Anchor Motel. 2332 River Rd.; 693–0850. 21 units. Pool; grounds located on the Niagara River.

Bel Aire Motel. 9470 Niagara Falls Blvd.; 297–2250. 23 units; pool.

Driftwood Motel. 2754 Niagara Falls Blvd.; 692–6650. 20 units; pool.

Henwood's Motel. 9401 Niagara Falls Blvd.; 297–2660. 30 units; pool.

Pelican Motel. 6817 Niagara Falls Blvd.; 283–9818. 14 units. Refrigerators, two efficiencies.

Sands Motel. 9393 Niagara Falls Blvd.; 297–3797. 17 units; pool.

Sharon Motel. 7560 Niagara Falls Blvd.; 283–5646. 22 units; pool.

 BED-AND-BREAKFAST TREASURES. Bed-and-breakfasts in the Niagara Falls–Buffalo area are organized under *Rainbow Hospitality,* 9348 Hennepin Ave., Niagara Falls, 283–4794 or 283–0228. They include historic homes close to Niagara Falls, an elegant Victorian home on the banks of the lower Niagara River, a working farm about 10 miles from Niagara Falls, and a private ski chalet about 30 miles south of Buffalo. Prices vary, but they average $35–$40 for a double. Some welcome children and one even offers a nursery and baby sitting services. Others do not accept children. Inquire in advance.

 CAMPGROUNDS. Because of weather conditions, campgrounds are open from May to October. Opening and closing dates vary. Following is a list of places with camping facilities:

Daisy Barn Campground, 3101 Lake Rd., Wilson; 751–9822.

Niagara Falls KOA, 2570 Grand Island Blvd., Grand Island; 773–7583.

Niagara Falls North KOA, 1250 Pletcher Rd., Lewiston; 754–8013.

Niagara's Lazy Lakes Campground, 4312 Church Rd., Cambria; 433–2479.

Norton's Motel & Campsite, 2405 Niagara Falls Blvd.; 731–3434.

 HOW TO GET AROUND. Airport. Shuttle buses between the Buffalo airport and major hotels in Niagara Falls are operated by *Niagara Scenic Bus Lines, Inc.;* 648–1500 or 282–7755. The shuttle runs from 7 A.M. to 8:30 P.M. and takes about an hour; fare $8 each way. Taxi service to Niagara Falls is also available; fare, $26. It is about 10 miles from the airport to downtown Buffalo, and average taxi fares are $12. Many hotels provide shuttle bus service. *The Niagara Frontier Transportation Authority (NFTA) MetroBus* also provides bus service with a fare of $1 or $1.50 depending on the terminal.

By Bus. NFTA provides bus service within the Buffalo area, including Niagara Falls. The fare is 80¢ within both cities. The cost between Buffalo and Niagara Falls is $1.40. The fare for children under 12 is 40¢. Transfers are 5¢ from bus to bus. Exact fare is required. Buses generally operate from 5 A.M. to 12:30 A.M. For information, phone 855–7211, or 285–9319 in Niagara Falls.

By Subway. *NFTA MetroRail* provides light rail rapid transit service in Buffalo. The system is partially above ground and partially underground. The above ground portion is free. For an underground ride the fare is 80¢ and tickets must be purchased at stations. There is no transfer charge from bus to train or train to bus. Art lovers should visit the subway stations even if they aren't riding, because each station is decorated with original paintings, photography, or sculpture. For information, phone 855-7211.

By Taxi. Taxi rates in Buffalo are $1.25 for the first mile and $1.25 for each additional mile. *City Service Taxi,* 852-4000; *Yellow Cab,* 832-9900; *Madison Taxi,* 853-3333; *Sheridan Cab,* 634-2600. Taxi rates in Niagara Falls are $1 for the first 1/10 of a mile and 10¢ for each 1/10 of a mile thereafter. *Niagara Dispatch Service,* 284-0436; *United Cab Co.,* 285-9331; *LaSalle Cab,* 284-8833.

By car. Buffalo and Niagara Falls are early towns and rush hours are generally 7-9 A.M. and 3-5 P.M. Parking is easy; 25¢ per half hour in Buffalo or 90¢ an hour in ramps. Along Main St. in downtown Buffalo there is a pedestrian mall—no cars. In Niagara Falls, parking is $2.50 in the state parking lots. Otherwise, parking meters have been removed from the street and parking is free. The ramp at the Rainbow Center is also free. There are designated handicapped spots in all lots, but the auto must have a special license plate.

By rental car. *Budget Rent-A-Car,* airport pickup, 632-4662; *Avis,* airport pickup, 632-1808; *Agency Rent-A-Car,* free pickup, 836-4847; *Hertz,* airport pickup, 632-4772. There are a number of limousine services for a special night or sightseeing in style. *Buffalo Limousine Service,* 835-4997; *Niagara Scenic,* 648-1500; *Arthur's Limousine Service,* 834-3291.

TOURIST INFORMATION. *The Niagara Falls Official Tourism Information Center,* 4th and Niagara sts., is open seven days a week 9 A.M.-7 P.M.; during the Festival of Lights, hours are 4 P.M.-10 P.M.; 284-2000. *The Niagara Falls Convention & Visitors Bureau,* 345 Third Sts., Niagara Falls, 278-8010, has guides, maps, and brochures. Their 24-hour telephone information service, 278-8112, provides a recorded message summarizing the day's events, plus suggestions on what to do and see in the city. There is an information center in both terminals at the Buffalo Airport. During off-hours a telephone number is provided for anyone needing information or assistance. *The Travelers Aid Society,* 181 Ellicott St., 854-8661 (633-8807 at the airport), provides emergency assistance to travelers. *The Buffalo Area Chamber of Commerce,* 107 Delaware Ave., 849-6677, provides maps, guides, and brochures on the Buffalo and Niagara Falls area. For information on the entire area, call New York State Tourism Information toll-free, 800-342-3810.

FOREIGN CURRENCY EXCHANGE. All local banks will exchange Canadian funds. The main office *M&T Bank,* One M&T Plaza, Buffalo, offers exchange facilities, 9 A.M.-4 P.M. Also, *Deak International Currency Exchange,* Rainbow Center, 284-0642, and *Factory Outlet Shopping Mall,* 297-0876, both in Niagara Falls, exchange foreign funds.

SERVICE CLUBS. *Rotary Club* meets Thursdays at 12:15 P.M. at Buffalo Convention center or Mondays at 12:15, Ramada Inn, Niagara Falls. *Kiwanis Club* meets Wednesday, 12:10 P.M., Buffalo Hilton; Thursday, noon, Friars Restaurant, 441 3rd St., Niagara Falls. *Lions Club* meets second and fourth Tuesdays, 6:15 P.M., Scalzo's Restaurant, 1602 Pine Ave., Niagara Falls, and Mondays at noon at the Holiday Inn, 620 Delaware Ave., Buffalo.

RECOMMENDED READING. All these books are easily available in Buffalo–Niagara Falls bookstores, and some are available nationally in bookstores or libraries: *Buffalo Architecture: A Guide.* Sponsored by Buffalo Architectural Guidebook Corp. MIT Press, Cambridge; 1981.

Country Inns of New York State. Robert W. Tolf, Roxane S. Rauch. 101 Productions, San Francisco; 1984.

Sander's Fishing Guide. John M. Sander. Sander's Fishing Guide & Service Directory Inc.; 1985.

Somewhere to Go on Sunday: A Guide to Natural Treasures in Western New York. Margaret Wooster. Prometheus Books; 1982.

Wilderness Weekends in Western New York. Compiled by Niagara Frontier Chapter Adirondack Mountain Club. Frank and Wilma Cipolla, co-editors. Niagara Frontier Chapter Adirondack Mountain Club; 1983.

SEASONAL EVENTS. January. The *Niagara Falls Festival of Lights* continues through the Sunday after New Year's Day. There are hundreds of thousands of colored lights, decorations, animated displays, entertainment, free events, and shows, combined with the special beauty of the freezing mist crystallizing the surroundings. Buffalo celebrates winter with the *Winter Carnival* the last weekend in January at Chestnut Ridge Park, Orchard Park. The *Blizzard Ball,* held the same weekend, remembers the "Great Blizzard of 1977."

March. Buffalo has the biggest *St. Patrick's Day* parade west of New York's Fifth Ave. on the Sunday before March 17. The whole town turns Irish and offers up corned beef and cabbage.

May. During the third weekend of the month a corner of Buffalo becomes a Greek island as the Hellenic Orthodox Church of the Annunciation, 150 W. Utica St., is transformed into a taverna and a Greek bazaar for the *Hellenic Festival.* At the end of the month, on the Sunday of the Memorial Day weekend, Niagara Falls sponsors the *Concert in the Sky* with synchronized fireworks and music above Prospect Point and Goat Island at the Falls.

June. On the first weekend in June, the *King's Birthday* is celebrated at Old Fort Niagara, with 18th-century military ceremonies, drills, music, cannon, and musket firings. During the second weekend, all of Allentown in Buffalo is turned into an outdoor art gallery and people-watching extravaganza as thousands flock to the area for the *Allentown Art Festival,* one of the largest outdoor art shows in the country. The following weekend is the *Juneteenth Festival,* a celebration of Afro-American culture. Parades and other activities are centered along Jefferson Ave. in Buffalo.

July kicks off a series of outdoor festivals and concerts throughout the area. Daily during the week through August there is noontime entertainment at 1 M&T Plaza, Buffalo. On the Fourth of July there is a celebration and fireworks at the E. Dent Lackey Plaza, in front of the Niagara Falls International Convention Center. This day also begins the *Niagara Summer Experience,* a series of outdoors weekend ethnic entertainments at the Lackey Plaza. The weekend after July 4, Buffalo celebrates its culinary diversity with a *Taste of Buffalo,* an outdoor food festival. The following weekend is celebrated at the Niagara Falls airport with the *Western New York International Airshow. The Waterfront Festival* also begins at the Waterfront Pavilion, LaSalle Park.

August. Entertainment continues at 1 M&T Plaza through the end of the month and the Niagara Summer Experience continues every weekend in Niagara Falls. For ten days in mid-August, Hamburg, 10 miles south of Buffalo, is home to the largest county fair in the country, the *Erie County Fair & Expo.* It features animals, foods, amusement rides, tractor pulls, and national entertainers. It was here in 1885 that the hamburger was born.

September. The second weekend is devoted to a celebration of Irish culture at the *Irish Hooley* at the Erie County Fairgrounds in Hamburg. On Sunday during the middle of September is the *Pulaski Day* parade, a celebration of Polish heritage, and the largest such parade east of Chicago. Mid-September is *Cityfest—Curtain Up,* the opening night celebration for Buffalo's theater district. The third Saturday in the month is the *Buffalo/Niagara Falls International Marathon* race through Buffalo and Canada to Niagara Falls, Ontario.

October. A *Revolutionary War Encampment* is held the third weekend of the month at Old Fort Niagara. The troops are garrisoned as they would have been during the Revolutionary War, with period clothing and living conditions.

November. The *Niagara Falls Festival of Lights* begins the Saturday after Thanksgiving with nightly entertainment and thousands of lights from 5 P.M. to 11 P.M.

December. The *Festival of Lights* continues nightly throughout the month.

FREE EVENTS. At Niagara Falls during the Festival of Lights in December, the E. Dent Lackey Plaza has an outside skating rink. Wintergarden, a seven-story, indoor tropical garden across from the Convention Center, is open every day of the year. The Niagara Power Project Visitor Center has displays and exhibits on the hydroelectric project. July brings Shakespeare in the Park performances near the Rose Garden in Delaware Park, under the direction the Department of Theater of the State University of New York at Buffalo. There are free weekday noon entertainments at 1 M&T Plaza in Buffalo throughout July and August. The newly renovated Buffalo & Erie County Botanical Gardens, S. Park Ave. and McKinley Pkwy., is open daily 9 A.M. to 4 P.M. The 28th floor observation tower of Buffalo's impressive City Hall provides a panoramic view of the city, the lake, and the suburbs. Open weekdays, 9 A.M.–3:30 P.M. Of course, the greatest sight of all, Niagara Falls itself, has been free to all since 1885. The view of the Falls is enhanced at night when the Falls are illuminated for 2½–3½ hours, depending on the season.

TOURS. Sightseeing is what Niagara Falls is all about. *Bedore Tours,* 454 Main St., 285–5261, has a 3-hour tour; adults, $18; children, $8; May–October. *Bridal Veil Tours,* 9470 Niagara Falls Blvd., 297–0329, has 4-hour tours; adults, $19.95; children, $10.50. *Gray Line,* 3466 Niagara Falls Blvd., 692–4288, provides tours of Niagara Falls and Buffalo. *International Honeymoon Tours,* 9393 Niagara Falls Blvd., 297–3797; *Niagara Scenic Tours,* S–5700 Maelou Dr., Hamburg, 648–1500; *Two Nation Tours,* 1260 95th St., 297–5038; and *Young Tours,* 850 Niagara Falls Blvd., 837–1188, all provide falls tours and pickups from major hotels. *Rainbow Helicopter,* 454 Main St., 285–0492, provides year-round helicopter tours of the falls area. *International Carriage Rides & Livery,* 6764 Walmore Rd., 731–3389, has horse-drawn carriage tours of the area.

Niagara Viewmobiles, sightseeing **trains,** may be boarded at several locations on Goat Island and at Prospect Point near the Observation Tower. Stopovers are permitted at five sites; daily June 24–October 15; adults, $2; children, $1; 282–0028.

The *Cave of the Winds Trip* allows visitors to almost reach out and touch the falls by taking the group on wooden walkways to within 25 feet of the base.

Rainbows abound here and in 1984 a Korean visitor was hit by a 15-pound chinook salmon trying to swim up the great cataract. Rain slickers and foot coverings are provided. Mid-May–mid-October; adults, $3; children, $2.50; 282–8979. In Buffalo, information on walking tours of Allentown can be obtained from *Allentown Association,* 45 Elmwood Ave., 881–1024. Guided two-hour walking tours depart from Wilcox Mansion, 641 Delaware Ave., May–October; adults, $2; children, $1; 884–0330. A self-guided tour of *Forest Lawn Cemetery,* 1411 Delaware Ave., final resting place of President Millard Fillmore and Indian Chief Red Jacket, is available at the cemetery office, 885–1600.

By boat. The most famous boat ride of all is the *Maid of the Mist,* which has operated since 1843. Just about every celebrity and head of state who has ever visited the falls has taken a ride on the *Maid of the Mist,* which travels to the very base of the falls where the waters roar and the mist swirls upward in an ascending cloud. Theodore Roosevelt said that a ride on the Maid was "the only way to fully realize the Grandeur of the Great Falls of Niagara."

The Maid boats have become as much a symbol of Niagara as the falls themselves. The diesel boats may be boarded on either the American or the Canadian side. To get to the boats there is a charge of 50¢ on the American side for the elevator and 60¢ for the incline railway on the Canadian side. The season opens mid-May and continues daily through October 24. The tour lasts approximately one-half hour with departures every 15 minutes. Heavy rain slickers are provided.

There has never been an accident with the boats, but in 1960 the Maid crew rescued seven-year-old Roger Woodward, who was thrown over the falls wearing only an orange life jacket. A fishing boat he was riding in developed engine trouble and broke up in the rapids above the Falls. Roger survived the plunge in good condition and remains the only person to have survived the trip without benefit of a barrel or other protective device. Adults, $5; children, $2.50; 284–8897.

In Buffalo, *Miss Buffalo Cruises* conduct a 2-hour narrated tour of the Buffalo harbor. The trips leave the Naval and Servicemen's Park at Marine Dr. and Erie St. and travel on Lake Erie and the Niagara River, returning through the locks of the Black Rock Canal. Tours are daily 12:30 P.M. and 3 P.M., July 1–Labor Day. Adults, $6.50; ages 6–16, $5.50; under 6, $1.50; 856–6696 for reservations and additional cruises. *Classic Yacht Cruises* provides dinner, cocktail, fall foliage, and other special cruises on a classic 1946 yacht; 837–0972.

 PARKS. No other individual has had a greater influence on the landscape and parks in Niagara Falls and Buffalo than Frederick Law Olmsted, architect of New York City's Central Park. He was the leader in the fight to free Niagara Falls for public viewing and he designed the *Niagara Falls Reservation,* the first state park in the nation. He resisted all pressure to surround the Falls with then-fashionable ornamental gardens, seeking to preserve the character of the Falls' natural environment. The 139 land acres (and 296 water acres) of the reservation include *Prospect Park, Upper Rapids Park,* and *Goat Island,* and provide the closest view of the falls. Goat Island is in the middle of the river on the brink of the falls and has spectacular viewing areas.

Near the Convention Center is the *Niagara Splash Water Park,* 700 Rainbow Blvd., complete with pools, hot tubs, five-story slide, wave pool. $10.50, adults; $9.50 children, 4–11; $6.95 nights.

In the center of the city is 600-acre *Hyde Park,* the largest of the city parks, with an 18-hole public golf course and a swimming pool. Along the lower Niagara River are the 42-acre *Devil's Hole* and 109-acre *Whirlpool* state parks.

Artpark is a 200-acre state park along the Niagara River gorge in the village of Lewiston that is a theater and arts complex. An artist-in-residence program features specialists of both the visual and performing arts, and visitors may observe them at work. Recreational facilities include nature trails, picnic areas, and fishing docks from which trout and salmon can be caught. Call 745–3377 for schedule and ticket information. All activities free except theater events, which average $5–$8. Vehicle use fee, $2.50. Open Memorial Day–Labor Day. The 952-acre *Beaver Island Park*, Grand Island, has beaches, golf, tennis, fishing, boating, restaurant, and skiing.

In Buffalo, there is an extensive Olmsted-designed system of parks with various units linked by parkways. In all, there are more than 500 parks and playgrounds in the area. The 359-acre *Delaware Park* is in the center of the city and includes a zoo, a golf course, tennis courts, baseball diamonds, and even lawn bowling. The 33-acre *LaSalle Park* is along the waterfront and includes baseball diamonds, tennis courts, and an outdoor theater. *Tifft Farm Nature Preserve*, 1200 Fuhrmann Blvd., is a 264-acre nature preserve three miles from downtown Buffalo with a 75-acre cattail marsh, lake, and ponds. It features hiking trails, cross-country skiing, bird watching, fishing, and picnicking; open year-round dawn to dusk; 826–0544. *The Naval and Serviceman's Park*, One Naval Park Cove, along the waterfront, allows visitors to board two front-line fighting ships, the guided missile cruiser *U.S.S. Little Rock* and the destroyer *U.S.S. Sullivans*. The museum and grounds contain aircraft and artifacts from all branches of the armed services. Open April 1–November 30; adults, $3.50; children and seniors, $2.50; family rate, $10; 847–1773.

Darien Lake Theme Park, 9993 Allegheny Rd., Darien Park, about 25 miles east of Buffalo consists of 1,200 acres, with 2,000 campsites including trailer sites. Among the more than 35 major amusement rides are the 165-foot-high ferris wheel from the 1982 World's Fair and a number of water rides. Nature trail, petting zoo, amphitheater. Daily, Memorial Day–Labor Day. Admission $13.95; 716–599–4501.

ZOOS. *Buffalo Zoological Gardens* in Delaware Park celebrated its first 100 years in 1975. This is home to the nation's oldest bison herd and is one of the country's oldest zoos. Special features include a tropical rain forest, a gorilla habitat, and a simulated Asian forest. A children's petting zoo is popular and includes camel and elephant rides. Open daily except Thanksgiving and Christmas. Adults, $2.50; ages 11–16; $1, ages 4–10, 50¢; over 65 and under 4, free; family $6. There are several free days a month; 837–3900.

GARDENS. The Niagara Parks Commission School of Horticulture on the Canadian side of the Falls oversees the area's most spectacular floral display. Flowers of the season bloom outdoors throughout the growing season, and the *Botanical Gardens* offers year-round displays; 356–2241. Six miles north of the Falls on the Canadian side, is the *Floral Clock*, one of the largest in the world with approximately 25,000 colorful plants that bloom from early spring to first frost. The timepiece keeps accurate time. The Horticulture School also maintains the elaborate floral gardens that fill the park along the Canadian side of the falls. In Buffalo, the newly renovated *Buffalo & Erie County Botanical Gardens*, S. Park Ave. and McKinley Pkwy., 828–1040, houses a large collection of exotic plants, fruit trees, flowers, and a cactus house. Open 9 A.M.–4 P.M. Free.

BEACHES. The Buffalo area and nearby southern Ontario are blessed with miles of fresh-water shoreline. In fact, there's as much beachfront within an hour's drive of Buffalo as there is near Los Angeles. Unfortunately for beach-lovers, many of the best are privately owned and not open to the public. *Beaver Island State Park,* Grand Island, has a nice beach, lifeguards, full bathing and picnic facilities, and bathhouse and boardwalk; $2.50 parking fee. *Wendt Beach, Evans,* and *Evangola State Park,* have lifeguards, bathhouses, and clean beaches on the American shore. On the Canadian side, *Sherkston Beach* and *Quarry,* about 10 miles from Buffalo (take Hwy. 3 after crossing Peace Bridge to Regional Rd. 98) has more than a mile of excellent sand beach and a deep quarry for swimming, bathhouse, camping, and restaurant; 416–894–0972. *Crystal Beach Amusement Park & Beach,* about 8 miles from Buffalo, offers an excellent sand beach and a huge amusement park featuring two roller coasters; take Hwy. 3, make left onto Gorham Road, go 2.5 miles. Admission $3 general (park and beach entry but rides not included), or $1.50 for beach only; $10.50 for unlimited rides; $8.50 for children 4–8; 877–0726.

BABY-SITTING SERVICES. *Kiddie Kare Baby Sitter Service,* Tonawanda, 836–2212, uses adults sitters only. Kiddy Kare charges $4 an hour with a 4-hour minimum and a $3 transportation charge unless pickup and dropoff is provided. Many hotels and motels can also provide names of sitters.

CHILDREN'S ACTIVITIES. Niagara Falls itself delights children of all ages, and exploring it from all angles can satisfy the child in all of us. Whether viewing the wonder of the falls from the deck of the *Maid of the Mist,* the Niagara Viewmobile, the Cave of the Winds trip, or from a tower or railing, children will be in awe. The *Aquarium of Niagara Falls,* Whirlpool St. at Pine Ave., has aquatic creatures from around the world, including performing dolphins and sea lions. Closed Jan. 1, Thanksgiving, and Christmas; adults, $4.50; over 60 $3; children $2.50; 285–3575. *Marineland,* 7657 Portage Rd. on the Canadian side, features killer whales, dolphins, and sea lions. On the grounds is an aquarium and a game farm with bear, deer, elk, and buffalo. Admission varies with season; summer, adults, $12.50; over 59 and children, $8.95; spring and fall, adults, $11.40; over 59 and children, $6.95; winter, adults, $5.95, and over 59 and children, $4.25; 416–356–8250. *Niagara Splash Water Park* on the U.S. side offers pools, water slides. (See *parks* for details.)

Maple Leaf Village, Clifton Hill and Falls Ave., on the Canadian side, is an amusement complex sporting a 350-foot observation tower and one of the largest ferris wheels on the continent; also rides, musical shows, and restaurants. Admission to the village is free. Outdoor rides are open June 15–September 15. Combination price of $9.95 includes unlimited use of rides and a number of attractions.

Buffalo Museum of Science, Humboldt Pkwy. at Northampton St., has a hands-on exhibit room for children 6–12. Children and their parents may handle prehistoric stone tools, touch a stuffed alligator, learn about snakes, play musical instruments, and wear African clothing. Adults, $1.50; students, senior citizens, and children, 75¢; 896–5200. *The Children's Zoo,* Buffalo Zoological Gardens, Delaware Park, has animals for petting and riding. Adults, $2.50; ages 11–16, $1; ages 4–10, 50¢; 837–3900.

Theater; of Youth (TOY) Company, Pfeifer Theater 681 Main St., performs several major children's shows per year; call 831–3742 for schedules and ticket information.

PARTICIPANT SPORTS. With the ample supply of lakes and rivers and plenty of wind, water sports of all kinds are popular, including **sailing, boating, windsurfing,** and **water skiing.** *Seven Seas Sailing School,* Erie Basin Marina, 856–4109, and *Serendipity Sailing Services,* 2493 Garrison Rd., Ridgeway, Ontario, 416–894–0696, provide sailboat rental and instruction. *Bouquard's Boat Livery,* 1581 Fuhrmann Blvd., 826–6189, and *Wolf's Boat House,* 327 S. Ellicott Creek Rd., Tonawanda, 691–8740, have motor boat rentals. *Niagara Scuba Sports,* 2048 Niagara St., 875–6528, provides scuba diving instruction, equipment rentals, and dive trips year round, including under the ice in winter. The nearly eight mile-an-hour current in the Niagara River provides a particularly exciting dive for experienced divers.

Fishing. After years of negative publicity regarding pollution in area lakes and rivers, conditions have improved enough so that lake trout and other freshwater fish have returned to Lake Erie, Niagara River, and Lake Ontario. *John M. Sander's Fishing Guide* is a detailed guide to area fishing; available in sporting goods stores and bookstores. There is still a health advisory regarding eating fish from Lake Ontario. Consult the State *Department of Environmental Conservation (DEC),* 847–4600, for health and license information. Write or call DEC, 50 Wolf Rd., Albany 12233; 518–457–5400, for booklets on Great Lakes fishing, trout and salmon fishing, and state boat launching sites. Bass, trout, muskie, salmon, and northern pike are being caught in large numbers. There are a number of charter fishing operators in the Buffalo, Lake Erie, and Niagara River area and Lake Ontario in Niagara County. They include *Great Lakes Fishing Charters,* 8255 West Point Dr., Amherst, 741–3453; *Olcott Charter Service,* Newfane, 434–9902; and *Downrigger Charters,* 2683 Grace Ave., Newfane, 778–7518.

Hunting. Excellent hunting opportunities for whitetail deer, wild turkey, upland birds, waterfowl, and small game exist within a 90-minute drive from Buffalo. For information on licenses, seasons, bag limits, permissible weapons, public hunting grounds, and private preserves, write Department of Environmental Conservation (DEC), 50 Wolf Rd., Albany 12233, or call 518–457–5400.

Skiing. There are 20 skiing areas within a 90-mile radius of Buffalo, with the nearest only a 45-minute drive from downtown. *Kissing Bridge,* Rte. 240, Glenwood, 592–4963, is the closest to Buffalo and one of the largest area ski centers. *Holiday Valley,* Rte. 219, Ellicottville, 699–2644, has been called "the Aspen of the East" and is the most extensive ski center in the area. There is cross country skiing in the city's parks. For ski conditions dial 800–CALL–NYS.

Tennis. There are more than 100 tennis courts in the area, and a number of public **golf** courses. Contact Buffalo Parks Dept., 855–4200 or Erie County Department of Parks & Recreation, 846–8352. There are jogging trails in the major parks and Buffalo is home of the Buffalo/Niagara Falls International Marathon held in mid-September, 885–RACE.

SPECTATOR SPORTS. Buffalo is a big sports town. The National Football League Buffalo Bills play at Rich Stadium, Orchard Park; 649–0015. The **Buffalo Sabres** professional hockey team plays at War Memorial Auditorium; 856–3111. The **Buffalo Bison** AAA baseball team plays at Pilot Field; 878–8055. **Buffalo Raceway,** Hamburg, 649–1280, has live harness racing. In Niagara Falls, the **White Sox,** a farm team of the Pittsburgh Pirates, plays baseball at Hyde Park.

 HISTORIC SITES AND HOUSES. Since 1726, *Old Fort Niagara,* Youngstown, 14 miles from Niagara Falls, has commanded a view of the Niagara River and Lake Ontario. The flags of three nations—Great Britain, France, and America—have flown over this fort, which was an active military post well into the 20th century. During the summer, authentically-clad militiamen give hourly cannon and musketry demonstrations and explain the fort's history. Closed Jan. 1, Thanksgiving, and Christmas. Adults, $3.75; over 65 and ages 13–18, $3; ages 6–12, $1.90; 745–7611.

Theodore Roosevelt Inaugural National Historic Site (Wilcox Mansion), 641 Delaware Ave., is a Greek Revival structure dating from 1838 when it served as military officers' headquarters. Restored and containing late Victorian furniture are the library, where Theodore Roosevelt was sworn in as the 26th President of the U.S., a morning room, dining room, and bedroom. Items related to the inauguration of Roosevelt and assassination of President McKinley in Buffalo in 1901 are displayed. Art gallery on second floor. Open daily except Sat., Jan.–Mar. adults, $1; under 12, 50¢; 884–0095.

Roycroft Campus, 40 South Grove St., East Aurora, 20 miles southeast of Buffalo. Home of the Roycroft Movement, founded in 1895 by philosopher and writer Elbert Hubbard, the 10-building campus is listed on the National Register of Historic Places. The Roycroft Inn has been renovated as it was in Hubbard's day and the campus has undergone a renaissance with art galleries, print shops, craft, and furniture shops. Tours available. Inn open daily for overnight lodging and fine meals; 652–9030.

Millard Fillmore Museum, 24 Shearer Ave., East Aurora. Millard Fillmore practiced law here and built a home for his bride in 1825 before going on to become the nation's 13th President. The house has been restored; 652–8875.

 ARCHITECTURE. Buffalo has achieved worldwide recognition for its rich architectural treasures. The architectural gem is one of the greatest skyscrapers ever built, *Louis Sullivan's Guaranty Building,* 30 Church St. Built in 1895 it was painstakingly restored in 1983. Tours available.

Nearby is the *City Hall,* Niagara Square, built 1929–31. It is one of the finest examples of Art Deco. The 28th floor observation deck offers views of the lake and city.

Frank Lloyd Wright's work is well represented with five houses. The most impressive is the *Darwin D. Martin House,* 125 Jewett Pkwy., which is owned by the State University of New York at Buffalo. Built in 1904, the house has much of the original Wright-designed furniture. Tours available, Saturdays noon and Sundays 1 P.M.; $2; 831–3485.

Stanford White was one of the greatest late-19th-century architects, and two fine examples of his work sit side-by-side on stately Delaware Ave. They are *Butler Hall,* 672 Delaware Ave., the one-time home of the Butler family, former owners of the *Buffalo News,* and *Pratt House,* 690 Delaware Ave., now the headquarters of the Snyder-Darien Corp. Buffalo businessman Paul Snyder restored this building and also transformed a landmark office building into the elegant Hyatt Regency Hotel.

LIBRARIES. *Buffalo & Erie County Public Library,* Lafayette Sq., Rare Book Room has an impressive collection of original manuscripts including the original of Mark Twain's *Adventures of Huckleberry Finn.* The State University of New York at Buffalo's *Capen Hall Rare Book Room* has the nation's top collection of manuscripts and first editions of 20-century poets and writers.

MUSEUMS. The Niagara Falls–Buffalo area has a wealth of museums ranging from the scientific and historical to the bizarre. All prices for admission to Canadian museums and attractions are listed in Canadian dollars.

NIAGARA FALLS

Niagara Reservation Visitor Interpretive Center. Niagara Reservation State Park. Information, exhibits, gardens, theater. Open daily; free. Among the attractions is a *Niagara Spectacular* film. Adults, $2.50; senior, $2; children, $1.50.

Power Vista, Rt. 104, four miles north of the falls; 285–3211. Observation, information center, and museum of Niagara Power Project with spectacular views of the river and gorge. Movies, working models, and dioramas explain how generators at Niagara Project operate. Closed Thanksgiving, Christmas, Jan. 1. Free.

Schoellkopf Geological Museum, Niagara Reservation State Park; 278–1780. Multi-media museum explains 500-million-year geologic history of the Falls. A geological garden and nature trail on grounds. Guided tours twice daily; 25¢.

The Turtle: Native American Center for the Living Arts, 25 Rainbow Mall; 284–2427. Houses a museum and art gallery focusing on American Indian heritage, culture, symbols, and art. Iroquois dance performances are held daily during summer season. Restaurant, gift shop. Adults, $3, senior citizens, $2.50; ages 6–12, $1.50.

NIAGARA FALLS, ONT.

Boris Karloff Wax Museum, 6546 Buchanan Ave.; 416–356–5220. Effigies of some of the notorious film characters played by Karloff. Closed Christmas. Adults, $2.75; ages 13–18, $1.50; ages 6–12, $1.25; family, $7.

Elvis Presley Museum, Maple Leaf Village; 416–357–0008. Billed as the largest private collection of Elvis memorabilia in the world. On exhibit are his jewelry, clothes, cars, furniture from Graceland, and his Hollywood home and personal effects including the first dollar bill he earned. Adults, $3.95; children, $2.50.

Guinness Museum of World Records, 4966 Clifton Hill, 416–356–2238. Hundreds of record-breaking exhibits including the tallest, fattest, longest, smallest. Adults, $4.50; students, $3.50; children, $2.50.

Houdini Hall of Fame, 4983 Clifton Hill; 416–356–4869. A record of Houdini's amazing career and paraphernalia used by other magic greats. Exhibits include the $100,000 Houdini handcuff collection, steel trunk used by Houdini for his dangerous underwater stunts, and Chinese water torture cell used in his famous escape. Adults, $4; students, $2.75; children, $2.

Louis Tussaud's Waxworks, Clifton Hill and Falls Ave., 416–354–7521. Life-size reproductions of the most famous and infamous people in historically accurate costumes and settings. Adults, $4.95; children, $2.75.

Niagara Falls Museum, 5651 River Rd.; 416–356–2151. Geological, zoological, and historical exhibits as well as "Daredevil Hall of Fame" with originals of devices that carried adventurers over the falls. Adults, $4; seniors and students, $3; children, $1.75.

BUFFALO AREA

Amherst Museum, 3755 Tonawanda Creek Rd., East Amherst; 689–1440. Niagara Frontier Aviation Hall of Fame and aviation history exhibits in technology building, plus St. John Neumann log chapel reconstruction. Gift shop. Daily, 1:30 P.M. to 4:30 P.M. Free.

Buffalo and Erie County Historical Society, 25 Nottingham Ct.; 783–9644. The only remaining building from the Pan American Exposition of 1901, with an emphasis on history of the area including Indian culture. Former U.S. President Millard Fillmore was first president of the society. Period rooms and shops. Tuesdays–Sundays. Closed Jan. 1, Thanksgiving, and Christmas. Adults, $1.50; seniors, 90¢; under 12, 75¢; family, $3.

Buffalo Museum of Science, Humboldt Pkwy. at Northampton St., 896–5200. Exhibits on anthropology, archaeology, astronomy, botany, geology, and zoology, including gigantic insect models and a children's discovery room. Museum shop. Daily, 10 A.M.–5 P.M., Fri., 10 A.M.–10 P.M. Kellogg Observatory open Fridays, dusk–9:30 P.M., September 1–May 31. Adults, $1.50; students, seniors, and ages 3–17, 75¢; family, $3.50.

MUSIC. Buffalo has had a long tradition as an important music town, both for classical and jazz. Although he doesn't play often in Buffalo, punk rock star Rick James was born in Buffalo and lives in nearby East Aurora. *Arts Council* in Buffalo and Erie County, 700 Main St., 856–7520, provides information about all area arts and music events on *ARTSline,* a 24-hour hotline, 847–1444. The renowned 87-member *Buffalo Philharmonic Orchestra,* 885–5000, celebrated its 50th anniversary season during 1985–86. Music directors have included Joseph Krips, Lukas Foss, Michael Tilson Thomas, and Julius Rudel. The orchestra plays symphony concerts in Kleinhans Music Hall, Symphony Circle, acclaimed as an acoustically perfect concert hall. The orchestra actually plays virtually year-round with concerts in area parks including Artpark during the summer. Pops Concerts are played by the philharmonic Fridays, October–April.

STAGE. Buffalo has long been known as a good theater town. Actress Katharine Cornell was born and played here. The theater district on Main St. between Virginia and Chippewa Sts. has undergone a renaissance. The showpiece of the district is *Shea's Buffalo Theater,* 646 Main St., 847–0050, an ornate, crystal palace which has been refurbished to its original grandeur. It boasts one of the largest Wurlitzer organs ever built. Theater, dance, opera, and music, national touring companies.

Studio Arena Theater, 710 Main St., 856–5650, is the city's resident theater, with live performances September–May. World premieres and pre-Broadway productions are staged here. This is the largest regional theater in the state.

The Pfeifer Theater, 681 Main St., 831–3742, is across the street, and is home to the State University of New York at Buffalo's Department of Theater and Dance. Performances October–December and February–May. The *Theater of Youth (TOY) Company,* 856–4410, also performs in the Pfeifer Theater.

The world renowned *Shaw Festival* hosts performances from May–Oct. in three theaters in nearby Niagara-on-the-Lake, Ont.; 416–468–2172.

ART GALLERIES. Buffalo's art scene has achieved worldwide acclaim largely through the efforts of industrialist Seymour Knox, who has contributed greatly to the *Albright-Knox Art Gallery,* 1285 Elmwood Ave., 882–8700. In particular, he is responsible for the gallery's top modern art collection.

The gallery is a handsome Greek revival building with a modern addition. Painting and sculpture dating from 3000 B.C. to the present. The collection of 20th-century art is internationally known. It was the first U.S. museum to buy works by Picasso and Matisse. Included in the collection is "The Mirrored Room," a life-size room, table, and chair made completely of mirrors. Museum shop and restaurant. Open Tuesdays–Sundays; donations.

Burchfield Art Center, 878–6011, is across the street on the campus of Buffalo State University College. Featured is a collection of watercolor paintings by the late Charles E. Burchfield, for whom the center is named. Concerts, lectures, recitals, films, and classes are held here. Tuesdays–Sundays; free.

The ArnakArt Gallery, 49 W. Chippewa St., 855–1834 specializes in North American Indian and Eskimo art. Free.

Buscaglia-Castellani Art Gallery, 3100 Lewiston Rd., Niagara Falls, 284–2816, has 19th and 20th-century art with major emphasis on contemporary works. Free.

G & R Wildlife Gallery, 2895 Seneca St., West Seneca, 822–0546, holds a collection of wildlife art and wood carvings by local artists as well as works by such well-known wildlife artists as Robert Bateman. Closed Wednesdays. Free.

SHOPPING. The shopping scene in the area largely revolves around malls and factory outlets, which have become tourist attractions themselves. Malls are open seven days a week and every evening except Sunday. Downtown stores are open Thursday evenings and Saturdays. Sales tax in Niagara County (Niagara Falls) is 7 percent and in Erie County (Buffalo area), 8 percent.

NIAGARA FALLS AREA

Artisans Alley, 10 Rainbow Blvd., 282–0196, features work of more than 400 American craftsmen, including local artists.

Factory Outlet Mall, 1900 Military Rd., 773–1797. More than 70 manufacturer outlets offering 20–70 percent savings.

Rainbow Centre Shopping Mall, 302 Rainbow Blvd., 285–9758. 60 shops and restaurants one block from the falls. Many outlet stores.

Summit Park Mall, 6929 Williams Rd., 297–0206. Niagara County's largest mall, with more than 90 stores and services.

BUFFALO AREA

Broadway Market, 999 Broadway, in the heart of the city's Polish neighborhood. The market is filled with small shops serving up such delicacies as Polish kielbasa, smoked hams, and fresh breads and pastries.

Eastern Hills Mall, 4545 Transit Rd., Williamsville, 631–5191. More than 100 department and specialty stores and services.

Factory Outlet Mall, 1881 Ridge Rd., West Seneca, 674–8920. More than 20 manufacturer outlets at 20-70 percent savings.

 DINING OUT. Buffalo has given the world two classic dishes—Buffalo chicken wings and beef on weck. The chicken wings are served mild, medium, or spicy hot, along with blue cheese dressing and celery. Beef on weck is roast beef carved on the spot and served on a freshly made flaky kimmelweck roll which is sprinkled with pretzel salt. Because of the rich ethnic diversity of the entire area there are a variety of restaurants reflecting the culture and background of the people. The price classifications of the following restaurants, from inexpensive to deluxe, are based on the cost of an average three-course dinner for one person, beverages, tax, and tip are extra. *Deluxe,* over $22; *Expensive,* $14–$22; *Moderate,* $7–14; *Inexpensive,* less than $7. There is currently a favorable exchange rate on American dollars in Canada, averaging more than 30 percent.

Abbreviations for credit cards are: AE, American Express; CB, Carte Blanche; DC, Diners Club; MC, MasterCard; V, VISA. Most restaurants that do not accept credit cards will cash traveler's checks. Sales tax in Niagara Falls (Niagara County) is 7 percent; in Buffalo (Erie County) it is 8 percent. Abbreviations for meal codes are B, breakfast; L, lunch; D, dinner. As restaurant hours and days of closing often change, you should call first to confirm the hours. What follows is only a selective list of dining possibilities in the area.

AMERICAN

Expensive

Asa Ransom House. 10529 Main St., Clarence; 759–2315. Fine country dining featuring local foods served by friendly waitresses dressed in early American costumes. Picture perfect country setting in historic house filled with antiques. Four bedrooms upstairs. Closed Fridays, Saturdays; L, Wednesdays only; D, Sundays–Thursdays. No credit cards.

Clarkson House. 810 Center St., Lewiston; 754–4544. A landmark since 1818, this is a special favorite during the Artpark summer theater season. Lobster is flown in daily from Maine and steaks are a favorite. Closed Mondays. D; AE, MC, V.

Lyon's Countryside Inn. 8255 Clarence Center Rd., Clarence; 741–3644. Fine country dining in garden setting with outdoor deck. L, D; Closed Mondays. AE, MC, V.

Old Orchard Inn. 2095 Blakely Rd., East Aurora; 652–4664. One-time hunting lodge in country setting transformed into handsome dining room with fine American food. Gift shop. L, D, daily. AE, MC, V.

Red Coach Inn Restaurant. 2 Buffalo Ave., Niagara Falls; 282–1459. A tradition since 1923, overlooking the spectacular upper rapids of the falls. Fireplaces, outside patio dining, prime ribs a specialty. L, D, daily. AE, MC, DC.

The Rib Cage. 1124 Main St., Niagara Falls, 282–1004. Home of the gourmet lovers; prime ribs are featured; flaming desserts and coffee prepared tableside. L, Tuesdays–Fridays; D, Tuesdays–Sundays; closed Mondays. Major credit cards.

Roycroft Inn. 40 South Grove St., East Aurora; 652–9030. Country inn featuring "new American cuisine" with local produce and New York wines. Inn dates from 1903 and has been renovated and filled with original Roycroft furniture. L, D, daily. AE, DC, MC, V.

Moderate

Table Rock Restaurant. Queen Victoria Park, Niagara Falls, Ont.; 416–354–3631. Though Canadians do sometimes object to being labeled American, this restaurant serves Canadian/American fare. While the food is quite good, it is the location that brings the diners. It is at the brink of the Horseshoe Falls and from your table you can view the falls on both sides of the border without the spray. B, L, D, daily. Major credit cards.

Top of the Falls Restaurant. Goat Island, Niagara Falls; 285–3311. The location is the big drawing card here. Each table gives the feeling of being on top of the falls. Cafeteria style. L, daily. MC, V.

Turtle Gallery Restaurant. 25 Rainbow Mall, Niagara Falls; 284–4867. A unique restaurant within the Native American Center for the Living Arts serving American Indian and usual American fare. L, D, daily. Closed Mondays, October–April. AE, DC, MC, V.

Inexpensive

McDonald's Frontier House. 460 Center St., Lewiston; 754–4041. While this is really a McDonald's, it certainly doesn't look like it. It is located in a National Historic Landmark. Built in 1824, it once hosted such notables as Lafayette, King Edward VII, President McKinley, and Charles Dickens in the days when it was a bustling stagecoach stop. The building has been restored to its glory days and McDonald's did forego its golden arches. B, L, D, daily. No credit cards.

CHINESE

Expensive

Ming Teh. 126 Niagara St., Fort Erie, Ont., just over the Niagara River from Buffalo; 416–871–7971. Along the river on Chinese restaurant row. The owner is also an artist and the artist's influence can be seen in the perfect dishes, greatly pleasing to the eye and the palate. A popular spot with area residents and visiting celebrities. L, D. Major credit cards.

Moderate

Lee Chu's Restaurant. Colvin Eggert Plaza, Tonawanda; 835–3352. Tucked into a shopping plaza, there is a real Chinese atmosphere inside. Specializing in Szechuan and Mandarin; Peking duck with advance notice. L, D, daily. Major credit cards.

May Wah Restaurant. 90 Niagara Blvd., Fort Erie, Ont.; 416–871–2422. In a prime location with a riverfront view. There is excellent cuisine including some specialties of the house and attentive service. L, D, daily. AE, MC, V.

Shanghai Village. 1465 Hertel Ave., Buffalo; 835–3300. Specializing in lunch and dinner Chinese smorgasbord (the ribs and eggrolls are superior) as well as traditional menu dishes. L, D, daily. Major credit cards.

Inexpensive

Parkview Tavern. 93 Niagara Blvd., Fort Erie, Ont.; 416–871–6571. Nothing fancy here, but Cantonese fare is good and there is plenty of it. L, D, daily. Major credit cards.

CONTINENTAL

Deluxe

Harlan's. 150 Theater Place, Buffalo; 842–6500. Intimate dining room in renovated Theater Place next to Shea's Buffalo Theater. Most popular spot for before or after theater dining; wine bar. L, Mondays–Fridays; D, Tuesdays–Sundays. AE, DC, MC, V.

Justine's. Buffalo Hilton at the Waterfront; 845–5100. Elegant dining room in beautiful surroundings with varied menu; jackets and ties required. D; closed Sundays. AE, CB, DC, MC, V.

Expensive

Cloister Restaurant. 472 Delaware Ave., Buffalo; 886–0070. Winner of multiple awards, this continues to be a special restaurant. It is built partly from a section of the home of Mark Twain, who served as editor of *The Buffalo Express.* Excellent selection of entrees served in several unique and attractively furnished dining rooms. The expensive tag doesn't apply to frequent dinner specials on steak and lobster. L, Mondays–Fridays; D, daily. AE, CB, DC, MC, V.

Crawdaddy's Restaurant. 2 Templeton Ter., Buffalo; 856–9191. On Buffalo's newly renovated waterfront area, overlooking the Erie Basin Marina. Very popular restaurant, usually packed on weekends and during the summer. Outdoor patio, expansive restaurant, ask for a water view. Varied menu with fresh seafood a feature. L, D, daily. Major credit cards.

E. B. Green's Restaurant. Two Fountain Plaza, in Hyatt Regency Buffalo; 856–1234. Named in honor of the architect who designed the Genesee Building, which was transformed into the hotel. Small elegant dining room. L, D, daily. Major credit cards.

Skylon Tower. 5200 Robinson Rd., Niagara Falls, Ont.; 416–856–5788. Take an outside elevator high up to the tower with some of the best views anywhere of the majestic falls. Dine in the revolving dining room with fine food and service. L, D, daily. Major credit cards.

Moderate

Rolf's. 3840 Main St., Niagara Falls, Ont.; 416–295–3472. Renovated old house is the setting for fine food prepared by European trained chef-owner Rolf. D, daily; closed Mondays. Major credit cards.

FRENCH

Deluxe

Rue Franklin West. 341 Franklin St., Buffalo; 852–4416. Housed in a 100-year-old Victorian brick house; every dish is extra fresh and prepared from scratch. Menu changes seasonally, but imaginative all year round. D, Tuesdays–Saturdays. Major credit cards.

GERMAN

Moderate

Deutsches Haus Restaurant. 2090 Genesee St., Buffalo; 895–4401. An old-world German atmosphere with home cooking and a variety of German beers and wines. L, D, daily. AE, DC.

Wurzburger-Hof Restaurant. 3250 Bailey Ave., Buffalo; 836–9303. Daily specials such as knockwurst and sauerkraut; discounts for seniors; entertainment on Fridays, Saturdays. L, D, daily. No credit cards.

GREEK

Moderate

Towne Restaurant. 186 Allen St., Buffalo; 884–5128. In the heart of the Allentown District, this restaurant started life as a hot dog stand specializing in dogs with spicy hot sauce. It just grew and grew in response to its loyal customers and now resembles a Greek taverna. The owner hails from Rhodes and knows the meaning of Greek hospitality. L, D, daily. AE, MC, V.

Yianni's Greek Restaurant. 581 Delaware Ave., Buffalo; 883–6033. Housed in an elegant old home with an outdoor patio; fine Greek food. L, D, daily. AE, MC, V.

ITALIAN

Expensive

Salvatore's Italian Gardens. 6461 Transit Rd., Cheektowaga; 683–7990. Salvatore's would be right at home on the Las Vegas strip. It's an extravaganza with life-size statuary, fountains, and colored lights. The dining rooms are as ornate and new ones are constantly appearing at the whim of owner Russ Salvadore. Wide selection of Italian dishes. Specialty of the house is steak a la Russell, tenderloin prepared at tableside. D, daily. AE, CB, DC, MC, V.

Moderate

Chef's Restaurant. 291 Seneca St., Buffalo; 856–9187. Long a popular spot with politicians, media folk, and just about anyone who works or visits downtown. Owner Louis Billittier personally oversees the kitchen, which serves fine dishes. Daily specials with friendly service. L, D, Mondays–Saturdays. Closed Sundays. Major credit cards.

Donna Felicia's. 490 Center St., Lewiston; 754–7901. Long-time favorite in Lewiston; popular with summer Artpark visitors. Traditional Italian menu. L, D, daily. Major credit cards.

Fortuna's. 827 19th St., Niagara Falls; 282–2252. Since 1945, a popular dining room with local residents. Italian home cooking. D; closed Mondays and Tuesdays. AE, MC, V.

JAPANESE/KOREAN

Ichi Hana. *Moderate.* 850 Niagara Falls Blvd., Buffalo; 832–1585; Authentic Japanese and Korean foods and the area's only sushi bar. Skylight Tea Room. L, D, daily; closed Tuesdays. All major credit cards.

MEXICAN

Chi-Chi's Restaurant. *Moderate.* Maple Rd., Amherst; 834–2281. This is part of a national chain and had immediate success as soon as it came to town. Macrame hangings and Mexican prints brighten the white stucco walls. The best margaritas in town along with some varied south-of-the-border offerings. L, D, daily. Major credit cards.

SEAFOOD

Expensive

Marie's Seafood House. 1 Lock St., St. Catharines, Ont.; 416–934–1677. Lobster is the specialty of the house here, and diners choose their own from the lobster tank. Worth the 30-minute drive from Niagara Falls. D, daily. Major credit cards.

Red Lobster. 7540 Transit Rd., Williamsville, 634–9195; 4010 Maple Rd., Amherst, 837–0202; and 1000 McKinley Mall, Hamburg, 823–2901. Part of national chain specializing naturally in lobster but featuring full range of fresh seafood. L, D daily. Major credit cards.

Moderate

Foit's Seafood Restaurant. 4437 Lake Shore Rd., Athol Springs; 627–3970. Attracts a most loyal following. Weekends are particularly busy. Located along the American shore of Lake Erie with fine views of sunsets over the lake. L, Mondays–Fridays; D, daily. AE, DC, MC, V.

Jafco Marine Restaurant. 2192 Niagara St., Buffalo; 877–9349. Located at a busy marina on the Niagara River with a fine view of the Canadian shore. Very popular during the summer, with an interesting selection of seafood and other offerings. L, D. AE, CB, DC, MC, V.

STEAK

Expensive

John's Flaming Hearth. 1965 Military Rd., Niagara Falls; 297–1414; and 1830 Abbott Rd., Lackawanna; 822–2448. Some of the finest steak in the country is served here in ornate dining rooms. The Niagara Falls location is the original and attracts area residents and tourists from all over the world, including visiting celebrities. Lobster and chicken also on menu. Pumpkin ice cream pie a dessert specialty. L, D, daily. AE, CB, DC, MC, V.

Scotch 'N Sirloin. 3999 Maple Rd., Amherst; 837–4900. Charcoal-broiled steak a feature here, but there are other specialties of the house. A popular spot and a busy bar area with a gas fireplace in the center. L, D, daily. Major credit cards.

Moderate

Danny Sheehan's Steak House. 491 West Ave., Lockport; 433–4666. Though steak is the featured item, the menu is a big one with more than 37 different dinner entrees and 17 seafood dishes alone. Good spot for families with children's menu. D, daily. AE, MC, V.

UNIQUELY BUFFALO

Moderate

Anchor Bar. 1047 Main St., Buffalo; 886–8920. This is the birthplace of Buffalo chicken wings, now famous around the country. They were invented in 1964 by the late owner, Dominic Bellissimo, and tons are served up every week. Anchor wings have been flown all over the country by former residents homesick for this delicacy. There are many other items on the menu but the wings remain a favorite. L, D. No credit cards.

Eckl's Beef & Weck Restaurant. 4936 Ellicott Rd., Orchard Park; 662–2262. This is beef on weck supreme. Housed in a renovated 100-year-old house, there is a varied dinner menu, but the beef on weck continues to be the favorite. Dale Eckl, the owner, personally carves the beef to order, dipping the weck roll deftly into the roast beef juices to retain the roll's flaky texture. D, daily. No credit cards.

Schwabl's Restaurant. 789 Center St., West Seneca; 674–9821. This is another long-time Buffalo favorite and loyal customers have been coming since this was farmland. Now no longer countryside, it is just outside the city, but little else has changed. Again, beef is carved to order and placed on freshly baked weck rolls. Small menu and dining room, very popular, especially on weekends. Fish fry is a hit on Fridays. Good old-fashioned German potato salad. L, D, closed Sundays. AE, MC, V.

NIGHTLIFE AND BARS. Buffalo has long been known as a city of taverns. But they are sedate places now compared to the 19th century when the two-block long Canal Street at the waterfront had 93 saloons and 15 dance halls. For utter depravity, toughness, and violence, the street had no equal. Neighborhood spots are favorite watering holes. *The Buffalo News* "Friday Gusto Magazine" has a comprehensive listing of entertainment in the area.

The Bakery, Niagara at 30th Sts., Niagara Falls, 282–9498, offers good opportunities to meet people. Beyond music and dancing all tables come equipped with phones to enable guests to call from table to table. *Club Exit,* 512 Third St., Niagara Falls, 282–0108, has a high-tech lighting and sound system for disco dancing.

Comedy clubs are springing up in the Buffalo area. *The Funny Farm,* 1840 Maple Rd., 688–1001; and *The Comedy Trap,* 1180 Hertel Ave., 875–9191, both have professional comics and an open mike Thursdays after the show. *Stuffed Mushroom,* 2580 Main St., 835–7971, has comedy nights several times a week.

Tralfamadore Cafe, Theater Place off Pearl St, 854–1414, is a long time **jazz** center and books nationally known artists. *Buffalo Irish Center,* 245 Abbott Rd, 825–9535, specializes in Irish folk singing, as does *Belle Watling's Eating and Drinking Establishment,* 1449 Abbott Rd., 826–8838.

Cafe Casablanca, 511 Rhode Island St., 881–9992; *Mickey Rats City* Bar, 3057 Main St., 836–9467; *Nietzsche's,* 248 Allen St., 886–8539; and *946 Elmwood,* 946 Elmwood Ave., 885–3570; are popular **rock** clubs.

EXPLORING THE CHAUTAUQUA AREA

Chautauqua County, which follows the shores of Lake Erie south of Buffalo to the border of Pennsylvania, is a region rich in rolling hills, vineyards and wineries, fish-filled lakes, and the area's oldest cultural asset—the world-famous Chautauqua Institution.

The county takes its name from the largest lake, which is 20 miles long and was called "Jad-dah-gwah" by the Indians. French explorers landed on the Lake Erie shores of the Chautauqua area in 1679. Their quest was a southward passage to the Ohio and Mississippi rivers, and the route connecting Lake Erie with Chautauqua Lake, known as the Portage Trail, offered an answer. The controversy between France and England over possession of the trail led to the French and Indian War. It later opened the area to settlement and industry.

It was on the shores of Chautauqua Lake in 1874 that John Heyl Vincent, a Methodist minister, and Lewis Miller, an industrialist, began a training center for Sunday school teachers. Their dream was a two-week meeting at which teachers could listen to self-improvement lectures and stroll by the lakeshore. The institution rapidly grew into a summer-long cultural encampment. Chautauqua became a household word as tent-show proprietors crisscrossed the country with their own version of Chautauqua's lectures, drama, and music. The Chautauqua circuit is part of history, but the Institution is well into its second century and very much alive. It has changed, but slowly, to keep pace with the times.

A More Placid America

Still, to visit Chautauqua is to enter another world, an older, more placid America. President Theodore Roosevelt called it "the most American place in America." The Institution, which is a National Register Historic District, occupies 856 acres and many of the early Victorian buildings are still standing in all their gingerbread splendor. The grand dame of them all is the renovated and improved Athenaeum Hotel, built in 1881 and wired for electricity by Lewis Miller's son-in-law, Thomas Alva Edison. At one time the hotel was the largest wood frame building in the country.

Psychologist William James called the institution "the middle-class paradise, without a sin, without a victim, without a blot, without a tear." From the beginning, alcohol of any sort was banned and it is still not sold on the grounds, although guests may partake in their rooms. Many visitors are repeaters and second-, third-, and even fourth-generation visitors are common. Tradition is one of the things that perennial visitors can count on.

The Institution strives hard to appeal to all ages by offering a unique mix of arts, education, religion, and recreation during the nine-week summer season. There are schools and day camps for children. Classrooms enroll more than 2,000 young and old people in subjects from archaeology to Zen. Popular, nationally known entertainers pack the 6,000-seat amphitheater, which also overflows for Sunday religious services.

Spiritualist Center

No cars are allowed on the grounds except for loading and unloading. It is a walking place with short streets or lined with old wooden houses with porches filled with wicker rockers. Flags fly freely from many houses.

Just five years after the founding of the Institution, the Lily Dale Assembly was started in 1879 on the nearby shores of Cassadaga Lake. It remains the spiritualist center of the world and attracts mediums from all over the U.S. and Canada. There is even a message service for those who believe in communicating with the dead.

The gentle Conewango Valley is southeast of Cassadaga and home to a thriving Amish community that hasn't yet been discovered by tour buses. Be careful of the slow-moving horse-drawn carriages that are the main mode of transportation. The people want to retain their old-world life styles and not become tourist attractions. But they do sell their delicious baked goods and handmade furniture from their homes and at auctions.

Vines Bear Concord Grapes

Chautauqua County is the largest grape area outside of California, and its vineyards produce more concord grapes than any other area in the country. The area is dotted with wineries with a growing reputation for fine wines. Just inland is the village of Fredonia, once known as the world's seed capital. It was settled in 1803 and in 1821 America's first gas well was tapped here. Ironically, considering the wineries in the area, the Women's Christian Temperance Union was formed here in 1873.

Continuing south along Lake Erie is Westfield, home of Welch's Foods and the self-proclaimed Grape Juice Capital of the World. It was founded by Charles Edgar Welch, who declared that "God did not mean the grape to be fermented." It is also an antique center with 20 dealers operating from historic 19th-century homes. The 1828 lighthouse at nearby Barcelona Harbor was the first in the world to be lit by natural gas.

PRACTICAL INFORMATION FOR CHAUTAUQUA

HOW TO GET THERE. Chautauqua is an area best explored by car although there is plane and bus service to the area. The Chautauqua Institution is about 75 miles southwest of Buffalo. It is in the westernmost corner of New York and about 450 miles from New York City. **By Air.** *USAir* and *Allegheny Commuter* serve the Jamestown Airport. *Jamestown Limousine Service,* 808 Allen St. 14701, (489–3470), serves the airport. *USAir, American, Eastern, United, Continental, Republic, Northwest, Piedmont,* and *Comair* all serve the Buffalo airport. With advance reservations, limousines meet planes in Buffalo for the $50 round-trip to the Chautauqua Institution. Contact *Sunburst Travel,* 305 Fairmont Ave., Lakewood 14750; 357–8363.

By train. There is no train service to the Chautauqua area. The nearest station is Buffalo.

By bus. Jamestown and Fredonia are served by *Greyhound Bus,* 485–7541; *Blue Bird Coach Lines,* 484–1900; and *D&F Transit,* 485–7541. Limousine and taxi service is available to the Chautauqua Institution and Chautauqua Lake via *City Air Bus Ltd.,* 489–3470, or contact *Sunburst Travel,* 357–8363. *Chautauqua Area Regional Transit System (CARTS)* provides two round trips daily between Jamestown and Westfield, 665–6466.

By car. Chautauqua is easily accessible from the north, east, or west via I–90, the New York State Thruway. It is also accessible from the east via Rte. 17. From the south, Rtes. 474, 69, or 62 provide access to the area. The Chautauqua Institution is 16 miles north of Jamestown.

TELEPHONES. The area code for all of Chautauqua County is 716. Information is 555–1212. Long distance rates apply between some areas within the county, such as between Fredonia and Jamestown and between Buffalo and anywhere else in the county. From outside the area, directory information can be obtained by dialing (716) 555–1212. Dial (800) 555–1212, directory information for toll-free 800 numbers, to see if there is an 800 number for the business you want to reach.

HOTELS AND MOTELS. Within the grounds of the Chautauqua Institution is a wide variety of accommodations: stately Victorian hotels, smaller hotels, guesthouses, apartments, houses, modern condos, and denominational houses operated by various religious bodies with rooms for rent. Some condos are available on a weekly basis, although most apartments are available only for the summer season. Since so many people return year after year to the same hotel or inn, reservations should be made early. A number of hotels and inns are open only during the nine-week summer season, although some are open throughout the year with low off-season rates. A referral service will assist in locating accommodations within the Institution. Call 357–6204 or write *Chautauqua Accommodations Referral,* Chautauqua Institution, Chautauqua 14722.

Outside the Institution are summer resorts, hotels, motels, condos, and inns scattered throughout the area.

Hotel rates are based on double occupancy, European Plan, although there are two Institution hotels that operate totally on the American Plan, providing three meals daily. Categories determined by price are *Deluxe,* $80–$100; *Expensive,* $66–$79; *Moderate,* $50–$65; *Inexpensive,* $40–$49; *Basic Budget,* under $40.

CHAUTAUQUA INSTITUTION

Deluxe

Athenaeum Hotel, Chautauqua; 800–821–1881 within New York, 800–862–1881 outside the state. 160 units. The grand dame of all Chautauqua hotels, it was built in 1881 and recently underwent a two-year, $2-million revitalization project. A National Historic site, which has hosted all manner of presidents and celebrities over the years. Ask to see Thomas A. Edison's table by the front window in the dining room. Overlooks lake with huge front porch and rows of wicker rocking chairs. American plan only with three fine and bountiful meals including traditional Athenaeum two-dessert dinner. Summer only.

Expensive

Hotel William Baker. Corner Lake and Miller sts.; 357–2805 (summer), 412–588–8995 (winter). American plan. Overlooking lake. Few rooms with running water only at lower rates.

Moderate

Cary Hotel. 9 Bowman Ave.; 357–2245 (summer), 688–1789 (winter). Another Victorian hotel, only one block from the amphitheater. Breakfast available but not included in rate. Summer only.

The Spencer Hotel. 25 Palestine Ave.; 357–3785 (summer), 505–434–3373 (winter). 34 rooms. Just 200 feet from amphitheater with long porches across front on all four floors. Pre- and post-season rates.

Basic Budget

Chautauqua Inn. 16 N. Terrace and 11 Whitfield; 357–3085 (summer), 216–795–1388 (winter). 17 rooms, five with private bath, rest shared bath. Open post-season.

The Cooper. 15 Roberts Ave.; 753–7722. Open all year.

The Gleason. 12 N. Lake Dr.; 357–2595. 28 rooms, lakefront location, kitchen available for season guests. One week or longer reservations.

The Shenango Guest House. 20 Ramble; 357–9211 (summer), 412–588–6335 (winter). Kitchenettes available. No smoking. Off-season rates.

OUTSIDE INSTITUTION

Moderate

1865 Vintage Inn. 435 East Main St., Fredonia; 673–1865. 7 units. Housed in a renovated 1865 house, full American breakfast included. Dining room.

Holiday Inn. 10455 Bennett Rd., Fredonia; 673–1351. Family plan, 135 units, pool, playground, dining room, cocktail lounge, pets.

Holiday Inn. 150 W. 4th St., Jamestown; 664–3400. Family plan, 149 units, indoor pool, dining room, cocktail lounge, entertainment.

Hotel Lenhart. Rte. 17, Bemus Point; 386–2715. Family plan, 20 units. This old fashioned hotel on the lake has been operating since 1880. Fine dining room, with a beach, park, and marina next door. During the summer the MAP plan with breakfast and dinner is mandatory. Free transportation from Jamestown Airport. Open Memorial Day to September 15. Off season rates June and September.

Inn at the Peak. Ye Olde Rd., Clymer; 355–4141. 60 units. Part of extensive year-round skiing and golf resort with indoor swimming and tennis. There are 16 slopes and trails and an 18-hole golf course. Elegant suites in English-style Tudor inn. Some suites have wood-burning fireplaces. Rates lower off-season.

Webb's Resort and Marina. Mayville; 753–2161. Family plan, 28 units, a complete resort with marina, bowling alleys, game room, goat-milk fudge factory with tours and tastings, gift shop, pool, restaurant with six dining rooms.

The White Inn. 52 East Main St., Fredonia; 672–2103. 20 units. Chautauqua County's oldest continuously operating hotel, it was a charter member of the elite Duncan Hines Family of Fine Restaurants in 1935. The house was built in 1868 and turned into a hotel in 1919. Since 1980 it has been totally renovated and transformed into an elegant inn filled with antiques and fine reproductions built in nearby Jamestown. Continental breakfast included.

The William Seward Inn. South Portage Rd., Westfield; 326–4151. Ten units. Dating from 1821, it was the home of Secretary of State William Seward. The home has been totally renovated and filled with antiques. It overlooks Lake Erie and is about 8 miles from Chautauqua Lake. Full breakfast included.

Inexpensive

Southshore Motor Lodge. 5040 West Lake Rd. (Rte. 5), Dunkirk; 366–2822. 20 units; on Lake Erie, pool, pets.

Basic Budget

Bemus Point Lakeside Cottages. 50 Lakeside Dr., Bemus Point; 386–2535. 22 units, including cottages; on lake, dock space, pool, by week only during the summer.

The Colony Motel. 620 Fairmount Ave., Jamestown; 488–1904. 45 units, including efficiencies; pool, dining room.

Dunkirk Motel. 310 Lake Shore Dr. W., Dunkirk; 366–2200. 46 units, including apartments, pool.

Quality Inn Vineyard. Vineyard Dr., Dunkirk; 366–4400. Family plan, 39 units, pool, playground, dining room, coffee shop, cocktail lounge.

 CAMPING. Camping facilities in the area include state and private campgrounds ranging from rustic woodland sites for tents only to those with all utilities and programs of entertainment and recreation. *Lake Erie State Park,* a 318-acre park with woods and hills along Lake Erie, has campsites, some with electrical hookup as well as cabins. Reservations may be made through *Ticketron* telephone outlets or by writing Ticketron, Dept. C.G., Avenue of the Americas, New York, NY 10019, or by contacting *Red House Rental Office,* Allegany State Park, Allegany. Commercial campgrounds listed below offer full hookup, laundry, and sanitary facilities.

Camp Chautauqua, Stow, 14785; 789–3435. Lakeside; open all year.

Camp Prendergast, Davis Rd., RD 2, Mayville, 14757; 789–3485. Pool; free boat launching nearby.

Forest Haven Campground, Box 175, Page Rd., Kennedy; 267–5902. Pool; recreation building.

Hidden Valley Camping Area, Off Rte. 62, South Jamestown, 14701; 569–5433. Pool; tennis.

KOA Lake Erie/Westfield Kampground, Rt. 5, Barclona; 326–3573. Two pools; fish pond.

Safari Camp Chautauqua Lake, Rte. 17 and Thumb Rd., Dewittville, 14728; 386–3804. Pool; open all year.

BED-AND-BREAKFAST TREASURES. *The Bed and Breakfast Association of Western New York,* Box 1059, Sinclairville 14782, handles information and reservations for bed-and-breakfast homes in the Chautauqua area. Members include **The Teepee,** a four-bedroom country home on the Cattaraugus Indian Reservation; the **1870 House** in Franklinville, a 115-year-old Victorian home furnished with antiques; the **Inn at Mayville,** a 150-year-old home just three miles from the Chautauqua Institution. Most do not accept credit cards. Several offer a complimentary bottle of local wine and all provide breakfast, some continental and others full American.

TOURIST INFORMATION. The *Chautauqua County Vacationlands Association,* 2 N. Erie St., Mayville, 14757 (753–4304), has free guidebooks, maps, and brochures. The association also operates an information center on the New York Thruway at Ripley. *Northern Chautauqua Chamber of Commerce,* 212 Lake Shore Dr. W., Dunkirk, 14048 (366–6200); *Lakewood Area Chamber of Commerce,* Box 51, Lakewood, 14750, (763–8557); *Southwestern Gateway Tourist & Visitors Bureau,* 101 W. 5th St., Jamestown, 14701 (484–1101), also have information and brochures. *Chautauqua Institution,* Chautauqua, 14722 (357–6200), has a complete set of booklets on events, concerts, summer school, accommodations.

SEASONAL EVENTS. February. The first Sunday of the month is the *Annual Chautauqua Overland Ski Marathon* with 1,000 skiers racing in the woodlands and trails in the Westfield area. During the third weekend, *Glacier Ridge Winter Weekend* is held at Woodbury Wineyards Winery, South Roberts Rd., Dunkirk, 14048; 679–WINE. Cross country skiing, food, and drink. **May** brings the *Wine & Apple Blossom Festival,* in the third weekend at Woodbury Vineyards. The next weekend, spring is celebrated at Chadwick Bay Wine Co., 10001 Route 60, Fredonia (672–5000), as *Spring Fling Weekend.*

June. Summer is ushered in at Bemus Point on Lake Chautauqua with a *Summer's Eve* party in the village park. The Chautauqua Institution begins its nine-week season of music, drama, summer schools, recreation, and religion the last week of the month.

July is kicked off with the traditional July *Flare Festival* on Chautauqua Lake. Since 1936, every Fourth of July at precisely 10 P.M., thousands of flares have been simultaneously lighted around the 56-mile shoreline of the lake. The flares burn for about 30 minutes. Independence Day is marked with a *Harborfest* in Dunkirk. During the first weekend Woodbury Vineyards celebrates its anniversary with a champagne party. Chadwick Bay Wine Co. holds a summer festival during the third weekend. The *Chautauqua County Fair* is held the last week of the month.

August. A *Hot Air Balloon Festival* turns the sky into a rainbow of color during the first weekend at Chadwick Bay Wine Co. The *Lake Erie Fishing Derby* tests fishing skills and luck the second weekend at Dunkirk Harbor, followed by the *Fredonia Farm Festival,* Barker Common. **September** is the harvest season in the vineyards and the *Harvest Festival* is celebrated the second weekend at Chadwick Bay, and *Septemberfest* is held the same weekend at Merritt Estate Winery, 2264 King Road, Forestville, 14062; 965–4800. The next weekend the *Festival of Grapes* is held in Silver Creek. **October** means apple harvest and *Apple Festival* is held the first weekend in Forestville. **November** is the time for the first wine of the season and *Nouveau Wine Weekend* is toasted at Chadwick Bay the second weekend of the month.

FREE EVENTS. In keeping with its traditional religious origins, Sundays are open to all at the Chautauqua Institution, otherwise there is a gate admission fee. The area's wineries offer tours and tastings. They include *Chadwich Bay Wine Co.,* 10001 Rte. 60, Fredonia; *Johnson Estate Vineyards & Winery,* U.S. Rte. 20, Westfield; *Merritt Estate Winery,* 2264 King Road, Forestville; *Woodbury Vineyards Winery,* South Roberts Rd., Dunkirk; *Schloss Doepken Winery,* Forsythe Dr., Ripley. *Webb's Candy Factory,* Rte. 394, Mayville (753–2161), has tours and samples of goat-milk fudge and other candy confections.

TOURS. Lake Cruises. Chautauqua Lake was a historic waterway as long ago as the 17th century, and there are a number of boat cruises that reflect another era. Although a bridge now spans Chautauqua Lake at Bemus Point–Stow, the ferry still operates during the summer as it has since 1811. Wire cable and diesel have replaced the rope and oxen treadmill. It still carries autos and passengers. The steamer *Chautauqua Belle,* complete with paddlewheel, still plies the waters for hour-long cruises or dinner or wine cruises. The *Sea Lion* was commissioned Aug. 18, 1985, after 15 years of research and construction and now provides summer cruises. It is an authentic replica of a 16th-century English merchant ship constructed from a treatise written in 1586. For information on all ships contact *Sea Lion Project,* One Sea Lion Dr., Mayville, 14757; 753–2403. The *Gadfly III* sails from the Bell Tower of the Chautauqua Institution. Fares: $3.50, adults; $1.64, children. Contact Box 362, Chautauqua, 14722; 753–2753.

Narrated tours of *Chautauqua Institution* are offered by **bus** during the nine-week summer season. Buses leave from the Colonnade Building at 6:30 P.M. weekdays and at 2 P.M. Saturdays and Sundays. There is a $1.50 charge and a gate ticket is needed to take the evening and Saturday tours. *Sunburst Travel Service,* 305 East Fairmount Ave., Lakewood, 14750 (763–0361), has tours of the area. *Cockaigne Ski Area,* RD 1, Cherry Creek, 14723 (287–3545), offers fall foliage tours and day tours through the Amish country.

PARKS. There is a $2.50 per car fee for state parks during the summer. *Long Point State Park,* Lake Chautauqua, off Rte. 17, has a marina and beach. *Lake Erie State Park,* Rte. 5, Dunkirk (792–9214) also has a beach and boating. *Allegany State Park,* off Rte. 17, with 65,000 acres is the largest in the state parks system. For hiking trails, lake and stream fishing, swimming, tennis, small and big-game hunting in season, call 354–2182. The following are some of the more unusual private parks:

Griffis Sculpture Park, Rte. 219, Ashford Hollow. Buffalo artist Larry Griffis has turned 400 acres into a sculpture garden. The metal figures provide an artistic backdrop for hiking, picnicking, or cross country skiing. Free.

Rock City Park, Rte. 16, Olean; 372–7990. Remains of prehistoric ocean, world's largest deposit of quartz conglomerate. Season, May 1–Oct 25.

Panama Rocks, Rte. 474, Panama; 782–2845. The rocks were formed over 300 million years ago and Indians used the rocks and caves for shelter long before the arrival of the French in the 1600s. Hiking trails, picnicking. Season, May–October.

CHILDREN'S ACTIVITIES. *Chautauqua Institution* has a complete program of activities for young people from 2½ years old to college age. There is a children's school for those up to 6 years old, and a summer day camp for ages 6–15. Both programs run weekdays during the season. The *Youth Activities Center* plans and coordinates activities for high school and college age youth. The *Gadfly III,* a cruise boat, sails from the Institution's Bell Tower daily except Monday during the season. The *Sea Lion Project Ltd.,* RD 1, Sea Lion Dr., Mayville, (753–2403), has boat rides on three craft that are popular with kids—the *Bemus Point–Stowe Ferry,* the Steamer *Chautauqua Belle,* and the *Sea Lion,* an authentic replica of a 16th-century English ship. *Webb's,* Rte. 394, Mayville (753–2161), is a mecca for candy lovers with tours of the candy-making factory and free samples of goat-milk fudge.

PARTICIPANT SPORTS. Fishing. Chautauqua Lake attracts serious anglers who come to challenge the native muskellunge, or "muskie," that is famous for its fight and size. The record catch for the lake stands at 51 lb 3 oz. Lake Erie and Cassadaga and Findley Lakes also provide good fishing. Although renowned for muskies, good-size walleyed pike, bass, and panfish are also caught in Chautauqua Lake. Ice fishing is popular during the winter. Some selected charter sportfishing outfits are:

Chautauqua Lake Charters, Box 1187, Chautauqua, 14722; 753–5255.

The Frenchman Boat, Box 231, Ashville, 14710; 763–8296.

J&C Charters, 4976 Webster Rd., Fredonia, 14063; 672–5674.

Pequod II Charters, 33 Newton St., Fredonia, 14063; 673–1117.

Salmon Tracker Charters, 6 Pennington Pl., Cassadaga, 14752; 595–3917

Golf. There are nearly 20 golf courses in the area including an 18-hole course at the Chautauqua Institution which overlooks the lake. There are golf packages available at several resorts.

Horseback Riding. There are stables that have lessons, rent horses, and provide well-marked trails for riding for about $8 an hour. They include *Carack-erjack Farms,* Bemus-Ellery Center Rd., Bemus Point, 14712 (386–5054); *Dane-ro Riding Stable,* Hewes Rd., Mayville, 14757 (789–4600); *Double D.A.B. Riding Stable,* Welch Hill Rd., Ripley, 14775 (736–4418).

Hunting. Good hunting for white-tailed deer, birds, and small game abounds in Chautauqua and adjacent Cattaraugus County with its 65,000-acre Allegany State Park, large tracts of which are open to public hunting by permit. For information on licenses, seasons, game limits, and permissable weapons, check with the *State Department of Environmental Conservation,* 128 South Street, Olean, 14760; 372–0645.

Skiing. Cross country skiing is popular, with well-marked trails at Allegany State Park, Chautauqua Institution, ski centers and campgrounds. The *Cross Country Ski Marathon* is held the first Saturday in February and attracts 1,000 skiers (the limit) from across the country, Canada, and Europe. *Holiday Valley,* Ellicottville, 699–2345; *Cockaigne,* Cherry Creek, 287–3223; and Peek 'n Peak, Clymer, 355–4141, are the area's largest ski resorts with both downhill and cross country skiing.

Windsurfing, parasailing, and water skiing. For lessons and equipment rentals, contact *Windsurfing Chautauqua,* Chautauqua, 14722; 789–2675.

MUSEUMS. The museums of the Chautauqua area reflect the history and culture of the area from the time of the era of steamboats to the culture of the Indians. *Dunkirk Lighthouse & Veterans Museum,* Point Drive N., Point Gratlot off Rte. 5, Dunkirk. April–June, 9 A.M.–4 P.M. daily; July–August, 9 A.M.–9 P.M. daily; September–November, 9 A.M.–2 P.M. weekdays. *Great White Fleet Museum,* The Casino, One Lakeside Dr., Bemus Point; 386–3661. Displays pertaining to the steamboat era on Chautauqua Lake. There is a collection of working steam whistles from a 6-inch baby whistle to its huge 5-foot tall brass brother. This museum has its own dock, so you can arrive by water.

Chautauqua County Historical Society, Village Park, Westfield. House was built in 1818–20 by James McClurg, a pioneer merchant and trader, and restored as an early-19th-century home and museum. Open Tuesdays–Saturday, 10 A.M.–noon; Sundays, 1 P.M.–4 P.M.; July–August, 2 P.M.–5 P.M.

Fenton Historical Center, 67 Washington St., Jamestown; 661–2296. Listed on National Register of Historic Places. Museum in Civil War period mansion built by New York Governor Reuben E. Fenton. Monday–Saturday, 10 A.M.–4 P.M.

Heritage Museum of Childhood, 314 W. 5th St., Jamestown; 484–1101. Antique and collectible dolls, antique toys, and displays in Victorian architectural setting. Doll-making demonstrations.

Seneca-Iroquois National Museum. Rte. 17, Allegany Indian Reservation; 945–1738. Exhibits on history and contemporary culture of Seneca Nation of Indians. May 1–October 1, Mondays–Saturdays 10 A.M.–5 P.M., Sundays, noon–5 P.M.

MUSIC. The *Chautauqua Institution* has a rich musical tradition and program during the summer season. There are concerts or rehearsals going on most every hour, and since practice sessions are often held outdoors there is music just about everywhere. For tickets and information, contact Chautauqua Institution, Chautauqua, 14722; 357–5635. Admission to the grounds is by gate ticket available by the day, week, weekend, or season. During the school season the *State University of New York College at Fredonia* is well known for its music program and presents both student and professional concerts.

Chautauqua Symphony Orchestra plays tri-weekly concerts with its 74-member symphony orchestra composed of outstanding professional musicians from across the nation. The concerts feature distinguished guest conductors and some top soloists.

Amphitheater Specials. Programming is varied with symphonic concerts as well as appearances by the *Music School Festival Orchestra,* made up of college and graduate music students from across the country who perform on most Monday evenings. Each Friday evening, as well as the entire first and ninth weeks, popular entertainers take the stage.

Chautauqua Opera presents four productions in English in the 1,400-seat Norton Memorial Hall. The opera also has an artist-in-residence program for young professionals.

The School of Music. Students may enroll in *Festival Orchestra,* or the *Youth Orchestra,* senior division for piano and voice. Adults may also enroll in chamber music. Auditions are required for acceptance into each program. Music workshops, special chamber orchestra, and master classes are all available for the amateur musician.

Michael D. Rockefeller Arts Center, State University of New York College at Fredonia. Concerts during the school year by *Fredonia Chamber Players* and student orchestras as well as such professional orchestras as the *Buffalo Philharmonic Orchestra.* In addition, nationally known musicians perform here. For information, call 673–3217.

 DANCE. The *Chautauqua School of Dance* offers talented dance students training in classical ballet and the Martha Graham technique. Performance opportunities include recitals and full programs with the orchestra. For the vacationer, open enrollment classes are available in ballet, modern, jazz, and character dance at beginning levels and beyond.

 STAGE. The *Chautauqua Conservatory Theater Company* stages five productions during the season under the direction of award-winning Broadway director and producer Michael Kahn. The theater school is organized into two studios. The Conservatory Theater Company is open to students 19 and over. Studio II is open to high school students ages 16 to 18. *Little Theater of Jamestown,* 101 W. 5th St., Jamestown, 14701 (484–1101), offers year-round musical and dramatic stage presentations.

 SHOPPING. The Chautauqua area is an antique lovers' and collectors' mecca. The Village of Westfield has 20 antique dealers. *Stockton Sales Antiques & Collectibles,* 6 Mill St., Stockton, has barns covering 30,000 sq ft packed full of an amazing collection of antiques, collectibles, furniture, and reproductions. The *Lock Stock & Barrel Country Store,* Rte. 62, Ellington, is a country grocery and antique store. *Good Morning Farm,* Rte. 394, Stow, is a 19th-century farm with a restaurant, bar, and barn with seven shops featuring local arts and crafts. *Chautauqua Institution* has a number of shops, including fine clothing stores and a well-stocked bookstore. The *Chautauqua Mall,* 318 E. Fairmount Ave., Lakewood, has 70 stores and restaurants.

 DINING OUT. Restaurants in the Chautauqua area are varied, with a predominance of coffee shops and cafes, and tend to have moderate prices. Reservations are important at many places in the summer, especially if you are planning on attending an evening performance at the Institution. Price classifications of the following restaurants are based on the cost of an average three-course dinner for one person; beverages, tax, and tip are extra. *Expensive* $14–$22; *Moderate,* $7–$14. Abbreviations for credit cards are: AE, American Express; CB, Carte Blanche; DC, Diners Club; MC, MasterCard; V, VISA. Most restaurants that do not accept credit cards will cash traveler's checks. Meal code abbreviations are B, breakfast; L, lunch; D, dinner. The following is only a selection of restaurants to give an idea of the range.

CHAUTAUQUA LAKE AREA

Expensive

Athenaeum Hotel. Chautauqua Institution; 357–4444. Large, gracious dining room overlooking lake. Set menu for one price; two-dessert dinner is an Athenaeum tradition. No alcohol; reservations required. Open only during nine-week summer season. B, L, D. No credit cards.

Moderate

Captain's Table. Rte. 394, Mayville; 753–2161. Part of the large Webb's complex, which includes marina, motel, candy factory. Attractive dining room and fine food. B, L, D, daily. AE, MC, V.

Good Morning Farm. Rte. 394, Stow; 763–1507. Restaurant is in 150-year-old farmhouse. Country-style home cooking. Everything made from scratch. Breads, muffins, and desserts a specialty. The chef is also an artist and her works are on display. L, D, daily. Memorial Day–Labor Day. Major credit cards.

Ye Hare 'N Hounds Inn. Rte. 430, Bemus Point; 386–2181. A charming old English style inn on the lake. Noted for fresh seafoods. Private dock for water arrivals. L, D, daily in summer; D, Wednesdays–Sundays, Labor Day–Memorial Day. AE, MC, V.

Italian Fisherman. 61 Lakeside Dr., Bemus Point; 386–7000. Serving pasta, steaks, seafood in lakefront patio dining room. Home of the "pasta bar." Lake cocktail cruises. L, D, daily, Memorial Day–Labor Day. Major credit cards.

Peking Restaurant. 12 W. Fairmount Ave., Lakewood; 763–9121. Widely acclaimed Peking, Szechuan, Cantonese-style dining room. Take-out available. L, D, daily. MC, V.

The Tally-Ho. Plaza, Chautauqua Institution; 357–3325. Two dining rooms, one serving charcoal-broiled steaks and the other a family-style dining room. Summer season only. B, L, D. No credit cards.

OUTSIDE CHAUTAUQUA LAKE AREA

Expensive

Bark Grill Restaurant. 14 E. Pearl St., Westfield; 326–2112. Continental menu specializing in French cuisine. L, Wednesdays–Fridays; D, daily. Major credit cards.

Inn at the Peak. Ye Olde Rd., Clymer; 355–4141. Elegant English-style Tudor restaurant; roast beef a specialty; varied wine list. Restaurant is part of complete ski and golf resort. B, L, D, daily. AE, DC, MC, V.

The White Inn. 52 East Main St., Fredonia; 672–2103. Inn was charter member of elite Duncan Hines Family of Fine Restaurants, and new owners are striving to reestablish its national reputation. It is well on its way with a fine dining room. Gourmet entrees featured on menu as well as local wines. Inn has been totally renovated and is filled with antiques. L, D, daily. AE, MC, V.

Moderate

The Galley. 2 Mullet St., Dunkirk; 366–3775. Great view of the harbor, popular restaurant and tavern. L, Mondays–Saturdays; D, Tuesday–Sundays; Sunday brunch. Major credit cards.

Portage Inn. 24–30 North Portage, Westfield; 326–4434. Old English decor and fine food in the center of historic Westfield. Specializing in ribs and steaks and Italian dishes. B, L, D, daily. Major credit cards.

THE FINGER LAKES REGION

by
DEBORAH WILLIAMS

Iroquois Indian legend says that the Finger Lakes region was formed when the Great Spirit placed his hand in blessing on this favored land. Geologists have a more scientific explanation: the lakes were created when Ice Age glaciers retreated about a million years ago. The intense pressure of those ice masses created the long narrow lakes lying side by side, the deep gorges with rushing falls, and the fertile, wide valleys that extend south for many miles. These features, found nowhere else in the world, make the area topographically unique.

Regardless of the explanation, there is universal agreement that the 11 Finger Lakes offer lush, scenic vistas from every turn in the road. The waters are deep and blue, yielding a bountiful harvest of fish. Some lakes are so pure that drinking water is pumped out directly without treatment. The lakes cover a 9,000-square-mile area from Conesus Lake due south of Rochester to Otisco Lake south of Syracuse. Their shorelines total more than 600 miles.

Cayuga, Canandaigua, Keuka, Hemlock, Honeoye, Otisco, Owasco, Canadice, Conesus, Skaneateles, and Seneca sound like a roll call for the Indians of the Iroquois Confederacy who dominated this area for more than two centuries. But these are the names of the Finger Lakes.

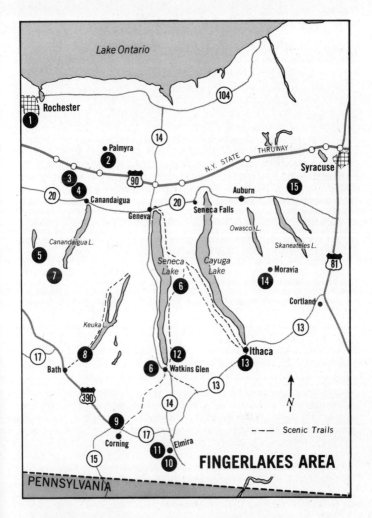

Points of Interest

1) Rochester Institute of Technology
2) Mormon Monument
3) Finger Lakes Racetrack
4) Sonnenburg Gardens
5) Harriet M. Spencer Memorial Park
6) Wine Cellars
7) Wineries
8) Glenn H. Curtis Museum
9) Glass Center
10) Burial Place of Mark Twain
11) National Soaring Museum
12) Motor Racing Museum
13) Cornell University
14) Millard Fillmore Birthplace
15) Railroad Station Museum

Another Lake—Plus 1,000 Cascades

There is another lake in this region that provides fine boating and some top fishing opportunities—Lake Ontario, the easternmost of the Great Lakes into which Niagara Falls drains. Coho and Chinook salmon and lake trout have been successfully reintroduced into the lake, and fishing enthusiasts are flocking there. For outdoor enthusiasts there is hot air ballooning, hunting, soaring, sailing, hiking, canoeing, polo, auto racing, horse racing, and skiing as well as a multitude of campgrounds and parks.

The ever-changing landscape is notched with gorges and dotted with waterfalls. There are more than 1,000 waterfalls splashing down these gorges. The highest is Taughannock at 215 feet (Niagara Falls is only 184 feet high). It is also one of 20 state parks in the region. Letchworth State Park, with a deep gorge and three waterfalls, has been aptly dubbed the "Grand Canyon of the East." At Watkins Glen State Park you can walk under a waterfall and sit spellbound while being whisked 45 million centuries into the past with lasers and special sound effects in "Timespell" a twice-nightly sound-and-light show which explains the birth and life of the famous glen.

Three Major Universities

Diversity is the keynote of the region, not only in the variety of natural landscapes but in the abundance of recreational, educational, and cultural facilities. Educational institutions include the universities of Cornell, Syracuse, and Rochester. In all there are 30 colleges and universities that contribute to the cultural and educational richness of the region. Museums abound and they are devoted to such diverse subjects as agriculture, auto racing, aviation, dolls, electronics, the Erie Canal, glass, Indians, the 19th century, photography, salt, soaring, and wine-making. The area has played a significant role in American social, economic, and political history as the home of statesmen, inventors, industrialists, and writers.

Mark Twain wrote most of his classics, including *The Adventures of Huckleberry Finn* while at his summer home in Elmira. Glenn H. Curtiss is responsible for putting Hammondsport on the aviation map. In 1908 his *June Bug* flew just under a mile—the longest distance of a preannounced flight. Harris Hill is considered the birthplace of soaring, and the National Soaring Museum there has the country's largest exhibit of classic and contemporary sailplanes.

Birthplace of Women's Rights

Seneca Falls is the home of the women's rights movement, and the National Women's Hall of Fame is located on the site of the first Women's Rights Convention held in 1848. Palmyra was the early home of Joseph Smith, who had a vision that led to the founding in 1830 of the Church of Jesus Christ of Latter-day Saints, the Mormons. Every summer late in July this event is celebrated with the presentation of the

Hill Cumorah Pageant, the oldest and largest religious pageant in the United States. Residents of Waterloo dreamed up the idea of Memorial Day for the dead of the Civil War and the country's first Memorial Day was celebrated May 5, 1866.

Rochester is the birthplace of the Kodak camera and film and the Xerox machine. George Eastman, a young bank clerk whose interest in photography led to the development of the photographic giant, was also an unflagging patron of the arts, medicine, and education. He helped turn the University of Rochester into an institution of national renown, particularly for its medical and music schools. Earlier in the 19th century, escaped slave Frederick Douglass established his newspaper, *The North Star,* here, and suffrage leader Susan B. Anthony helped lead the fight for women's rights.

Fine Glass Products

Corning is famous as the home of Corning Glass Works and its Steuben Glass division, which produces fine works of art. The Steuben masterpieces have been presented as gifts to foreign heads of state and are in museums around the world. The Corning Museum of Glass houses the world's foremost collection of glass. The city's downtown Market Street has been restored in its 19th-century glory and is listed on the National Register of Historic Places. Free English-style double decker buses provide transportation to the Glass Center and down Market St.

Ideal Conditions for Vineyards

Not only did retreating glaciers create the Finger Lakes, but they also created ideal conditions for grapes by depositing a shallow layer of topsoil on sloping shale beds above the lakes. The deep lakes also provide protection from the climate by moderating temperatures along their shores.

It all began in 1829 when the Rev. William Bostwick planted a few grapevines near the shore of Keuka Lake in Hammondsport. He transplanted vines from the Hudson Valley to make sacramental wine for his parishioners at the St. James Episcopal Church. The grapes grew well and within a few years grapevines could be found around Keuka, Canandaigua, and Seneca lakes. In 1860, 13 Hammondsport businessmen resolved to form a company "for the production and manufacture of native wine." The Hammondsport and Pleasant Valley Wine Company was the first commercial winery to open in the region. It became Great Western and was later merged with the giant Taylor Wine Co.

The success of the vineyards and wines created new jobs. Young carpenter Walter Taylor arrived in the late 1870s to make barrels for the wineries. He began planting grapevines and making wines himself and in time his winery became the largest in the region. Since 1976, when the state legislature eased regulations for anyone creating a winery producing 50,000 gallons a year or less, some 20 small farm wineries have opened in the region, and new techniques and grapes are earning medals for the area's wines at international and national competitions. Recently the federal government recognized an official "Finger Lakes Wine District."

EXPLORING THE FINGER LAKES REGION

Our tour of the Finger Lakes Region takes us on an eastward journey between the two largest cities in the region—Rochester and Syracuse. But we don't travel in a straight line. Instead, the trip makes a wide southern arc, skirting the southern tips of the lakes to Hammondsport and on to Elmira near the Pennsylvania border, then heading northeastward to Ithaca and up to Syracuse. Following is a sampling of what a visitor might expect to find at each of these communities.

Rochester

The state's third largest city anchors the region on the west and north. Although not nearly as large or dramatic as Niagara Falls, there are two 100-foot waterfalls in the middle of the city, which is well situated on the Genesee River. Lake Ontario serves as the city's northern boundary. Early in the 19th century Rochester was considered the flour capital of the nation. But as the sources of grain moved westward, Rochester became a nursery and seed capital and acquired the nickname "Flower City," which has stuck to this day. Lilacs are the most prominent flower. The annual 10–day Lilac Festival in late May draws thousands to see and smell the heavenly aroma of 22 acres of lilacs in Highland Park.

The city is internationally known as the birthplace and home of the Kodak Company. The International Museum of Photography at the George Eastman House has the world's largest collection of photographic art and technology. At her death in 1969, Margaret Woodbury Strong was the largest single Kodak shareholder, and she contributed her considerable fortune and her lifetime collections to a museum named in her honor. Opened in 1982, it houses the country's foremost collection of Victorian furniture; vast collections of 19th-century glassware, ceramics and silver, an extensive doll collection with nearly 20,000 dolls, and an array of miniatures, antique toys, and dollhouses.

The Seneca Indians—keepers of the western door of the Iroquois Six Nations—called the area Genesee, meaning beautiful valley. But it wasn't until the 19th century that the area saw a real flowering as pioneers settled the rich land. The 19th century in the Genesee Valley has been recreated in Mumford, 20 miles southwest of Rochester. The museum opened in 1976, and there are now approximately 50 restored buildings in the 125-acre open-air village. The buildings are all original. They were gathered from the Genesee Valley and represent various stages in the development of the frontier. The museum has been called the "Williamsburg of the North," but unlike Virginia's famed recreation of early America, this museum attempts to show life of the average person engaged in everyday activities. Like Williamsburg, costumed interpreters are on hand to explain and demonstrate pioneer life.

They also perform crafts demonstrations such as spinning, weaving, quilting, and working with pottery and tin.

Hammondsport

This Keuka Lake community is not only the center of the Finger Lakes Wine Region but served as its birthplace more than 150 years ago. The lake's "Y" shape is unique among the lakes, and 19th-century settlers called it Crooked Lake and "the Lady of the Lakes." Keuka comes from the Indian name "O-go-ya-ga" or "cliff jutting out into the water," which aptly describes the great bluff dividing the northern branches of the lake. Many consider it the most spectacular of all the Finger Lakes.

This is home to the giant Taylor and Great Western Wine Company and down the road, the much smaller but fascinating Bully Hill Winery, which is the most talked-about winery in the region. Bully Hill's owner, Walter S. Taylor, grandson of the founder of Taylor Wine, is certainly the closest the wine world has to a folk hero, albeit a most controversial one. The Bully Hill Taylor lost the right to use the family name in a lengthy court battle with Coca-Cola, the previous owners of Taylor Wine. He turned his loss into a public relations bonanza, receiving international publicity for his wines. His Greyton H. Taylor (named after his father) Wine Museum, the first of its kind in the country, has an extensive collection of antique wine-making equipment, a large wine-making library, and art works by Bully Hill's multi-talented owner. The view from the Bully Hill Winery with a magnificent sweep of vineyards, lake, and—on a clear day—a glimpse of Seneca Lake, some 40 miles away, is one of the most superb in the region.

The village was the home of aviation pioneer Glenn H. Curtiss. A museum named in his honor tells the history of early American aviation and includes some of the Curtiss' airplanes and other early aircraft.

Elmira

Southeast of Keuka Lake is Elmira, site of an important Revolutionary War battle. The Newtown Battlefield Reservation marks the location of the battle won by Major General John Sullivan over a large force of Indians and Tories. It is also where Samuel Clemens, better known as Mark Twain, spent more than 20 summers and where many of his classics were written, including *The Adventures of Huckleberry Finn*. His wife, Olivia Langdon, grew up here and Twain loved the Chemung Valley area, which he called "the garden of Eden." Twain's study was moved from Quarry Farm, just outside town, to the campus of Elmira College in 1955. It sits there today, complete with a typewriter like Twain's (he was one of the first to submit a typed manuscript to a publisher) and some original furniture. Twain and his family are buried here in a grave marked by a 12-foot granite monument.

Elmira has been considered the soaring capital of America ever since a national soaring contest was held in 1930 on a mountaintop outside town. The area's hills and valleys created ideal soaring conditions. The

National Soaring Museum features movies and displays on gliding and exhibits of classic and contemporary sailplanes. There are walking tours of the Near Westside Neighborhood, the largest concentration of 19th-century architecture in the state.

Ithaca

Situated at the southern tip of Cayuga Lake, the longest of the Finger Lakes, Ithaca is northeast of Elmira. It is a city of spectacular natural beauty with deep gorges and more than a hundred waterfalls. Its picturesque qualities made it the nation's movie capital of the silent era. Ice cream lovers might know it as the birthplace of the ice cream sundae.

But it is probably best known as the home of Cornell University, founded by Ezra Cornell in 1865. The campus, one of the most beautiful in the nation, is situated on a hill overlooking Cayuga Lake and Ithaca. The campus now encompasses 13,000 acres, including farms and experimental lands. Triphammer Bridge offers a splendid view of Fall Creek Gorge, Triphammer Falls, and Beebe Lake. Cornell Plantations lie along gorges bordering the Cornell campus. There are trails, an arboretum, botanical gardens, a lake, ponds, streams, woodlands, and swamps. The area boasts three major state parks, including Taughannock Falls with the highest straight drop east of the Rockies.

Syracuse

The Indian chief Hiawatha chose this location as the capital of the Iroquois Confederacy in the 16th century. Salt brought the Indians, the French, and later settlers to boil the brine. For many years the bulk of the salt used in America came from here. The Salt Museum has exhibits and a reconstructed 1856 salt factory demonstrating salt processing. The Onondaga Indian Reservation at Nedrow is now the seat of the Indian Confederacy.

The state's fourth largest city, Syracuse anchors the region on the east and north and is ethnically diverse. The city's Tipperary Hill district is one of the last enclaves of militant Irish in the state. Here traffic signals have the green on top of the red; a concession the city made years ago when the red light was broken nightly. This is a college town with one of the country's largest private universities—Syracuse University. The university's Carrier Dome is the only university domed stadium of its kind in the nation.

The city has been the home of the New York State Fair since 1841. The Canal Museum is a former weighlock station through which boats passed when the Erie Canal ran through Syracuse. It is the last remaining of the seven weighlock buildings in the state. The Syracuse Area Landmark Theater (SALT) is the famous "Fantasy Palace" built in 1928 and is now a National Historic Landmark. The interior is dripping in reds and golds with gold-domed ceilings and extravagant chandeliers. This is also the smallest city in the nation to support a major symphony orchestra.

PRACTICAL INFORMATION FOR
THE FINGER LAKES REGION

HOW TO GET THERE. By air. *American, United, USAir, Piedmont, Continental, Eastern, Mall,* and *Brockway* all serve the Rochester and Syracuse airports. USAir and Empire also serve airports at Ithaca and Elmira/Corning. **By train.** *Amtrak* serves both Rochester and Syracuse. **By bus.** *Greyhound* provides service to cities and towns in the region. The *Rochester-Genesee Regional Transportation Authority* and *Syracuse & Oswego Motor Lines* provide service within their regions.

By car. All major car rental agencies operate in Rochester and Syracuse. Most area visitors tour by car. From east to west use Rte. 17, the Southern Tier Expressway; I–90, the New York State Thruway; or the northern trail of Rte. 104. Primary north and south highways are I–81 and Rtes. 15 and I–390.

TELEPHONES. There are three area codes in the region. The area code for Rochester, Letchworth State Park, and Canandaigua is 716; Syracuse and the northern Finger Lakes is 315; and southern Finger Lakes is 607. Information (directory assistance) is 555–1212. An operator will assist you on person-to-person, credit card, and collect calls if you dial "0" first. From outside the area directory assistance can be obtained toll-free by dialing the area code and then 555–1212.

HOTELS AND MOTELS in the Finger Lakes Region are a varied lot, catering to a wide range of tastes. Country inns have hosted visitors in the area since the 19th century, and there has been a recent resurgence in their popularity. Many lakeside motels have lower rates off-season and some close after November 1 and do not reopen until May. The peak season is summer. Sales tax throughout the region is 7 percent. In Monroe County (Rochester) there is an additional 2 percent occupancy tax on room charges; there is an additional 3 percent occupancy tax in Onondaga County (Syracuse). Rates in this listing are based on double occupancy. European Plan Categories determined by price are: *Deluxe,* $80 and up; *Expensive,* $60–$79; *Moderate,* $50–$59; *Inexpensive,* $40–$49; and *Basic Budget,* under $40.

In this listing area codes are specified for the hotels in the Cayuga Lake, Keuka Lake, and Seneca Lake areas. Codes for other areas are: Canandaigua Lake, Letchworth State Park, and Rochester areas, 716; Corning-Elmira Area, 607; and Skaneateles Lake and Syracuse areas, 315.

CANANDAIGUA LAKE AREA

Sheraton Canandaigua Inn. *Expensive.* 770 S. Main St.; 394–7800. 147 units. Family plan, rates lower off-season, pool, dining room, cocktail lounge.

Jimmie Miller's Thendara on Canandaigua. *Inexpensive.* 346 E. Lake Rd.; 394–4868. 7 units. Cottages, mobile homes, beach, lunch and cocktails in boathouse, dining room and cocktail lounge. Weekly only in summer; closed January and February.

Campus Lodge. *Basic Budget.* Lakeshore Dr.; 394–1250. 40 units. Kitchen units; adjacent to Performing Arts Center.

Lakeside Motor Lodge. *Basic Budget.* 100 Lakeshore Dr.; 394–4640. 32 units. Pool.

CAYUGA LAKE AREA

Aurora Inn. *Expensive to Inexpensive.* Main St., Aurora; 315–364–8842. 17 units. On lake, just down the road from Wells College; guests may use the college's golf course and tennis courts. 1983 was the 150th anniversary of this landmark hotel which has two fine dining rooms overlooking the lake. Continental breakfast included. Closed December–March.

Holiday Inn. *Expensive.* 2310 N. Triphammer Rd., Ithaca; 607–257–3100. 119 units. Family plan. Pool, dining room, cocktail lounge; pets.

Howard Johnson's Motor Lodge. *Expensive.* N. Triphammer Rd., Ithaca; 607–257–1212. 72 units. Family plan. Pool, dining room, cocktail lounge; pets.

Ramada Inn. *Expensive.* 222 S. Cayuga St., Ithaca; 607–272–1000. 180 units. Family plan. Indoor pool, sauna, dining room, cocktail lounge; pets.

Rose Inn. *Expensive.* 813 Auburn Rd., Ithaca; 607–533–4202. Four units. A perfect country inn with a striking carved mahogany circular staircase. Continental breakfast with freshly baked croissants included.

Sheraton Inn & Conference Center. *Expensive.* 1 Sheraton Dr., Ithaca; 607–257–2000. 105 units. Family plan. Indoor pool, sauna, dining room, cocktail lounge; pets.

Statler Inn. *Expensive.* Cornell University Campus, Ithaca; 607–257–2500. 51 units. Operated by School of Hotel Administration. Three restaurants and cocktail lounge.

The Gould. *Moderate.* 108 Falls St., Seneca Falls; 315–568–5801. 7 units. Family plan. Renovated 1920s hotel, all with kitchens. Dining room and cocktail lounge.

CORNING-ELMIRA AREA

Best Western Lodge on the Green. *Expensive.* Rte. 417 W., Painted Post; 962–2456. 135 units; ten rooms with steambaths; dining room, cocktail lounge, pool.

Corning Hilton Inn. *Expensive.* Denison Pkwy. E., Corning; 962–5000. 126 units. Family plan, indoor pool, dining room, cocktail lounge, next to Historic District.

Holiday Inn. *Expensive.* Rte. 17, Painted Post; 962–5021. 105 units. Family plan, pool, dining room, cocktail lounge.

Holiday Inn. *Moderate.* 1 Holiday Plaza, Elmira; 734–4211. 150 units. Family plan, pool, dining room, cocktail lounge.

Best Western Marshall Manor. *Inexpensive.* Rte. 14, Horseheads; 739–3891. 40 units. Family plan. Restaurant adjacent.

Colonial Motel. *Inexpensive.* 1122 S. Main St., Horseheads; 739–3831. 60 units. Family plan, pool, restaurant, cocktail lounge.

Huck Finn Motel. *Basic Budget.* Rtes. 17 and 328, Horseheads; 739–3807; 30 units. Pool, coffee shop, pets.

Stiles Motel. *Basic Budget.* RD 2, Painted Post; 962–5221; 16 units; playground.

KEUKA LAKE AREA

Viking Resort Apartment Motel. *Basic Budget to Moderate.* 680 E. Lake Rd., Penn Yan; 315–536–7061. 38 units. Apartments and cottages, pool, beach, free cruises. Closed October–April.

Colonial Motel. *Basic Budget.* 175 Lower West Lake Rd., Penn Yan; 315–536–3056. Just down road from Keuka College; kitchenettes, lake access.

Hammondsport Motel. *Basic Budget.* William St., Hammondsport; 607–569–2600. 17 units. On lake, open April–December.

Towne Motel. *Basic Budget.* 206 Elm St., Penn Yan; 315–536–4474. 24 units. Near Keuka College.

Vinehurst Motel. *Basic Budget.* Rte. 54, Hammondsport; 607–569–2300. 32 units. Just ¼ mile from Taylor-Great Western winery. Two miles from lake.

LETCHWORTH STATE PARK AREA

Genesee Falls Inn. *Inexpensive.* Rte. 436, Portageville; 493–2484. 11 units. Just a half mile from the entrance to the park, this landmark has been housing guests since 1870. Pleasant dining room. Closed January.

Glen Iris Inn. *Inexpensive.* Letchworth State Park, Castile; 493–2622. 20 units in two buildings. This is the one-time home of Buffalo industrialist and philanthropist William Pryor Letchworth, who donated his home and lands to form Letchworth State Park in 1910. The inn overlooks Middle Falls. The excellent restaurant draws diners from Buffalo and Rochester. Heavily booked far in advance especially, for fall foliage season. Open Easter Sunday–first weekend in November.

ROCHESTER AREA

Marriott Airport Inn. *Deluxe.* 1890 Ridge Rd. W.; 225–6880. 210 units. Family plan, indoor pool, sauna, whirlpool, pets.

Marriott Inn–Thruway. *Deluxe.* 5257 W. Henrietta Rd.; 359–1800. 307 units. Two pools, one indoor, hot tub, suites, dining room, cocktail lounge.

Rochester Hilton. *Deluxe.* 175 Jefferson Rd.; 475–1910. 170 units. Indoor pool, saunas, whirlpool, dining room, cocktail lounge.

Rochester Plaza. *Deluxe.* 70 State St.; 546–3450. 364 units. Pool, valet garage, Riverview Cafe, cocktail lounge.

Strathallan. *Deluxe.* 550 East Ave.; 461–5010. 150 units. Family plan. An elegant European-style hotel which began life as an apartment building. One- and two-bedroom efficiency suites. French restaurant.

Genesee Country Inn. *Expensive.* 948 George St., Mumford, 20 miles south of Rochester; 538–2500. Ten units. Built in 1833, this inn began life as a plaster mill and has two-foot thick walls. Now a lovely inn with a stream and waterfalls outside. Rate includes full American breakfast.

Holiday Inn–Airport. *Expensive.* 911 Brooks Ave.; 328–6000. 283 units. Family plan, indoor pool, exercise room, dining room, cocktail lounge.

Holiday Inn–Genesee Plaza. *Expensive.* 120 Main St. E.; 546–6400. 467 units. Family plan, pool, dining room, cocktail lounge.

Rose Mansion and Gardens. *Expensive.* 625 Mt. Hope Ave.; 546–5426. Ten units. An elegant country inn just a block from Highland Park in the center of the city, this is the former home of the nursery owner who donated the park land. It has five fireplaces, a working pipe organ, grand piano, and lovely gardens including 100-year-old roses and many lilacs. Rates include continental breakfast.

East Avenue Inn. *Moderate.* 384 East Ave.; 325–5010. 139 units. Family plan, dining room, cocktail lounge.

Howard Johnson's Motor Lodge. *Moderate.* 3350 Henrietta Rd.; 475–1661. 100 units. Family plan, pool, dining room, cocktail lounge.

Best Western Highlander Inn. *Inexpensive.* 4600 W. Henrietta Rd.; 334–1230. 69 units. Pool, dining room, cocktail lounge.

Luxury Budget Inn–Brighton. *Basic Budget.* 797 E. Henrietta Rd.; 427–0130. 100 units. Family plan, pets $3 extra.

Luxury Budget Inn–Greece. *Basic Budget.* 1635 W Ridge Rd.; 621–2060. 100 units. Family plan, pets $3 extra.

SENECA LAKE AREA

Geneva On The Lake. *Deluxe.* 1001 Lochland Rd., Geneva; 315–789–7190. 29 units. Family plan. A replica of Rome's Lancelotti Villa, this elegant and unique hotel is listed in the National Registry of Historic Places and formerly served as a Capuchin monastery. All units have kitchens, some have fireplaces. Pool, formal gardens, weekend and holiday specials. Continental breakfast included.

Belhurst Castle. *Expensive.* Rte. 14, Geneva; 315–781–0201. 12 units. 1985 marked the centennial of this magnificent Gilded Age mansion on 25 acres, filled with carved mahogany and oak and stained glass. Each room is special and the suites are quite extraordinary with 20-foot ceilings, a Jacuzzi overlooking the lake, working fireplaces. The tower suite has a spiral staircase leading into castle tower. Elegant dining rooms with fine food.

Glen Motor Inn. *Moderate.* Rte. 14, Watkins Glen; 607–535–2706. 40 units. Family plan. Dining room, cocktail lounge. On lake, pool, boat rental, tennis court, pets.

Rainbow Cove Motel. *Inexpensive.* Rte. 14, Himrod; 607–243–7535. 24 units. On lake, pool, beach, boat launching, game room and recreation hall. Scuba diving school. Dining room overlooking lake. Open mid-May–October.

Showboat Motel. *Inexpensive.* Plumpoint Rd., Himrod; 607–243–7434. 45 units. On lake, pool, swimming dock, fishing, boats, bicycles. Dining room overlooking lake. Open April–October.

Clark's Motel. *Basic Budget.* 824 Canandaigua Rd., Geneva; 315–789–0780. 10 units. Restaurant opposite.

SKANEATELES LAKE AREA

Sherwood Inn. *Expensive.* 26 W. Genesee St., Skaneateles; 685–3405. 16 units. Begun as a way station between New York City and Niagara Falls back in 1807 and was totally refurbished in 1974. Filled with antiques. Overlooks lake; fine dining room.

Birds Nest Motel. *Inexpensive.* U.S. 20, east of Skaneateles; 685–5641. 25 units. Pool, on lake, refrigerators. Open May 15–November 1.

Whispering Winds Motel. *Inexpensive.* Rte. 20E, Auburn; 685–6056. 12 units. Pool, refrigerators. Open May 25–October 15.

Bel-Air Motel. *Basic Budget.* 797 W. Genesee St.; 685–6720. 13 units. Restaurant adjacent. Open June 1–October 30.

Colonial Motel. *Basic Budget.* U.S. 20; 685–5751. 15 units. Pool, rental bicycles.

Skaneateles Steamboat Motor Lodge. *Basic Budget.* U.S. 20; 685–8925. 13 units. Pets.

SYRACUSE AREA

Marriott Inn. *Deluxe.* Marriott Dr. and Carrier Pkwy.; 432–0200. 250 units. Family plan, indoor/outdoor pool, exercise room, dining room, cocktail lounge.

Hilton at Syracuse Square. *Expensive to Deluxe.* 500 S. Warren St.; 471–7300. 201 units. Family plan, dining room, cocktail lounge, nightclub; shares facilities with Hotel Syracuse.

Holiday Inn–Downtown. *Expensive.* 701 E. Genesee St.; 474–7251. 290 units. Family plan, indoor pool, dining room, cocktail lounge.

Hotel Syracuse. *Expensive.* 500 S. Warren St.; 422–5121. 510 units. Family plan, dining room, cocktail lounge, nightclub; shares facilities with Hilton.

Best Western Dinkler Motor Inn. *Moderate.* 1100 James St.; 472–6961. Family plan, indoor pool, dining room, cocktail lounge.

Holiday Inn–Exit 39–Fairgrounds. *Moderate.* State Fair Blvd. and Farrell Rd.; 457–8700. 152 units. Family plan, pool, dining room, cocktail lounge, pets.

Howard Johnson's Motor Lodge. *Moderate.* Thompson Rd. and Carrier Circle; 437–2711. 90 units. Family plan, pool, dining room, cocktail lounge, pets.

Ramada Inn. *Moderate.* 1305 Buckley Rd.; 457–8670. 144 units. Family plan, pool, dining room, cocktail lounge.

 BED-AND-BREAKFAST TREASURES. Bed-and-breakfast inns have been growing in the region recently in response to demand. Most are in historic houses or farmhouses. Some accept major credit cards but many do not; be sure to inquire in advance when making reservations. Rates range from budget to moderate. *Cherry Valley Ventures,* 315–677–9723, handles reservations for a number of bed-and-breakfast establishments. The following is a selection of some in the area:

Bed & Breakfast Rochester. Box 444, Fairport; 716–223–8877.

Bristol Bed & Breakfast. 4861 Rte. 64; Canandaigua; 716–229–2003.

Bully Hill Bed & Breakfast. RD 2, Hammondsport; 607–868–3226.

Buttermilk Falls B & B. 110 E. Buttermilk Falls Rd., Ithaca; 607–272–6767.

The Cecce House. 166 Chemung, Corning; 607–962–5682.

Four Seasons Country Inn. 470 W. Lake Rd., Branchport; 607–868–4686.

Fox Run Vineyards Bed & Breakfast. Rte. 14, Penn Yan; 315–536–2507.

Laurel Hill Guest House. 2670 Powderhouse Rd., Corning; 607–936–3215.

 CAMPING. The region is a favorite for family camping, and most of the 20 state parks provide camping facilities. Among the outstanding public campsites are *Letchworth State Park,* Castile; *Taughannock Falls,* Ithaca; and *Buttermilk Falls,* Ithaca. For a complete list of camp sites contact the *Finger Lakes Association,* 309 Lake St., Penn Yan, 14527. In addition, there are a number of private campgrounds ranging from the very rustic to the most deluxe:

Canandaigua KOA Kampground, 5374 Farmington Town Line Rd., Candaigua, 14424.

Conesus Lake Campground, 2202 E. Lake Rd., Conesus, 14435.

Smith Park & Campground on Seneca Lake, off Rte. 414, Hector, 14841.

Watkins Glen KOA Kampground, Rte. 414 South, Box 4F, Watkins Glen, 14891.

Willowwood Campsites, Off Rte. 327, Box 583, Ithaca, 14850.

TOURIST INFORMATION. The *Finger Lakes Association,* 309 Lake St., Penn Yan, 14527 (315–536–7488), has free brochures, booklets, and maps. *Rochester Convention & Visitors Bureau,* 120 East Main St., Rochester, 14604 (716–546–3070), and *Syracuse Convention & Visitors Bureau,* 100 East Onondaga St., Syracuse (315–470–1343), also have information, brochures, and maps on their areas. In Rochester, phone 546–6810 for a listing of daily events. In addition, 25 smaller communities operate information centers during the summer, and centers in Canandaigua, Elmira, Geneva, Waterloo, Watkins Glen, and Camillus operate year round.

 RECOMMENDED READING. All these books are available in Finger Lakes bookstores, and some are available nationally in bookstores or libraries. *A Finger Lakes Odyssey.* Lois O'Connor. North Country Books, Lakemont, NY. 1977. *Country Inns of New York State.* Robert W. Tolf, Roxane S. Rauch. 101 Productions, San Francisco. 1984. *20 Bicycle Tours in the Finger Lakes.* Mark Roth, Sally Walters. Backcountry Publications, Woodstock, VT. 1983. *Wineries of the Finger Lakes.* James M. Morris, Jack Sherman. Isidore Stephanus Sons, Ithaca. 1985.

 SEASONAL EVENTS. March. The Bristol Mountain Ski Center, Canandaigua, celebrates St. Patrick's Day and spring the second weekend of the month with Irish *Spring Carnival Weekend.* The annual *Central New York Maple Festival* heralds maple syrup the fourth weekend of the month with pancake breakfasts, arts and crafts displays, samples, tours, and train excursions.

April. The Empire State/Lake Ontario *Trout and Salmon Derby* along the shores of Lake Ontario is held on the last weekend. **May** brings blossoms and flowers, and mid-month is the *Annual Dogwood Festival* in Dansville. For 10 days beginning the third week of the month, the *Lilac Festival* is held in Rochester to honor the city's 22 acres of lilacs, 1,600 bushes, and 550 varieties in Highland Park. There are parades, concerts, and other flower shows.

June. The first weekend is the *Salt City Hot Air Balloon Festival,* Jamesville Beach, Syracuse. The *National Lake Trout Derby,* Seneca Lake, Geneva, is held the last weekend. The last week is *Rose Week* at the elaborate Sonnenberg Gardens, Canandaigua. Mid-June is the *Civil War Reenactment Battle and Camp,* Emerson Park, Seward Home and City Hall, Auburn. The last week is also the *Irish Festival* in Rochester at the downtown festival site.

July. The *Fourth of July* explodes throughout the region. There are fireworks and a concert at MacArthur Stadium, Syracuse; in Rochester, a festival in Sodus Point; a parade and party in Branchport; the Fly-in Breakfast at the Penn Yan Airport; a trip back to the 19th century with parades, band concerts, cannon firings, and games at the Genesee Country Museum, Mumford; Americana Weekend–Military Encampment units depict the French and Indian War, Revolutionary War, War of 1812, and Civil War, at Sonnenberg Gardens, Canandaigua. During the middle of the month, the *Corn Hill Arts Festival* is held in Rochester's restored Third Ward. The third weekend is the annual *Central New York Firemen's Association Convention and Parade* with antique fire apparatus muster, downtown Elmira. It is also the anniversary of *Women's Rights Convention* and is commemorated with a run, bike and boat tours, parade, fireworks, and a street dance at Women's Rights National Historical Park, Seneca Falls. This weekend is also the re-creation of the Battle of Gettysburg with 400 Union and Confederate troops at the Genesee Country Museum, Mumford. Weekends in July and August, the *Pleasure Faire* of the Renaissance and Summer Marketplace, a re-creation of a late-16th-century English Village, is held in Sterling. For nine days during the end of July and beginning of August, the *Hill Cumorah Pageant* is presented by the Mormons in Palmyra.

August. Phelps' tribute to sauerkraut is the annual *Sauerkraut Festival,* held on the first four days. The first weekend is Ithaca's Cayuga Lake *Bass Tournament,* an air, sea, and land show and fishing tourney. The *Green Corn Festival* with Indian dances, handicrafts and food is held in mid-August on the Onondaga Indian reservation. The *Monroe County Fair,* south of Rochester, is also held in mid-August. Late in August are the annual *Civil War Days* in Elmira with a battle reenactment in period dress by Ward's Brigade. The *New York State Fair* is held the last 12 days of the month in Syracuse with name entertainment, midway, sports, and displays of agriculture, livestock, arts and crafts, business, and industry.

September. The *Free Spirit Hang Gliding Festival* is held Labor Day at Draught Hill, Elmira. Seneca Park *Zoo Fest* draws thousands to the zoo, St. Paul Blvd., Rochester, on Labor Day with concerts and special programs. Rochester Memorial Art Gallery's two-day *Clothesline Art Show,* one of the country's largest outdoor art shows, is held early in the month at the Gallery Building, 490 University Ave. The *Golden Harvest Festival* is an old-fashioned country fair held the second weekend with food, arts and crafts, hayrides, and nature walks at the Beaver Lake Nature Center, Baldwinsville. *Canal Town Days* are held in the middle of the month in Palmyra. The *Wine Folk Festival* is presented in Hammondsport the third weekend with parades, blue grass festival, and wine-making and tastings.

October. The *Fall Flight Foliage Festival* is the first weekend at the Harris Hill Soaring Site, Elmira. The *Agricultural Society Fair,* a recreation of a 19th-century fair is also the first weekend at the Genesee Country Museum, Mumford. The same weekend is a *Wine, Water, and Wilderness Festival* at Watkins Glen. Columbus Day weekend is the Lafayette *Apple Festival* at the Lafayette Elementary School, with crafts and all types of apple products for sale.

November. The annual *Great Nouveau Race* takes place in the middle of the month at Turback's Restaurant, Rt. 13, Ithaca. New York State wineries beat the arrival of French nouveau wines in the U.S. The *Snowbird Meet* with soaring competitions and demonstrations is held Thanksgiving weekend at the Harris Hill Soaring Site.

TOURS. Boat cruises: *Capt. Bill's Lake Ride,* Seneca Lake, Rte. 14, Watkins Glen, ten-mile cruise leaving every hour; 607–535–4541. *Capt. Gray's Lake Tours,* Roseland Park, Canandaigua, tours every hour, C. Gray Hoffman, 92 Park Ave.; 716–394–5270. *Mid Lake Navigation Company* offers mail, dinner, and luncheon cruises on Skaneateles Lake and cruises on the Erie Canal, Box 61, Skaneateles; 315–685–5722. *Seaviewer Sip-N-Sail,* Seneca Market, Watkins Glen, Jack and Harriett McCormack, Burdett; 607–546–5063. *M/V Corinne,* lunch and dinner cruises, Oldport Harbour, Ithaca; 607–272–6550.

Freewheeling Adventures offers **bicycle** tours in the area; for brochure write them at 84A Durand Dr., Rochester, 14622; 716–323–2657.

The Dining Car Train, Box 666, Syracuse, 13201 (315–458–5907), offers a 3- or 5-hour **rail tour** south to Homer or Marathon departing Jamesville Town Square, Syracuse. *Historic Onondaga Lake Tram Tours,* Onondaga Lake Park, Liverpool, 13088 (315–457–5715), offers lake tours on a motorized tram.

Escorted **bus** tours of the region are provided by *Upstate Sightseeing Tours,* Box 189, Watkins Glen (607–535–7382), and *K-Ventures Minicoach,* Box 522, Penn Yan (315–536–7559).

City tours of Rochester and surrounding area are offered by *Rochester Sightseeing Tours,* 585 Winona Blvd., 14617 (716–342–8346); *Personal Tours of Rochester,* Box 18055, 14618 (716–442–9365); and *Greater Rochester Tours,* 86 Shepard St., 14620 (716–442–9435).

Dockside Aviation, 716–396–2311, will pick up at most lakes for **seaplane** tours.

Special interest tours. *Eastman Kodak Company,* 343 State St., 716–724–4000, offers tours of its plants. *Carrier Dome,* Syracuse University, 315–423–4634, offers tours of the Northeast's largest domed stadium. *L. & J. G. Stickley, Inc.,* 300 Orchard St., Fayetteville, 315–637–3171, has factory tours of its plant manufacturing handcrafted cherry furniture, Tuesdays–Thursdays. 10 A.M.–2 P.M.

Winery Tours. There are more than 35 wineries in the region, the largest concentration in the eastern United States. The following have tours or welcome visitors and have wine tastings, free unless otherwise noted:

CANANDAIGUA LAKE

Canandaigua Wine Co., Sonnenberg Gardens, 716–394–7680, tastings. *Widmer's Wine Cellars,* Rte. 21, Naples, 716–374–6311, tours, tastings.

CAYUGA LAKE

Americana Vineyards, 4367 East Covert Rd., Interlaken, 607–387–6801, tours, tastings. *Knapp Farms,* Ernesberger Rd., Romulus, 315–549–8865, tours, tastings, $1.50. *Lakeshore Winery,* 5132 Rte. 89, Romulus, 315–549–8461, tours, tastings. *Lucas Winery,* RD 2, County Road 150, Interlaken, 607–532–4825, tours, tastings, $1. *Plane's Cayuga Vineyard,* RD 2, Ovid, 607–869–5158, tours, tastings, $1.

CORNING

Wine Center & Market, Baron Steuben Pl., Corning, 607–962–6072, tours of center that provides introduction to wine-making and its history and lore; tastings, 50¢ to 75¢ per tasting in what was once former hotel's ballroom. Wine Market downstairs.

HEMLOCK LAKE

Eagle Crest O-Neh-Da Barry Wine, 7107 Vineyard Rd., Conesus, 716–346–2321, tours, tastings; groups only.

KEUKA LAKE

Bully Hill, Greyton H. Taylor Memorial Dr., Hammondsport, 607–868–3610, has tours, tastings, Champagne Country Cafe, gift shop and Greyton H. Taylor Wine Museum. *DeMay Wine Cellars,* Rte. 88, Hammondsport, 607–569–2040, tours and tastings. *Finger Lakes Wine Cellars,* 4021 Italy Hill Rd., Branchport, 315–595–2812, no tours of winery but haywagon tour of vineyards. $1.50, adults; tastings, $1. *Heron Hill,* Middle Road, Hammondsport, 607–868–4241, tours by appointment, tastings. *Konstantin Frank & Sons,* Rt. 76, 607–868–4884, tastings, tours, by appointment, wine shop. *McGregor Vineyard,* 5503 Dutch St., Dundee, 607–292–3999, tours, tastings, $1. *Taylor-Great Western-*

Gold Seal Wine Company, Hammondsport, 607–569–2111, tours, tastings, gift shop.

SENECA LAKE

Glenora Wine Cellars, RD 4, Dundee, 607–243–5511, slide show, no tour, tastings. *Hazlitt 1852 Vineyards,* Rte. 414, Hector, 607–546–5812, tours, tastings. *Poplar Ridge,* RD 1, Valois, 607–582–6421, tours, tastings. *Rolling Vineyards,* Rte. 414, Hector, 607–546–9302, tours, tastings. *Wagner Vineyards,* Rte. 414, Lodi, 607–582–6450, tours, tastings, Ginny Lee Cafe, open mid-May–mid-October; musical entertainment during summer. *Wickham Vineyards,* 1 Wine Pl., Hector, 607–546–8415, tours, tastings, haywagon tours of vineyard. $2, adults; $1, children. *Hermann J. Wiemer,* Rte. 14, Dundee, tours, tastings, $1.

PARKS. There are more than 20 state parks in the region, with a $2.50–$3.50 per car admission during the summer depending on whether there are swimming facilities. The 14,344-acre *Letchworth State Park* has been called "the Grand Canyon of the East," and has few rivals in the East for spectacular beauty. It includes 17 miles of the Genesee River, dramatic cliffs, some of which approach 600 feet in height; three major waterfalls, one of which is 107 feet high; lush woods; the Glen Iris Inn, which was the country home of the park's donor, William Pryor Letchworth. The park has extensive camping facilities, fishing, hunting, swimming, and cross-country skiing. The Pioneer and Indian Museum tells the story of the early days of the area with artifacts, books and displays. There is also an original Iroquois Council House moved here from a nearby location. For information and reservations for camping facilities contact Letchworth State Park, Castile, NY 14427; 716–493–2611. For the Glen Iris Inn call 716–493–2622, or write to the Glen at the park address.

Just outside Ithaca is *Taughannock Falls State Park* with 215-foot high falls in a rock amphitheatre with 400-foot walls. It is the highest straight-drop falls east of the Rocky Mountains. The 737-acre park has complete camping facilities as well as swimming, fishing, boat launching, hiking trails, and cross-country skiing. Contact the park at Trumansburg, NY 14886; 607–387–7041. Also outside Ithaca is the 733-acre *Buttermilk Falls* on Rte. 13. It has complete camping facilities, fishing, swimming, and cross-country skiing. Contact the park at Trumansburg, NY 14886; 607–387–7041.

The 669-acre *Watkins Glen State Park,* Rte. 14, adjoins the village at the south end of Seneca Lake. The glen drops about 700 feet in two miles and is highlighted by rock formations and 18 waterfalls. Cliffs rise 200 feet above the stream; a bridge 165 feet above the water spans the glen. Taxis are available for those who wish to avoid climbing. The glen is lit at night. Phone 607–535–4511. *Timespell,* a dramatic sound and laser light show traces 45 million centuries of natural and human history in the gorge. A 45-minute show is presented twice nightly, beginning at dusk, May 1–October 31. Admission $4; 607–535–4960.

The *Green Mountain National Forest,* in the southern Seneca Lake area, is the only national forest land in the state. There are campgrounds within the preserve, 25 miles of trails, 80 ponds (many of which contain trout, bass, catfish, and panfish), excellent hunting, snowmobiling, and cross country skiing. Hector Ranger District, Green Mountain National Forest, Box W, Montour Falls, 14865; 607–594–2750.

Rochester's 155-acre *Highland Park* is unique with its 22 acres of lilacs and the Lamberton Conservatory, designed in 1911 along the lines of a Victorian greenhouse. This is the scene of the annual 10-day Lilac Festival in May, and during the winter there is cross country skiing. In the Syracuse area, the *Onondaga Lake Park,* Liverpool, 315–457–2990, has a marina, fishing, and all types of winter sports. The 560-acre *Beaver Lake Nature Center,* East Mud Lake Rd., Baldwinsville, 315–638–2519, is a nature preserve, a resting stop for Canadian geese, with a 200–acre wilderness lake, guided walks, and canoe tours. The 1,087-acre *Green Lakes State Park,* Rtes. 290 and 5, Fayetteville, 315–637–6111, has camping, a beach, boat rentals, golf course, and cross country skiing.

ZOOS. Rochester's *Seneca Park Zoo,* 2222 St. Paul St., is in Seneca Park, which has hiking trails along the east side of the Genesee River. The aviary, and its uncaged birds, polar bear enclosure, and elephant exhibit are especially popular. Open 10 A.M.–5 P.M. daily; summer weekends and holidays to 7 P.M.; 716–266–6846. Adults, 50¢; children, 10–15, 25¢; under 9, free. Syracuse's *Burnet Park Zoo,* S. Wilbur Ave., reopened after a $13-million modernization. On 36 acres, there are more than 1,000 animals and birds in nine separate complexes re-creating their natural habitats from arctic tundra and desert to tropical rain forest. Daily 10 A.M.–4:30 P.M., closed Christmas, New Year's Day; 315–425–3774. Adults, $2.50; children ages 5–14, $1.25; seniors, $1.25; family, $8.

GARDENS. *Sonnenberg Gardens,* Canandaigua, was built in 1887 as the summer home of Frederick and Mary Clark Thompson. Mrs. Thompson was the daughter of New York Governor Myron Holly Clark, and was born in nearby Naples. The gardens were reborn in 1972 through the efforts of local citizens and they have been recognized by the Smithsonian Institution as "one of the most magnificent late Victorian gardens ever created in America." Nine gardens, including rose, Japanese, Italian, rock, secret, and colonial, surround the mansion, which has restored period rooms with some original furnishings. The Canandaigua Wine Company Tasting Room is located on the 50-acre estate and offers wine tastings. Tea room, gift shops. Admission; adults, $4.25; seniors, $3.75; children, $1.25. Open daily 9:30 A.M.–4:30 P.M., mid-May to Mid-October. Guided tours offered at 10 A.M., 1 P.M., and 3 P.M.; 716–394–4922.

Cornell Plantations, Ithaca, 1,500 acres of university lands include collections of azaleas, lilacs, peonies, wildflowers, rhododendrons, and viburnums. There are lakes, ponds, streams, bogs, swampland, wooded areas, and an arboretum as well as a magnificent collection of Japanese tree peonies. Of special interest is the Walter C. Muenscher Poisonous Plants Garden with a unique collection of poisonous plants. The Robison York State Herb Garden has more than 800 herbs. Open daily; 607–256–3020.

Highland Park, Rochester, is famous for its 1,600 lilac bushes covering 22 acres as well as gardens filled with magnolias, azaleas, crabapples, hawthorns, peonies, and other plants. A spectacular pansy bed holds more than 5,000 plants. The Lamberton Conservatory has five major displays throughout the year. Open daily; 716–244–4640.

Legg Dahlia Gardens, off Pre-Emption Rd., Geneva, has over three acres of dahlias with 600 varieties. Free tours daily, August–October; 315–789–1209.

Tioga Gardens, Rte. 17C in historic village of Owego, which is a National Historic District. Solar-domed conservatory, water gardens, lily ponds, herb, wild flower garden, flower/gift shop. Open daily year round; 607–687–5522.

BEACHES. The Finger Lakes have very few beaches, mostly small patches of sand scattered along some of the lakes. However, there are some wide, sandy beaches at *Ontario Beach Park,* at the northern edge of Rochester, with bathhouses and snack bar. Free. *Durand Beach,* also on Lake Ontario, is across from Durand Eastman Park, on Lakeshore Blvd.; no bathhouse or snack bar. Free. *Hamlin Beach State Park,* Rte. 19, 20 miles from Rochester, on Lake Ontario, has a nice beach, with camping, bathhouses, snack bars; $3.50 admission.

CHILDREN'S ACTIVITIES. *The Margaret Woodburg Strong Museum,* 1 Manhattan Sq., Rochester, has an extensive collection of dolls, dollhouses, and antique toys. Open Tuesdays-Saturdays, 10 A.M.–5 P.M.; Sundays, 1–5 P.M. Adults, $2; seniors, $1.50; children 17 and under, 75¢; under 4, free; 716–275–3221. *The Victorian Doll Museum,* 4332 Buffalo Rd., North Chili, 10 miles west of Rochester, has more than 1,000 collector dolls, toy circus, puppet show, doll hospital, and gift shop. Open Tuesdays–Saturdays 10 A.M.–5 P.M.; Sundays 1–5 P.M. Adults, $1; children, 50¢; 716–247–0130. *Wild Winds Farms and Village,* Naples, has gardens, log fort, petting zoo, nature center, maple sugar house, restaurant. Open daily June–October; weekends in May; 716–374–5523. Most wineries provide grape juice for children at the wine tastings.

Syracuse's *Discovery Center of Science & Technology,* 321 South Clinton St., 315–425–9068, is a hands-on museum. There are visiting exhibits from science centers around the country and permanent "please touch" exhibits. The center's Science Store sells solar energy kits, star charts, fossil charts, rock collections, build-it-yourself electric motors. Planetarium. Open Tuesdays–Saturdays, 10 A.M.–5 P.M., Sundays, noon–5 P.M. Adults, $1; children under 12, 50¢.

PARTICIPANT SPORTS. The Finger Lakes region, with its hills, lakes, and valleys, offers the outdoor enthusiast a great range of sports and recreation. Water has long been a top asset of this area. Beyond the Finger Lakes there is Lake Ontario and the Barge Canal for **boating.** There are numerous boat launching sites throughout the area. The two longest lakes, Seneca and Cayuga, are connected by a canal that in turn is connected to the Erie Canal. These lakes are thus connected to the waterways of the world. All lakes provide great **sailing.**

The region has long attracted **fishing** enthusiasts who flock here for fishing derbies and record-breaking lake trout, rainbow trout, bass, pike, pickerel, salmon, and panfish. Opportunities include deep trolling in lakes, off-shore spin-casting, stream fishing, smelting, and ice fishing in winter.

Lake Ontario has been successful with a restocking program for Chinook and Coho salmon. Be sure to check the latest Health Department advisory on eating fish from Lake Ontario; there are restrictions because of chemical contamination. Call *Lake Ontario Hotline,* 716–473–1824 or 716–589–9211, for latest fishing update. The *New York State Fish Hatchery,* Rte. 16, 16 North St., Caledonia, was built in 1865 as the first in North America and is the state's largest producing hatchery. It now raises rainbow trout, Chinook, and Coho salmon. Hatchery is open daily for tours; 716–538–6300. For information on licenses, seasons, and limits contact the Department of Environmental Conservation, 6274 East Avon–Lima Rd., Avon, 14414; 716–372–8676.

There are nearly 30 **golf** courses in the region that welcome visitors. In Elmira courses are available at the 18-hole *Chemung Valley* ($7–$11 greens fees) and 18-hole *Mark Twain* ($7–$8 fees). Ithaca's *Cornell University* 18-hole Golf Club's fees are $15. The 9-hole *Newman Course,* Ithaca, has fees of $3.75–$6. In Rochester there is both a new 18-hole *Genesee Valley* course and an old 18-hole course with fees of $5–$8. In Syracuse, the 18-hole *Tanner Valley* has fees of $6–$7. Geneva has a 9-hole *Big Oak* course with fees of $6–$7, and Cayuga has a 9-hole course with fees of $4.50–$5.50. Watkins Glen has the 9-hole *Lake Breeze* with fees of $4.50–$6.50.

A multitude of well-marked **hiking** trails are in the area. The *Finger Lakes Trail* is an east-west footpath running from the Catskill Mountains westward into the Allegheny Mountains. The trail's major trunk spans nearly 350 miles. There are an additional 300 miles of branch trails. Much of the trail passes over private land, so hikers must obey trail rules. Contact *Finger Lakes Trail Conference,* Box 18048, Rochester, 14618; 716–288–7191.

Hot air **ballooning** is especially popular in the Syracuse area. For rides: *Adventure Air Sports,* 106 Evelyn Terr., Syracuse, 13208, 315–446–1891; *Cloud Cruises,* 113 Edgemere Lane, Fayetteville, 13066, 315–637–9785; *Serendipity Balloons,* 108 Rugby Rd., Syracuse, 13206, 315–437–6086.

Great **hunting** abounds in the region. Deer is the most popular big game, and small game includes waterfowl, grouse, rabbit, pheasant, squirrel, raccoon, fox, and wild turkey. Steuben County, where Corning is located, alternates with Allegany and Cattaraugus counties in western New York for the largest deer harvest in the state. The ruffed grouse is considered "king of the game birds" in the southern Finger Lakes. Wild turkey, which has made a fantastic comeback in the region, is also a much sought-after game bird. To the north there is excellent goose hunting adjacent to federal and state game refuges. The area is part of the Eastern Flyway for migratory birds. For information on licenses, seasons, and bag limits contact the Department of Environmental Conservation, 6274 East Avon–Lima Rd., Avon, 14414; 716–372–8676.

Skiing is a popular winter sport, with cross country skiing available in the state and local parks as well as the Green Mountain National Forest. The largest downhill ski centers are *Bristol Mountain,* Rte. 64, Canandaigua, 14424, 716–374–6331; and *Greek Peak,* Rte. 90, Cortland, 13045, 607–835–6111. Both have lessons and rentals.

The Elmira area is the "Soaring Capital of America." The area's hills and valleys present ideal **soaring and gliding** conditions. For rides and instruction contact *Harris Hill Gliderport,* RD 1, Elmira, 14903, 607–734–3128, or *Schweizer Soaring School,* Chemung County Airport, Rte. 17, between Elmira and Corning, 607–739–3821. In Syracuse contact *Right Brothers, Inc.,* 7248 Roumare Rd., East Syracuse, 13057, 315–656–2871; or *Thermal Ridge Soaring,* 115 Kittell Rd., Fayetteville, 13066, 315–446–4545.

Just about every community in the region provides **tennis** courts, and most are free. Some are lit for night play and in a few cases lights are on all night so you can play at 4 A.M. if you wish.

 SPECTATOR SPORTS. If you have never seen a **polo** game you can do it for free on a summer Sunday afternoon at the Skaneateles polo grounds, which overlook this lovely lake. In Rochester the Rochester Americans **hockey** team, a farm team for the Buffalo Sabres, plays at War Memorial Stadium, December–March. The Rochester Red Wings **baseball** team, a farm team of the Baltimore Orioles, plays at Silver Stadium, April–September.

The Syracuse University **football** team plays at the *Carrier Dome* each fall; university **basketball** appears there November–March, and university lacrosse,

March–May. The *Syracuse Chiefs* AAA baseball team plays April–September at MacArthur Stadium.

For **horseracing** fans, there is the *Finger Lakes Race Track,* Thruway Exit 44 and Rte. 96; April–Nov.; 716–924–3232. Harness tracks are the *Batavia Downs,* Batavia, and *Syracuse Mile,* Syracuse. Check local newspapers for post time and dates.

Watkins Glen International has professional **road racing** June–October. Events include Camel Continental, Trans-Am Nationals, Supervee, Vintage Cup, and 24-hour Firestone Firehawk. For schedules, contact Watkins Glen, Box 500, Watkins Glen, 14891; 607–974–7162.

HISTORIC SITES. A wealth of historic homes and sites can be viewed in the region. The biggest concentration of historic homes is at the *Genesee Country Village and Museum,* Flint Hill Rd., Mumford, 20 miles south of Rochester. There are 50 buildings, including an elegant 1870 octagonal house and a unique two-story 1814 log house, all gathered from the region. Open daily from mid-May to mid-October, 10 A.M.–5 P.M. Adults, $7.50; seniors, $3.50, Mon.–Fri. only; children 6–14, $3.50; children under 6, free; 716–538–6822.

AUBURN

Seward House, 33 South St. Home of William Seward, New York Governor, U.S. senator, and secretary of state for Presidents Lincoln and Johnson. He was a leading figure in purchasing Alaska and founding Republican party. Original furnishings. Guided tours: adults, $2.50; seniors, $2; children 7–18, $1; under 7, free. Open March–December; Mondays–Saturdays, 1 P.M.–5 P.M.; 315–252–1283.

Harriet Tubman Home, 180 South St. Used by Tubman as "underground railroad" way station for more than 300 slaves she led to freedom. During Civil War, she served as Union Army spy and scout. Donation. Special tours by appointment; 315–253–2621.

CANANDAIGUA

Granger Homestead and Carriage Museum, 295 N. Main St. Restored 1816 Federal mansion of Gideon Granger, U.S. Postmaster-General for Presidents Jefferson and Madison. Collection of 40 horse-drawn vehicles, 1820–1930. Admission to the homestead: adults, $2; children 12–16, 75¢. Museum: adults, $1; children 12–16, 75¢. Combined admission: adults, $2.50; children 12–16, $1. Open March–December, Tuesdays–Saturdays, 10 A.M.–5 P.M.; closed Mondays; 716–394–1472.

CORNING

1796 Benjamin Patterson Inn, 59 West Pulteney St. Restored furnished frontier inn. De Monstoy Log Cabin, built in 1784, and furnished in early style, and 1878 Browntown School House, adjacent. Adults, $1; students, 50¢. Open Mondays–Fridays; 10 A.M.–noon, 1 P.M.–4 P.M.; 607–937–5281.

ELMIRA

Mark Twain Study, Elmira College campus. Twain's famous octagonal study was moved here from his farm outside town. It contains some original furniture and a typewriter like the one Twain used. Open daily in summer, rest of year by appointment; 607–734–3911.

GENEVA

Rose Hill Mansion, Rte. 96A. Greek Revival restoration, built 1839, decorated in elegant Empire style, 21 rooms open to public. Carriage house, slide show, boxwood gardens. Adults, $1.50. Open May 1–Oct. 31; Mondays–Saturdays, 10A.M.–4 P.M., Sundays, 1 P.M. –5 P.M.; 315–789–3848.

PALMYRA

Mormon Historic Sites, Rte. 21, north of Thruway exit 43. Includes burial site of ancient records translated by Joseph Smith into Book of Mormon. Site of Angel Moroni Monument. Visitor center, movies, guided tours. Free; daily, 8 A.M.–6 P.M.; 315–597–5851.

Joseph Smith Home, Stafford Rd. Restored farm homestead of Mormon Church founder. Free. Summer, 8 A.M.–9 P.M.; rest of year, 8 A.M.–6 P.M.; 315–597 –5851.

Martin Harris Landmark Cobblestone House, 2095 Maple Ave. 1850 Erie Canal cobblestone farmhouse. Free. Summer, daily, 8 A.M.–9 P.M.; rest of year, 8 A.M.–6 P.M.; 315–597–5851.

ROCHESTER AREA

Susan B. Anthony House, 17 Madison St. The home of the women's rights activist is filled with antique furnishings of the 19th century. It was in the third floor workroom that she wrote *The History of Woman Suffrage.* Open Wednesdays–Saturdays, 1P.M.–4 P.M. Adults, $1.50; seniors, 75¢; students, 50¢; children under 17, 10¢; 716–235–6124.

The Campbell-Whittlesey House, 123 S. Fitzhugh St., is in the historic Third Ward and is one of America's finest examples of Greek Revival architecture. Operated by Landmark Society of Western New York. Adults, $1.50; seniors, 75¢; students, 50¢; children under 17, 10¢. Open February–December; Tuesdays–Fridays, 10 A.M.–4 P.M.; Sundays, 1 P.M.–4 P.M.; 716–546–7028.

The Stone-Tolan House, 2370 East Ave., is believed to be the oldest surviving building in the county, with one wing dating to 1790. Its four-acre site has vegetable and herb gardens and orchards. Adults, $1.50; seniors, 75¢; students, 50¢; children under 17, 10¢. Open February–December; Wednesdays–Fridays, 10 A.M.–4 P.M.; Saturdays and Sundays, 1 P.M.–4 P.M.; 716–442–4606.

SYRACUSE AREA

Sainte Marie de Gannentaha or *French Fort,* Onondaga Lake Pkwy., Liverpool. A re-creation of an original French Jesuit colonial settlement established on the shore of Onondaga Lake in 1656. Authentically costumed interpreters perform traditional craft demonstrations. Free; daily; May–October; 315–457–2990.

 MUSEUMS. There is a wide diversity of museums and they hold some of the world's largest collections of their specialties. They are spread out through the area and even some of the smallest towns and villages boast collections worth a stop.

CORNING

Corning Museum of Glass, off Rte. 17. Houses the world's largest collection of glass objects—more than 22,000 in all. The present building designed by architect Gunnar Birkerts opened in 1980. Part of Glass Center, which also includes the Hall of Science and Industry with push-button exhibits, live demonstrations, and films. Exhibits illustrate how glass is made and used in science, industry, and the home. Steuben Glass Factory here allows visitors to watch craftsmen create works of art. Gift shops, including Steuben shop and separate shop just for Corning products with a large selection of discount items. Snack shop and cafe. Adults, $2.50; seniors, $2; children 6–17, $1.25; under 6, free; family maximum, $6. Open daily, 9 A.M.–5 P.M.; 607–974–8814.

Rockwell Museum, Denison Pkwy. and Cedar St. Largest collection of western American art in the East. Also Carder Steuben glass and antique toys in the restored 1893 Old City Hall. Museum shops. Adults, $1.50; seniors, $1; children, 75¢. Open Mondays–Saturdays, 10 A.M.–5 P.M.; Sundays, 1 P.M.–5 P.M. July and August, open until 8 P.M. weekdays; 607–937–5386.

ELMIRA

National Soaring Museum, Harris Hill. Displays over a dozen fully assembled, historic gliders and sailplanes as well as artifacts pertaining to motorless flight. Films and slides. Adults, $1.50; seniors and students, 75¢; children under 12, free. Open daily, 10 A.M.–5 P.M.; 607–734–3128.

HAMMONDSPORT

Glenn H. Curtiss Museum of Local History, Lake and Main sts. Relive early history of aviation. Displays accomplishments of local citizen, Curtiss, a pioneer in aviation and other fields. Famous "June Bug" and "Curtiss Jenny" planes and other historic local memorabilia. Adults, $2; children 13–18, $1.50; 7–12, 50¢; family rate, $6. Daily, 9 A.M.–5 P.M., July and August; closed Sundays rest of year; 607–569–2160.

Greyton H. Taylor Museum, Bully Hill Rd., adjacent to Bully Hill Vineyards. 100-year old wood and stone building houses antique equipment used in tending vineyards and making wines. Coopers' tools and local historical memorabilia. Adults, $1; seniors and children 8–14, 75¢. Open May–October, Mondays–Saturdays, 9 A.M.–4:30 P.M.; Sundays, 1 P.M.–4:30 P.M.; 607–868–4814.

ROCHESTER AREA

Margaret Woodbury Strong Museum, One Manhattan Sq. The city's newest museum features the country's foremost collection of Victorian furniture, a vast collection of 19th-century glassware, ceramics and silver, Oriental objects, antique dollhouses, toys, miniatures, and nearly 20,000 dolls. Museum shop. Adults, $2; seniors and students, $1.50; children under 17, $.75; under 4, free. Tuesdays–Saturdays, 10 A.M.–5 P.M., Sundays, 1 P.M.–5 P.M.; 716–263–2700.

Rochester Museum & Science Center, 657 East Ave. Exhibits on natural science, anthropology, human biology, and regional history. Iroquois Indian artifacts and period rooms depicting 19th-century life in city. The Strassenburgh Planetarium has daily star shows under a 60-foot dome. Museum shop. Adults, $2; seniors and students, $1.50; children under 17, 75¢; under 4, free. Planetarium fee varies with show. Museum open Mondays–Saturdays, 9 A.M.–5 P.M.;

Sundays, 1 P.M.–5 P.M. Planetarium shows nightly, weekend and summer matinees; 716–271–4320.

International Museum of Photography at George Eastman House, 900 East Ave. The world's largest collection of photographic art and technology is housed in a 50-room mansion built by George Eastman, founder of Eastman Kodak Company. Survey of art of photography and exhibits tracing development of photographic technology. The archives contain a library with more than 35,000 books and hundreds of thousands of photographs. Museum shop. Adults, $2; students, $1; children under 17, 75¢; open Tues.–Sun., 10 A.M.–4:30 P.M.; 716–271–3361.

SYRACUSE AREA

Erie Canal Museum, 315 East Water St. The Weighlock Building, which houses permanent and special exhibitions, is a National Register Landmark and the only remaining canal boat weighing station of its kind in the world. Permanent exhibits include Weighmaster's Office which offers audiovisual overview of Canal history. Free. Open Tuesdays–Fridays, noon–5 P.M.; Saturdays, 10 A.M.–5 P.M., and Sundays, noon–5 P.M.; 315–471–0593.

Salt Museum, Onondaga Lake Park, Liverpool. Illustrates the salt industry during the period 1788–1926 when the city earned the name "Salt City." Exhibits include partial reconstruction of an 1856 boiling block. Free. Open daily, May–October; 315–457–2990.

Discovery Center of Science & Technology, 321 South Clinton St. A hands-on museum with displays on gravity, perception, chemistry, light, sound, electricity, optics, magnetism, mechanics, space, and human body. Planetarium; museum shop. Adults, $1; children under 12, 50¢. Open Tuesdays–Saturdays, 10 A.M.–5 P.M.; Sundays, noon–5 P.M.; 315–425–9068.

WATKINS GLEN

National Motor Racing Museum, 110 N. Franklin St. Displays relating to the history of motor racing, including motor cars. Adults, $1; children under 15, 50¢; under 5, free. Open Mondays–Saturdays, 9 A.M.–9 P.M.; Sundays, noon–8 P.M.; June–September; 607–535–2481.

FILMS. *Dryden Theatre,* 900 East Ave., Rochester, adjacent to George Eastman House, shows classic movies from the museum's vast film library throughout the year. Check with Rochester *Democrat & Chronicle* and *Times-Union* newspapers for schedule. 716–271–3361.

MUSIC. Except for colleges and universities with campus music programs, the music scene is largely centered in Rochester and Syracuse. *The Rochester Philharmonic Orchestra,* which performs at Eastman Theater, is one of 20 major orchestras in the U.S. The orchestra also travels to neighboring counties for Friday evening concerts. During the summer the orchestra's home is Finger Lakes Performing Arts Center, Canandaigua. Tickets and information, 716–454–7091.

Opera Theatre of Rochester, also performing in Eastman Theater, presents three major operas with the Philharmonic. Tickets and information, 716–461–5839.

Eastman School of Music and Theatre of the University of Rochester, Main St. East at Gibbs St. is one of the nation's most prestigious schools of music and presents various concerts and recitals; 716–275–3037.

The *Syracuse Symphony Orchestra,* Civic Center of Onondaga County, is a major symphony orchestra that performs in the Civic Center of Onondaga County, the first building complex in the West to combine a performing arts center with government offices. Tickets and information, 315–425–2155.

STAGE. Several theaters in the area present productions, some of them geared for the tourist season. *GeVa Theater,* Naval Armory, Rochester, is a resident professional theater presenting eight productions during season. Tickets and information, 716–232–1363. *Masonic Temple & Auditorium Theater,* 875 Main St. East, Rochester, offers touring Broadway productions, concerts, and one nighters; 716–454–7743. *Stage III Holiday Theater,* 120 Main St. East, Rochester, is the city's first residential musical theater company; 716–546–6230.

Salt City Center for the Performing Arts, 601 South Crouse Ave., Syracuse, presents drama, comedy and musicals; 315–474–1122. The *Syracuse Area Landmark Theater,* 326 South Salina St., Syracuse, is a National Historic Landmark which was built in the 1920s and is filled with carvings, gold leaf, and ornate decorations. Presents concerts, plays, dances, and classic movies; 315–475–7980.

Syracuse Stage, 820 East Genesee St., Regent Theater Complex, Syracuse, is the professional theater in the city; 315–423–3275.

Samuel L. Clemens Performing Arts Center, Clemens Center Pkwy. and Gray St., Elmira, presents year-round theater, dance, jazz, and classical artists; 607–734–8191.

Smith Opera House For the Performing Arts, 82 Seneca St., Geneva, presents year-round professional and amateur productions as well as films in a restored 1894 opera house. 315–789–2221.

Corning Summer Theater, Glass Center, Corning, presents professional companies during July and August in the center's auditorium; 607–974–8271.

ART GALLERIES. Galleries are scattered throughout the region and sometimes turn up where least expected, such as the Rockwell Department Store in Corning. *Memorial Art Gallery* of the University of Rochester, 490 University Ave., Rochester is the city's major art museum. It covers 5,000 years of art history and has special strengths in Renaissance and 17-century art, 19th century and early-20th-century French paintings, American folk art and contemporary prints. Housed in a splendid Italian Renaissance-style building. Open Tuesdays, 2 P.M.–9 P.M.; Wednesdays–Saturdays, 10 A.M.–5 P.M.; Sundays, 1 P.M.–5 P.M. Free Tuesdays, 5 P.M.–9 P.M. Adults, $2; students and seniors, $1; children free with adults, otherwise, 25¢; 716–275–3081.

Everson Museum of Art, 401 Harrison St., Syracuse. This was the first museum designed by architect I. M. Pei. It houses one of the largest collections of contemporary ceramics in the nation, as well as a fine collection of American paintings, sculpture, prints, and drawings. Donation. Open Tuesdays–Fridays, noon–5 P.M.; Saturdays, 10 A.M.–5 P.M.; Sundays, noon–5 P.M.; 315–474–6064.

Rockwell Gallery in Gates-Rockwell Department Store, 23 W. Market St., Corning, is not your usual art gallery. This is a real department store with a fine collection of Navajo rugs, western paintings, and antique guns on the walls.

Free. Open Mondays–Saturdays, 9:30 A.M.–8:30 P.M.; Sundays, 12:30–4:30 P.M.; 607–962–2441.

Much of the Rockwell collection is at the *Rockwell Museum* just down the street. It boasts the largest collection of western art in the East, as well as more Navajo rugs and glass masterpieces by Frederick Carder, founder of Steuben Glass; 607–937–5386.

Arnot Art Museum, 235 Lake St., Elmira, is a restored 1880 picture gallery. It houses a collection of Flemish masters, French Academy painters, 20th-century artists. Free. Open Tuesdays–Fridays, 10 A.M.–5 P.M.; Saturdays, 9 A.M.–5 P.M.; Sundays, 2 P.M.–5 P.M.; 607–734–3697.

Hagerton Gallery, 75 East Genesee St., Skaneateles, is an 1813 colonial home with antique furniture and an extensive collection of Dresden porcelains. Free. Open Fridays–Sundays, 1 P.M.–4 P.M.; 315–685–3849.

SHOPPING. Antique shops, as well as the increasingly popular factory outlet stores, are scattered throughout the region. Both Rochester and Syracuse have major department stores and large malls. The *Marketplace Shopping Mall,* W. Henrietta and Jefferson Rds., Rochester, has more than 140 shops and stores and is the largest mall between Long Island and Cleveland. Ithaca has an 80-store mall and a number of boutiques and book stores. Sales tax is 7%. Syracuse is home to *Syracuse China* and its factory retail store, Lyncourt Plaza. The *Market Place,* 5701 East Circle Dr., Clay, has more than 50 factory outlet stores. Corning has discount Corning products at the Glass Center and the *Corning Store,* with the largest collection of Corning products available anywhere.

DINING OUT. Restaurants in the Finger Lakes are as varied as the lakes and communities. Rochester and Syracuse boast some fine dining rooms, and so do the smaller cities and towns. Ithaca on Cayuga Lake has a surprisingly large assortment of top restaurants, in part due to the large universi-ty community and hotel school. Reservations are recommended especially at lakeside establishments during the summer. The price classifications of the following restaurants, from deluxe to inexpensive, are based on the cost of an average three-course dinner for one person; beverages, tax (7%) and tip are extra. *Deluxe,* over $22; *Expensive,* $14–$22; *Moderate,* $7–$14; *Inexpensive,* less than $7. Abbreviations for credit cards are: AE, American Express; CB, Carte Blanche; DC, Diners Club; MC, MasterCard; V, VISA. Abbreviations for meals are: B, breakfast; L, lunch; D, dinner.

CANANDAIGUA LAKE AREA

Naples Hotel. *Expensive.* Main St., Naples; 716–374–5630. A local tradition since 1895. Step back in time in the "Gay 90's" Tap Room. Traditional Ameri-can fare. L, D, daily. AE, MC, V.

Redwood Restaurant. *Expensive.* 6 Cohocton St., Naples; 716–374–6360. Large menu featuring seafood, steaks, and prime ribs; casual atmosphere. Popu-lar with families. Closed January–March 12. B, L, D, daily. MC, V.

Bob's and Ruth's. *Moderate.* Rtes. 21 and 245, Naples; 716–374–5122. Local favorite. Varied menu with homemade soups and pies. B, L, D, daily. MC, V.

Wild Winds Farms & Village. *Moderate.* Clark St. and Rte. 36, Naples; 716–374–5523. Features all natural foods, fresh baked breads and pastries, crepes and quiches, fresh vegetables grown on grounds. Country store, sugarhouse, nature trail, greenhouses, and gardens. Open May 25–October 27. L, daily; D, Fridays and Saturdays. Major credit cards.

CAYUGA LAKE AREA

Aurora Inn. *Expensive.* Main St. and Rte. 90, Aurora; 315–364–8842. 1983 marked the 150th year of this landmark overlooking Cayuga Lake. Menu is an ambitious one with fresh seafood daily. Closed December–March. L, D, daily. Major credit cards.

L'Auberge Du Cochon Rouge Restaurant. *Expensive.* Rte. 3 96B, Ithaca; 607–273–3464. French restaurant with intimate dining rooms, superb food and service. A real dining experience. *Travel-Holiday* Magazine Award winner. D, daily; brunch, Sundays. Major credit cards.

Oldport Harbour. *Expensive.* 702 W. Buffalo St., Ithaca; 607–272–6550. Seafood with fresh selections flown from Boston. Dine at dockside tables. Arrive by boat if you wish. Lunch and dinner cruise boat leaves from dock, spring–early fall. L, D, daily. Major credit cards.

The Station Restaurant. *Expensive.* 806 W. Buffalo St., Ithaca; 607–272–2609. National Historic Landmark. Dine in reconstructed Lehigh Valley Railroad Passenger Station or a real train car. Traditional American fare. D, Tuesdays–Sundays. Major credit cards.

Taughannock Falls Inn. *Expensive.* State Rd. 89 and Gorge Rd., Trumansburg; 607–387–7711. Close attention to detail in the four dining rooms of this 1873 Victorian mansion. All-American fare with sweet-lover's dessert menu, all prepared on premises. D, daily; April–November 24. No credit cards.

Turback's. *Expensive.* Rte. 13, Ithaca; 607–272–6484. Long-established restaurant, considered the "Grand Dame of Ithaca." Dine in a converted 19th-century mansion that features regional foods and wines. D, daily. Major credit cards.

CORNING–ELMIRA AREA

Lodge on the Green. *Expensive.* Rte. 15S at Gang Mills exit, Corning; 607–962–2456. Continental menu with pleasant atmosphere and service. Features Finger Lakes wines. L, D, daily. Major credit cards.

Genghis Khan Chinese Restaurant. *Moderate.* 84 E. Market St., Corning; 607–962–6176. Famous for its Mongolian barbecue. Extensive Cantonese/Szechuan menu. L, D, daily. Major credit cards.

Moretti's Restaurant. *Moderate.* 800 Hatch St., Elmira; 607–734–1535. Popular Italian menu with friendly service. D, daily. AE, DC, MC, V.

Pierce's 1894 Restaurant. *Moderate.* 228 Oakwood Ave., Elmira; 607–734–2022. Long-established restaurant with variety of American, continental, and Chinese dishes. Extensive wine cellar. D, Tuesdays–Sundays. No credit cards.

Pierri's Restaurant. *Moderate.* 58 Ferris St., Corning; 607–936–3171. Seafoods, steaks, and Italian specialties. B, L, D, Mondays–Fridays; L, D, Saturdays. Major credit cards.

Sorge's Restaurant. *Moderate.* 66–68 W. Market St., Corning; 607–937–5422. A long-established Italian restaurant that attracts a loyal following with its good, plentiful meals, friendly service, daily specials, and pasta buffet. B, L, D, daily. No credit cards.

KEUKA LAKE AREA

Pleasant Valley Inn. *Expensive.* Rte. 54, Bath–Hammondsport Rd., Hammondsport; 607–569–2282. Lovely inn and grounds. Vineyard in front. Elegant

Victorian-style dining room with fine food and imaginative menu. Local wines featured. L, D, Tuesdays–Sundays. Major credit cards.

Switzerland Inn. *Expensive.* 1249 East Lake Rd., Hammondsport; 607–292–6927. Lakeside, docking, daily specials, Finger Lakes wine list. Gift shop. L, D, daily, Tuesdays–Sundays. Major credit cards.

The Vintage. *Expensive.* Rte. 54A between Hammondsport and Branchport; 607–868–3455. Picture window view of the bluff and lake. Private docks for diners who arrive by boat. Popular spot with beef and seafood specialties. L, D, daily. Open May–October. MC, V.

The Keuka. *Moderate.* 12 Main St., Penn Yan; 315–536–805. Popular spot especially with families. B, L, D, daily. Major credit cards.

Lakeside. *Moderate.* Rte. 54A, 7 miles north of Hammondsport; 607–868–3636. On lake, nautical atmosphere. Steaks, seafood, Italian food. Large dock. L, daily July and August; D, daily. AE, DC, MC, V.

ROCHESTER AREA

Rio Bamba. *Deluxe.* 282 Alexander St., downtown; 716–473–2806. Distinctive and popular dining room since 1950. Classic food and service with extensive wine list. D, Mondays–Saturdays. AE, DC, MC, V.

The Strathallan. *Deluxe.* 550 East Ave. in Strathallan Hotel; 716–461–5010. French gourmet cuisine; boeuf Wellington is a specialty. L, D, daily. AE, DC, MC, V.

The Budapest Restaurant. *Expensive.* 253 Alexander St., downtown; 716–325–3700. Authentic Hungarian food and atmosphere, entertainment. D, Mondays–Saturdays. AE, CB, DC, MC, V.

The Changing Scene. *Expensive.* 120 First Federal Plaza, downtown; 716–232–3030. Revolving rooftop restaurant offering a panoramic view and fine dining. L, Mondays–Fridays; D, Mondays–Saturdays, brunch, Sundays. AE, DC, MC, V.

Lesley's Cafe and Wine Bar. *Expensive.* 200 S. Plymouth Ave., in the historic Corn Hill area; 716–232–5100. Wonderful homemade soups and fresh foods. Wine bar. Light jazz, Friday nights. L, Mondays–Fridays; D, Tuesdays–Saturdays. Major credit cards.

Royal Scot. *Expensive.* 657 Ridge Road East, Irondequoit; 716–342–4220. Dine in a Scottish castle on steaks, prime ribs, seafood, and veal specialties. Live entertainment Fridays and Saturdays in Scot's Pub. L, Mondays–Fridays; D, daily; brunch, Sundays. AE, CB, DC, MC, V.

Spring House. *Expensive.* 3001 Monroe Ave.; 716–586–2300. Traditional American menu served in restored 1829 colonial inn. L, D, Tuesdays–Sundays. AE, MC, V.

SENECA LAKE AREA

Belhurst Castle. *Expensive.* Rte. 14, Geneva; 315–781–0201. A most elegant 100-year Romanesque mansion overlooking Seneca Lake with fine goods. Finger Lakes wines featured. Eat on terrace in summer months. L, buffet, D, daily. AE, DC, MC, V.

The Dresden. *Moderate.* Rtes. 14 and 54., Dresden; 315–536–9023. Long-established popular dining room that features king crab and prime ribs. L, D, Tuesdays–Sundays. Major credit cards.

Glen Motor Inn Wine Country Restaurant. *Moderate.* Rte. 14, Watkins Glen, 607–535–2706. Italian and American dishes with an extensive New York State wine list. B, L, D, daily. MC, V.

Town House Restaurant. *Moderate.* 108 N. Franklin St., Watkins Glen; 607–535–4619. Varied menu with casual atmosphere. Local favorite. D, daily. Major credit cards.

Wing Tai Oriental Restaurant. *Moderate.* Castle and Main sts., Geneva; 315–789–8892. Extensive Cantonese, Hunan, and Szechuan menu with large selection of Finger Lakes wines. L, D, Mondays–Saturdays. AE, MC, V.

SKANEATELES

The Krebs. *Expensive.* 53 W. Genesee St., Skaneateles; 315–685–5714. This has been a landmark since 1899, and is operated by the third generation of the founding family. The seven-course dinners are what made Krebs famous, but there are lighter dinners for those with smaller appetites. Open May–October. D, daily; brunch, Sundays. CB, DC, MC, V.

Mandana Inn. *Expensive.* Rte. 41A, 6 miles south of Skaneateles; 315–685–7798. Seafood featured in this pleasant colonial inn. Closed January–March. D, Wednesdays–Mondays. AE, CB, DC.

Sherwood Inn. *Expensive.* 26 W. Genesee St., Skaneateles; 315–685–3405. Overlooking the lake and continuing the hospitality that began back in 1807 when it opened as a stagecoach stop. Fine American and French fare in handsome dining rooms. L, D, daily. AE, CB, DC, MC, V.

Doug's Fish Fry. *Moderate.* 8 Jordan St., Skaneateles; 315–685–3288. Local favorite. Fish is direct from Boston and chowder is fresh and delicious. L, D, daily. No credit cards.

SYRACUSE AREA

Barbuto's. *Expensive.* 50 Presidential Plaza; 315–474–3000. Intimate atmosphere with continental and Italian cuisine. L, Mondays–Fridays; D, Mondays–Saturdays. Major credit cards.

Daphne's Steakhouse on the Green. *Expensive.* 200 Waring Rd.; 315–445–1976. Despite name, features continental and American cuisine. Country setting overlooking greens at Tecumseh Hills Club. Rustic elegance. L, D, daily. AE, DC, MC, V.

Nikki's Downtown. *Expensive.* 201 S. Salina St.; 315–424–1171. Continental dining with tableside cooking at LeGueridon or dine in casual elegance at New Orleans Bistro with Cajun–Creole cuisine. Wine bar. L, D, daily. AE, DC, MC, V.

Pascale Wine Bar & Restaurant. *Expensive.* 304 Hawley Ave.; 315–471–3040. Award-winning restaurant featuring French and northern Italian cuisine. Extensive wine list. D, Monday–Saturday, 6 P.M.–10 P.M., lounge menu 6–midnight. Closed Sun. Major credit cards.

Garfield's Restaurant. *Moderate.* 831 W. Genesee St.; 315–479–6621. All-you-can-eat crab legs a specialty. Featuring seafood, steaks, Italian food, pizza, giant sandwiches. L, D, daily. Major credit cards.

Trivet House. *Moderate.* 7 North St. and Buckley Rd.; 315–451–1040. Early American atmosphere with most generous portions. L, Mondays–Fridays; D, daily. AE, DC, MC, V.

CENTRAL LEATHERSTOCKING
REGION

by
DIANE GALLO

The Central Leatherstocking region is one of New York's "roads less traveled." Whereas tourists have left deep ruts in other areas, in Leatherstocking they've left mostly wildflowers in wagon tracks. The area's simple rural character is its biggest charm. Although there's plenty to see and do, many areas of this region are less "tourist-sophisticated" than others.

As you move deep into Leatherstocking, towns are fewer and farther between. Industry leaves less and less of a mark, and time slows down. New pictures come into focus. Rivers, streams, and brooks glitter like diamond necklaces upon emerald hillsides. Forests of hardwood and pine and fields of corn and alfalfa form a living patchwork. Farmers on tractors slow traffic down to a hay-chopping crawl.

Leatherstocking Country, which takes its name from the leather leggings worn by early-day pioneers, is a nine-county, 7,000-square-mile area in New York's agricultural and dairy heartland. It is quintessential country, the kind of country that glossy magazines like to sell. In the kitchens of the white frame farmhouses, kettles steam on woodstoves. In the small towns and hamlets, politics are conservative. Entertainment usually means church suppers and firemen's picnics. Canning jars and blue-ribbon preserves are easier to come by than imported wines.

Picturesque countryside glues together the region's three major tourist centers of the Mohawk Valley–Utica region, the Cooperstown area, and the Binghamton area.

The Mohawk Valley

The Mohawk Valley runs east and west through the center of Leatherstocking Country, forming the only natural divide in the Appalachian mountain chain. This "passing zone" made it of strategic importance to warring colonial factions because whoever controlled the Mohawk Valley controlled the heart of the North American continent. As a result, some of the bloodiest battles of the American Revolution were fought here. Of major interest are the Oriskany Battlefield, Fort Stanwix—a reconstructed Revolutionary War outpost—and the Erie Canal Village where the first shovelful of dirt was turned in 1817 for the Erie Canal.

With the opening of the canal, the Mohawk Valley became a center of industrial development. Utica, Leatherstocking's largest city, became a focus for that development. Utica is now home to the Children's Museum of History, Natural History, and Science, the Utica Zoo, and the widely known and highly respected Munson-Williams-Proctor Institute.

While in Utica, tour F.X. Matt's Brewery, interesting, opulent, and free. At the nearby Herkimer "Diamond" mines, try your luck prospecting for quartz crystals. If breaking rock is not your idea of fun, prospect for bargains at the Charlestown Factory Outlet Center.

Cooperstown

South of the Mohawk Valley region is Leatherstocking's most famous attraction—Cooperstown. This exquisitely historic area was made famous by James Fenimore Cooper in his *Leatherstocking Tales.* Lake Otsego, Cooper's beloved Glimmerglass (and a source of joy to bass fishermen), provides a beautiful backdrop for some unique attractions.

Enjoy the great moments of an American obsession at the National Baseball Hall of Fame. Vibrate along with the high notes sung by the nationally acclaimed Glimmerglass Opera which has its new home in the Alice Busch Opera Theater. Nearby, at the Farmer's Museum and Village Crossroads, get a first hand look at how early Americans really lived. At the Fenimore House, see one of the country's finest collections of American Folk Art.

Binghamton Area

In the southwest corner of Leatherstocking Country is Binghamton, the region's gateway city and center of the Tri-Cities area which in-

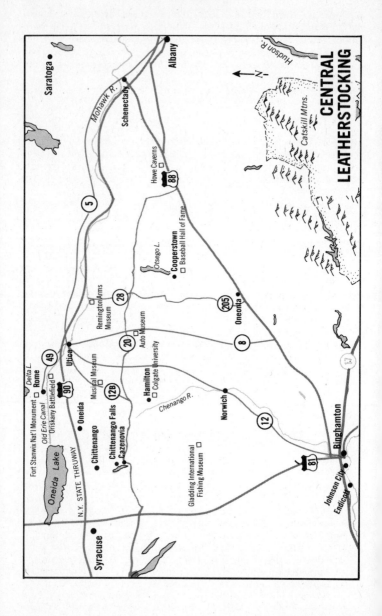

cludes Johnson City and Endicott. As the region's "front parlor" business center at the turn of the century, Binghamton bristled with smokestacks. Today, however, Binghamton is located in what has become known as the "Valley of Opportunity." The city was recently cited as a national example of a community that's made the successful transition from smokestack to high-tech economy.

Binghamton enjoys a reputation for safety and a high quality of life. The city offers a little of everything you might expect of a proper city—museum, galleries, zoo, performing arts centers, cultural and sporting events, restaurants, and shopping. High on the list are Roberson Center for the Arts and Sciences, Anderson Center for the Performing Arts, and Ross Park Zoo. In neighboring Vestal Center is New York's largest celestial observatory, Kopernik. Binghamton also offers pleasant surprises, such as a beautifully planned and renewed urban center and an unusual variety of onion dome churches.

Regional

Between the major tourist areas are scattered many regional attractions, like the spectacular Howe Caverns—the underground geological wonder of the Northeast—and the battle-scarred walls of the Old Stone Fort at Schoharie.

In the less touristy areas, a little patience unearths pleasing Yankee towns like Norwich (impressive Greek Revival courthouse and historic preservation district) and Hamilton (pay attention to the architecture and tour Colgate College's idyllic ivy-covered campus). Other good regional bets are Cazenovia (the lake, the town, charming country inns, and Lorenzo) and nearby Chittenango Falls (wonderfully refreshing).

PRACTICAL INFORMATION FOR THE
CENTRAL LEATHERSTOCKING REGION

HOW TO GET THERE. Leatherstocking Country is about 200 miles northwest of New York City and can be reached by bus, plane, train and car. **By Bus.** Bus service is available throughout all areas of this region. Routes crisscross the region and provide effective point-to-point service. However, buses lack the door-to-door service required by rural "roads." Carriers include *Adirondack Trailways, Broome County Transit, Capital Trailways, Central New York Coach, Chenango Valley, Greyhound, Short Line (Hudson Transit), Syracuse & Oswego, Utica-Rome,* and *Trailways.*

By Air Three airports serve the Leatherstocking region. Utica–Rome and Oneonta (Cooperstown) are served by *Catskill Airways,* 607–432–8222 or 800–252–2144 and *Piedmont Airlines,* 800–251–5720. Binghamton (Broome County's Edwin A. Link Field) Airport is serviced by *Continental Express,* 607–770–9462; *Piedmont Airlines,* 800–251–5720, and *USAir,* 607–729–6111.

By Train. Amtrak services Amsterdam, Utica, and Rome.

By Car. The region is framed by the rough triangle formed by Interstates 90, 81, and 88. I–90 (the New York State Thruway) is a major east-west route that cuts across the northern part of Leatherstocking and connects Albany with Utica and other Mohawk Valley towns before leading west to Syracuse and Buffalo. Because of a bridge collapse on I–90 (the Thruway) near Amsterdam, travelers should use alternate Rtes. 5 or 20 around that area. A temporary bridge is scheduled to be in place by mid-1988. However, it would be wise to get a status report as you enter the region. Intersecting I–90 at Syracuse is I–81, a north-south connection to Binghamton. For a direct (and incredibly scenic) route from Binghamton to Albany, take I–88. The region is less than four hours from New York City via the New York State Thruway.

TELEPHONES. There are three area codes for the Leatherstocking Region. In the southern part—the counties of Broome (Binghamton), Chenango, and Otsego (Cooperstown)—the area code is 607. In the northern part—Madison, Oneida, and Herkimer (Mohawk Valley)—the area code is 315. In the northeastern sections—Montgomery, Hamilton, and Schoharie counties —the area code is 518.

When dialing a number from within the same area code as the number, you don't need to use the area code. An operator will help you with person-to-person, credit-card, and collect calls if you dial "0" first. For information within the same dialing area, dial "1," then 555–1212. For information outside the dialing area, dial "1," the area code, and then 555–1212. There is a one-minute initial minimum period on all coin toll calls plus a 50¢ surcharge.

ACCOMMODATIONS. "You get what you pay for" is a good rule in Leatherstocking. With few exceptions, most accommodations fall within the inexpensive-to-moderate range. Generally, rates remain the same the year round. One exception, however, is Cooperstown, a summer resort area that shuts down in mid-October. Here the Memorial Day–Labor Day rates are 10–15 percent higher than off-season rates. Except during winter when only a few motels and bed-and-breakfasts remain open, Cooperstown always requires reservations at least six weeks ahead of time. There is no room surcharge.

In Broome County (Binghamton) the room surcharge is 1 percent of the room rate and the rates remain constant year round. The only time you'll have trouble finding a room here is when your trip coincides with a State University of New York function—late May graduations or early-to-mid-October parents weekends. The same is true in outlying university towns like Oneonta, Cobleskill, and Hamilton.

In the Mohawk Valley region, it's almost always possible to get a hotel room even in the busy June–September season. The rates remain constant throughout the year and the room surcharge is 2 percent. Depending upon the area, sales tax in the Leatherstocking region ranges between 4 and 7 percent.

Central Leatherstocking hotels and motels are what you might expect from their moderate price range. They are very clean, quite comfortable, and fairly unremarkable.

Rates for double occupancy average as follows: *Deluxe,* $80–$100; *Expensive,* $70–$79; *Moderate,* $60–$69; *Inexpensive,* $50–$59; *Basic Budget,* under $50.

MOHAWK VALLEY REGION

Moderate

Best Western Little Falls Motor Inn. 20 Albany St., Little Falls, 13365; 315–823–4954. 56 rooms. Midtown. Everything you'd expect from a Best Western: cafe, cocktail lounge, twin cinemas.

Sheraton Inn & Conference Center. 200 Genesee St., Utica, 13502; 315–797–8010; 800–325–3535. 156 large, modern rooms. Indoor heated pool, whirlpool, and sauna; game room, health club, lounge, skylit dining room with a bamboo and jungle decor.

Basic Budget

The Beeches–Paul Revere Lodge. Rte. 26, Turin Road, Rome, 13440; 315–336–1776. 52-acre resort with 74 rooms in Early American decor, restaurant, breakfast room, golf course.

Carriage Motor Inn. Thruway Exit at Rte. 233, Westmoreland, 13490; 315–853–3561. 22 rooms. Quiet country setting, spacious grounds and gardens.

Family Inns of America. 145 E. Whitesboro St., Rome, 13440 (across from Fort Stanwix); 315–337–9400. 57 rooms. Within walking distance of Revereware Factory Store. Tour planning assistance.

Herkimer Motel. I–90 exit 30 and Rte. 28, 100 Marginal Rd., Herkimer, 13350; 315–866–6080. 60 rooms.

Ramada Inn. 1710 Burrstone Rd., Utica, 13413; 315–735–9231, or 800–2–RAMADA. 79 rooms.

Utica Travelodge. 1700 Genesee St., Utica, 13502; 315–724–2101, or 800–255–3050. 47 rooms.

COOPERSTOWN AREA

Expensive

The Otesaga Hotel. Lake Street, Box 311, Cooperstown, 13326; 607–547–9931. Resort hotel with golf, tennis (complimentary), heated outdoor pool, and sailing, boating, and fishing on Otsego Lake. Summer season: $66–$70 per person double occupancy. Spring and fall seasons: $64–$68. No charge for children under 2. Rates, subject to 6 percent tax, include breakfast and dinner daily. Dress code; no pets.

Moderate

The Cooper Inn. Lake and Chestnut Sts., Cooperstown, 13326; 607–547–2567. 20 rooms. July–Labor Day, $66–$70; spring/fall seasons, $62–$66; cot or crib, $8. Otesaga facilities available to guests.

Deer Run Motel. RD 2, Box 722, Cooperstown, 13326; 607–547–8600. Year-round. 46 acres. Enjoys excellent ratings.

Hickory Grove Motor Inn. RD 2, Box 896, Cooperstown, 13326; 607–547–9874. Open May 15–October 15; lake frontage.

BINGHAMTON AREA

Expensive

Best Western Hotel de Ville. 80 State St., Binghamton, 13901; 607–722–7272. 63 exceptional rooms. Downtown location, complimentary garage parking, exercise room, Valet, restaurant, cocktail lounge, banquet and meeting rooms. The hotel is the Old City Hall building, an outstanding example of French Renaissance architecture in the late Beaux Arts style listed on the National Register of Historic Places.

Holiday Inn–Arena, 8 Hawley St., Binghamton, 13901; 607–722–1212. 250 rooms. Downtown location, restaurant, cocktail lounge, indoor pool overlooking Riverside Promenade, indoor/outdoor dining, banquet and meeting rooms.

Moderate

Howard Johnson's. 700 Front St., Binghamton, 13903; 607–724–1341. 106 rooms, restaurant, cocktail lounge, outdoor pool, banquet room.

Ramada Inn. 65 Front St., Binghamton, 13905; 607–724–2412. 135 rooms, restaurants, three cocktail lounges, indoor pool, banquet and meeting rooms.

Inexpensive

Scott's Oquaga Lake House. Oquaga Lake, Deposit, 13754; 607–476–3094. 114-room-resort. Lake with swimming, water skiing, canoeing, sailing, fishing, cruises, golf, tennis, entertainment/dancing nightly. Banquet and meeting rooms. Rates include three meals daily and all recreation and entertainment. No-tipping policy. Rates: double, $53–$59 per person per day. Special rates by the week or for children.

Quality Inn Endicott. Delaware Avenue, Endicott, 13760; 607–754–7570. 142 rooms. Restaurant and lounge.

Basic Budget

Binghamton Days Inn. I-81 and Front Street, Binghamton, 13901; 607–724–3297. 106 rooms, new lodge with a mauve and pastel lobby, outdoor pool.

Fireside Motor Lodge. 1156 Front St., Binghamton, 13905; 607–722–5353. 70 rooms, 24 efficiencies.

REGIONAL

Deluxe

Brae Loch Inn. U.S. Rte. 20, 5 Albany St., Cazenovia, 13035; 315–655–3431. Only 9 rooms, but special, with great big four-poster beds; foil wrapped chocolates on the pillows.

Expensive

Lincklaen House. 79 Albany St., Cazenovia, 13035; 315–655–3461. 27 rooms; double, $50–85.

Inexpensive

Colgate Inn. On the Green, Hamilton, 13346; 315–824–2300. 40 rooms; restaurant.

Holiday Inn of Oneonta. Rte. 23, Oneonta, 13820; 607–433–2250. 120 rooms, restaurant, cocktail lounge, banquet and meeting rooms, heated outdoor pool, adjacent to bowling and roller skating.

Howard Johnson's Motor Lodge. 75 North Broad St., Norwich, 13815; 607–334–2200 or 800–654–2000. 82 rooms, restaurant, lounge.

 BED-AND-BREAKFASTS. The more highly organized tourist areas of Leatherstocking tend toward hotels and motels, whereas bed-and-breakfasts appear mainly in the rural regions. Those listed here are just a representative sampling of what's available. For more information, write or call the *Leatherstocking Bed & Breakfast Association of Central New York,* Brockway Road, Frankfort, 13340 (315–733–0040) or check with local chambers of commerce (see *Tourist Information* section below) for the area you plan to visit. As with any B & B, reserve rooms well in advance. Prices vary within a

Moderate ($60–$69) range. Make sure you inquire about credit card policies when making reservations. Many B & B's do not accept them.

REGIONAL

The Brewster Inn. Cazenovia, 13035; 315–655–9232. Nestled on the southern shore of Cazenovia Lake. Not quite a B & B, but not quite a hotel, the Brewster is billed as an elegant country inn. Under continual restoration, the inn limits itself to eight guests. Well known for its fine dining, the inn serves lunch and dinner Tuesdays–Sundays.

Brook Willow Farm, RD 2, Box 514, Cooperstown, 13326; 607–547–9700. Inn with Victorian "cottage house," restored barn, Victorian gardens. Full country breakfast included.

Cedar Court. Polkville Hill, Norwich, 13815; 607–336–3333. Unusual for this part of the country—California-style architecture overlooking the picturesque Yankee-style town of Norwich. The hosts have a flair for making guests feel special and very welcome.

 HOW TO GET AROUND. When you think Leatherstocking, think distance. Travel between any given point and any given airport or bus terminal can be time consuming. On balance, however, there are rarely any traffic jams or parking problems in the region. Although there are limousine and taxi services, don't plan to depend upon them. You need a car. Leatherstocking's airports are fairly small, so there's no chance of getting lost in any of the terminals. The region's only mass transit carrier is *B.C. Transit,* (607) 722–3692, which operates within Binghamton and Broome County. Fares are 50¢ during peak hours, 25¢ in off hours.

MOHAWK VALLEY–UTICA

Brognano Airport Limousine. Oneida County Airport, Oriskany; 315–736–9601 or 315–337–5454. From the airport to downtown Utica is 12 miles. Fee: $10 to hotels, $12 to residences for one person; $14 for two people (same destination); three people or more, $6 each. Call for out-of-town trip rates.

Avis, 315–797–5255 or 800–331–1212, will rent you a mid-size late model car for $56.88 per day with unlimited mileage. Advance reservations and valid driver's license required. All major credit cards.

BINGHAMTON

Airlines Limousine Service. 750 Harry L. Drive, Johnson City; 607–729–3111. Edwin A. Link Field is 8 miles northwest of Binghamton. Cost of a trip from airport to downtown Binghamton, Johnson City, or Endicott is $9; for local continual use, $25 per hour. Out-of-town rates: $1 per mile one-way. These rates are at or just below average for limo/cab service in the Binghamton area.

Budget/Sears Rent-a-Car. The Sheraton Binghamton/Sears, 607–723–8281, and Broome County airport, 607–729–0833 or 800–527–0700. Mid-size car $35.95 per day and 100 free miles; 20¢ for each additional mile. Call for weekend and weekly specials. Reserve in advance. All major credit cards.

ONEONTA (Cooperstown Area)

Ken's Taxi Service. Pony Farm Road, Oneonta 607–432–0046 or 433–2005. This service shuts down after 11 P.M. unless otherwise reserved in advance.

Charge for trip from airport to downtown Oneonta is $5.50 per person, 50¢ for each additional person going to the same destination. Out-of-town trips: $1 per mile.

Car rentals are available at *Country Club Chevrolet,* 70 Oneida St., Oneonta; 607–432–6190 or 800–621–7333. All major credit cards honored. A mid-size car is $15 per day and 18¢ per mile; weekly rate is $98 a week plus 18¢ per mile. Reserve in advance for airport pickup.

TOURIST INFORMATION The Binghamton, Cooperstown, and Mohawk Valley–Utica areas have visitors and tourist bureaus that publish a variety of free maps, booklets, and brochures containing information about accommodations, restaurants, shopping, and entertainment. In other areas, the local chamber of commerce usually functions as a center for information and referral. Offices listed here with addresses are usually open Mondays–Fridays, 9 A.M.–5 P.M.

Association of Cazenovia Businesses, Box 66, Cazenovia, 13035; 315–655–3856.

Broome County Convention & Visitors Bureau, Security Mutual Building, 80 Exchange St., Box 995, Binghamton, 13902; 607–772–8860.

Boonville Area Chamber of Commerce, 119 Main St., Boonville, 13309; 315–942–2459.

Chenango County Chamber of Commerce, 29 Lackawanna Ave., Box 249, Norwich, 13815; 607–334–3236.

Cooperstown Chamber of Commerce, Chestnut Street, Box 46, Cooperstown; 607–547–9983.

Herkimer County Chamber of Commerce, 19 W. Main St., Box 25, Mohawk, 13407; 315–866–7820.

Leatherstocking Country, 200 N. Prospect St., Herkimer, 13350 315–866–1500.

Montgomery County Chamber of Commerce, 9 market St., Amsterdam, 12010; 518–842–8200.

Oneida County Convention & Visitors Bureau, Box AA, Oriskany, 13424; Utica, 315–736–2999; Rome, 315–865–8600; Information for the entire Mohawk Valley Region, 800–237–0100 within the state, and 800–426–3132 out of state.

Otsego County Chamber of Commerce, 58 Market Ave., Oneonta, 13820; 607–432–4500.

Otsego County Tourism Bureau, 197 Main St., Cooperstown, 13326; 607–547–4225.

Schoharie County Promotion Department, Box 548, Schoharie, 12157; 518–295–8522.

FOREIGN CURRENCY EXCHANGE in Leatherstocking Country is iffy at best. Depending upon what type of currency you need to exchange, the wait can be anywhere from a week to 10 days. If you've got to convert, do it in New York City or another major metropolitan area.

SEASONAL EVENTS. In addition to all the traditional holidays, Leatherstocking celebrates the changing seasons with events both major and minor. Aside from those listed here (most of which are free), many smaller events and activities occur all year long. Most towns have farmers' markets

(Saturday mornings on the village greens), church suppers, firemen's picnics, and day-long observances of historical or other events. Check local newspapers and shoppers' bulletins for these happenings. Most "open town" events, like harvest festivals, Utica's Good Old Summertime Festival and Norwich's Fourth of July Balloon Festival, are free. Other events charge only a nominal fee.

Start off the New Year right at the *Annual Winter Festival* in Richfield Springs in **January** and get out your winter woolies for the *Annual Winter Carnival* in Cooperstown in **February.**

March is a quiet month in Leatherstocking, but keep the long johns out and an eye open. Local maple sugar events (New York outproduces Vermont) throughout the region and at Timian's Maple Farms in Sauquoit. In **April** when spring is busting out all over, visit the *Annual Cheese Festival* at the Erie Canal Village in Rome.

In **May,** Utica's Memorial Auditorium features music, arts, crafts, dances, and foods of 20 national heritage groups during its *Celebration of Nations,* and Oneonta hosts the *Annual Blue Grass Festival.*

In **June,** Old Forge is hopping when competitors brush off their best frogs for the *Frog Jumping Contest* and Binghamton explodes with fireworks for the *BC Pops on the River* concert.

July is Leatherstocking's busiest month. Binghamton celebrates summer with the *July Fest,* one of Broome County's biggest events. Lighten up at the Fourth of July *Balloon Festival* in Norwich and hold on to your horses at the *Horse and Carriage Driving Competition* at Lorenzo in Cazenovia. Utica has a 10-day *Good Old Summertime* Festival with parades, sidewalk crafts and performances, and an art show. The last weekend in July, try the *Americana Village Arts and Crafts Fair* in Hamilton.

In **August,** the National Baseball Hall of Fame has its Induction Ceremonies and *Hall of Fame Game* in Cooperstown and Madison-Bouckville has its annual *Antique Show* (usually the third weekend in August).

On Labor Day weekend in **September,** the SUNY campus in Cobleskill hosts the *Iroquois Indian Festival.* Later in the month Cooperstown holds the *Annual Beaver Valley Bluegrass Festival* and the *Farmers' Museum Autumn Harvest Festival.*

Throughout Leatherstocking Country, **October** is ripe with *harvest festivals, Oktoberfests,* and other autumn celebrations.

In **November,** Herkimer hosts the annual Herkimer County *Arts & Crafts Fair* and Rome prepares for the holidays with its *Christmas Craft Workshop.*

December offers very special Christmas observances and exhibitions at Roberson Center in Binghamton, Lorenzo in Cazenovia, and at the Farmers' Museum in Cooperstown.

For more information about seasonal events, contact *Leatherstocking Country,* 200 North Prospect St., Herkimer, 13350; 315–866–1550. Or contact the appropriate local visitors bureau or chamber of commerce (see *Tourist Information* section above).

 RECOMMENDED READING. In this listing, books not available through libraries can be obtained through publishers or through local historical associations. Among fictional titles, the best are any of James Fenimore Cooper's *Leatherstocking Tales.* Also: *Drums Along the Mohawk,* Walter Edmonds, Little, Brown, Boston: 1936; and *Tall Tales of the Catskills,* Frank L. Dumund, New York State Historical Association, Cooperstown: 1968.

Other selections: *Diary of a Binghamton Boy in the 1860's,* Morris Treadwell, Union Press, Endicott: 1982.

Broome County Heritage: An Illustrated History, Lawrence Bothwell, Broome County Historical Society, Binghamton, 1983.

Cherry Valley Country, Emily Williams, Brodock Press, Utica, 1978.

Landmarks of Otsego County (photo guide), Diane Schull, Syracuse University Press, Syracuse: 1980.

Cooperstown: Where Baseball's Legends Live Forever, Sporting News Publishing Co., St. Louis: 1983

Pages and Pictures From the Writings of James Fenimore Cooper, Susan Fenimore Cooper, Castle Books, Secaucus, NJ: 1980

Cooperstown, Louis C. Jones, New York State Historical Association, Cooperstown: 1985

Happy Valley—the Elegant 80's in Upstate New York, Pauline Dakin Taft, Syracuse University Press, Syracuse: 1965.

Through Poverty's Vale—A Hardscrabble Boyhood in Upstate New York, 1832–1862, Henry Conklin, Syracuse University Press, Syracuse: 1974.

TOURS Although there are chartered bus tours for groups in Leatherstocking Country, few are suitable for individual or family sightseeing. However, being on your own should present no problem with this list of things to do and see.

Cherry Valley Historical Association. Main St., Cherry Valley, 13320; 607–264–3303. Walking tours of the site of the infamous Revolutionary War massacre. By appointment.

Colgate University. Hamilton, 13346; 315–824–1000, Ext. 401. Idyllic ivy-covered walls, beautifully landscaped grounds, striking architecture on campus and off. Today's dorms were the gracious 19th-century homes that lined Hamilton's Main Street in years past. By appointment.

Harden Furniture Factory. Mill Pond Way, McConnellsville, 13401; 315–245–1000. Tours (no sales) give a fascinating look at the manufacturing process of fine wood and upholstered furniture. Follows the process from choosing the right wood to finishing. A similar tour is conducted at Ethan Allen Furniture Factory, Grove St., Boonville, 13309; 315–942–4471. Write or call for arrangements.

Howe Caverns, Howes Cave, 12092; 518–296–8990. Open all year, 9 A.M.–6 P.M. Cavern tour includes a quarter-mile underground boat ride. Howe Caverns is Leatherstocking's underground natural wonder. Underneath the deceptively picturesque countryside lies a hidden prehistoric world. Guided tours through caverns that wind for nearly a mile-and-a-half along paved walkways and over manmade and natural bridges. Knowledgeable guides describe and explain the many unique rock formations like the Titan's Temple with its Chinese Pagoda. Adults, $7; children 7–12, $3.25; under 6, free.

Lake Otsego Boat Tours. Box 787, Cooperstown, 13326; 607–547–5295 or 607–547–9606. One-hour cruise tours of James Fenimore Cooper's Glimmerglass Lake on the 55-foot *Chief Uncas.* Frequent departures July–Labor Day. Adults, $6; children 3–12, $3; under 3, free. Charters upon request.

Timian's Maple Farms. Between Rtes. 8 and 12, 8 miles south of Utica, Sauquoit; 315–839–5585. Learn about the history of the maple sugar industry. Sugarhouse tour includes operation of traditional working farm with sheep shearing, cow milking, farm animals. Gift shop and picnic area. March 15–October 31, or by chance or by appointment. Free.

Upstate Sightseeing Tours. 13 Syosset Lane, Cazenovia, 13035; 315–655–8790. Offers guide service and preplanned custom package tours of the entire Leatherstocking Region.

SPECIAL-INTEREST SIGHTSEEING. Griffiss Air Force Base. 416th Bomb Wing, Public Affairs, Rome, 13441; 315–330–3057. Reservations must be made three days in advance by calling the Wing Public Affairs Office. Griffiss is a Strategic Air Command base. Free tours take about an hour. They're conducted Wednesdays and Fridays June–September and begin at 1 P.M. at the Floyd Avenue gate parking lot. The KC-135 Strato-tanker and the B-52 Stratofortress are impressive.

F. X. Matt Brewery Tour. 811 Edward St., Utica, 13503; 315–732–3181. In June, July, and August, Mondays–Saturdays, 10 A.M.–5 P.M. September–May, Mondays–Saturdays, noon–4 P.M. (reservations required during this period) Tours offer visitors a warm welcome at the beginning and a cold beer or root beer at the end. The brewery tour, trolley shuttle, and a visit to an 1888 tavern takes about an hour. Best of all, it's free.

Rogers Environmental Center, Box Q, Sherburne, 13460; 607–674–2861. The 571-acre center is dedicated to the appreciation and conservation of natural resources. A receptionist and educators are on hand to answer questions. Interpretive nature trails, exhibits, demonstrations, and public information programs. Open year round. Outdoors, sunrise–sunset; buildings, weekdays 8:30 A.M.–4:45 P.M.; weekends 1–5 P.M. Free.

Susquehanna Urban Cultural Park. Self-guided walking tours of Binghamton, Johnson City, and Endicott. An urban cultural park gives visitors the opportunity to enjoy the natural features and the historic buildings and setting that reveal the story of a community's growth. Points of interest focus on historic preservation and recreational and educational potential. Pick up guide folders at the Broome County Chamber of Commerce, 80 Exchange St., Binghamton 13902; 607–772–8860.

PARKS. Visitors to the Leatherstocking Region have ample opportunity to relax, picnic, or take part in recreational activities in parks scattered throughout the region. In the Mohawk Valley–Utica area, the **Edward A. Hanna Park,** downtown Utica, features daily entertainment on five acres of landscaped gardens, a 100-foot Tower of Hope musical clock, a 50-foot waterfall, children's play area, and snack bar. Also in the area, there's the **Old Erie Canal State Park** right on the canal. Flat for a bike, picnic tables. Trails to bike, hike, and ski. Kirkville; 315–687–7821. In other areas:

BINGHAMTON AREA

Chenango Valley State Park. Rte 369, Chenango Forks; 13 miles north of Binghamton; 607–648–5251. Open year round. Parking $3.50 in summer. 1,071 acres. Offers boat rental, fishing, hiking, picnicking; 18-hole golf course; Bathing beach, camping, children's playgrounds.

Nathaniel Cole Park. Colesville Road, Harpursville; 607–693–1389. Twin arcs of white sand frame the beautiful 53-acre lake. Sand beach, lifeguards, changing areas with hot showers, restrooms, and coin operated lockers. Picnicking, nature trails, boat rentals, playing field, guided nature walks, recreational equipment, free parking.

COOPERSTOWN

Glimmerglass State Park. 4 miles south of Rte. 20 RD 2, Cooperstown; 607–547–8662. 593 acres for swimming, picnicking, camping, hiking, biking, fishing. Historic site here is the George Hyde Clark Estate. Parking $3.50 in summer.

REGIONAL

Bowman Lake State Park. Rte. 220, Oxford; 607–334–2718. Parking $3.50 in summer. 650 acres, ½ developed. Camping, picnic areas, boat rentals, fireplaces, hiking trails, 36-station interpretive nature trail, sand beach, swimming, lifeguards. Entertainment on park grounds throughout summer.

Chittenango Falls State Park, Chittenango; 315–655–9620. 192 acres with a 167-foot-high waterfall. Picnicking, hiking, restrooms; parking $2.50 in summer.

Gilbert Lake State Park. RD 1, Laurens; 607–432–2114. Parking $3.50 in summer. This huge (1,569 acres) park offers camping, picnicking, fishing and boating, hiking, bicycling, nature center recreation program, winter activities. Sand beach and swimming area, lifeguards, boat rentals, bathhouse with hot showers and a first aid room, rest rooms, and concession stand.

Verona Beach State Park. Rte. 13 (east shore of Oneida Lake), Verona Beach; 315–762–4463. Parking $3.50 in summer. Fishing, hiking, bathhouse, picnicking, swimming.

 ZOOS. Ross Park Zoo. 185 Park Ave., Binghamton, 13903; 607–724–5461. Open 10 A.M.–5 P.M. daily, late April–early November; weekends, November–April. Opened in 1875, it is one of the country's oldest zoos. With its varied terrain, rock ledges, and shale strata, the heavily wooded 25-acre compound exhibits animals in their natural habitat. Exhibits are identified with the animal's common and scientific name, regional distribution, feeding and mating patterns, and other vital information. (If you get a fancy for one of the animals, you can't take it home, but you can adopt it with Ross Park's Adopt-an-Animal program.) The compound also has a waterfowl pond, gift shop, amphitheater, and picnic facilities.

The woodland waters exhibit provides a naturalistic setting for beaver, otters, native waterfowl, and fish. Presently under construction is a cat country exhibit that will display cougars and other species. Visitor areas will be glass enclosed and the cats will live in natural settings with plantings, rock work, and a pool. Special crowd-pleasers include the timberwolf pack that thrives in a 2-½-acre wolf compound, and a children's petting zoo. Admission to zoo: adults, $2; children, $1; seniors, 75¢; under 2, free.

Utica Zoo. Steel Hill Rd., Utica, 13501; 315–738–0472. Open daily year round 10 A.M.–5 P.M. Children's Zoo operates from spring to fall. Features mammals, birds, reptiles, a children's zoo (domestic and wild) with petting area, picnic facilities. Located in Roscoe Conkling Park, which was designed by Frederick Law Olmsted, the zoo serves as a regional recreational and learning center. On its beautifully landscaped grounds, the zoo displays over 300 animals from all continents, habitats, and latitudes. Collection includes polar bears and Siberian tigers as well as tropical birds and primates. In Zoolab children and parents explore the contents of 10 self-discovery boxes dealing with such subjects as animal coverings, reptiles, and zoo animal diets. Most popular exhibits are the big cats and the California sea lions. Admission: adults, $2; children 2–12, $1.

GARDENS. Ross Park Zoological Gardens. 185 Park Ave., Binghamton, 13903; 607–724–5461. Open 10 A.M.–5 P.M. daily late April–early November; weekends, November–April. Animal and plant collections from major North American areas with emphasis on Northeastern ecosystem; waterfowl pond, varied terrain, rock ledges, and shale strata. Heavily wooded 25-acre compound exhibits animals in their natural habitat. Admission: adults, $1.25; children, 75 cents; under 2, free.

Root Glen. College Hill, Clinton. Perennial garden and arboretum. Nature walks spring to fall. No motorized equipment except motorized wheelchairs. Year round, dawn–dusk.

George Landis Arboretum. 2 miles north of town of Esperance; 518–875–6935. 50 acres of marked rare trees and shrubs and gardens. April–November 1, dawn–dusk.

BEACHES. Lacking oceanfront property, Leatherstocking does very well with lakeside beaches. A sampling: **Bowman Lake State Park,** Rte. 220, Oxford, 13830; 607–334–2718. Sand beach, swimming, lifeguards. Entertainment on park grounds throughout summer. Admission $3.50. **Gilbert Lake State Park,** Box 145, RD 1, Laurens, 13796; 607–432–2114. Sand beach and swimming area, lifeguards, boat rentals, bathhouse with hot showers and first aid room, rest rooms, concession stand, plenty of parking. Admission $3.50 per car til 4 P.M. on weekdays, $1.50 per car on weekends.

Nathaniel Cole Park. Colesville Rd., Harpursville, 13787; 607–693–1389. Twin arcs of white sand frame the beautiful 53-acre lake. Sand beach, lifeguards, changing areas with hot showers, restrooms, and coin operated lockers. Picnicking, nature trails, boat rentals and free parking.

Sylvan Beach. Box 515, Sylvan Beach, 13157; 315–762–9934. Conveniently located near the attractions of the Utica–Rome area, Sylvan Beach is a 4-mile public beach on the east shore of Oneida Lake with free swimming, bathhouse, fishing pier, picnic area, and village park with playground. An amusement park is adjacent to the beach.

Verona Beach State Park, Rte. 13 (east shore of Oneida Lake), Verona Beach, 13162; 315–762–4463. Swimming, bathhouse, comfort stations, picnicking, fishing, and hiking. Parking $3.50 in summer.

CHILDREN'S ACTIVITIES. Leatherstocking Country is family oriented. Although some attractions might be a bit esoteric for very young children, most let kids participate. The attractions listed here by area feature a "please touch me" policy.

BINGHAMTON

The Discovery Center The Discovery Center for children was moving from its location on Hawley St. in Binghamton to the Ross Park Zoo at press time. Sources say the center will be offering the same hands-on learning and fun experiences such as the computer corner and Nature Area, it has always had. Call the Ross Park Zoo for information at 607–724–5461.

UTICA–ROME AREA

Children's Museum, 311 Main St., Utica; 315–724–6128. A beautifully restored building houses what's billed as the finest children's museum between

New York City and Toronto. Free parking in the lot diagonally across from the museum. Open July 1–Labor Day, Tuesdays–Fridays, 10 A.M.–5 P.M.; Saturdays and Sundays 1–5 P.M. Labor Day–July 1, Wednesdays–Sundays 1–5 P.M. Closed most major holidays. Admission, $1; children under 2, free.

Erie Canal Village, Rome; 315–336–6000. Canal boat and steam rail rides; reconstructed 19th-century village; staff wears period dress. Demonstrations, seasonal events, visitors reception center, gift shops, and snack bar. Adults, $6; children 7–14, $3.50; under 6 free. Open daily 9:30 A.M.–5:30 P.M. from the last weekend in April through October 31.

Fort Rickey Game Farm, Rome; 315–336–1930. Exotic and native animals on exhibit, large petting and feeding area. Pony rides, picnic area. Open daily mid-May–Labor Day, 10 A.M.–6 P.M.; September–October, Saturdays and Sundays, same hours (Depending upon weather). Admission: adults, $2.50; children 3–13, $1.50.

REGIONAL

Howe Caverns, Howe Cave; 518–296–8990. Underneath the deceptively picturesque countryside lies a hidden prehistoric world of underground caverns that will fascinate people of all ages. Cavern tour includes a quarter-mile boat ride. Open all year, 9 A.M.–6 P.M. Adults, $7; children 7–12, $3.25; children under 6 free when accompanied by adults.

The Musical Museum, Rte. 12B, Deansboro; 315–841–8774. Seventeen rooms of "hands-on" music experience. Kids can crank, pump, and play restored music boxes, melodeons, nickelodeons, grind organs, and jukeboxes as well as other musical instruments. Don't miss the giant calliope in the parking area. Open daily April–Dec. 31, 10 A.M.–4 P.M. Adults, $4; children under 12 (accompanied by parent), free.

National Baseball Hall of Fame, Cooperstown; 607–547–9988. Open seven days a week year round including all holidays except Thanksgiving, Christmas, and New Year's. May 1–Oct. 31, 9 A.M.–9 P.M. November 1–April 30) 9 A.M.–5 P.M. Adults, $4; children 7–15, $1.50. If the kids are baseball fans, the Hall of Fame is for them. Most youngsters will enjoy the Hall, but a few of the younger non-fans may miss its charm.

Rogers Environmental Center, Sherburne; 607–674–2861. Here's one good thing in life that really is free. The 571-acre center is dedicated to the appreciation and conservation of natural resources. Interpretive nature trails, exhibits, demonstrations, and public information programs focus on young people learning about nature. Open year round. Outdoors: sunrise to sunset; buildings; weekdays, 8:30 A.M.–4:45 P.M.; weekends, 1–5 P.M. Free.

 PARTICIPANT SPORTS. The Leatherstocking region offers opportunity to enjoy a variety of sports. Almost every town has swimming pools and tennis courts open to the public, either free of charge or for a slight fee. The fishing is excellent with public access areas spotted along rivers and streams. Local and state parks (see Parks section above) also provide ample opportunity for **hiking, jogging, biking, swimming, boating, fishing,** and cross country **skiing** either for free or for a small fee.

Canoeing. *Canoes Along the Mohawk,* Rte. 46, Rome; 315–337–5172. Canoe or kayak rentals for 9–mile white- and still-water trip along historic Mohawk. Transportation return to starting point. Call for season, rates.

Horseback Riding. Brush up your equestrian skills at *H. Bar D. Ranch* (lessons; English and western styles) in Norwich; 607–334–9752; the *Thunder-*

bolt Farm (lessons; English) on Stokes Hill in Rome; 315–339–0661; *Paradise Ranch* (lessons; western) on Rte. 29A in Caroga Lake, 518–835–8331; and *Fieldstone Farm* (lessons; western) in Richfield Springs, 315–858–0295.

Golf. Since 9- and 18-hole courses abound in the area, those listed here are 18-hole courses. Call for current (modest) fees and starting times. *Afton Golf Club,* Afton, 607–639–2454; carts, rentals, bar, restaurant, and pro shop. *Seven Oaks Golf Club,* Hamilton, 315–824–1432; carts, bar, restaurant, and pro shop. *Canasawacta Country Club,* Norwich, 607–336–2685; carts, rentals, bar, restaurant, and pro shop. Golfers with short attention spans should try *Fort Putt Miniature* Golf on Rtes. 46 and 49 in Rome, 315–339–3333.

Skiing. Skiers can find downhill action at *Shu-maker Mountain* in Little Falls, 315–823–1111, which offers rentals, ski school, snow-making, night skiing, cafeteria, and lounge. *Snow Ridge Ski Area* in Turin, 315–348–8456 or 800–962–8419, offers a complete north country ski resort with 21 slopes, night skiing, cross country, ski school, rentals, restaurants, and lounge. *Ironwood Ridge* in Cazenovia, 315–655–9551, offers 7 slopes and trails, snowmaking equipment, and rentals. There is also great cross-country throughout Leatherstocking.

 SPECTATOR SPORTS. Canoe Race. On Memorial Day, cheer on the stalwart paddlers in the *General Clinton Canoe Regatta,* the nation's largest whitewater race, in Bainbridge. Sponsored by the Bainbridge Chamber of Commerce; 607–967–8700.

Baseball comes into full swing April–October, with the *Oneonta Yankees* (New York Yankees' Class A farm team) at Damaschke Field in Oneonta; 607–432–4500. Also the annual National Baseball *Hall of Fame Game* is played in July at Abner Doubleday Field in Cooperstown.

Motocross. In mid-July, the pace heats up with *U. S. Grand Prix Motocross* action at the Unadilla Valley Sports Center in New Berlin. Contact Ward Robinson, Box 5119F, Edmeston, 13335; 607–965–8784 or 607–847–8186.

Golf. Labor Day Weekend—$400,000 *Open PGA Golf Tournament.* For tickets, contact En-Joie Golf Club, Endicott, 13760; 607–754–2482.

Billiards. In late August–early-September is the Open 9-ball professional billiard tournament at the arena. American Productions, 225 Lester Ave., Johnson City, 13790; 607–729–4504.

Horse Racing. *Vernon Downs,* Vernon; 315–829–2201. Place your bets on spirited trotters and pacers competing for almost five million dollars in purses. Season mid-April–early November. Post times 1:30 and 7:30 P.M.

Polo. Here's a surprise—World class championship polo at *Village Farms Polo Club,* Gilbertsville; 607–783–2764 or 607–783–2737. Summer season runs from early June through early September. Starting times are 3 P.M. Sundays. Adults, $3; children under 12, free. Call for schedule.

Hockey. Check out the hockey action at the Arena, home of the Binghamton Whalers; 607–723–8937.

 HISTORIC SITES AND HOUSES. Chenango County Court House, Broad Street, Norwich. The carefully renovated and restored courthouse is the crown jewel of Norwich's downtown historic district. With four massive Corinthian columns, the 1837 courthouse is an outstanding example of Greek Revival architecture. For more information, contact *Chenango County Historical Society,* Rexford Street Museum, Norwich, 13815; 607–334–9227

Fort Stanwix National Monument, 112 East Park St., Rome (off Thruway exit 33 at the intersections of Rtes. 365, 49, and 69); 315–336–2090. Fort Stanwix stands on what was once a major artery linking the Great Lakes with the Atlantic Ocean. Originally a British post, it was abandoned and later taken over by the Americans during the Revolutionary War to defend the Mohawk Valley. On Sunday, Aug. 3, 1777, forces commanded by British Colonel Barry St. Leger laid siege to the fort. Six days into the siege, Colonel Peter Gansevoort wrote to St. Leger, "It is my Determined resolution with the Forces under my Command, to defend the Fort to the last Extremity. . . . " Fortunately, Gansevoort's last extremity was not required. After a siege of 21 days, the British retreated in the face of advancing relief troops. This outpost is an accurate reconstruction which includes barracks, storehouse, bastion, museum, Indian Trade Center, and officers' quarters. Self-guided walking tour. Open every day 9 A.M.–5 P.M., April 1–December 1. Free.

Herkimer Home, Rte. 169 and Thruway Exit 29A; 3 miles southeast of Little Falls; 315–823–0398. Home of General Nicholas Herkimer, known for his bravery during the crucial summer of 1777 when he rallied 800 men and boys to defend the besieged Fort Stanwix. Ambushed and surrounded by Loyalists and Indians at Oriskany, and despite a serious leg wound from which he later died, he managed to hold his ground in savage hand-to-hold combat. Activities include orientation exhibit, audiovisual show and house tours. Demonstrations of early farm activities every Sunday, Memorial Day–Labor Day. "Sugaring off" held on a Sunday in March or early April. Open Mid-April–mid-October; Wednesdays–Saturdays 10 A.M.–5 P.M. Sundays, 1–5 P.M. Free.

Lorenzo, Rte. 13, Cazenovia; one-quarter mile south of Rte. 20; 315–655–3200. "Situation superb, fine land." Those were the words of John Lincklaen, agent for the Holland Land Company, when he first viewed his future homesite at the foot of Cazenovia Lake. Built in 1807, Lorenzo is an elegant mansion from the Federal period with 20 acres of lawns, formal gardens, and wooded groves. Collection of horse-drawn vehicles and restored carriage house. Guided tours of house, picnicking, cross country skiing, and temporary exhibits. Special events: Annual Driving Competition, Harvest Day, Christmas Open House. Open May–Labor Day, Wednesdays–Saturdays and Monday holidays, 10 A.M.–5 P.M.; Sundays, 1–5 P.M. Grounds open all year 8 A.M.–sunset. Free.

Old Stone Fort, Rte. 30, Schoharie County Historical Society, Schoharie; 518–295–7192. Built in 1771 as a house of worship by the Reformed Protestant High Dutch Church Society. Six years later, the American Revolution made Schoharie Valley a frontier outpost and the church a fortress. Sharpshooters stationed in the steeple repelled more than 800 British, Tory, and Indian attackers who were tr. The troops traveling down the valley destroying everything in their path. The fort and its inhabitants were virtually unharmed. Open Saturday before Easter through October 31, 10 A.M.–5 P.M. Sundays, 12–5 P.M. Closed Mondays in April, May, September, and October. Admission includes two museums and carriage house: Adults, $1.50; students 50¢.

Oriskany Battlefield, Rte. 69, 2 miles west of Oriskany. (From Thruway exit 32 take Route 223 to Route 69); 315–768–7224. Here, in what was the bloodiest battle of the American Revolution, Mohawk Valley militiamen engaged in hand-to-hand combat and thwarted one flank of the British three-pronged invasion of New York. Audiovisual program, panoramic photographs, guided walking tours, special events include battle reenactments and the annual observance of the Battle of Oriskany. Open early May–Labor Day; Wednesdays–Saturdays and Monday holidays, 10 A.M.–5 P.M.; Sundays, 1–5 P.M. Free.

Shrine of Our Lady of Martyrs, Rte. 5S, Auriesville; 518–853–3033. Site of St. Isaac Jogues' martyrdom and birthplace of Blessed Kateri Tekawitha. Guided tours weekdays, 9 A.M.–4:30 P.M.; shrine office open daily from first Sunday of May to last Sunday of October. Free.

LIBRARIES. *Margaret Reaney Memorial Library,* 19 Kingsbury Ave., St. Johnsville; 518–568–7288, contains a good eclectic collection of local history, farm and home implements, Robert M. Hartley military button collection, paintings, bronze sculpture, and other historical artifacts. Open year round, Mondays–Fridays, 1–5 P.M.; Saturdays, 1–3 P.M. *National Baseball Library,* Main Street, Cooperstown; 607–547–9988, just behind the Hall of Fame (see *Museums* below), has an outstanding collection of baseball reference material. On display is the George Weiss baseball collection. A special room is set aside in recognition of the news media for their contributions to the game. Baseball movies are shown periodically throughout the day.

CHURCHES. Leatherstocking churches reflect the lives and times of the people who built them. After the urgent needs of the body were taken care of, hard-working settlers turned their attention to matters less worldly, but no less urgent. As congregations grew, especially in the more prosperous commercial towns, impressive churches were built of brick or stone. But the churches that reflect Leatherstocking's spirit best are the woodframe churches whose spires point heavenward from wooded valleys and swelling meadows. These churches express a sturdy and simple faith directly connected to the earth.

Throughout Leatherstocking you'll find churches both elaborate and simple, built in the diverse and pleasing architectural styles of the 19th and 20th centuries. For listings of churches and services, see the *Yellow Pages* of the local telephone book.

MUSEUMS. History is alive and well throughout Leatherstocking Country. You can't turn your head in Leatherstocking without bumping into a museum. Aside from the museums clustered in the region's major tourist areas, most towns have historical societies or some repository for historical artifacts and information. Some museums are formal. Others, like Topsy, "just growed" with a collection of local artifacts.

Erie Canal Village. Rome; 315–336–6000. "Low bridge—everybody down!" Relive the canal days when that warning was commonplace. The Erie Canal Village is a ca. 1840 village reconstructed near the spot where the first shovelful of dirt was turned for "Clinton's Folly." Ride the 1840 horse-drawn passenger packet boat along a refurbished section of the original Erie Canal. Take the narrow-gauge steam train ride and explore the village, a cluster of buildings typical of a 19th-century canal village. These include Bennett's Tavern (still serving a cold draft or root beer), a church meeting house, blacksmith's shop, weaving and spinning house, a train station schoolhouse, a ladies' furnishings shop, and a settlers cabin. The *Harden Carriage Museum* houses an extensive collection of antique vehicles. The *Canal Museum* offers a complete exposition of the history of the canal. Unique demonstrations, seasonal events at the village amphitheater; visitors reception center, gift shop, and snack bar. Hours: 9:30 A.M.–5:30 P.M. daily from the last weekend in April through October 31. Adults, $6; children 7–14, $3.50; under 6, free.

The Farmers' Museum. Lake Road, Rte. 80, one mile north of Cooperstown. A living historical farm complex with permanent exhibits. Daily demonstrations include blacksmithing, food preparations, spinning, and weaving. Visitors can play 19th-century games, take a wagon ride, or sample the food cooked in the fireplace of the Lippitt Farmhouse. Step back into history at the village cross-roads, a harmonious group of 19th-century buildings. The Main Barn, once a working dairy barn, features an introductory exhibit, weaving loft, and wood-working areas. Hours: 9 A.M.–6 P.M. daily, May–October. Adults, $4; children 7–15, $1.50.

The Fenimore House, close to the Farmers' Museum on Lake Road, is the museum and headquarters of the New York State Historical Association. It houses an extensive collection of James Fenimore Cooper memorabilia and is home to one of the country's finest collections of American Folk Art—billed as the extraordinary creations of ordinary people. The collection includes 19th- and 20th-century paintings, sculptures, textiles, ceramics, decoys, weather-vanes, and other decorative objects. An audiovisual program complements and provides a background for viewing the collection. Adults, $2.50, children 7–15, $1.25. Open daily 9 A.M.–6 P.M. from May through October. Combination tickets are available with The Farmers' Museum and the Baseball Hall of Fame. For more information about the Farmers' Museum and the Fenimore House, contact the *New York State Historical Association,* Lake Road, Box 800, Coopers-town, NY 13326; 607–547–2533.

Gladding International Sport Fishing Museum. South Otselic; 315–653–7287. Brush off your fish stories and sink your hook into this truly off-the-beaten-track museum. The Gladding reels in diehard fishers with bait from all over the world. Handcrafted trolling rigs used by Greenland Eskimos. The 1819 rod that once graced the cabin of Robert Fulton's steamboat. Specialty rods inlaid with ebony and engraved silver handles. Rare reels and creels and lures. There's also a library of old and new books, including *The Treatyse of Fysshnge* written by Sister Juliana Berners in 1496. Bring your fishing pole, for the museum offers 25 wooded acres with pond, picnic tables, and hiking trails. The season runs from Memorial Day through Labor Day; Tuesdays–Sundays, 10 A.M.–5 P.M. Children welcome if accompanied by an adult. Free to all.

The Musical Museum. Rte. 12B, Deansboro; 315–841–8774. "Hands-on" policy invites you to crank, pump, and play restored music boxes, melodeons, nickelodeons, grind organs, and much more. (The renowned composer Ros-topovich often stops in just to see what's new.) Whether your musical tastes run to Paderewski playing Chopin's rousing "Polonaise in A" or Elvis singing "You Ain't Nothin' But a Hound Dog," the Musical Museum will strike just the right note for you. Seventeen rooms, picnic area (don't miss the giant calliope), and a workshop that stocks parts, special fabrics, and information on repairing pump organs, nickelodeons, melodeons, grind organs, and other musical an-tiques and exotica. The Old Lamplighter shop specializes in old lamps, lamp parts, repairs, and restorations with an impressive variety of china shades. Open daily from April through December 31; 10 A.M.–4 P.M. Adults, $4; children under 12 (accompanied by parent), free.

National Baseball Hall of Fame. Cooperstown; 607–547–9988. A visit to the Hall of Fame is the ultimate experience for the baseball fan. It's all here, down to the last strike. A statue of "The Babe" dominates the entry area. Large displays, photographs, paintings, and audiovisual presentations trace the origin of the game and the development of the museum from a one-room exhibit to today's 50,000-square-foot display area. Enjoy Abbott and Costello's engaging "Who's on First?" routine and the nostalgic radio broadcast from a 1950s World Series game. Even if you're not a baseball fan, you'll like the Hall of Fame. Modern gift shop. National Baseball Library, on which baseball movies are shown periodically throughout the day.

Remington Firearms Museum. Catherine Street, off Rte. 5S, Ilion; 315–894–9961. Annie Oakley wasn't called "Little Miss Sure Shot" for nothing. She hit the mark every time with a Remington .22 rifle. Here you'll find a collection of handguns, rifles, and shotguns including flintlocks, percussion rifles, Civil War muzzle-loaders, and "transition rifles" that led to modern repeaters. The gallery features guns belonging to the famous and the infamous. Open all year Mondays–Fridays, 8 A.M.–5 P.M.; Saturdays and Sundays, noon–5 P.M. Free.

The Roberson Center for the Arts and Sciences. 30 Front St., Binghamton; 607–772–0660. Roberson Center is a complex of museums, galleries, ballet studios, and classrooms, and includes a planetarium and a 300-seat theater. The center's collections and exhibitions represent and interpret the region's history, art, and sciences. Exhibits range from ancient pottery to swords and armor to paintings of American masters. The center's headquarters and the Broome County Historical Society's museum are located in the restored Roberson Mansion, a handsome Renaissance structure. Roberson offers classes in all phases of arts and crafts, sponsors an annual Holiday and Arts Festival in early September and a Christmas Forest each December, and publishes a monthly calendar of events. Open year-round, Tuesday–Thursday and Saturday, 10 A.M.–6 P.M.; Friday, 10 A.M.–9 P.M.; Sunday, noon–5 P.M.; closed Mondays and major holidays.

 FILM. Although the occasional art or foreign film series shows up in college campus theaters or local arts centers, film is not especially distinguished in Leatherstocking Country. These listings are representative. Check the entertainment pages of local newspapers and *Yellow Pages* in local phone books for a more comprehensive listing of theaters.

Mall Cinemas, Riverside Mall, Utica; 315–735–9223.

Sangertown Square Cinemas 1–6, Sangertown Square Mall, Utica; 315–797–2121.

Oakdale Mall Cinemas, Johnson City (near Binghamton); 607–729–9391.

Cinema 1 & 2, Binghamton Plaza, Binghamton; 607–724–2464.

Cooperstown Theater, 137 Main St., Cooperstown; 607–547–8888

Oneonta Theater, 47 Chestnut Street, Oneonta; 607–432–2820.

Colonia Theater, 35 South Broad St., Norwich; 607–334–2135.

 MUSIC. From country to opera, Leatherstocking Country's satisfyingly diverse musical community hits all the right notes. Opera lovers, take note: Enjoy fine repertoire performances of the *Tri-Cities Opera* in Binghamton, the *Glimmerglass Opera* in Cooperstown (summer), traveling productions at the *Earlville Opera House* in Earlville (summer), and the *Stanley Center for the Performing Arts* in Utica. In the regional areas between the major cultural centers, country and western, bluegrass, and a variety of other small grassroots bands flourish. Small roving groups like the Del-Se-Nango Olde Tyme Fiddlers are regional favorites whose performances are often listed in the entertainment and good-time guides of local newspapers.

The B. C. Pops, Station Square, 45 Lewis St., Binghamton; 607–724–0007, is a 50-piece professional orchestra that keeps Binghamton humming with popular music from country to light classical. The B. C. Pops plays several performances a year at The Forum. A highlight of the entertainment season is the "Pops on the River with Fireworks" concert on the Chenango River. This is the kind of energetic, interesting, and bright group that makes people feel good about their town.

Binghamton Symphony and Choral Society, Press Building, 19 Chenango St., Binghamton; 607–723–8242. This professional orchestra performs major symphonic works whose roster of guest soloists includes artists of international renown as well as young American performers.

Broome County Veterans Memorial Arena, Box 1146, Binghamton, 607–772 –2611, is the focal point for a wide range of activities and performing arts. Big name tours include Neil Diamond, Kenny Rogers, The Oak Ridge Boys, and musical productions like *The Wiz, The Sound of Music,* and *Showboat.*

The Earlville Opera House, Earlville, 315–691–3550, hosts a summer season of mostly musical performances that range from opera to string quartets to sacred music. Call for schedule.

Floyd E. Anderson Center for the Performing Arts, University Center at State University of New York, Binghamton; 607–798–2174. Here's a brand new campus center getting ready to break into the big time. Performances range from the Orpheus Chamber Orchestra to Slam Stewart and Friends to the North American premiere of the Central Ballet of China.

The Forum, 228 Washington St., Binghamton; 607–722–5369, is the center for the Broome County Performing Arts. A former vaudeville house, The Forum is home to the B. C. Pops, the Tri-Cities Opera, the Binghamton Sym-·phony and Choral Society, and the Broadway Theater League.

The Glimmerglass Opera in Cooperstown, 607–547–5704, enjoys a growing reputation for its classics sung in English. Summer season with performances at the Alice Busch Opera Theater, Box 191, Cooperstown.

Stanley Center for the Performing Arts, Munson-Williams-Proctor Institute, 310 Genesee St., Utica; 315–797–0000. Hosts a variety of national and internationally known musicians, including such greats as flautist Jean-Pierre Rampal and the Netherlands Chamber Orchestra.

Tri-Cities Opera, 315 Clinton St., Binghamton, 607–797–6344, has achieved national recognition with its productions of such classics as *La Traviata, The Marriage of Figaro, Lucia di Lammermoor,* and newer works. *New York Times* critic Harold Schonberg commented on Tri-Cities' production of *Galileo Galilei:* "Produced with style, taste, imagination, and a strong group of young American singing actors . . . the production could have held its own in any company."

DANCE. Regional centers host a variety of cultural programs which occasionally include performances by nationally known ballet companies. They include the *Stanley Center for the Performing Arts,* Munson-Williams-Proctor Institute, 310 Genesee St., Utica; 315–797–0000; and *The Forum* (Center for the Broome County Performing Arts), 228 Washington St., Binghamton; 607–722–5369.

STAGE. *Cider Mill Playhouse* is the State University of New York's off-campus theater. Located at 2 South Nanticoke Ave., Binghamton, the playhouse is a 300-seat cabaret theater presenting a year-round bill of about dozen performances. Box office: Through May 16, Anderson Center, SUNY Binghamton, Mon.–Sat., 12–5:30 P.M., 607–777–ARTS. Beginning May 18 at the Mill, Mon.–Sat., 12–5:30 P.M., 607–748–7363. Beginning June 3 at the Mill, days of performance 12–9 P.M., other days 12–5:30 P.M.

Broadway Theater League Box 1921, Binghamton, 607–772–1429, presents programs such as *Biloxi Blues, La Cage aux Folles,* and *Can-Can* at the Forum theater from September through March.

Broadway Theater League of Utica presents four performances a season at the Stanley Center for the Performing Arts, 259 Genesee St. Box office: 315–724–7196

ART GALLERIES Leatherstocking's art scene can best be described as eclectic. The variety runs from exhibits by native regional artists to artists who have migrated from metropolitan areas. Although Binghamton, Utica, and Cooperstown have more to offer, don't ignore the regional galleries. They are listed here following those of the three cities.

Munson-Williams-Proctor Institute, 310 Genesee Street, Utica; 315–797–0000. This modern cultural gallery complex has what's billed as one of the Northeast's finest collections. The internationally recognized museum contains 18th–20th century American and European artwork. Picasso, Dali, Calder, Moore, Pollock, Burchfield in permanent collection. On permanent view is Thomas Cole's allegorical painting of *The Voyage of Life.* Open year round; Tuesdays–Saturdays, 10 A.M.–5 P.M.; Sundays, 1–5.

Rome Art and Community Center, 308 W. Bloomfield St., Rome; 315–336–1040. Galleries, gift shop, and classes. Tuesdays–Saturdays, 9 A.M.–5 P.M.; Sundays, 2–4 P.M.; closed holidays.

Plaza Gallery, Binghamton City Hall, Governmental Plaza, Binghamton; 607–772–7000. Features noted regional artists, touring shows. Also home to a small police museum and sculpture garden. Mondays–Fridays, 9 A.M.–5 P.M.

Roberson Center for the Arts and Sciences, 30 Front Street, Binghamton, (see Museums above.)

Canajoharie Art Gallery (in library), Canajoharie; 518–673–2314. Outstanding collection of American paintings. Changing exhibits. Open year round, Mondays–Fridays, 9:30 A.M.–4:45 P.M.; Saturdays, 9:30 A.M.–1:30 P.M.

Cooperstown Art Association Gallery, 22 Main St., Cooperstown; 607–547–9777. Permanent collection of paintings, sculpture, and crafts. Open year round, Mondays–Saturdays, 10 A.M.–4 P.M.

The Gallery, Anderson Center for the Arts, Hartwick College, Oneonta. Paintings, sculpture, VanEss collection of Renaissance and Baroque works. Open year round, Mondays–Fridays, 10 A.M.–4 P.M.

The Gallery, 9–11 Maple St. Norwich 607–336–5227, is run by the Chenango County Council of the Arts and displays a variety of work by regional artists. Weekdays, 10 A.M.–5 P.M.

SHOPPING. Binghamton and Utica have the usual variety of plazas, malls, and shopping districts. Depending upon the county, sales tax ranges from 4 percent to 7 percent. Like everything else in Leatherstocking, shopping is done at a slower pace. This is not the place to go looking for haute couture. It is, however, the place for savvy shoppers to turn up bargains in outlet stores and antique shops. Many worthwhile factory outlets are clustered near Binghamton and Utica. Try Charlestown Factory Outlet in Utica and the Vestal Plaza in Binghamton. Both offer name brands at substantial savings. Although factory outlets and antique shops are listed in the local *Yellow Pages,* many regional antique shops are not listed, and finding them may require a bit of detective work. When driving through a new area, pay attention to the signs because every town has its antique dealer. Some dealers offer fine antiques. (The region is ripe with 19th-century Americana.) Others offer what might be best described as junk-tiques. (When in Binghamton, don't miss Clinton Street's antique row. Those nondescript storefronts hide a multitude of treasures.) It's always wise to call ahead. Many antique dealers do not have set hours and are open by inspiration or by appointment. For information about dealers in the eastern section of Leatherstocking, call *Stagecoach Route Antique Dealers Association,* Butternut Road, Richfield Springs; 315–858–0964.

BINGHAMTON AREA

Oakdale Mall, Route 17, Harry L. Drive, Johnson City; 607–798–9388. Over 120 specialty shops and services and four department stores; tree-lined, climate-controlled environment. Mondays–Saturdays, 10 A.M.–9:30 P.M.; Sundays noon–5 P.M.

Ship 'n' Shore Outlet, Vestal Plaza, Binghamton; 607–729–9158. Full line of women's apparel from this famous maker includes mix & match separates, suits, and blouses. Also Izod for men and women. Mondays–Saturdays, 10 A.M.–9 P.M.; Sundays, noon–5 P.M. Visa and Mastercard.

REGIONAL

China Factory Outlet, 30 Genesee St., Rte. 5, Oneida; 315–363–4231. Nationally advertised stonewear at discount prices. Specializing in Noritake china. Large selection of handcrafted mugs and many gift items. Open daily, 9 A.M.–5 P.M. Personal checks, Visa, and MasterCard accepted.

Fownes Gloves Factory Store, off E. Main St. and Elk Sts., Amsterdam, 518–842–0640. Handwear and knit accessories. Women's and men's dress and sport gloves and mittens, leathers and knits, overproductions, discontinued styles, samples, and irregulars. Weekdays, 10 A.M.–5 P.M.; Saturdays 10 A.M.–3 P.M. closed Sundays.

Herkimer Family Treasure House, Rte. 51 South, Ilion; 315–895–7832. Wholesale Herkimer aged cheddar cheese (which was famous before the Erie Canal opened). Cheese, cheese spread, cheese balls, and cheese gift packages. Mondays–Fridays, 9 A.M.–5 P.M.; Saturdays, 11 A.M.–3 P.M.; Sundays by chance.

Oneida Silversmith's Factory Store, Sherrill Rd. at Noyes Blvd., Sherrill; 315–361–3661. Outlet for the famous Oneida silversmiths. Features silver, stainless, pewter, silverplate, flatware, cutlery, holloware, china, glass. Monthly specials. Personal checks, Visa, and MasterCard accepted. Mondays–Saturdays, 9 A.M.–4:30 P.M.

UTICA–ROME AREA

Charlestown Factory Outlet Center, 311 Turner St., Utica; 315–724–8175. Over 40 famous manufacturer's factory outlet stores under one roof. Quality brand merchandise for men, women, children, and the home as well as specialty and gift shops, and restaurants. You might easily get lost in this huge old munitions plant with its 13 interconnected buildings, but don't worry. At the south entrance information center, pick up a color-coded guide. Then, like Dorothy in the land of Oz, just follow the yellow brick—make that plastic—road. Open every day except Christmas, New Year's Day, Easter, July 4, and Thanksgiving. Visa and MasterCard accepted.

Cluett Apparel Outlet, 501 Bleeker St., Utica; 315–797–2618. Full line of men's, women's, and children's apparel. All manufacturers owned by Cluett. Open Sunday noon–5 P.M. Mondays–Saturdays 9:30 A.M.–5:30 P.M. Visa and MasterCard accepted. Cluett also has a Mohawk branch at 100 E. Main St. that is open Mondays–Thursdays, 10 A.M.–5:30 P.M.; Fridays 10 A.M.–9 P.M., and Sundays, noon–5 P.M.

Daniel Greene Shoe Store, Main St., Dolgeville; 315–429–3131. Slippers and shoes. Weekdays, 10 A.M.–5:30 P.M.; Saturday, 9 A.M.–1 P.M.

The Erie Peddler, 7567 Gifford Rd., Rome; 315–336–7597. Antiques and collectibles.

Revere Factory Store, Railroad St., Rome; 315–336–4398. Famous Revere-ware pots, pans, and cooking and kitchen utensils. Open stock, seconds, close-outs, and overstocks. Monday–Friday, 9 A.M.–5 P.M.; Saturdays, 9 A.M.–3 P.M. Also located at the Charlestown Mall, Utica.

 DINING OUT. Eating out in Leatherstocking Country is an experience in middling American cuisine, decor, and price. The food and service are good, but unremark-able. Although a few ethnic restaurants achieve varying degrees of success, most lack credibility. If you're on a budget, you won't have any trouble finding inexpensive restaurants with good food and no pretensions. Every major town has the usual assortment of fast food places and inexpensive eateries. Most restaurants fall into the moderate range. (You'll be hard pressed to find a deluxe—or even an expensive—restaurant.) The only regional delicacy, the spiedie (chunks of grilled beef, pork or chicken marinated in a top-secret marinade) hails from Binghamton. Binghamton puts out a travel guide that features a diner's section which can be obtained from the Convention & Visitors Bureau, Broome County Chamber of Commerce, 80 Exchange St., Binghamton 13902; 607–772–8860. Another helpful diner's guide is available from *Leather-stocking Country, N.Y.,* 200 North Prospect St., Herkimer 13350; 315–866–1500.

The price classifications of the following restaurants are based on the cost of an average three-course dinner for one person; beverages, tax, and tip are extra. *Deluxe,* over $25; *Expensive,* $15–$25; *Moderate,* $8–$15; *Inexpensive,* less than $8.

Abbreviations for credit cards are: AE, American Express; CB, Carte Blanche; DC, Diners Club; MC, MasterCard; V, VISA. For restaurants that do not accept credit cards, cash will probably be more readily acceptable than travelers checks or personal checks.

Abbreviations for meals are: B, breakfast; L, lunch; D, dinner. Restaurant hours vary. Check first to confirm hours.

The restaurants listed here are fairly representative of Leatherstocking.

Expensive

Eaton Place. Hotel de Ville, 80 State St., Binghamton; 607–722–7272. Huge brass lamps with globe fixtures, vaulted ceilings, tiled floors, linen tableclothes, fresh flowers, French doors. Meals are brought down a grand staircase to the strains of classical music. Selections include dishes like fusilli with duck sauce, chicken and raspberries, and veal piccata. It all spells ambience. Continental cuisine with daily specials. B, L, D, daily. V, DC, AE.

Trinkaus Manor. Rte. 69, Oriskany; 315–736–5205. Family-owned restau-rant, famous locally for elegant dining. Lots of windows, winter Christmas scene, little waterfall, linen tablecloths, American cuisine. With a seating capaci-ty of 750, it's billed as one of the most popular restaurants in the state. Cocktails, full menu, entertainment. L, D, daily. All credit cards.

Moderate

Atrium Cafe. 2–8 Hawley St. (in the Holiday Inn Arena), Binghamton; 607–722–1212. Skylight, airy decor. Outdoor cafe in summer. Pasta garden, deli buffet. Open daily 6:30 A.M.–midnight. B, L, D.

Brae Loch. 5 Albany St., Cazenovia; 315–655–3431. A bit o' Scotland. The staff wears kilts and host Grey Barr sports full Highland regalia. The menu features Scotch steak (steak and kidney) pie, muckle sow (sugar cured ham), cock o' the north (rock Cornish hen), and American cuisine selections. Dessert is extra special in the Victorian parlor. (After dinner, browse the Wee Gift & Antique House gift shop, which stocks lovely tartans and other fine imports.) D, daily. Most major credit cards.

Cathedral Farms. Rtes. 205 and 23 Morris exit, Oneonta; 607–432–7483. Features champagne brunch, seafood, prime ribs, and steaks. Great desserts— watch out for the deep fried ice cream. Pink tablecloths, lots of brass, and Tiffany peacocks. After dinner, take a stroll on the beautiful grounds and watch the real peacocks strut their stuff. D, daily; champagne brunch Sundays. Most major credit cards.

Colgate Inn. On the Green, Hamilton; 315–824–2300. Work up an appetite for dinner with a walk though this ivy-covered college (Colgate University) town and admire the outstanding examples of 19th-century architecture. The inn serves traditional American cuisine with some continental offerings, and features veal dishes like veal Francaise with lemon butter and wine sauce. L, D, daily, except Sunday brunch 11 A.M.–2 P.M. Major credit cards.

The Flotilla Restaurant, Rte. 12 North, Barneveld; 315–896–6821. A 1930s house artfully converted into a restaurant that serves "good food, simply prepared." All soups, bread, and desserts made in-house. Accent on seafood. Comfortable atmosphere with plants, candlelit tables. D, daily except Tuesdays. Most major credit cards.

Hickory Grove Inn. Rte. 80, Cooperstown; 607–547–8100. This renovated stagecoach stop has been providing refreshment for travelers since 1804. American and continental cuisine. House specialties include shrimp tempura (outstanding) and veal piccata. Every meal gets off to a sweet start with a little basket of tiny crisp apple muffins for which the management will gladly give you the recipe. D, daily in summer. Most major credit cards.

Mohawk Station Restaurant and Cocktail Lounge. 95 E. Main St., Mohawk; 315–866–7460. Pleasing railroad station decor with lots of brass. Casual and comfortable. Steak and seafood specialties. Large salad bar. L, D, daily. MC, AE, V.

Surf & Turf, 1202 Campville Road, Endicott; 607–754–2333. Home-style American food, and lots of it, served in a warm and informal atmosphere. They take "from-soup-to-nuts" seriously here. Courses include soup, tossed salad, assorted breads, cheese, and crackers. Main course is served with family-style vegetables. Dessert is a huge and wonderful chocolate chip cookie. Most major credit cards.

Whiffletree Inn. 345 E. Main St., Rte. 5S, Ilion; 315–895–7777. Beautifully decorated restaurant with antiques, plants, and flowers. Full range of American cuisine. Great place for indecision—but with the custom built buffet and salad bar, you can have it all. L, Tuesday–Friday; D, Tuesday–Saturday, from 5 P.M. Sunday buffet, noon–6 P.M. Closed Mondays. Major credit cards.

Inexpensive

Crystal Chandelier. Middleville; 315–891–3366. Although this restaurant is part of the Herkimer "Diamond" Development, it offers a satisfying menu and service at an easy-to-swallow price. American cuisine features baby back ribs, steak, chicken, and seafood. Seasonal hours. Casual dress. Reservations appreciated. AE, V, MC.

GERMAN-AMERICAN

Inexpensive

Deller's German-American Restaurant. 33 Schuyler St., Utica 315–732–9611. German and American dishes specializing in sauerbraten. Closed Tuesdays. No credit cards.

Obie's Brot Und Beer. Pioneer Alley, Cooperstown; 607–547–5601. Superb sandwiches and cold beverages served in a charming German-style sandwich and beer restaurant. Al fresco dining in summer on a flower-laden porch. Daily in summer. Closed Sundays in winter. No credit cards.

ITALIAN

Moderate

Grimaldi's. 418–424 Bleecker St., Utica; 315–732–1184. Billed as one of Utica's oldest, largest, and finest restaurants and cocktail lounges, Grimaldi's serves a traditional Italian-American menu specializing in veal and pasta dishes. Open daily, 11 A.M.–2 A.M. AE, V, MC, DC, CB.

 NIGHTLIFE. If it's night life you want, go to New York City. With a few sophisticated exceptions, the atmosphere in outlying regional bars falls heavily in the honky-tonk range. Lots of fiddler's fests, bluegrass, and rednecks. There is, however, a core of warm-bodied nightlife surrounding Utica and Binghamton. The atmosphere in city bars is usually split between the disco crowd and the pin-striped suits.

BINGHAMTON AREA

Number 5. 33 South Washington St., Binghamton; 607–723–0555. Downstairs, have drinks in one of the classiest lounges in town, then retire upstairs to the supper club whose menu offers a truly satisfying variety of continental and American cuisine. D, daily. All major credit cards.

Esprit. 65 Front St., Binghamton; 607–773–8390. Major night spot (bar and dancing) with dress code—proper attire (no shorts or mid-riffs for ladies, dress jeans for men; shoes, no sneakers); disc jockey; Tuesday–Friday shrimp buffet during happy hour; closed Mondays. No cover.

UTICA AREA

Lily Langtry's. 700 Varick St., Utica; 315–724–5219; live entertainment Tuesday evenings; Wednesdays happy hour (5–7 P.M.); and Thursdays, Fridays, and Saturdays evenings; open noon–3 A.M.; no cover, no minimum; all major credit cards.

Lemons and Limes. Ramada Inn, Burrstone Road, New Hartford; 315–735–9231; lighted dance floor with disco music, garden theme; no cover, no minimum. AE, MC, V, DC.

Promenade. Sheraton Inn, 200 Genesee St., Utica; 315–797–8010; live music, Tuesdays–Sundays. Monday is football night in season. Videos 7 nights a week fill band breaks; all major credit cards.

Livingston's Ale House. Limberloft Road, Clinton; 315–853–8073. Live entertainment Fridays, Saturdays, and ocassionally week nights; cover charge varies according to the entertainment; no minimum; no credit cards.

INDEX